KU-409-544

Charles Allen was born in India, where six generations of his family served under the British Raj. After being educated in England, he returned to the Indian sub-continent in 1966 to work with Voluntary Service Overseas in Nepal. He ended his service with a long walk through the Himalayas that won him the *Sunday Telegraph* Traveller of the Year trophy in 1967. Since then he has trekked and climbed extensively in the Himalayas and in other corners of the world.

Praise for Charles Allen and *Soldier Sahibs*:

'Charles Allen is an excellent guide through this fascinating territory. Along with John Keay and Peter Hopkirk, Allen is one of a triumvirate of brilliant narrative historians who have attempted to retell the story of the Raj in northern India and the Himalayas for an age that regards imperial history as an embarrassing skeleton in the cupboard' William Dalrymple, *Sunday Times*

'Allen has written a marvellous book in the best traditions of narrative history: colourful, informative and splendidly readable. I can give it no greater praise than to admit I would like to have written it myself' Saul David, *Daily Telegraph*

'Allen is one of the most ... consistently enjoyable writers of his generation ... producing well-researched, well-written and eminently readable works of narrative history which have illuminated ... previously unwritten corners of British Indian history' *Guardian*

'Charles Allen is a master of his genre' *Military Illustrated*

SOLDIER SAHIBS

The men who made the
North-West Frontier

Charles Allen

JOHN MURRAY

First published in Great Britain in 2000 by John Murray (Publishers)
An Hachette UK Company

This paperback edition published by John Murray 2012

2

A CIP catalogue record for this title is available from the British Library

B format paperback ISBN 978 1 84854 716 2
Ebook ISBN 978 1 84854 720 9

Printed and bound by Clays Ltd, St Ives plc

John Murray policy is to use papers that are natural, renewable and recyclable products
and made from wood grown in sustainable forests. The logging and manufacturing
processes are expected to conform to the environmental regulations of the country of
origin.

John Murray (Publishers)
338 Euston Road
London NW1 3BH

www.johnmurray.co.uk

Contents

Contents

Illustrations

The author and publishers would like to thank the following for permission to reproduce illustrations: Plates 4, 5, 11, 12, 13, 14, 17, 18, 19 and 20, the Director, National Army Museum, London; 6, 7, 8 and 10, National Portrait Gallery; 9, 15, 16 and 22, Oriental and India Office Collection, British Library. Plates 1, 2, 3, 21 and 23 are taken from the author's collection.

A Note on the East India Company and its Bengal Army

This book concerns itself chiefly with events in north-west India between July 1839, when seventeen-year-old John Nicholson landed at Calcutta as a cadet in the East India Company's Bengal Native Infantry, and September 1857, when that same John Nicholson died of his wounds in the British camp below Delhi Ridge – eighteen busy years which saw the British East India Company extend its conquests to the very edge of the mountain barriers which define the northern boundaries of the Indian sub-continent.

In moments of pomposity the East India Company liked to refer to itself as 'the Honourable Company'; for brevity it became 'EICo' or 'Hon EICo'; its servants referred to it more familiarly as 'John Company', *'Jan Kampani'* or even *'Jan Kampani Bahadur'* ('Heroic John Company', as a local interpretation of 'Honourable John Company'). During this period the EICo's Indian territories were divided into the three presidencies of Bengal, Madras and Bombay, each with its own civil service and army but under the supreme control of a Governor-General, his Commander-in-Chief, and a Council based at Calcutta in the Cold Weather (October–March) and Simla during the Hot Weather months and the Rains. Although very much the *'Lat Saheb'* ('Lord and Master') in India, the Governor-General was always answerable to the Court of Directors at the EICo's head offices in Leadenhall Street in the City of London.

The three presidency armies operated as three separate forces, but as the EICo continued to extend westwards from Bengal across and beyond the Gangetic plain, so its Bengal Army grew until it eclipsed the other two in strength and numbers. The greater part of this army was made up of several score of infantry regiments known as Bengal Native Infantry (BNI), composed of local recruits under the command of British officers and numbered in accordance with their original order of formation – for example, the 27th BNI, John Nicholson's original regiment. These BNI regiments were strengthened by a number of infantry battalions made up entirely of British and Irish soldiery, known as European Infantry – for example, the 1st Bengal Fusiliers. The Bengal Artillery was also largely composed of British gunners and gunner officers and included highly mobile horse artillery, as well as elephant- and bullock-drawn guns. The rest of the Bengal Army comprised the Bengal Cavalry, chiefly formed of regiments of light horse, and two support units, a Corps of Sappers and Miners and a Corps of Pioneers.

All the British officers of the Bengal Army were recruited directly by the EICo and carried Company rather than Queen's Commissions – a big social and military disadvantage. A major distinction was that there were far fewer British officers per unit in the Bengal Army: a ratio of one officer for every ninety men, as compared with one per thirty in the British Army (known then as the 'Queen's Army'). This was only possible because of the extensive reliance placed on the 'Native Officers', as they were known until 1885, who played a vital intermediary role between the British officers and the men under their command. Nominally, the most senior Native Officer was junior in rank to the lowliest British sub-altern, although in practice no junior British officer worth his salt would do other than confer with and defer to his Native Officers, many of whom were twice or even three times his age. Cavalry units had four ranks of such Native Officers: *rissaldar-major, rissaldar, rissaidar* and *jemadar*. The equivalent in the infantry units were *subedar-major, subedar* and *jemadar*. No equivalent of the Native

Officer existed in the Queen's Army, but the two armies could be compared in the lower ranks: the infantry *havildar* and the cavalry *duffadar* of the Bengal Army were the equivalent of the Queen's Army sergeant-major, the infantry rifleman or private soldier was known as the *sepahi* or sepoy, and the cavalry trooper as the *sowar*.

In times of war – which in the Indian context meant most of the time – the Bengal Army was strengthened by British troops drawn from the Queen's Army – for example, HM 24th Foot, which fought alongside the Bengal Army throughout the Sikh Wars – as well as local irregular forces, both infantry and cavalry, raised by special order. These irregulars often went by the name of their commander, or the region in which they were raised – for example, Daly's Horse (also known as the 1st Punjab Cavalry) or Coke's Rifles (1st Punjab Infantry) – and came under the direct command of the provincial governor rather than of the Commander-in-Chief. The whole ethos of these locally recruited irregulars was different from that of the regular regiments. Their first loyalties were to the men who had recruited them, rather than to their regiment. A further difference between these and the regular units of the Bengal Army was that the irregulars had even fewer British officers, an average of one per two hundred sepoys or sowars, usually represented by the commander, the adjutant, the quartermaster and an assistant surgeon.

One final point about the composition of the Bengal Army of this period: its Native Infantry regiments were very largely made up of recruits from Bihar, Oude and Rohilkand, nearly all high-born Hindus from the Brahmin and Rajput upper castes. The result was that the men in these corps put caste and religious loyalties first. Only after the final defeat of the Sikh army in 1849 did Sikhs and Muslims from the north-west border regions begin to join the Bengal Army in large numbers. Units then formed, both regular and irregular, tended to be made up of different combinations of Hindus, Muslims and Sikhs brought together into one unit but put into their own companies, squadrons or troops. Thus a typical infantry regiment raised in the Punjab after 1849 might have two companies of Punjabi Muslims, one of Sikhs, and one of Hindu Dogras. Loyalties in such units were first and foremost to the battalion or regiment, rather than to caste or class.

In my text I have, as a general rule, followed the usage of the period. It makes no sense, for example, to call a battalion of Punjabi soldiers 'Indian': this was not a term employed by the native peoples of the subcontinent to describe themselves, although – curious as it now seems – it was sometimes used by the British in India about themselves. Where a group cannot be identified precisely, I have preferred 'native' – thus, 'native troops' and 'British troops'. Similarly, I refer to the 1857–8 uprising as the 'Sepoy Mutiny' or the 'Mutiny', with a capital M. The Mutiny began as a series of mutinies by regulars of the Bengal Army and was waged by sepoys and former sepoys, and I see no reason to sacrifice accuracy to the political correctness of modern revisionists.

Furthermore, in describing the most significant racial group of eastern Afghanistan and Pakistan's North-West Frontier Province, I have abandoned the well-known term 'Pathan' in favour of 'Pakhtun', for two good reasons. The first is accuracy, again: 'Pathan' is simply wrong, a corruption of *Pakhtanah*, the plural of Pakhtun, picked up and promoted by the British. The second is that the word irritates the hell out of a people who set great store by *Pakhtunwali*, the Pakhtun way of life, and by *Pakhtunkhwa*, the land of the Pakhtun people. So Pakhtun it is, and I hope that others will follow suit.

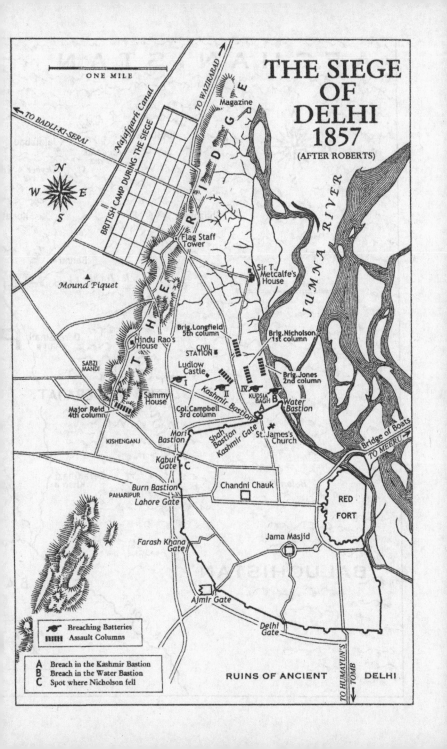

THE SIEGE OF DELHI 1857
(AFTER ROBERTS)

ONE MILE

TO WAZIRABAD

← TO BADLI-KI-SERAI

Najafgarh Canal

BRITISH CAMP DURING THE SIEGE

N
W — E
S

Magazine

JUMNA RIVER

Flag Staff Tower

Sir T. Metcalfe's House

Mound Piquet

Brig. Longfield 5th column

Brig. Nicholson 1st column

CIVIL STATION

Hindu Rao's House

Ludlow Castle

I

Brig. Jones 2nd column

SABZI MANDI

II

IV

KUDSIA BAGH

Sammy House

Kashmir Bastion

A B

Water Bastion

Major Reid 4th column

Col. Campbell 3rd column

Mori Bastion

Shah Bastion

Kashmir Gate

St. James's Church

Bridge of Boats

KISHENGANJ

TO MEERU →

Kabul Gate

C

Burn Bastion

Chandni Chauk

RED FORT

PAHARIPUR

Lahore Gate

Farash Khana Gate

Jama Masjid

Ajmir Gate

Delhi Gate

🦘 Breaching Batteries
▮▮▮ Assault Columns

A Breach in the Kashmir Bastion
B Breach in the Water Bastion
C Spot where Nicholson fell

RUINS OF ANCIENT

TO HUMAYUN'S TOMB

DELHI

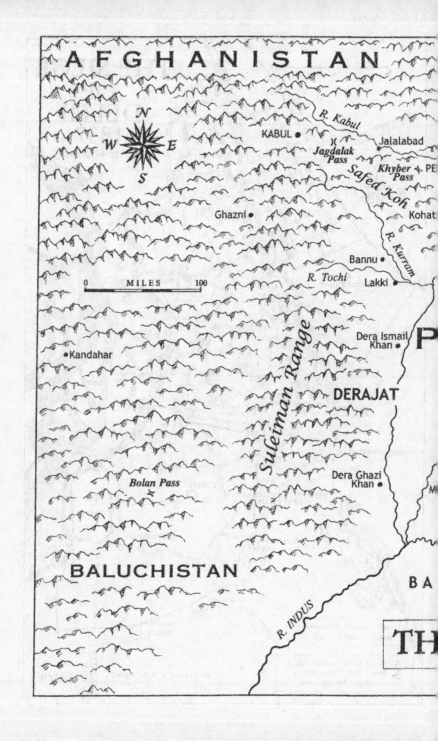

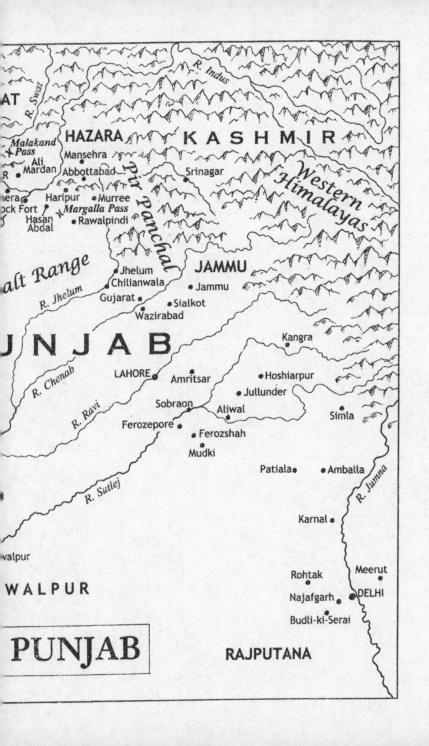

Prologue

'The type of the conquering race'

LISBURN, 1903

A rainy day in September 1903 – not 'Irish mist', but a 'continuous and drenching downpour of rain unparalleled since the Lord Lieutenant visited the city', rain that has turned the red, white and blue bunting into so many rags. At five minutes past one precisely the 12.45 local train from Belfast's Great Northern Terminus steams into Lisburn railway station to the accompaniment of a series of explosions caused by detonators placed on the line in lieu of a gun salute. As a reserved saloon carriage draws up beside a specially erected dais the Lisburn Amateur Brass Band, strategically placed on the balcony of the Lisburn court-house, strikes up 'See! The Conquering Hero Comes'. A dense crowd gathered on the arrival platform breaks into loud cheers.

Out steps a small, elderly, white-haired old gentleman: Field Marshal Lord Roberts, VC, Earl Roberts of Kandahar, Pretoria and Waterford, KG, KP, GCB, GCSI, GCIE, PC, Commander-in-Chief of the British Army and former C-in-C of the Army in India, where he was known to the troops as 'Bobs' or 'Bobs Bahadur' (Bobs the Hero). He stands smartly to attention as the band plays 'God Save the King', a diminutive figure but every inch a soldier.

In reply to an address presented by the town council, the Field Marshal explains that for many years it has been his wish to visit

Lisburn. An unknown scribe representing the *Hillsborough Parish Magazine* stands at his elbow and then shadows him throughout his visit, noting down his every word. 'It has been my desire to see the birthplace of a man for whom I had a most profound respect and admiration – John Nicholson,' proclaims Lord Roberts, to loud applause. 'It was my great privilege to serve for a short time on General Nicholson's staff, and I perhaps had opportunities which few others had of understanding his great military genius and of appreciating his many noble qualities. He did great things in Delhi and gave up his life there in defence of his country. (*Applause.*) I am proud to think that I was associated with General Nicholson, and I am very much obliged to you. (*Loud applause.*)'

After luncheon the Field Marshal is driven in an open carriage by way of Clonavon Park, Antrim Road, Bow Street and Market Square to the parish church, the cathedral of the diocese of Connor, his route lined all the way by cheering crowds and sodden bunting. Perhaps the downpour speeds his progress, because Lord Roberts arrives at the sacred edifice 'considerably in advance of the programme time'. The canon and churchwardens conduct him in solemn procession up the left transept to the foot of a large tablet of white marble set high on the wall. It consists of a broad base bearing fourteen long lines of inscription, sur-mounted by a large bas-relief, the work of J.H. Foley, RA. This portrays the storming of the breach in the Kashmir Bastion on the walls of Delhi on the morning of 14 September 1857. The glacis is piled with British and Indian dead, and the fusiliers pushing forward at the top with musket and bayonet are waved on by a figure in the left forground: it is John Nicholson, mortally wounded, heaving himself up on one elbow to urge the troops forward.

Bobs Bahadur gazes at the carving for some moments. The unknown Hillsborough parishioner, still at his side, notes the 'emotion too deep perhaps for utterance' that crosses the face of the 'war-torn veteran, so deeply loved by his countrymen'. The Field Marshal then turns his attention to the inscription, written by Nicholson's friend Herbert Edwardes at the request of his mother. He begins to read it aloud, from time to time adding his own interjections: ' "He had an iron mind and frame, a terrible courage, an indomitable will" – an extraordinary good expression, that – "a terrible courage" – and that – "an indomitable will".'

He reads on:

His form seemed made for an army to behold; his heart, to meet the crisis of an empire; yet was he gentle most exceedingly, most loving, most kind. In all he thought and did, unselfish, earnest, plain, and true; indeed, a most noble man. In public affairs he was the pupil of the great and good Sir Henry Lawrence, and worthy of his master. Few took a greater share in either the conquest or the government of the Punjab, perhaps none so great in both. Soldier and civilian, he was a tower of strength; the type of the conquering race. Most fitly in the great siege of Delhi he led the first column of attack and carried the main breach. Dealing the deathblow to the greatest danger that ever threatened British India, most mournfully, most gloriously, in the moment of victory, he fell mortally wounded on the 14th, and died on the 23rd of September, 1857, aged only 34.

Lord Roberts now turns again to his escort. 'The memorial is somewhat at fault,' he says, to a murmur of disquiet. He points out that Nicholson did not fall at the breach, as the bas-relief shows: 'He got them over the Kashmir bastion and was two or three hours inside the city when he was shot.' 'Bobs Bahadur' should know, of course, because he was there. And it was he – then a 25-year-old lieutenant – who found Nicholson abandoned by his stretcher-bearers. His memoirs tell the full story:

I observed by the side of the road a doolie [covered stretcher], without bearers, and with evidently a wounded man inside. I dismounted to see if I could be of any use to the occupant when I found, to my grief and consternation, that it was John Nicholson, with death written all over his face . . . He was lying on his back, no wound was visible, and but for the pallor of his face, always colourless, there was no sign of the agony he must have been enduring. On my expressing a hope that he was not seriously wounded, he said: 'I am dying; there is no chance for me.' The sight of that great man lying helpless and on the point of death was almost more than I could bear. Other men had daily died around me, friends and comrades had been killed beside me, but I never felt as I felt then – to lose Nicholson seemed to me at that moment to lose everything . . . Having with difficulty collected four men, I put them in charge of a sergeant of the 61st Foot. Taking down his name, I told him who the wounded officer was, and ordered him to go direct to the field hospital. That was the last I saw of Nicholson.

Having paid his tribute, the Field Marshal makes a quick tour of the church before returning once more by train to Belfast. It continues to rain for the rest of the afternoon.

On my eighth birthday a kind aunt gave me a boy's adventure book and told me to read it very carefully: it was about a distant forebear of mine, of whom I should be very proud. The book's title was *Nikkal Seyn: A Tale of John Nicholson, Hero of Delhi, Saviour of India*, its author was Ernest Gray, and it was published in the same year that partitioned India and Pakistan gained independence. It must have been one of the last examples of a genre, pioneered by Captain Marryat and greatly reinforced by G. A. Henty and other Victorian authors, which helped to despatch generations of young English, Scots and Irish Protestant gentlemen off to do their bit in the farthest reaches of the British Empire.

The book's hero is a young drummer-boy known, with the innocence of the period, as Lanky Dick. The year is 1856, and a detachment of Dick's regiment, HM 78th Foot, is set upon by 'wolves of Pathans' while manning an isolated fort on India's North-West Frontier. Dick is rescued by the man whom the natives call 'Nikkal Seyn, the mighty one, the tramp of whose war horse is heard from Attock to the Khyber' – John Nicholson, Deputy Commissioner of Peshawar:

Into the flickering firelight stepped a tall man dressed in grey trousers and a grey, semi-military frock-coat, with a broad pale blue sash swathed round his muscular throat. From all he had heard of him, Dicky had imagined the famous John Nicholson to resemble some craggy prize-fighter, but the newcomer was as graceful as a mountain ash. Long glossy black hair fell to his shoulders; his eyes were dark and sparkling, and beneath an aquiline nose the points of a sweeping black moustache ran into a thick spade-shaped beard. His forehead was white and lofty. The grey frock-coat strained over a chest like a barrel, and its sleeves were taut over the rippling arm muscles. His hands and feet, though sinewy, were narrow and small. Fingers crossed over the hilt of a curved sword . . .

Dick becomes John Nicholson's protégé and is transferred to his office as a clerk, which allows the reader to follow the last year of Nicholson's short but action-packed life to its close on Delhi Ridge. Towards the end of the tale young Lanky Dick rather fades into the background of this ripping yarn, full of blood and guts.

The novel closes with a quote from John Nicholson's patron, the future Viceroy John Lawrence: 'As long as an Englishman survives in India, the name of John Nicholson will not be forgotten.' Other admirers also did their bit to perpetuate the Nicholson legend by erecting monuments and memorials extolling his virtues and achievements. The first was a marble tablet set into a wall of the little church close beside the Deputy Commissioner's bungalow at Bannu, its text written by the same man who composed the words on the Nicholson memorial in Lisburn church, Herbert Edwardes. Its sentiments encapsulate his image of his dearest friend, as he wished it to be preserved:

Gifted in mind and body, he was as brilliant in government as in arms. The snows of Ghazni attest his youthful fortitude; the songs of the Punjab his manly deeds; the peace of this frontier his strong rule. The enemies of his country know how terrible he was in battle, and we his friends have to recall how gentle, generous and true he was.

The indefatigable Captain Lionel Trotter did his best to preserve this same romantic image with his uncritical *Life of John Nicholson, Soldier and Administrator*, written in 1897. A few years later Rudyard Kipling's *Kim* helped to bolster the mystique of 'Nikal Seyn' as an avenging spirit revered by his Sikh enemies. A second biography, *The Hero of Delhi*, published in 1939 by Hesketh Pearson, was scarcely less adulatory than the first – as, indeed, was that ripping yarn of 1947.

The post-1947 mood was very different, however. Heroes of Empire were no longer required, and the rising generation of historians had no time for them. I can still remember the *frisson* of shock I felt when I first opened a popular history of British India written in the mid 1970s and saw my family paragon described as a bully, a racist, a religious bigot and, to cap it all, a homosexual sado-masochist. Nicholson was indeed remembered, but not at all as his colleagues would have wished him to be. More than half a century after Independence, moral confusion still colours our attitudes to men like Nicholson, and to British rule in India in general. This book represents, in part, my own attempts to come to grips with this uncertainty; however, what began as a search to pin down the true nature of my illustrious/infamous relation very quickly grew into something more ambitious.

Although anything but a team player, Nicholson was an inextricable part of a small band of military officers-cum-civil administrators – the Soldier Sahibs of my title – who between them shaped what is still to this day known in Pakistan as the North-West Frontier Province – the NWFP, for short. Effectively, they drew lines with their sabres along the mountain tops that mark today's border between Pakistan and Afghanistan. They secured the allegiance of the fiercely independent-minded tribespeople who had settled east and south of that line, and saw to it that their divided loyalties remained – for the most part – pro-Raj rather than pro-Afghanistan. They also established a style of loose-reined government which is still, almost a century and a half later, the hallmark of the NWFP and sets it apart from all other forms of local administration.

It soon became clear to me that I could not write about John Nicholson without also covering the personalities, actions and motives of those other pioneer frontiersmen. Some years after the death of Herbert Edwardes, his wife Emma wrote of the deep bond that had existed between her husband and John Nicholson, declaring that 'they became more than brothers in the tenderness of their whole lives henceforth'. A similar attachment existed between the young Henry Daly of Daly's Rifles and his brother-

officer William Anderson. 'We were much to each other,' Daly
wrote after Anderson's murder at Multan. A very close friendship
also grew up between the four men who formed what was almost
an inner circle on the Frontier – Edwardes, Nicholson, Harry
Lumsden and Neville Chamberlain. Such close friendships,
between lonely men who lived many miles from each other,
finding open expression only in the event of the death of one of
their company, were very much the order of the day. This was a
brotherhood of young men who shared a vocation: they saw
themselves very much as a band of brothers, Paladins at the court
of their master and mentor Henry Lawrence.

This brotherhood divides into two distinct age-groups. The
older generation is represented by three father-figures in the form
of the three Lawrence brothers: the above-mentioned Henry, born
in 1806; his elder brother George (1804); and his younger brother
John (1811). Along with the Lawrences are two others of their
generation, James 'Uncle' Abbott (1807), himself one of four
brothers who each made his own mark on the Punjab, and a
second 'Uncle', Frederick Mackeson (1807), often overlooked, the
outsider in the pack.

Separated from these five by about a decade are the Paladins
themselves, the younger generation who became widely known as
'Henry Lawrence's young men', junior officers of the Bengal
Army who in nearly every case learned their administrative skills at
the feet of Henry Lawrence as his political assistants before going
on to exercise them more fully under John Lawrence. Their names
and attributes were conveniently listed by Henry Lawrence himself
in a letter sent to a military friend, the future historian John Kaye,
shortly before his death in Lucknow in 1857:

> I was very fortunate in my assistants, all of whom were my
> friends, and almost every one was introduced into the Punjab
> through me. George Lawrence, Macgregor, James Abbott,
> Edwardes, Lumsden, Nicholson, Taylor, Cocks, Hodson,
> Pollock, Bowring, Henry Coxe, and Melvill are men such as
> you will seldom see anywhere, but when collected under one
> administration were worth double and treble the number taken
> at haphazard.

Add to this list the names of four whom Henry Lawrence omits, three because they were full-time military men rather than administrators, and the fourth for pettier reasons – Neville Chamberlain, Henry Daly, John Coke and Frederick Mackeson – and you have a comprehensive roll-call of the men who laid the foundations of the Punjab and North-West Frontier Provinces in that pioneering phase between the close of the First Sikh War in January 1846 and the outbreak of the Sepoy Mutiny in May 1857.

For reasons of space alone this book follows the fortunes of only the most prominent of Henry Lawrence's Young Men: mainly James Abbott (the old man of the pack), Herbert Edwardes (born in 1819), Neville Chamberlain (1820), Henry Daly (1821), Harry Lumsden (1821), William Hodson (1821), Reynell Taylor (January 1822) and John Nicholson (the youngest, born in December 1822). What old *Kaka* Abbott did at forty and these seven younger men in their twenties and early thirties, both individually and together, is the stuff of legend.

Would that I could say the same for their womenfolk but, alas, the Frontier has always been a male-dominated theatre in which women, whether native or foreign, play only walk-on parts. In pre-Mutiny days very few European wives ventured into the Punjab beyond Ferozepore, partly because it was frowned upon but also because there were not many of them to do so, it being customary in those days for East India Company officers to delay marriage until their first home furlough, usually after completing ten to twelve years' service, after which they took 'leave of absence' for perhaps two years or more. The Frontier, which initially included the whole of the Punjab, was not considered a fit place to take a wife, certainly for anyone junior in rank to a captain, or a mere Assistant to the Political Agent. When Herbert Edwardes returned to India in 1851 at the age of thirty-two, having married his childhood sweetheart Emma Sidney, he failed to get the long-coveted Commissionership of Peshawar – and wrote to warn his friend John Nicholson, who had been best man at his wedding, that if he returned to India still a bachelor it would be in his favour. Nicholson made no effort to find a bride, and in the normal course of events would then have had to wait another decade for a second bite, the course followed by Harry Lumsden,

Neville Chamberlain and Reynell Taylor, who all married comparatively late in life.

The odd one out was – as always – William Hodson. Like others, he left a childhood sweetheart behind; she married someone else, a man twice her age, but, fortunately for Hodson, the couple came out to India, where the husband died. As soon as he heard the news, Hodson travelled post-haste to her side in Calcutta, and married her. All the surviving indications suggest that they loved each other dearly for the few years they had together, writing daily when they were apart; regrettably, I have been unable to find evidence of this correspondence beyond the few letters from William Hodson quoted by his brother, the Reverend G.S. Hodson. Susan Hodson died in 1884 in the grace-and-favour apartment at Hampton Court given her by Queen Victoria 'out of consideration for the distinguished services of her husband'. Some fine 'last words' have been preserved from this time, but none do I find more moving than Hodson's gasp, as a musket fired at close range tore open his chest – 'Oh! My wife!' – and his dying whisper: 'My love to my wife. Tell her my last thoughts were of her. Lord, receive my soul.'

Of the older generation, James Abbott was recently widowed when he first appeared on the Punjab scene, and Frederick Mackeson, a shadowy figure, appears to have been a lifelong bachelor. All three Lawrence brothers, however, were very happily married to wise and down-to-earth women always prepared – though frequently forbidden – to follow their husbands through thick and thin, who brought up (or, in several instances, lost) children in circumstances that no gentlewoman of the day expected to have to endure. Of these three sisters-in-law a later memsahib, the novelist Maud Diver, wrote that their marriages were 'as decisive as entering a convent'. One in particular, Henry Lawrence's wife Honoria, was an exceptionally observant and perceptive woman. Her writing positively throbs with life when set beside the work of the more learned menfolk whose diaries, letters, journals and reports I have drawn upon. 'She and her children became camp equipment,' writes Diver, 'jolted in bullock-carts and on the backs of camels, exposed to dust, sun, heat, cholera and malaria, moving always from tent to bungalow and back again, gypsies without a home, hearth beneath the stars. They must expect hard wear and a short life, and, if they survive that, years of anxious, deadening separation.' What kept these wives going was their faith: 'To accept such a life without some sense of spiritual dedication would almost inevitably mean a coarsening of the fibres, but the wives of the Lawrences and their followers were vowed to God just as definitely as their husbands, were as closely knit in a community of work and religion.' But theirs is quite another story, and one that in Honoria Lawrence's case at least has been well told by others.

It comes as a shock to discover how very young most of these Young Men were when they first went to the Punjab, and what power they exercised; for example, Harry Lumsden, aged twenty-five, leading a force of 3,500 Sikhs, but lately his enemies, against 7,000 Hazarawal tribesmen, or Herbert Edwardes at twenty-nine leading an army of Afghan tribesmen against Dewan Mulraj of Multan. But this has always been the way of things in times of war – and the North-West Frontier has always been a cockpit of war. It is also true to say that, from the British perspective, India was always a young man's country. The striking exception to this rule was its generals, allowed to stagger on into their dotage as field commanders, often with near-disastrous consequences. Time and again, it was the young men under them who saved their skins and reputations – as these pages will demonstrate.

The Victorians saw the Lawrences and their lieutenants as a special breed of British hero: saints militant fired with Christian grace; *beaux sabreurs, sans peur et sans reproche*. Today we are more judgemental: to our eyes they come across as young men of strong convictions and unlimited self-confidence, driven to do extraordinary things quite as much by their upbringing and motivation as by their personal qualities. They were, after all, recruited locally in the field from a fairly small pool of officers serving in the EICo's Bengal Army – a pool that was never more than three thousand strong at any one time. However, it is worth bearing in mind that these officers were all gentlemen and, even if they called themselves Englishmen, mostly Scots, Scots-Irish or Anglo-Irish: in the main, younger sons of small country squires, lairds and vicars who lacked the means to set them up at home. The Queen's Army, the Navy, the clergy – and India: these were the classic outlets that might, if fortune (and patronage) smiled, bring advancement and 'genteel enrichment' sufficient to retire on at fifty. India, as that well-known Borderer Sir Walter Scott wrote, had become 'the corn chest for Scotland where we poor gentry must send our youngest sons as we send our black cattle to the South'. As a group, these poor gentry were well-educated, hardy and ambitious.

Another common factor was religious conviction, ranging from the fervid evangelicalism of such as Herbert Edwardes, who saw himself as a 'pioneer of Christian civilisation', to the sin-ridden gloom of the kirk which gripped men like John Nicholson. Somewhere in between were the bluff, no-nonsense C. of E. Christians like Neville Chamberlain; God-fearing rather than devout, but whose rock-solid convictions were a bastion in danger-ous times. 'A horse and a sword were all that were needful,' Neville Chamberlain wrote of those times in later years, 'and one never gave a thought as to danger. Not that there was any levity in facing death; it was simply that one was possessed of a light heart to meet any-thing that came. There was nothing but God above and duty below.'

We have to make a leap of imagination, from our own faithless age, back to an era when the promise of the Heavenly Kingdom for those who had fought the good fight was still very real. Contemporaries on both sides of the racial divide write of the extraordinary recklessness with which the British soldiery – men and officers – went into battle at this time. Drink played its part, to say nothing of fighting spirit and military discipline, but for many it was the confidence born of unshakeable faith that enabled them to look death in the face – if not actually to seek out danger. Think of the youngster Quintin Battye, recently-joined subaltern of the Guides' Cavalry, sketching on the walls of the new billiard room in the officers' mess at Hoti Mardan a spirited mural of the Guides at full tilt, the officers brandishing their swords and the sowars their lances – and then adding underneath the words of the Roman poet Horace: '*Dulce et decorum est pro patria mori*'. Two years on, slipping into death on Delhi Ridge, he whispers his last words to his friend William Hodson: 'Ah well, old fellow, "*Dulce et decorum est pro patria mori*". That's how it is.'

Along with religious conviction came the sense of a divine mission. This is best illustrated by Henry Lawrence's answer when asked by Maharaja Gulab Singh of Jammu and Kashmir to explain how it was that the British always conquered their foes. Lawrence at first refused to be drawn, but when the Maharaja pressed him for an answer he marked on a sheet of paper the mystical letters which had become more or less synonymous with the Evangelical Movement then sweeping through the Church of England, and which can be seen carved on Victorian pulpits in parish churches all over England: IHS. He did not trouble to explain to Gulab Singh that these letters represented the Latin form of 'Jesus Saviour of Men', so that the maharaja took them to be some cabalistic sign of good fortune and even had them stamped on the silver rupee coins for his newly-acquired kingdom of Kashmir.

One other quality these young Paladins also had in common was luck, the attribute Napoleon always demanded in his generals. The Indian subcontinent – and the Frontier, in particular – is littered with half-forgotten graveyards filled with the bones of the unlucky, their lives extinguished before they had a chance to shine. Among those whose luck ran out before their time we might list Alexander 'Bokhara' Burnes, assassinated by the Afghans at Kabul in 1841; Charles Stoddart and Arthur Conolly, both beheaded by the Amir of Bokhara in 1842; George Broadfoot and Elliott D'Arcy Todd, blown to pieces at the savage battle of Ferozshah in 1845; and twenty-one-year-old Patrick Vans Agnew and his equally youthful military assistant Lieutenant William Anderson, whose murders at Multan in April 1848 set off the Second Sikh War. One wonders, too, what kind of career might have been followed by John Nicholson's younger brother, Alexander, had he not been ambushed by Shinwari tribesmen in the Khyber Pass within weeks of arriving at Peshawar in November 1842. Rudyard Kipling's 'Arithmetic on the Frontier' could almost have been written for poor seventeen-year-old Alexander:

> A scrimmage in a Border Station –
> A canter down some dark defile –
> Two thousand pounds of education
> Drops to a ten-rupee *jezail* –
> The Crammer's boast, the Squadron's pride
> Shot like a rabbit in a ride!

It was a particularly violent period, in a theatre where warfare and killing was and is endemic. But the violence was emphatically bilateral, with both sides giving as good as they got, and this balanced equation of strong men on both sides lies at the heart of the Frontier story.

It has been said by a much later frontiersman – Sir Olaf Caröe, last British Governor of the NWFP in 1946–47 (at whose feet I had the honour of sitting, as a young man from the BBC, in the summer of 1974) – that the British political officers who served in the NWFP were 'more than half Pathans themselves'. Caröe and others like him have written of the shared bonds between themselves and the people of the North-West Frontier. These were bonds not so much of friendship as of mutual respect, a respect encapsulated by Rudyard Kipling in his much misunderstood poem 'The Ballad of East and West', and constitute the third element in this book.

One can no more write about John Nicholson without reference to Henry Lawrence's Young Men than one can write about the latter without reference to the tribespeople of the Frontier, the *Pakhtuns* (Pathans), and to *Pakhtunwali*, the way of the Pakhtuns – an uncompromising social code so profoundly at odds with Western mores that its application constantly brings one up with a jolt. Pakhtunwali still forms the single most powerful guiding and unifying force in Frontier life today, while at the same time being the most divisive force in NWFP politics. Standing shoulder-to-shoulder with Pakhtunwali is Islam. The issue of *Shariat* law versus secular law remains a matter of the hottest dispute in Pakistan, while on its western borders the hard-line fundamentalist *Talib* government of Afghanistan – whose followers, the Taliban, believe profoundly in the sixth pillar of Islam, *Jihad* or 'holy war' – is both a source of inspiration and a threat. It is also a reminder that, on the Frontier, Islam has always been forceful and uncompromising.

Lastly, there is that Frontier itself: as a border, an imaginary line demarcated by Sir Henry Durand in 1893 that runs for about a thousand kilometres from one mountain top to another between Pakistan and Afghanistan – and in so doing cuts right through the homelands of a dozen major Pakhtun tribes, from the Afridi to the Waziri; as a province of Pakistan, an area of approximately 100,000 square kilometres separated from the Punjab by the River Indus (give or take a couple of pockets of land on the wrong side of the river) and largely made up of poor soil, sandy scrub and rocky mountainside. These highlands, however, overlook a number of fertile valleys, of which the largest, the Vale of Peshawar, watered by the Kabul and Swat rivers, is one of the most productive agricultural regions of Pakistan.

The first westerner to leave a detailed description of the Vale of Peshawar was Mountstuart Elphinstone, writing at a time when the Indus formed the boundary between India and Afghanistan. Set down in his *Account of the Kingdom of Caubul*, it is as valid today as it was in 1809, the year of his diplomatic mission to the court of the Amir of Kabul. 'The plain', he writes, 'is nearly circular, and about thirty-five miles in diameter. Except for a small space on the east, it is surrounded with mountains, of which the range of the Indian Caucasus [the Hindu Kush] on the north, and the Peak of Suffaidcoh [the Safaid Koh range] on the south-west, are the most conspicuous.' His party entered the Vale of Peshawar in springtime, when the countryside is at its loveliest:

The plain was clothed with the richest verdure, and the climate was delicious . . . The numerous gardens and scattered trees were covered with new foliage, which had a freshness and brilliancy never seen in the perpetual summer of India. Many streams ran through the plain. Their banks were fringed with willows and tamarisks. The orchards scattered over the country contained a profusion of plum, peach, apple, pear, quince, and pomegranate trees, which afforded a greater display of blossom than I ever before witnessed; and the uncultivated parts of the land were covered with a thick elastic sod, that perhaps never was equalled but in England. The greater part of the plain was highly cultivated, and irrigated by many water-courses and canals. Never was a spot of the same extent better peopled.

This fertile paradise was the lure which throughout history had drawn plunderers down from the mountains of Afghanistan in search of the three great prizes of *zan*, *zar* and *zamin* – women, gold and land. Today it is still a lure, but hardly a paradise: the highway first laid across the Vale from the mouth of the Khyber to the river Indus at Attock by the Mughal invader Babur in the six-teenth century, and then modernised by Lieutenant Alexander Taylor and his sappers in the 1850s, is now built up on both sides all the way from the sprawling military depot of Nowshera to the city of Peshawar, and on almost up to the foot of the mountains. Peshawar itself now extends far across the plain on all sides, its pop-ulation quadrupled in the last two decades by a huge influx of Afghan refugees fleeing first the war against the Russians and then the civil war that followed. During the day its streets are crowded and clamorous with pedestrians, motorised rickshaws, lorries and buses, the air fouled by diesel exhaust fumes. But walk a few yards into any back-street and, with a little imagination, you can see how it might have looked to Elphinstone when he first rode through one of its gates in 1809, into a walled city some five miles in circumference, with no more than 100,000 inhabitants. 'The houses', he wrote, 'are built of brick (generally unburnt), in wooden frames: they are commonly three storeys high, and the lower storey is generally occupied by shops. The streets are narrow, as might be expected, where no wheeled carriages are used . . . The shops were all open. Dried fruits, and nuts, bread, meat, boots, shoes, saddlery, bales of cloth, hardware, ready-made clothes, and posteens [sheep-skin coats], books, etc., were either displayed in tiers in front of the shops, or hung up on hooks on the roof. Amongst the handsomest shops were the fruiterers' (where apples, melons, plums, and even oranges, though these are rare in Peshawar, were mixed in piles with some of the Indian fruits); and the cookshops, where every thing was served in earthen dishes, painted and glazed so as to look like china.'

Large sections of the bazaar area of the old city remain almost unchanged, still thronged by passers-by as varied and picturesque as they were in Elphinstone's day:

The streets were crowded with men of all nations and languages, in every variety of dress and appearance . . . people carrying greens, curds, etc., and men carrying water in leathern bags at their backs, and announcing their commodity by beating on a brazen cup, in which they give a draught to a passenger for a trifling piece of money. With these were mixed people of the town in white turbans, some in large white or dark blue frocks, and others in sheep-skin cloaks; Persians and Afghauns, in brown woollen tunics, or flowing mantles, and caps of black sheep-skin or coloured silk; Khyberees, with the straw sandals, and the wild dress, and air of their mountains; Hindoos, uniting the peculiar features and manners of their own nation to the long beard and the dress of the country; and Hazaurehs [people of Hazara], not more remarkable for their conical caps of skin, with the wool, appearing like a fringe round the edge, and for their broad faces and little eyes, than for their want of the beard, which is the ornament of every other face in the city. Among these, might be discovered a few women, with long white veils, that reach their feet . . . Amidst all this throng, we generally passed without any notice, except a salaam alaikum [greetings] from a passenger, accompanied by a bow, with the hands crossed in front, or an application from a beggar, who would call out for relief from the Feringee Khauns [Frankish or foreign lords], admonish us that life was short, and the benefit of charity immortal, or remind us that what was little to us was a great deal to him.

What has changed most are the means of transport. Today pedestrians are assailed by the roar and stink of thousands of customised buses, public-carriers and motor-rickshaws with hand-painted panels and gaudy decorations. In Elphinstone's day the sounds were easier on the ear. 'Sometimes a troop of armed horsemen passed,' he writes, 'and their appearance was announced by the clatter of their horses' hoofs on the pavement, and by the jingling of their bridles. Sometimes, when the King was going out, the streets were choked with horse and foot, and dromedaries bearing swivels [mounted guns], and large waving red and green flags; and, at all times, loaded dromedaries, or heavy Bactrian camels, covered with shaggy hair, made their way slowly through the streets; and mules, fastened together in circles of eight or ten, were seen off the road, going round and round to cool them after their labour, while their keepers were indulging in an eating-house, or enjoying a smoke of a hired calleaun [chillum, or hookah] in the street.'

Babur, first of the Mughal Emperors, gave the city its present name and its meaning: 'frontier town'. Peshawar is still a frontier town – but it is also the hub about which the North-West Frontier turns. To many, the NWFP is simply 'the Frontier'; there is no other. And its romance is unquestionable. Pakhtuns will say that the romance was started by the great seventeenth-century warrior-poet of the Khatak tribe, Khushal Khan. Fans of the Mughals might say it was Emperor Babur, writing in that neglected masterpiece among memoirs, *Baburnama*. However, from a British perspective, the Frontier legend begins with Herbert Edwardes's *A Year on the Punjab Frontier in 1848–9* – now long out of print but a classic of its time. Within a decade of the publication of Edwardes's book in 1850 the Frontier had carved out a special niche for itself in British folklore – and with good cause. It had, after all, been the frontier from which thousands of young men had marched off into the dark defiles of Afghanistan, and into oblivion, in the First Afghan War. It had taken two fiercely-fought wars against the Sikhs to secure – and from that time onwards became the ultimate testing-ground for generations of professional soldiers from both the British and Indian Armies, a posting to be feared by the greenhorn and the timid, but one eagerly sought-after by the ambitious and by those who liked their soldiering to carry a whiff of gunpowder and cordite. This remained true of those who followed in the footsteps of Henry Lawrence's Young Men, the officers of the Indian Political Service who served in the NWFP, an élite cadre drawn from both the Indian Army and the Indian Civil Service. Again I turn to Sir Olaf Caröe, for a quotation (taken from *Plain Tales from the Raj*) that sums up the Frontier ethos:

I remember Lord Ronaldshay saying that 'the life of the frontiersman is hard and he treads it daily on the brink of eternity'. That was the sort of feeling one had about the landscape there, which was sometimes gloriously beautiful – green and lovely and verdant – and sometimes stark and horrible and beset with duststorms. The stage on which the Pathan lived out his life was at the same time magnificent and harsh – and the Pathan was like his background. Such a contrast was sometimes hard to bear but perhaps it was this that put us in love with it. There was among the Pathans something that called to the Englishman or the Scotsman – partly that the people looked you straight in the eye, that there was no equivocation and that you couldn't browbeat them even if you wanted to. When we crossed the bridge at Attock we felt we'd come home.

The North-West Frontier was to Britain and British India what the Wild West was to the United States of America. Service on the Frontier always carried risk. It was (as it remains) a hard country of hard men, who bore arms almost from the moment their mothers first set them on the earth, who were merciless to the loser yet always offered hospitality whenever it was asked, who would go to the ends of the earth to settle old scores, who stuck to their own code through thick and thin, and who refused to become part of the fold, even when this meant bringing the wrath of government down on their heads.

Throughout the period of British crown rule in India, from 1858 to 1947, scarcely a year passed without some form of military force or punitive expedition having to be raised and sent into the Tribal Areas of the NWFP to bring one or other of the clans to heel. But once a settlement had been reached and punishments or fines levied, those same punitive forces always marched away again – out of the Tribal Areas and back into the Settled Areas. And throughout the British period the Pakhtuns in the Tribal Areas, uniquely, retained a high degree of independence. They never paid taxes, other than collective fines, and even received what they regarded as tribute from the Raj to keep the peace – danegeld, in the form of cash payments as well as lesser favours such as gun licences. So when the British troopships finally sailed away from Karachi in August 1947 they left behind, in the NWFP, one of the biggest of their headaches.

With Partition, the Pakhtuns of the NWFP threw in their lot with Pakistan, but remained as determined as ever to preserve their quasi independent status and their traditional way of life. How the government of Pakistan has managed the Frontier since 1947 and gue

what goes on today in those same divisions and districts that
Nicholson and the rest of Henry Lawrence's Young Men first governed is a story in itself – but one which, regrettably, falls outside
the confines of this book. But the romance continues; and today, as
yesterday, the politics of the NWFP tread daily on the brink of
eternity.

'The land of the Afghans'

JOHN NICHOLSON AND AFGHANISTAN, 1839–1841

> This is the land of the Afghans and the sons of this soil
>   cannot be deceived,
> Therefore withhold your hands, as your agents cannot
>   succeed.
> Listen, oh child of imperialism, to my views and thoughts:
> Don't play with fire, and sit quietly,
> For I am the Afghan who made the British flee.
>
>   Old Afghani song

DOMINATING THE Market Square in the former linen town of Lisburn is a figure of John Nicholson, cast in the best statuary bronze and, at nine foot six inches, a third larger than life-size. He stands feet apart, brandishing a sabre in his right hand and a pistol in his left. Ever since it was erected in 1922 the Nicholson statue has provided a rallying point for the town's largely Loyalist community. During the summer marching season a two-tiered wooden arch is erected across the Market Square and covered in a variety of Loyalist flags and symbols surmounted by a cardboard cut-out of King Billy on a white charger and a large crown picked out in light-bulbs. The statue faces the arch and is linked to it by several strings of bunting: one tied to its right heel, another to the top of its scabbard and a third looped round the hand holding the revolver, so that the figure appears to be struggling to fight its way clear of the red, white and blue. To reinforce its status as an Orange Order totem, a bright orange sash is draped over its right shoulder and pinned together at the waist.

One face of the large block of Aberdeen granite upon which John Nicholson stands carries the marks of a Republican car-bomb. In that same explosion, what was thought to be a spanner went through the window of a nearby dentist's surgery: it was later found to be the end of Nicholson's sword scabbard. During the time of troubles another far larger car-bomb in nearby Seymour Street caused so much damage that a number of houses had to be pulled down. One of these was the Hogg house, in which John Nicholson had lived as a boy.

John Nicholson was born on 11 December 1822 into a family colonial to the core, descended from the Protestant Scottish Lowland and Border immigrant stock which settled in the Ulster Plantations after the English Crown's appropriation of some two million acres of prime Irish land in 1607. In 1622 the Reverend William Nicholson, rector of Derrybrughas, built himself a fine manse at Tallbridge, Cranagill; in 1641 he and most of his family were among the thousands of Protestant settlers massacred in the uprising known as the Old Irish Rebellion. One daughter-in-law and one infant grandson survived, saved by a faithful Irish Catholic servant who hid them under a pile of brushwood while their home was burned to the ground – an act of courage that puts one in mind of the scores of British memsahibs and children saved by Indian ayahs and servants in the 1857 Mutiny. The Old Irish Rebellion, characterised by horrific acts of cruelty perpetrated by Irish peasants desperate to reclaim their land and followed by equally savage reprisals, burned itself into the Protestant consciousness. Although long forgotten on the British mainland, it is the hidden trauma that lies at the root of all Orangery in Northern Ireland. Prejudices conceived in 1641 were merely nourished by the Glorious Revolution of 1688–9.

The surviving grandson had by then rebuilt the family house and converted to Quakerism, so becoming known in family history as William the Quaker. This new faith failed to prevent three of his sons from being caught up in the 105-day siege of

Londonderry. It is odds on that at least one of the three was among those who stood on the walls of Londonderry on the morning of 18 April 1689 to shout what become thereafter the rallying cry of all Ulster Protestants: 'No Surrender!' Two of the three were killed in the siege, and the recently-restored ancestral home at Cranagill was again burnt to the ground. Nevertheless, the Nicholson line survived, several of the Quaker's great-grandsons and great-grand-daughters doing what many other Ulster folk were doing at that time – emigrating to Massachusetts, New Hampshire, Vermont and Maine.

But some stayed on, and in 1795, six generations after William the Quaker, Alexander Nicholson was born to John and Isabella Nicholson of Stamore House, Gilford, County Down. He studied at Trinity College, Dublin, became a doctor, and in 1820 married Clara Hogg of Lisburn.

The Hoggs were late arrivals in Ulster compared to the Nicholsons, having come across the water with William III's army. They were also genteel folk, but Clara Hogg's father, having ruined himself in unwise ventures in the linen industry in his native town, had then compounded his family's misfortune by dying, leaving a widow, two sons and four daughters in very tight circumstances.

Dr Nicholson's choice of Clara Hogg for his bride led to a split in his family, not because of the lack of a dowry but because she was a Presbyterian and he a Quaker. This was probably why he moved to Dublin and took a post as assistant physician at the Lying-in Hospital, where he soon gained a reputation as a skilled and caring practitioner.

Over the ten years of their marriage Clara Nicholson gave birth to seven children: Mary (1821), John (1822), Alexander (1824), Lily (1826), James (1827; he died in 1840), William (1828), and Charles (1831). However, soon after John's ninth birthday his father picked up a fever from one of his patients, and died. Mrs Nicholson now found herself once more in very reduced circum-stances, having only the rents from a few smallholdings to live on. Yet by every account she was a survivor, a woman of strong will and determination who gave her children a strict, disciplined, God-fearing upbringing. One of the many stories recorded of the young John Nicholson – the majority emanating from his mother and having more than a tinge of *Lives of the Saints* about them – tells how she once found the three-year-old John flicking a knotted handkerchief frenziedly in the air around him. 'What are thee doing, John?' cried Mrs Nicholson. 'Oh, mother dear,' replied the boy gravely, 'I'm trying to get a blow at the devil. He is wanting to make me bad. If I could get him down, I'd kill him.' This tale may have charmed Victorian readers, but it also reveals something of the dark side of John Nicholson. He could be said to have spent much of his life wrestling with the devil.

In 1833 Mrs Nicholson's circumstances changed dramatically for the better, entirely due to the efforts of her elder brother, James Weir Hogg, who had established himself in Calcutta as an extremely successful lawyer. In 1809 he had sailed for India armed with a passport from the Duke of Buckingham which allowed him to practise law within the EICo's trading monopoly in Calcutta. He had then borrowed heavily from Indian *banyas* in order to send back money to support his mother, younger brother and four sisters in Lisburn, but within the space of five years had paid off his debts. By 1820 he was making £15,000 a year at the Calcutta bar – a sum which must be trebled and have another nought added to reflect its value in today's terms. In 1822 he became Registrar of the Calcutta Supreme Court and continued to earn a very handsome annual income until 1833, when he retired from India at the age of 43 with a nabob's fortune.

As 'Uncle Hogg', it was James Weir Hogg who opened the door to India for the Nicholson boys. As a first step he invited his widowed sister and her brood to move into the large late-Georgian house which he had bought for his mother in Seymour Street, Lisburn. When John Nicholson reached the age of twelve, Uncle Hogg paid for him to board at the Royal School, Dungannon. More honeyed tales are told of John's four years here: of his inability to tell a lie, his strong sense of justice and honour, his hatred of bullies and all mean practices, his premature manliness. Although they speak of him as a retiring boy of few words, underlying these stories are hints of a violent disposition and a fiery temper. Perhaps an unguarded remark, made in her old age by John's elder sister Mary to an enquirer – that he was 'just a great big bully' – may be nearer the mark. At any rate, the teenaged John found his greatest expression in physical activity, throwing himself into games, rough-housing and fights, where his great size and strength gave him the upper hand.

John left the Royal School very soon after his sixteenth birthday. Uncle Hogg was by then a Member of Parliament and a leading figure in the City of London, with a pile of East India stock in his name and a large house in Grosvenor Street. He was also on the board of directors of the East India Company and in line to be its next chairman. This enabled him to secure for his nephew a direct cadetship in the EICo's Bengal Infantry, one that circumvented the requirement to attend one or other of the EICo's two colleges – Haileybury for its cadet administrators, still known then as 'writers', and Addiscombe for its artillery and engineer officer cadets.

In January 1839 John said farewell to his family – promising his mother that he would read a chapter a day from the Bible given him by his elder sister Mary – and travelled to London. Here he spent several weeks in Grosvenor Street, being tutored in Indian ways and manners by Uncle Hogg, kitted out at his expense, and presented to the EICo's Court of Directors in Leadenhall Street to be sworn in as a Company cadet. Finally, he was taken down to Gravesend to board the East Indiaman *Camden*, which sailed for India in mid February.

On board the *Camden* John shared the great cabin with a number of young writers and cadets much like himself in background, if not in temperament. Most had a head start over him by virtue of the schooling they had received at the Company's colleges, where they had been given a good grounding in the military arts and the basics of Hindustani, the lingua franca of Northern India (also known as Urdu, the language of the camp, being primarily the common language spoken among Muslims in India). They had studied James Mill's eight-volume *History of British India*, which taught them that the Indian subcontinent was 'cursed from one end to the other by the vice, the ignorance, the oppression, the despotism, the barbarous and cruel customs that have been the growth of ages under every description of Asiatic misrule'. They had also been introduced to the new 'liberal' thinking of Thomas Macaulay, James Mill's disciple, which gave them a three-point mission statement: firstly, to rule 'a great people sunk in the lowest depths of slavery and oppression' so as to make them 'desirous and capable of all the privileges of citizens'; secondly, 'to bestow on the swarming millions of India the blessings of rudimentary legislation'; and thirdly, to create as intermediaries between themselves and these swarming millions 'a class of persons, Indian in blood and colour, but English in taste, in opinions, in morals, in intellect'. John Nicholson did his best to fill the gaps in his professional education by means of shipboard reading. As for political indoctrination, he had his own set of prejudices, shaped by the entrenched Presbyterian colonist culture in which he had grown up.

A speedy, uneventful voyage brought the *Camden* up the Hoogly River in mid July 1839 – giving John his first views of a Bengal countryside revived and newly-greened by the Rains – and on to moorings beside Fort William at Calcutta. Uncle Hogg's name carried much weight there. A letter of introduction to a wealthy lawyer enabled John to avoid the discomforts of messing in Fort William while awaiting his instructions. On the Indian subcontinent, contacts and influential friends were everything, then as now. Talent and application had their place, but came a poor second to that vital bundle of sealed letters wrapped in oilskin which said, 'He is one of us. Do what you can to keep it that way.'

In August John was instructed to proceed up-river for temporary attachment to the 41st Regiment of the Bengal Native Infantry (41st BNI) at Benares – the first staging-post in a young officer's progress from unattached cadet to a subaltern gazetted as on the strength of a regiment which would be 'his' for as long as he remained a field officer. In Benares he made contact with a Nicholson uncle, a younger brother of his late father, employed in the EICo's Opium Department at nearby Mirzapur. It was at this point that Uncle Hogg's usefulness seems to have run out, for it was the Nicholson uncle who provided John with his most valuable item of kit: a horse.

John Nicholson was a man of few words, and fewer letters. By Victorian standards, he was a wretched correspondent – and a significant number of the comparatively few letters he did write after leaving Ulster were destroyed in a fire in the study of the historian Sir John Kaye. Accidental fires in studies do happen, of course, but anyone who has explored the lives of other awkward nineteenth-century heroes – Lord Byron and Sir Richard Burton, for example – must view such an accident with suspicion, wondering whether here, too, some tidying-up of a reputation was not taking place.

A surviving letter from this early period, dated 13 October 1839, is full of just those concerns one would expect from a lonely and homesick seventeen-year-old newcomer to India – a 'griffin', in Anglo-Indian parlance. John is 'all alone' in a little bungalow in the cantonments – the military area of the civil station of Benares, where the local British community lived, at some distance from the native city. He is being looked after by servants who 'cannot speak one word of English'. He worries about money. If he stays where he is he can save on his pay, but if ordered to move to another post he will have to borrow: 'I may be ordered to-morrow to join a corps some hundreds of miles up country; then I have to buy a tent, to hire camels, etc . . . I must incur heavy expenses: a tent costs 400 rupees, which it would take me a year to pay up; if I am ordered to march tomorrow, I have not 400 rupees to buy one, for I have been only two months receiving pay. However, I am very well off, and have no reason to complain. On the contrary, I am thankful for having got such a good appointment. I am getting very steady, and am beginning to learn the language.'

John asks for a full account of things at home, wonders how each of his brothers and sisters is doing, and assures his mother that he is indeed reading a chapter from sister Mary's Bible every day, as well as going to church on Sundays. His letter closes on a sad note that will strike a chord with anyone who has ever been separated from home and family at an early age: 'I often, when I am sitting alone here in the evening, think of you all at home, and say to myself there is no place like *home*.'

Neither in this nor in any subsequent letter is a word written about Nicholson's social or regimental life. We must assume that he went through the same regime as other military cadets: being taught drill by the battalion adjutant and the sergeant-major, studying Hindustani under a native *munshi* and taking on his share of regimental duties. We know, however, that after four months of 'holding' with the 41st he was ordered to proceed up-country to join his future regiment, the 27th BNI, at Ferozepore. This was the Company's newest station, in the process of being established a few miles short of the river Sutlej. The river marked the north-western limits of the EICo's territories. On its far side lay the homelands of the Sikhs, the EICo's last and most potent rivals for power in the Indian subcontinent.

British India at this time was on a roll, committed to expansion on the grounds that it had no other choice. Whatever Parliament and the EICo's Board of Directors might have to say back in England, the rallying cry of the policy-makers on the ground was still Robert Clive's famous dictum: 'To stop is dangerous, to recede ruin.' What became known as the 'Forward' policy had been first promulgated by Marquess Wellesley at the turn of the century, and enthusiastically applied by his former lieutenants in the ensuing thirty years, most notably by the three Scots, Mountstuart Elphinstone, Thomas Munro and John Malcolm, and the Englishman Charles Metcalfe. All four had worked to extend the territories of the EICo deep into the Indian hinterland. In some areas the Company ruled directly, installing its own civil adminis-trators; elsewhere it ruled indirectly, through treaty arrangements with local rulers and landowners.

By the time John Nicholson first set foot on the soil of Bengal the Forward policy had seen the EICo's pink carpet rolled all the way across the Gangetic plain as far as the waters of the Sutlej. The Maratha Confederacy had been destroyed, the Pindari freebooters broken up and numerous treaties signed between the Company and local rulers, Moslem, Jat and Rajput, none powerful enough to pose any individual threat. In the palace of his ancestors within the Red Fort at Delhi, the Mughal Emperor Bahadur Shah ruled in name only, having been deprived of everything but title and household. Only one power to rival that of the EICo remained: the Sikh Empire, centred on the Land of the Five Rivers, the Punjab (from the Persian *punj*, five and *ab*, water).

The Sikhs are a reformed sect of Hindus rather than a particular racial group, but drawn from the predominantly peasant and yeoman stock who farmed the fertile lands watered by the five tributaries of the Indus which together form the Punjab: from north to south, the Indus, Jhelum, Chenab, Ravi and Sutlej. In 1699, in the face of constant Moslem oppression inaugurated by the bigoted Mughal emperor Aurangzeb and enthusiastically pursued thereafter by a succession of Mughal and Afghan rulers, the tenth and last of the Gurus or teachers of Sikhism, Gobind Singh, initiated a section of his followers into a casteless community known as the *Khalsa* or 'pure'. In part a self-defence brotherhood, which developed into an increasingly self-confident confederacy of ten *misls* or groupings to form the *Khalsa Dal*, the army of the Sikhs, this eventually proved a match for the Afghan invaders who had occupied and settled in large tracts of the Punjab: in 1764 it defeated the army of the Afghan king of Kabul and captured Lahore, the ancient capital of the region. In 1799 a charismatic, one-eyed general named Ranjit Singh became its undisputed leader, consolidating his power base around the two cities of Lahore and Amritsar. A decade later Mountstuart Elphinstone noted that Ranjit Singh 'had acquired the sovereignty of all the Siks in the Punjaub and was assuming the title of king . . . he is busy in subjugating his weak neighbours by the same mixture of force and craft that he so successfully employed against the chiefs of his own nation.'

Prevented from expanding down into the Gangetic plain by the military superiority of the EICo, Maharaja Ranjit Singh secured his southern borders by conceding a slice of Sikh territory south of the Sutlej to the EICo – an area known as the Cis-Sutlej. This allowed him to concentrate his efforts on extending the Sikh state northwards across the Punjab, so that by 1813 the 'Lion of the Punjab' had gained control of all the so-called *doabs* – the five areas of land lying between the five rivers and the Indus. In that same year he took the great fort built by Akbar which guards the crossing-point of the river Indus at Attock, so gaining a base from which to launch an invasion of Afghan territory on the western bank of the Indus.

Ranjit Singh has been called the Napoleon of the Punjab, but the comparison does not hold: he remained in power twice as long as Napoleon, and never relinquished any of the territories he had acquired, except where it suited him. And unlike Napoleon, the illiterate Ranjit Singh was not the least interested in reform, or model administration. But what he and Napoleon did have in common was an understanding that power rested in the possession of a disciplined, modern army. His dealings with the EICo had shown Ranjit Singh the absolute necessity of modelling his Khalsa Dal on European lines if his empire was to survive, and his opportunity arose with the ending of the Napoleonic Wars in Europe, when large numbers of battle-hardened military officers with no love of the British – mostly French, but including Italians and even Americans – came on the market as mercenaries. Ranjit Singh hired no fewer than two hundred foreigners, ranging from generals (most notably Jean-François Allard, Jean-Baptiste Ventura and the Italian Paulo Avitabile) to hands-on gunnery corporals. Nor were the men who made up the rank-and-file of Ranjit Singh's Khalsa Dal exclusively Sikh: large numbers of Hindu Dogras and Gurkhas served in his infantry, which was organised, trained, dressed and armed very much along French lines. 'They are a fine-looking body of men,' wrote an English observer in 1840, 'dressed in white jackets and trowsers, with black belts and pouches, and wear the yellow Sikh turban . . . They work in three ranks, and do everything to the beat of the drum, according to the French fashion; are not what are called well set up, but beautifully steady on parade, and fire with greater precision and regularity, both volleys and file firing, than any other troops I ever saw.'

Ranjit Singh had been shocked to the core by a display of rapid unlimbering, loading and firing staged by the EICo's Horse Artillery in 1831. Intended to overawe him, it had the opposite effect, making him determined to match the EICo in firepower. To this end he secured the services of Claude Auguste Court, another French refugee from Napoleon's army, and charged him to build an artillery force capable of taking on his rivals. By the time of Ranjit Singh's death in 1839 his army had more than four hundred cannon – many recovered from the forts at Lahore, Attock, Multan and elsewhere – ranging from huge 48-pounder siege guns drawn by elephants or trains of bullocks to 3-pounder swivel guns mounted on camels. General Court trained up as artillery officers a number of Sikhs drawn from the leading families of the Khalsa but, out of Ranjit Singh's fear that the guns might be turned against him by one or other faction within the Khalsa, the gun crews themselves were made up almost entirely of Punjabi Muslims. Virtually every

British account of the two Sikh wars refers to the extreme accuracy and high rate of fire of these Sikh guns.

All three armies – Queen's, Company's and Khalsa Dal – looked upon their cavalry as the cream of their forces. In Ranjit Singh's army only the cavalry remained wholly Sikh, led by Gorchurras, land-owning 'knights' who each raised and brought their own bands of horsemen with them. As proud of their martial traditions and fighting skills as the Rajputs, the Gorchurras clung to feudal tradition, taking the field clad in chain mail and shining armour, banners flying from their lances, their mounts draped in brightly coloured quilts and shawls. The Gorchurra squadrons were masters of hit-and-run and of the surprise ambush. In set-piece battles, however, they proved no match for the EICo's cavalry brigades, whose strength lay in their ability to manoeuvre and turn to order, and to impact as one disciplined mass.

This 'new model army' had its first test in 1823 on the plains outside what is now the large military cantonment of Nowshera, on the outskirts of the Vale of Peshawar, when it confronted and defeated a massed force of Ghazi, Yusufzai and Khattak tribesmen. The victory was followed by the sack of the city of Peshawar, long regarded by the Afghans as their winter capital, and the surrounding countryside was ravaged – the first bout in a fierce struggle between the Sikhs and the Afghans for ownership of the Vale of the Peshawar that continued for over a decade. The plains country lying between the mountains of Afghanistan and the Indus was finally annexed to Ranjit Singh's Sikh dominions in 1834.

The fertile Vale of Peshawar now became the fiefdom of Ranjit Singh's army commander, Hari Singh, whose four-year governorship was characterised by looting, vandalism and rapine. It ended with his death near the mouth of the Khyber Pass during an abortive attempt by the Afghans to recapture Peshawar, but the memory of his reign of terror lived on for decades in the expression *'Raghe Hari Singh* – Hari Singh is here', employed by Yusufzai mothers to hush their children to silence. No doubt the oppressiveness of a quarter-century of Sikh misrule became more exaggerated in the telling with every year that passed thereafter, but the term *Sikha shahi* – Sikh rule – is still used today in Pakistan Punjab to describe the very worst kind of misgovernment.

Ranjit Singh's advance beyond the Indus had only been made possible by internecine squabbling among the Afghan chiefs, which culminated in the ousting of the Amir of Kabul, Shah Shuja, by a rival, Dost Mohammad Khan, in 1812. Shah Shuja was then imprisoned in Kashmir until he was rescued by Ranjit Singh, who used him as a pawn by encouraging him in his ambition to regain his throne in Kabul, while at the same time bleeding him of much of his wealth, including the famous Koh-i-noor diamond. By degrees, the British authorities in India – particularly in the persons of Lord Auckland, Governor-General since 1836, and his Chief Secretary, Sir William Macnaghten – were sucked into this process, a fatal involvement in large part resulting from their concern over what Macnaghten assured his all-too-credulous master was growing Russian influence in Afghanistan, a concern which rapidly developed into paranoia. The arrival in Kabul in December 1837 of a mysterious character named Vitkevich bearing what purported to be letters of introduction from Tsar Nicholas I led to a frenzy of comings and goings in Calcutta and Simla, the Cold and Hot Weather seats of EICo government in India. Sound advice from those who knew best was ignored. The Governor-General chose to listen only to Macnaghten, who urged nothing less than the invasion of Afghanistan and the restoration of their man, Shah Shuja, to the throne of Kabul.

Such an invasion could only be achieved with the support of Maharaja Ranjit Singh, who was delighted to learn from Macnaghten that the British proposed to take on his enemy Dost Mohammad Khan. Macnaghten's original proposal was that the Sikhs should do most of the fighting with the British lending only token assistance; but by the time his negotiations with the wily Sikh emperor had been concluded, these positions had been reversed. As an additional and equally unlooked-for bonus, the unfortunate Shah Shuja was required, as the price for his restoration to the throne of Kabul, to confirm Maharaja Ranjit Singh's title to Peshawar and to other Afghan territories west of the Indus held by the Sikhs.

So it came about that in March 1839 – as John Nicholson's Indiaman was approaching the Cape of Good Hope – the EICo's Army of the Indus marched into Afghanistan by way of the Bolan

Pass. In July of that year, when Nicholson was taking his first uncertain steps ashore in Calcutta, the great citadel of Ghazni was stormed and Kabul occupied. With as much pomp as the British could muster, Shah Shuja was reinstalled as the Amir of Kabul – in reality a puppet ruler, with Macnaghten at his elbow as 'Envoy and Minister to the Court of Shah Soojah-ool-Moolk'. The Amir's old rival, Dost Mohammad Khan, attempted to wage a guerrilla campaign against the invaders but was eventually forced to surrender. He and his family were sent into comfortable exile in India – all except his eldest son, Akbar Khan, who slipped off into the mountains.

This was how things stood beyond the Sutlej in December 1839 when John Nicholson, now eighteen, received his orders to proceed north to Ferozepore to join his battalion. One might think that the prospect of service on the Company's front line would have set racing the pulse of any newly gazetted young officer, but John seems to have been preoccupied with the difficulties of travelling up-country on his own. 'I am afraid it will prove a very unpleasant march to me,' he wrote to his mother, 'as I go alone and am unacquainted with the language and country.'

The six-hundred-mile journey by horse and bullock-cart proved just as bad as Nicholson had feared: at Meerut, thieves slashed a hole in his tent and made away with a trunk containing a brace of pistols, a dressing-case which had belonged to his father, and most of his savings; at Karnal he had to be physically restrained from fighting a more senior officer who had been unnecessarily officious; and on the open road between Ludhiana and Ferozepore he found the Sikh population unpleasantly hostile. In a letter full of complaints, he wrote to tell his mother how the authority of Colonel Wade, the British Political Agent in Ludhiana, had been defied by the village chiefs who were supposed to supply him with food: 'The Jemadars [Sikh police officers] desired the people to give me nothing, adding, "What do we care for Colonel Wade? We are Sikhs." ' But John's response, as he recounted it, suggests that he was beginning to develop the Nicholson touch: 'By threatening these refractory Sikhs with a good flogging, I managed to procure enough to eat.'

Ferozepore had been selected as the ideal site for a brigade headquarters, so placed as to provide a base for any future military adventures across the Sutlej. An area for a cantonment – the Anglo-Indian term for a standing camp, based on the template of a tented encampment wherein cavalry, infantry and artillery lines were laid out side by side in neat rectangles, together with all the supporting elements such as officers' messes, hospital, commissariat, armoury, powder magazine, treasury, parade ground, latrines and so forth – had been marked out. As was now standard Company practice, this was a few miles outside the native town of Ferozepore, and separated from it by a cleared expanse of open ground known as the *maidan*. It kept the local native population at a distance and, although designated an area for military exercises, also provided an open field of fire for the camp's artillery and a 'killing field' for its cavalry, thus doing away with the need to turn the cantonment into a fortress or walled camp. This helps to explain why British civil stations and cantonments in India always appeared so open and vulnerable to attack: piquets at each corner and check-posts at the main gates were normally all that were required in the way of security.

When John Nicholson's little convoy of bullock-carts finally arrived at Ferozepore cantonment he was dismayed to find it set in 'a perfect wilderness: there is not a tree or a blade of grass within miles of us; and as to the tigers, there are two or three killed in the neighbouring jungle every day.' Although they did not meet for another two years, his future chief Henry Lawrence was also newly arrived in Ferozepore, as its civil administrator or, more properly, the 'Assistant to the Agent of the Governor-General for the Affairs of the Punjab and the North-West Frontier'. His wife Honoria and their infant son Alexander had accompanied him, and the three were then living in two 'little pigeon-holes' in a dilapidated mud-and-brick fort, the only 'pukka' building on the plain, which Mrs Lawrence described rather more eloquently than John Nicholson as 'a wilderness of cacti, prickly scrub, sandy hillocks and the bleached bones of camels and bullocks'.

Nicholson found the officers and men of his new regiment, the 27th BNI, hard at work building their own living quarters in the patch of land designated for the infantry battalions: small bungalows for the officers and long, high-ceilinged barrack blocks for the men. As the most junior officer in the regiment, his was the last bungalow to be built, so that for several months he had to make do with a stable. Before he could move in, the Punjab Hot Weather had arrived, a time of fearful dry heat that the later chronicler of British India, Maud Diver, described as 'that pitiless destroyer of youth and beauty'. With the Hot Weather came the mosquitoes – and Nicholson's first attack of what soon became notorious as the 'Punjab fever'. 'I have just recovered from a severe attack of fever, brought on by the want of proper shelter,' John writes to his mother in July 1840. 'But my new house will soon be finished, and then I hope I shall enjoy my usual health. You can have no idea how the hot weather enervates the body, and, if you do not take special care, the mind also.'

From this time onwards bouts of fever, together with the annual purgatory of the Hot Weather – four blistering months from mid April to about mid July, followed by the two suffocatingly humid months of the Rains – became regular features of his life.

However, Nicholson was pleased to find himself among officers and men he could respect. 'The corps is considered a first-rate one,' he wrote. Like other infantry regiments of the Bengal Army, the 27th was composed of high-caste Hindus – Brahmins and Rajputs recruited from Oude and Bihar. Caste obligations dominated their thinking and affected their military performance in ways that Nicholson must have found almost incomprehensible at first. Before taking meals they had to purify themselves by bathing, changing their clothes and performing prayers. The meal itself had to be fresh, cooked by persons of the same caste as themselves, and eaten in ritually pure circumstances without risk of pollution. All this could take hours, so that no fast marches were possible. For all the martial qualities of the men themselves and their smartness of parade, their potential for effectiveness as a modern fighting force was bound to be a matter of concern to anyone who cared to look a little deeper.

However, the only issue that really mattered to Nicholson, along with every other officer on the station, was the prospect of military action – for action in the field was the only sure means of advancement in their military careers. 'We are on the qui vive for intelligence from the frontier,' he wrote to his Uncle Hogg. 'Kabul by all acounts is quite quiet, and has almost ceased to afford us any interest.' However, at the start of the Cold Weather orders came through that the 27th BNI was to relieve one of the infantry regiments which had entered Afghanistan as part of the Army of the Indus. In November 1840 John Nicholson's regiment began its march across the Punjab.

The Punjab Cold Weather, from October through to March, is a delight: warm, sunny days and, for the most part, clear nights which in December and January bring a touch of frost. This is ideal marching and camping weather, so much so that in ancient days the kings of India were said always to start their military campaigns after celebrating the warriors' festival of Dassera in the early autumn. The military route-march might last for a month or more, but it was by no means a hard slog. The distances covered each day were not great, being regulated by the pace of each unit's transport animals, usually bullocks. The routine was unchanging. Long before first light the camp began to stir. Tents were struck and loaded onto bullock-carts and camels while the officers washed, shaved and snatched a quick breakfast by lamplight. By 5 a.m. at the latest the first columns would be played out of camp by the regimental band, the officers following on horseback at their own pace. For an hour or more the regiment marched in the dark, its front-markers guided by burning torches. A short halt an hour or so after sun-up allowed the men a chance to consume a cold breakfast of the chappatis carried in their packs. Then the men returned to their columns and settled down to a long, steady march that grew warmer and dustier by the hour. In the meantime, an advance party would have hurried on ahead to mark out the lines at the day's camping-ground and to organise all the necessary supplies. By midday at the very latest the columns would march into camp one behind the other, again played in by the fifes and drums of the regimental band. Camp-fires would be lit and rice boiled up in large *dekshies*, so that the men could have their main meal of the day: curried vegetables, lentils and rice. By mid afternoon the last of the bullock-carts would have arrived, so that the mess-tent could go up and each officer's camp furniture and kit be set out in his tent.

While all this was going on the officers themselves would probably leave camp for a spot of local *shikar*, taking a few of the sportier sepoys out with them as *shikaris* and beaters, walking the local scrub jungle in the hopes of putting up *chikor*, the Indian partridge, or sandgrouse, or perhaps some deer. The local village elders were always on hand, only too willing to point the sahibs towards bigger game which in their eyes constituted a nuisance: wild boar ravaging their corn or sugarcane, or a tiger threatening their livestock. If the officers were adventurous enough and well mounted, they might go after both such prey with well-sharpened lances rather than shotguns.

The Punjab then was not what it is now – a countryside transformed into a vast mosaic of well-tilled fields by an extensive canal system engineered under the British administration. A hundred and sixty-odd years ago much of the country was untouched jungle, cultivated only in the stretches adjoining the five great rivers and their side tributaries. These rivers made natural divisions of the land and natural halting-points. Some had bridges made up of boats tied together, but others had to be crossed either by fords or by the laborious process of ferrying. When a thousand or so soldiers arrived at such a crossing-point, together with several times that number of camp followers and all their beasts of burden, it served as a welcome opportunity for the regiment to clean itself up: for the men to wash and bathe as required by their caste rules, and for the dhobies to do their dubious laundering – by bashing their cottons on flat rocks before laying them out to dry.

So, stage by stage, the 27th BNI made its way north and west across the Punjab: first across the Sutlej to the Sikh stronghold of Lahore, and then along the well-shaded Mughal highway by way of Gujranwala, Wazirabad, Gujarat and Rotas to Rawalpindi, at that time nothing more than a village and a bazaar under the shadow of the Pir Panchal range and the mountains of Hazara. From here on the character of the country began to change, becoming hillier and wilder with every day that passed. Half a day's march west of Rawalpindi they came to the Margalla or 'cut-throat' Hills, a mountain spur jutting out into the plains which formed a natural defensive barrier. This was breached at one point by a narrow defile, the Margalla Pass, guarded by a small hill upon which stood a stone watchtower known as a *burj*. As he passed by,

Nicholson will have noted that here was a place of obvious strategic importance.

Two days later they came to the banks of the Indus, at the point where that great river narrows to force its way through the two-hundred-yard-wide gorge at Attock. The crossing-point was dominated by the battlements of Akbar's Fort, which now guarded a newly-built bridge constructed from a number of boats lashed side by side. Always vulnerable, that bridge of boats was replaced in 1883 by a twin-storey Meccano-like structure – railway line above, road below – which in turn has been superseded by a magnificent modern road-bridge. As you drive off it, you pass under an arch supported on two crenellated towers of stone and bearing the sign 'Welcome to NWFP'. This is the famous Gateway to the Frontier. The sepoys in John Nicholson's regiment will have needed no such sign; they knew that they had now left Hindustan and entered notably hostile territory – the land of the Afghans. Another two days' march brought the regiment to the city of Peshawar, where its officers were made welcome by the governor, the Italian mercenary General Avitabile.

After only a brief stay, the regiment marched out of Peshawar to the point where the plains of India end and the mountains of Afghanistan begin. The Pakhtuns say that when Allah created the world he had a pile of rocks left over, out of which he created Afghanistan. Some fifteen miles west of Peshawar that pile of rocks is cut by a dark ravine out of which a river debouches onto the plain. This is the mouth of the Khyber Pass, although 'pass' suggests a high crossing-point over a mountain range, whereas this is really a trail that leads up the bed of a river which has cut itself a deep, narrow defile of more than twenty miles through the mountains. Although only one of a number of fissures in the mountain chain which provides India with a natural defensive wall to west and north, the Khyber has always provided the subcontinent with its main invasion and trade route. It also long served as the chief highway between what the Afghans had come to regard as their summer and winter capitals, Kabul and Peshawar. Yet even the Afghans were forced to recognise that passage through the Khyber could only be obtained with the agreement of its guardians, the local Khybari tribespeople, who had held it for centuries and who made their living by exacting heavy tolls from every traveller. To secure safe passage through the Khyber without the approval of the Khybari tribes meant holding the high ground on both sides of the caravan trail. But before high ground can be held it has to be seized and piquets set up on all the strategic points – an enormous undertaking in the case of the Khyber Pass, which is serrated by scores of ravines and side-valleys and overlooked by hundreds of peaks and crags. Many conquerors with mighty armies have come this way, but all have found that, if they fail to pay their dues, they suffer for it. In 1841 it became the turn of the British to learn this painful lesson.

The custodians of the Khyber were made up of three different Afghan tribes, the Afridi, Shinwari and Orakzai, each controlling their own sector. In appearance and characteristics they were typically Pakhtun: 'lean, muscular men, with long gaunt faces, high noses and cheekbones'. But they were also masters of the ambush, adept at using their long-barrelled jezails to bring a man down at five hundred paces and then closing with their curved tulwars and daggers to finish him off. During his mission to Peshawar, Mountstuart Elphinstone learned that even among the Afghans themselves these Khybari had an awesome reputation as the 'greatest robbers' in the land:

> Such are their habits of rapine, that they can never be entirely restrained from plundering passengers; and when there is any confusion in the state, it is impossible to pass through their country. In quiet times, the Khyberees have stations in different parts of the pass, to collect an authorised toll on passengers, but in times of trouble, they are all on the alert: if a single traveller endeavours to make his way through, the noise of his horse's feet sounds up the long narrow valleys, and soon brings the Khyberees in troops from the hills and ravines.

In January 1841 the 27th BNI made its way up the twenty-six miles of the Khyber and on to the town of Jalalabad without incident – for the very good reason that Sir William Macnaghten was then paying the Khybaris a notably generous annual toll of £8,000 (again, add a nought and multiply by three to get some idea of its worth today) for the safe movement of all the Company's troops. A few months later the regiment marched back down to Peshawar to collect a convoy of six hundred women of Shah Shuja's harem and then escort them back up the Khyber and on to Kabul – an extremely tedious exercise which, if nothing else, taught them how narrow and dangerous was this passage.

No sooner had the regiment delivered its precious cargo to the Amir in Kabul than it was ordered to proceed over the mountains to Ghazni – a five-day march south from Kabul on the road to Kandahar – to relieve the 16th BNI and take over garrison duties at its great citadel. At Ghazni Nicholson met Neville Chamberlain, a subaltern in the 16th BNI, two years his senior, and made his first real friend in India.

The second son of an English baronet, Neville Chamberlain was a military officer in an almost classic British mould. He and his younger brother Crawford, also serving in the Bengal Army but as a cavalry officer, had come to India determined to cover themselves with glory in the field. Both had already seen action in Afghanistan with the Army of the Indus, and Neville carried the scar of the first of a quite prodigious tally of wounds to be inflicted on his person over the next few years. Fiercely competitive as well as protective of each other, the two brothers shared the same temperament: cheerful, outgoing and always game for a hazard. However, Neville's letters home to his mother, written in the form of a journal which he copied and sent back in instalments, show him to be an unusually thoughtful and sensitive young man. His *Journal of the Afghan War*, never published, provides an exceptionally frank account of that bizarre and unhappy first encounter between Britain and Afghanistan.

On the face of it, Chamberlain and Nicholson had very little in common, other than the fact that they were both junior infantry ensigns. But perhaps it was significant that both had been brought up by strong-minded widowed mothers, and both had turbulent natures. At the age of fifteen Neville Chamberlain had been expelled from the British Army's academy for engineer officers at Woolwich for fighting, and it was only through the intercession of influential family friends in India that he obtained a cadetship in the EICo's Bengal Army. His brother Crawford, with this same rebellious streak, had rejected the chance to go to Haileybury in favour of a military career alongside Neville. The patronage of the Commander-in-Chief had secured posts for both Neville and Crawford in the Army of the Indus, and the brothers had been involved, with their respective regiments, in the storming of the citadel at Ghazni.

Thrown together in an isolated outpost in a strange country, Neville Chamberlain and John Nicholson became – as the former was to write many years later – 'friends at first sight'. He remembered John Nicholson at nineteen as 'a tall, strong, slender youth, with regular features, and a quiet, reserved manner. We were constantly together during the short time that intervened between his regiment taking over the fort and my regiment leaving for Kandahar. After my arrival at that place occasional correspondence passed between us, but neither of us was given to letter-writing, and what most occupied our minds was the events taking place in our respective neighbourhoods.'

These events began with the British envoy, Sir William Macnaghten, calling a halt to the payment of the subsidy which had kept the Khybari friendly, and ordering the return to India of one of the two brigades which were helping to keep Shah Shuja's increasingly unpopular regime in power – in effect, a fifty per cent reduction of his occupying force. When the troops of the withdrawing brigade and the thousands of native camp-followers who accompanied them began to retire through the Khyber defile, they were blocked and pinned down for two weeks by Shinwari marksmen furious at the loss of their toll fees. This should have given Macnaghten ample warning of what would follow. Dismissing the advice of his political advisers as 'alarmist', however, he continued to deceive both himself and his masters in Calcutta. The scene was now set for the greatest military disaster in the history of British India – a 'signal catastrophe', as a participant later described it.

It began in early November 1841 with an attack on the British Residency in Kabul city by an Afghan mob, in which a number of British officers were killed. Sir William Macnaghten and the reduced British garrison soon found themselves besieged in the new cantonment area outside the city where they were now quartered. The arrival of Dost Muhammad's son Akbar Khan with a large army from Turkestan sealed their fate. Late in December Macnaghten, riding out into the snow almost unattended to parley with Akbar Khan, was shot by him before being stabbed to death by his followers. Two weeks later the British garrison, numbering some 4,500 fighting men but encumbered with 12,000 non-combatants made up of camp-followers and several dozen British wives and children, was permitted to leave Kabul to march through heavy snow towards Jalalabad.

Over the next few days a terrible revenge was exacted on these remnants of the Army of the Indus. At first it was only stragglers who were picked off, but as each day passed and the column grew more extended, so the attacks became bolder. Eventually the column was broken up into a series of isolated groups, each pinned down by marksmen or surrounded by large bodies of horsemen. On the afternoon of the sixth day a lone rider was seen from the walls of the fort at Jalalabad: the unhappy Dr Brydon, who had been permitted to escape the slaughter in accordance with Akbar Khan's boast that he would 'annihilate the whole army except one man, who would reach Jalalabad to tell the tale'.

This defining moment, which marks a nadir in the fortunes of the British in the East unparalleled until the surrender of Singapore in 1942, was frozen in purple prose by the Victorian historian Sir John Kaye in his multi-volumed *History of the War in Afghanistan*, and in oils by that great military painter Lady Butler:

A sentry on the ramparts looking out towards the Cabul road, saw a solitary white-faced horseman struggling towards the fort. The word was passed; the tidings spread. Presently the ramparts were lined with officers looking out with throbbing hearts, through unsteady telescopes, or with straining eyes tracing the road. Slowly and painfully, as though horse and rider were in an extremity of mortal weakness, the solitary mounted man came reeling, tottering on. They saw that he was an Englishman. On a wretched weary pony, clinging, as one sick or wounded, to its neck, he sat, or rather leant forward; and there were those who, as they watched his progress, thought he would never reach, unaided, the walls of Jellalabad. A shudder ran through the garrison. That solitary horseman looked like the messenger of death . . . The messenger was Dr Brydon, and he now reported his belief that he was the sole survivor of an army of some sixteen thousand men.

2

'Respect the British soldier'

AFGHANISTAN, 1841–1842

> Then we marched to Chalazan
> And we met the wild Afghan,
> And made him for to run boys,
> Run boys oh!
> And we marched into Kabul
> And we took the Bala Hissar,
> And made them to respect the British soldier.
>
> Chorus:
> Bang upon the big drum, clash upon the cymbal,
> We'll sing as we go marching along, boys, along.
> And although on this campaign there's no whiskey or
>   champagne,
> Still we'll keep our spirits flowing with a song, boys.
>
> British Army marching song

WHEN NEWS of the Afghan disaster was brought to Lord
Auckland in Calcutta he screamed and raved and then took
to his bed. When he eventually emerged, it was said that he had
aged ten years in as many hours. It seems probable that he had
suffered a stroke. Although part-paralysed, he still had enough of
his wits about him to order a relief force to be assembled in
Peshawar under the command of Major-General George Pollock.

However, this Army of Retribution, as it came to be known, was forced to kick its heels in camp for three months until the winter snows had cleared.

In the meantime, the defenders of the military garrisons at Jalalabad, Kandahar and Ghazni, together with prisoners taken by the Afghans in Kabul, waited impatiently for news of rescue. At Ghazni, despite the battering they had received two years earlier, the citadel's defences were still immensely strong. The British garrison was also well armed, so that, despite severe shortages of food and the bitter cold, its officers were confident they could hold out until a relieving force arrived in the spring. But in mid February 1842 the commanding officer of the 27th BNI, one Colonel Palmer, received a written order from the imprisoned British army commander in Kabul requiring him to evacuate the fort and hand it over to the Afghans. Similar orders were received by the besieged garrison commanders in Jalalabad and Kandahar – and ignored. At Ghazni, however, Colonel Palmer complied. He negotiated with the Afghan leaders and obtained from them a solemn assurance sworn on the Koran that, provided he vacated the fort, they would be allowed to proceed unmolested to Peshawar as soon as the snows had cleared. On 6 March he led his men out of the safety of the citadel and into quarters prepared for them below in the town. Scarcely had they settled in before they were attacked by a mob of yelling Ghaznavi.

John Nicholson and two other junior officers, together with two companies of infantry, were almost immediately isolated from the rest of the garrison. They held off their attackers for two days until the building they occupied was fired, which forced them to retreat from one blazing room to another until eventually they were able to escape the flames by using their bayonets to hack a hole through the back wall of their position. From here the survivors were able to rejoin the rest of the garrison, now crowded into two buildings, where the guns of the citadel were brought to bear on them, firing almost directly onto their heads.

Nothing of this period survives from Nicholson's pen, but we have a detailed account of events from Lieutenant Crawford, a young officer of the 3rd Bombay Native Infantry, also part of the garrison: 'You cannot picture to yourself the scene these two houses presented,' he wrote in a *Narrative* later published in a Bombay newspaper. 'Every room was crammed, not only with Sepoys, but camp-followers – men, women and children; and it is astonishing the slaughter among them was not greater, seeing that the guns of the citadel sent round shot crashing through and through the walls.'

Fortunately the powder for the guns soon ran out, so that those who survived the initial cannonade were able to hang on behind their makeshift defences for two weeks. But once their food and water had gone they were forced to accept the Afghans' terms of surrender. Once again the Afghan chiefs, in Crawford's words, 'swore by all that was holy that, if we laid down our arms, we should be honourably treated and sent to Kabul to the Shah as soon as possible'. John Nicholson was one of a number of officers who argued long and passionately against surrender, since it meant abandoning their Hindu sepoys. When the order was given to lay down their arms he refused to comply, clinging to a musket and threatening with his bayonet any Afghan who came near him. When finally commanded by Colonel Palmer to obey, he flung his sword at the feet of his captors and burst into tears. As he had feared, the sepoys were immediately assaulted by a mob of armed men and all those who refused to convert to Islam on the spot were hacked to death. The horror of this double betrayal, in which he believed he had played a part through failing in his duty of care to the men in his charge, cut very deep.

The ten surviving British officers were taken back to the citadel and imprisoned in a small room, where they remained for six weeks. 'When we lay down at night we exactly occupied the whole floor,' wrote Crawford, 'and when we wanted to take a little exercise, we were obliged to walk up and down (six paces) in turns. Few of us had a change of linen, and the consequence was that we were soon swarming with vermin, the catching of which afforded us an hour's employment every morning. I wore my solitary shirt for five weeks, until it became literally black and rotten.'

On 7 April news reached Ghazni that Amir Shah Shuja had been killed, and from that day their conditions grew worse. 'The severities of our confinement were redoubled,' Crawford writes in his *Narrative*. 'They shut and darkened the solitary window from which we had hitherto derived light and air, and they also kept the door of our room constantly closed, so that the air we breathed became perfectly pestiferous.' Their captors also threatened torture and death to make them reveal the whereabouts of treasure they had supposedly concealed, carrying out these threats to the extent of pinning the colonel to the floor of the cell and twisting his foot with a rope. All their personal belongings and valuables were taken, – with the single exception of a locket belonging to John Nicholson. Although loath to say anything else about his captivity, in a letter written a full year after the event John did trouble to tell his mother how this had been achieved: 'I do not know whether I mentioned to you that I had managed to preserve the little locket with your hair in it. It was the only thing worth a shilling that was kept by any of us; and I was allowed to keep it because, when ordered to give it up, I lost my head and threw it at the sirdar's [chief's] head – which was certainly a thoughtless and head-endangering act. However, he seemed to like it, for he gave strict orders that the locket was not to be taken from me.'

In early May 1842 General Pollock's Army of Retribution fought its way through the Khyber to relieve the garrison at Jalalabad, and this setback for the Afghans immediately brought about a change of attitude on the part of the gaolers in Ghazni. 'Indeed,' writes Crawford, 'we could always form a pretty shrewd guess of what our troops were about by the treatment we experienced at the hands of our captors.' As a consequence of the relief of the British garrison at Kandahar they were allowed an hour's exercise during Friday prayers, which was followed by a change of quarters. Then quite suddenly, on the night of 19 August, they were hurried out of the fort and bundled into the side-panniers of a number of camels. Three days of bumpy riding brought them to Kabul, where they were immediately taken to the fortress of the Bala Hissar and ushered into the presence of Akbar Khan, the son of Dost Mohammad, now governing Kabul in his father's name.

Reduced to nine after the death of one of their number from typhus fever, the prisoners found themselves, verminous and dressed in little more than rags, sitting down to dine with the man who seven months earlier had shot down Envoy Macnaghten with his own pistol – an indignity John Nicholson *was* prepared to recount. Describing the occasion in a letter to his mother, he first admitted that he 'never was in the company of more gentleman-like, well-bred men. They were strikingly handsome, as the Afghan sirdars always are.' But he would not allow himself to forget even for a moment what these same Afghans had done. Opposite him at dinner sat a nobleman named Saltan Jan, 'the handsomest man I ever saw in my life, and with a great deal of dignity in his manner. He had with his own hand murdered poor Captain Trevor in the preceding winter, but that was nothing. As I looked round the circle I saw both parricides and regicides, whilst the murderer of our envoy was perhaps the least blood-stained of the party.' Akbar Kahn played the perfect host throughout, chattering and joking, doing all he could to make his guests feel at ease. At the best of times Nicholson was not a man given to dinner-party small-talk, so we can take it that he had little to say to the men who, for all their charm and good manners, were still his captors.

The next morning the nine were taken to a small fort outside Kabul where the rest of the British prisoners held by the Afghans were confined in conditions which Lieutenant Crawford found a 'small paradise' after what they had endured. The shirt John Nicholson had worn for months was now no more than a rag hanging from his shoulders, so that when an older prisoner presented him with a crisp new shirt he himself had just received in a parcel, John was almost overcome with gratitude.

The donor of the shirt was Captain George Lawrence, at thirty-eight the oldest of five brothers then serving in India, of whom three were to have considerable influence over Nicholson, as mentors and father-figures. Although only half-Ulstermen by birth, George, Henry and John Lawrence had all spent their for-mative years among their mother's relatives in the province, so that in John Nicholson's eyes they were men like himself. They had been schooled at the Foyle College in Londonderry, a tough, no-nonsense, God-fearing institution that produced boys ideally matched to the East India Company's needs. George and Henry were two years apart, while five years separated John from Henry. This gap was accentuated by their later education: George and Henry both went to Addiscombe and thence into the Bengal Army as military cadets, whereas John, despite his protestations, was sent to Haileybury College and so joined the EICo as a writer, to become a civil rather than a military officer. These distinctions of age and occupation, compounded as they were by differences of temperament – for the two older brothers were more 'Irish' than John – ensured that Henry and George could always work comfortably together, but never Henry and John.

Henry and John Lawrence are numbered among the 'greats' of British India: Henry is probably best remembered today for the circumstances of his death, as the man 'who tried to do his duty' and was killed at the start of the epic siege of the Residency at Lucknow in the summer of 1857; John as Lord Lawrence of the Punjab, a thoroughly solid post-Mutiny Viceroy who believed strongly that Afghanistan was a poisoned chalice best left untouched and whose name is synonymous with the frontier policy known as 'masterly inactivity'. Both have their champions, but it is fair to say that Henry was the warmer of the two, the more emotional and the more imaginative, and that he inspired far greater devotion among those who served him than John ever did. John was far thicker-skinned, far slower to praise or to criticise, and not given to showing his emotions. John was respected, Henry was loved, and both overshadowed their elder brother George, who led the way.

George Lawrence had come out to India as a cavalry officer, followed two years later by Henry, a gunner officer. In 1839 George was attached to the Army of the Indus, first as a political assistant and then as military secretary to Sir William Macnaghten, while Henry in that same year was appointed an assistant to the Political Agent at Ludhiana, but based at Ferozepore, where he remained for three years in charge of civil affairs. In late December 1841, in the fatal confrontation between Sir William Macnaghten and Akbar Khan in the snow outside Kabul, George Lawrence had seen both his master and a fellow political assistant, Captain Robert Trevor, hacked down at his side. He had survived to become a prisoner of the Afghans, although in easier circumstances than John Nicholson. His younger brother Henry, meanwhile, had joined the Army of Retribution as a Political Agent. For some time he was based at Peshawar, working in partnership with another political officer, Captain Frederick Mackeson, in an abortive attempt to break the Khybari's grip of their domain with the aid of local Sikh troops. Both he and Mackeson then played leading roles in the successful breaching of the pass by General Pollock's column.

As the Army of Retribution closed on Kabul on two fronts, so the Afghan alliance began to fall apart. In mid September all the British prisoners held by the Afghans were freed, and escorted into the British camp outside Kabul to cheers and gun salutes. The two Lawrence brothers were reunited, and Henry was soon introduced to John Nicholson, the young man who was to become his most difficult disciple.

A reunion also took place between Nicholson and Neville Chamberlain, who had come through the siege of Kandahar with two new scars to show for it. 'As I was passing not far from a tent apparently surrounded by Affghans I was struck by a stone,' wrote Chamberlain later. 'I put my hand to my sword and approached the man, who was stooping to pick up another stone, when to my surprise who should my assailant be but John Nicholson, surrounded by other rescued officers, dressed in their Affghan prisoner's dress, when of course we both burst out laughing, and shook hands heartily.'

Here in Kabul Nicholson and Chamberlain both made the acquaintance of another junior officer, with whom they later formed a close-knit inner circle within Henry Lawrence's group of political assistants. This was young Lieutenant Harry Lumsden, known to his close friends as 'Joe'. Joe Lumsden had the unusual distinction of being India-born yet not 'country-born', as the old Anglo-Indian term had it, since his birth had occurred at sea in the Bay of Bengal on the East India Company's ship *Rose*, in November 1821. He also had the distinct advantage of having spent his first six years in Bengal, where his father was serving as an artillery officer, before being sent home to Scotland to be educated. A happy childhood in Aberdeenshire in the care of his grandmother had left him with a great love of the outdoors and a passion for field-sports. He had returned to India at sixteen to be commissioned as a cadet into the 59th BNI. His Indian childhood had left him with a particular aptitude for native languages, and it was as an interpreter that he had been attached to General

Pollock's army. How and when he first met John Nicholson in Kabul is unrecorded – not surprisingly, for Joe Lumsden was hardly more of a letter-writer than Nicholson. The tone of those he did write is very different from Nicholson's – short on personal detail they assuredly are, but, in keeping with the man himself, always bursting with good cheer and optimism.

After more than ten months of isolation from the outside world, John Nicholson was able to catch up on news from home. He had known that his younger brother Alexander was due to sail out to India in the spring to follow him into the Bengal Infantry, and now learned that he was already on his way up-country to Peshawar with his regiment.

British accounts of the First Afghan War invariably make much of the cruelties perpetrated by the Afghans; what is not dwelt upon is the way the Army of Retribution more than evened the score. Though it was intended for his mother's eyes, Neville Chamberlain's Journal makes grim reading today. In every region where British or Indian troops had been killed or maltreated, the male inhabitants were shot, bayoneted or put to the sword in the name of 'signal punishment', and their houses fired. 'I suppose I need not tell you that no males above fourteen years were spared, and some of the men (brutes except in form) wanted to wreak their vengeance on the women,' Chamberlain writes of one such instance of retribution in which his own soldiers participated with enthusiasm. Many of the inhabitants of Kabul had fled with their possessions to the town of Estalef in the mountains north of the capital, hoping the fighting would pass them by. But the avenging troops showed little mercy and, after storming the town, embarked on an orgy of killing and looting 'The scenes of plunder were dreadful,' notes Chamberlain:

Every house filled with soldiers, both European and native, and completely gutted. Furniture, clothes, merchandise of all sorts flung from windows into the streets and scrambled for by those below . . . It was curious to see the various tastes displayed in the selection of booty. Some took arms, some jewels, some books! Some, again, fancied silks and satins, shawls etc. . . . On forcing open a large house in the town we found it contained merchandise of the most valuable description, which immediately fell a prey to my followers, a motley band, composed of men of all regiments and all colours – British, Hindu, Mussulmans, Goorkha! . . . Many a musket shot was also heard which sent some male of the family who had not been fortunate enough to conceal his hiding place into the next world. Several were killed before me. Tears, supplications were of no avail, fierce oaths were the only answer; the musket was deliberately raised, the trigger pulled, and happy was he who fell dead! . . . These horrible murders (for such alone must they be in the eyes of God) were truly wicked; the only thing to be said in their extenuation is, that the Affghans who then suffered were the very men who had inflicted every kind of torture on our own countrymen and Hindustanees.

Early the next morning Chamberlain returned to the sacked town, and found a scene of utter desolation:

Furniture of all description, wearing apparel, provisions, books, arms, everything made by the hand of man and for his use, lay scattered and destroyed, trampled into the mud, soiled and broken. Here and there the crackling of fire was to be heard and the smoke issuing from windows and crevices of the houses, told that the pillager, after sacking it of everything, had committed it to the flames. At one place my eyes were shocked by the sight of a poor woman lying dead, and a little infant of three or four months by her side still alive, but with both its thighs pierced and mangled by a musket-ball. The child was conveyed to camp, but death soon put an end to its sufferings. Further on was another woman in torture from a wound, and she had been exposed to the cold of the night without any covering; she clasped a child in her arms, and her affection appeared only to be increased by the agonies she endured. She was placed on a doolie and sent into our camp, and our doctor attended her. Sitting outside a shop was a little girl of three or four years of age . . . apparently quite unconscious of what had happened, or what was passing around her; while scattered about the streets lay the bodies of old and young, rich and poor.

As Chamberlain, saddened, returned to camp he met another wounded Afghani woman dragging herself towards a stream with a water-pot in her hand. 'I filled her vessel for her,' he writes, 'but all she said was, "Curses on the Feringees!"' He continued on his way 'disgusted with myself, the world, and above all, with my cruel profession. In fact we are nothing but licensed assassins.'

In mid October 1842, with the flames of the burning bazaar lighting the sky, the Army of Retribution marched away from Kabul to begin the process of extricating itself from Afghanistan with as much loot, and as few casualties, as it could manage. Although it was presented to the British public as a triumphant withdrawal after giving the Afghans a damned good thrashing, Chamberlain's journal makes it plain that this was more in the nature of a second retreat, following the same Via Dolorosa through the mountains as General Sale's ill-fated army had taken 21 months before.

The trail was still littered with the corpses of thousands of men and animals. 'I rode through the [Jagdalak] pass and the sight that presented itself was truly lamentable,' recorded Chamberlain of the first defile on the road. 'The miserable remains of thousands of that doomed force lay scattered about in all kinds of positions and states of decomposition. The skeletons of men, women and children, horses and camels, etc., heaped together in one confused mass. The European would always be distinguished from the Indian by the colour of the hair; and the skull of the former was invariably battered in with stones.'

Two days on, their path was still 'strewn with skeletons of men and animals . . . Our gun-wheels ground to dust the bones of the dead, the pass being so narrow it was impossible to avoid them. In some places the Affghans, to add insult to all the misery they inflicted, had placed the skeletons one in the arms of the other, or sometimes sitting or standing against the rocks as if they were holding a consultation! The soldiers in retaliation, wherever they killed an Affghan, placed the skeleton of one of our poor fellows over him as a mark of victory or derision.' To make matters worse, the trail was also littered with the living – sick or exhausted camp-followers abandoned by the military units which they had accompanied into Afghanistan, so that 'every march we passed the bodies of those abandoned by the columns ahead of us'.

Chamberlain's regiment formed part of the rear-guard and was subject to almost incessant sniper fire from *jezailchis*, sharpshooters armed with long-barrelled jezails which in range and accuracy far exceeded the old-fashioned muskets with which the sepoys were armed. Unable to get to grips with an elusive, hidden enemy, the 16th BNI had no option but to keep on the move: 'The only way we escaped so well was by never standing still, and always going in a zigzag direction.' Chamberlain had already received three slight wounds to date and now, on 16 October, he was wounded a fourth time: 'I was walking in rear of all with my orderly, rifle in hand, taking shots at the rascals, when my orderly's horse close by me was riddled through the neck. I had not gone many paces when I was struck myself. I spun round and fell to the ground, but soon got up again and staggered on in great pain, but was determined the Affghans should not have even the satisfaction of thinking they had done for me. On putting my hand to my back I thought it was all over with me, but on getting into camp we found the ball had only penetrated the skin, and it tumbled out on the doctor touching it.'

The withdrawal continued without pause across the Jalalabad plain, where Chamberlain and his men were briefly able to turn the tables by hunting down on horseback some of their attackers. On 1 November they reached Dakka, at the head of the long descent through the mountains that constituted the Khyber. On this same day, John Nicholson was briefly reunited with his younger brother, Alexander. John left no account of what followed, but Chamberlain's diary shows that both his own and John Nicholson's regiments stayed back as part of the final rear-guard party, while Alexander's unit proceeded down into the pass as rear-escort to General McGaskill's division.

Just below the present fort of Ali Masjid, perched on a high outcrop, the defile closes in to its narrowest point before widening out into a small valley. Here, on 3 November, McCaskill's rear-escort was ambushed, trapped and overwhelmed.

It is not known what were the exact circumstances of Alexander's death – only that by cruel fate it fell to John to find his body as he himself rode down through the Khyber the following day. As John Nicholson and Ensign Julius Dennys emerged onto the open ground at Ali Masjid they spotted what appeared to be a pale, naked body lying among the rocks. Disobeying the order not to leave the line of march, the two officers galloped across, and found the corpse of Alexander Nicholson, hacked to pieces. In accordance with Afghan custom, his genitalia had been cut off and stuffed in his mouth.

The body was placed in a doolie and taken down to a camping-ground below Ali Masjid, where it was subsequently buried, under cover of darkness, and a large fire lit over the grave. The object, as Julius Dennys wrote later, was to cover the grave with ashes, 'so that the Afghans might suspect nothing, as they were very fond of disinterring our dead and heaping indignities on the bodies. Poor Nicholson felt it deeply, and the tears coursed down his cheeks.' Chamberlain's account makes it clear that their rear-guard party was under attack throughout this night and for the next twenty-four hours, as their tormenters continued in pursuit right to the point at which the Khyber river emerges onto the plains of Peshawar. With Fort Jamrud and safety in sight, Neville Chamberlain received his fifth and most serious wound:

All the heights, with the exception of those at the exit of the pass, had been crowned by our troops; from one of these the Khyberrie opened upon us as we passed beneath it. My horse was restive, and he not liking to be in the rear, I was riding a few paces in advance of the corps, the balls striking about me rather close. I turned round and said to an officer, 'These fellows do not fire badly.' And true enough, for the moment afterwards I was struck (in the thigh). The ball hit me so hard that my friend answered, 'You are hit, old fellow', but I needed not to be told to make me aware of it. The regiment galloped on to get from under the fire. I was obliged to dismount, or rather I half fell from my horse, and dragged and supported by my groom and a sepoy, I lay down behind a piece of rock which sheltered me from the fire, until after some time a doolie was brought for me and I was carried into camp at Jamrood.

When the rear-guard and its wounded finally reached Peshawar, John Nicholson wrote to his mother to tell her the dreadful news:

It is with sorrowful heart that I sit down to write to you now, after a silence of more than a twelvemonth. Indeed I should scarcely dare to do so now, were I not encouraged by the knowledge that God will enable you to bear your sad loss with Christian resignation, and comfort you with His Holy Spirit. Poor Alexander is no more. He was killed in action on the rearguard on the 3rd inst . . . Now my dearest mother, let me entreat you not to grieve more than you can help. Alexander died a soldier's death, in the execution of his duty, and a more glorious death he could not have died. He was a great favourite with the officers of his corps, who all spoke in high terms of his courage and amiable qualities. Indeed, I never saw a boy more improved than he was, and deeply do I feel his loss. You may imagine we were both happy at meeting after so long a separation. Three days after, I placed him in his grave; but it is a consolation to me that he met a glorious death. It will be a consolation to you to know that he was buried by a clergyman of the Church of England; few have been who have perished in this country.

On the subject of his own misfortunes, Nicholson had little to say other than that he was 'not in spirits to write about anything at present'. He viewed his own survival in Afghanistan as 'little less than a miracle', for which 'to God alone thanks are due'. Many months later, his family having asked for more details of the siege of Ghazni and his imprisonment, he referred them to a newspaper article. However, he also railed bitterly against the 'ideas of people at home' about the Afghans, and against the British press that had given rise to them. This was not an episode of his life that Nicholson ever wrote about, as we have seen, or willingly discussed. It left him with the deepest loathing of the Afghans – 'the most vicious and bloodthirsty race in existence, who fight merely for the love of bloodshed and plunder'. He viewed them thereafter as a people without any redeeming qualities other than good manners: 'I cannot describe their character in language sufficiently strong . . . From the highest to the lowest, every man of them would *sell* both country and relations.' His experiences also engendered in him a profound distrust of those in authority, whether Afghan, Sikh, Hindu or British – feelings which were shared by many who came through the débâcle of the Afghan War and which help to explain the marked anti-authority, trust-nobody, act-first-and-do-everything-yourself line taken by men like Nicholson, Chamberlain and Lumsden in the years that followed.

Afghanistan hardened traits in Nicholson's character which had been apparent at school. Taciturn before, he was now silent in company, to the point of rudeness; his self-confidence was now absolute, to the point of arrogance. If the Lord of Hosts had spared him, where so many other Christian souls had been snatched away, then it had to be for a purpose. John Nicholson at twenty years of age was no longer a callow, ungainly youth looking about for a means to restore the fortunes of his family, but a war-hardened adult with a sense of destiny. What that destiny might entail had still to be revealed, but from this time onwards it was as if he sought it with an energy and single-mindedness that sometimes bordered on the manic. To his contemporaries he now appeared a man apart: Julius Dennys, with whom he shared a bungalow for some months, writes of him as being 'reserved almost to morose-ness', but also touched by some indefinable but unmistakable trace of genius: 'He made me feel that he had probably in him what must make him a man of mark. Fear of any kind seemed unknown to him, and one could see that there was a great depth behind his reserved and at times almost boorish character.'

While Nicholson's regiment stayed on in Peshawar, the 16th BNI returned to Ferozepore with its sick and wounded, Neville Chamberlain among them:

The whole of the road through the Punjab I was carried in a litter, and I was too ill to be amused or to see the country. Hundreds of our men died during our march from fatigue and wounds. I used to pity the unfortunate wounded who were carried on camels for want of better conveyance, and were sometimes exposed for twelve or fourteen hours to the cold at night and to the heat of the sun during the day, and often it was not possible to dress their wounds for a day or two. Comparatively speaking I was well off, for my wound was dressed three times during the twenty-four hours! But I hope I shall never again go through what I then suffered.

Lieutenant Joe Lumsden also returned to Ferozepore, pleased to have earned himself a campaign medal and six months' extra pay. As he crossed the river Indus at Attock he wrote to his parents to say what fun it would be to 'peacock about' before his old regiment with a medal on his chest 'where no other officer has anything of the sort!' He also apologised for not writing from Afghanistan, claiming as an excuse that only married officers had been allowed to send letters. 'Never mind,' he added, 'they will not make me on that account marry a bit sooner; but now that young hopeful is to have a medal, there may be some hope of his being able to pick up a sound and quiet creature one day.' In the event, it was a quarter of a century before he found that 'creature', and in the meantime he had earned a chestful of campaign medals to add to his first.

For two months Ferozepore was a 'whirl of reviews, parades, festivities' as a new Governor-General presided over celebrations to mark the triumph of the Army of Retribution. In England, a chastened Lord Auckland returned to his former sinecure as First Lord of the Admiralty; in Afghanistan, Dost Mohammad Khan was quietly restored to the throne which his son Akbar Khan had regained for him.

3

'First comes one Englishman'

THE FIRST SIKH WAR, 1845–1846

> First comes one Englishman, as a traveller or for shikar; then
> come two and make a map; then comes an army and takes
> the country. Therefore it is better to kill the first
> Englishman.
>
> Pakhtun proverb

'LAHORE IS Lahore', says the old Punjabi proverb, and to many Pakistanis it is still the prince of cities. In outward appearance it is cheerfully secular, not least because of its many lurid cinema hoardings that climb like ivy, three and four storeys high, hiding the dull colonial architecture underneath. But above the traffic's roar, from the city's mosques you can hear the crackling, tape-recorded calls to prayer of the muezzins. No one seems quite sure of Lahore's current population, but the general understanding is that the Islamic Republic of Pakistan has some one hundred and thirty-two million souls, of which about six million have made this city their home. In the traumatic division of the Punjab that was part of the price of the creation of Pakistan in 1947, Lahore gained far more Muslims than it lost Sikhs and Hindus.

The city has ancient roots and some fine Mughal architecture – most notably a great fort laid out by Akbar, and a grand mosque raised by Aurangzeb – but its golden age ended with the arrival of that wily, one-eyed, hard-drinking genius Ranjit Singh, one of history's great despoilers. For seventy years Lahore was the capital of the Sikh Empire he created. It then became the capital of the Punjab Province in the years of the British Raj, and remains today the capital of a Punjab province – albeit a shrunken one that has lost to India part of the headwaters of the five great rivers.

What was known in British times as the 'civil station' is now the heart of downtown Lahore, south-west of the old city walls, with The Mall as its main artery. To the majority of Lahore's present-day inhabitants it is still 'The Mall', although officially and on maps it is Sharah-e-Qaid-i-Azam, while what was once the Lawrence Gardens is now the Bagh-e-Jinnah, and Montgomery Hall is now Jinnah Hall. All three names commemorate the creator of Pakistan, Mohammad Ali Jinnah, the 'Great Leader' or *Qaid-i-Azam*. By some quirk of fate or happy oversight, however, Nicholson Road is still Nicholson Road.

The civil station was founded here, rather than at a safe distance from the city, because the first Britons came not as administrators but as envoys to the Sikh court. They were allotted an area outside the city walls, known today as Islampura but formerly called Anarkali or 'pomegranate blossom'. At the time this was open country dotted with imposing Mughal tombs and country mansions surrounded by formal gardens. To the young Rudyard Kipling, who came here as a cub journalist in 1882 to work on *The Civil and Military Gazette*, there was always something spooky about it: he called it a 'crowded Golgotha', laid over 'vast forgotten Muslim cemeteries, with the tombs of the dead at every point'. But the British, like the Sikhs, thought nothing of cannibalising the best of the Muslim sepulchres and unused mosques and putting them to practical use.

The first to suffer this fate was the Tomb of Anarkali. The building still stands, a great whitewashed pile in a corner of the grounds of the Punjab Civil Secretariat; robbed of its outer casing of marble, it is not a pretty piece of architecture. It is now the home of the Secretariat's historical records archive, but in one corner of the central chamber is a white marble cenotaph upon which are carved in Arabic the ninety-nine Names of God. Under these is the inscription *Majnun Salim-i-Akbar*, which translates as 'the enamoured Salim, son of Akbar', while on another side can be seen two lines of verse: 'Ah, could I but behold the face of my beloved once again, I would offer thanks unto Allah until the day of the resurrection.'

The English traveller Ralph Fitch visited Lahore in 1611 and tells us that Anarkali, Pomegranate Blossom, was the pet name bestowed by Emperor Akbar on his favourite concubine, a young beauty named Nadira Begum. Anarkali had the misfortune to be caught by the emperor exchanging smiles with his son, the young Prince Salim, and for this crime was buried alive – entombed by bricks laid around her as she stood. In time, her youthful admirer succeeded his father and became the Emperor Jehangir. Having never forgotten his first love and its fatal consequences, he built Anarkali a cenotaph and caused the melancholy distich to be incised on her tomb, together with his name. He also ordered a fine mausoleum to be raised over her sepulchre, octagonal in shape with eight arches supporting a vast dome some sixty feet in diameter, and four lesser domes at each corner supported on four hectagonal towers. This became known as Anarkali's tomb – although there are spoil-sport revisionists who now say that it was actually raised to Sahiba Jamal, one of the wives of Emperor Jahangir, rather than to one of his father's mistresses.

The Tomb of Anarkali was first used as a dwelling-place by one of Ranjit Singh's sons, who stripped its walls of their marble, a mutilation widely practised on Islamic mosques and tombs in the Punjab during Ranjit Singh's time. It next became the home of the Italian General Ventura, one of the most able and cruel of Ranjit Singh's foreign mercenaries. The third occupant was Henry Lawrence.

In June 1839 Maharaja Ranjit Singh died of a stroke brought on by excessive drinking. With his death the Sikh Empire he had built up with such skill over forty years began to unravel. Fratricide among his natural heirs left a minor, Maharaja Dalip Singh, to succeed him and a number of factions at court jockeying for power, none strong enough to take command and hold the Empire together. Its strength had always rested in the Khalsa Dal, which now became increasingly dominant but also increasingly divided. While the commanders quarrelled among themselves, misl against misl, a soldiery which in many cases had not been paid for months took to running its own affairs: regiments began to elect their own committees, and soon it was they and not their generals who were giving the orders. Within three years of his death Ranjit Singh's mighty army had become a headless behemoth, and the Punjab had descended into a state of anarchy. The EICo's civil and military officers watched and waited with ever-growing apprehension, few doubting that confrontation with the Sikhs was now inevitable – and that they would, in Neville Chamberlain's phrase, 'prove an enemy worthy to meet'.

Those prophetic words were written as Chamberlain prepared to board ship in Calcutta in February 1845. His shattered thighbone had refused to heal, and after a series of painful operations he had been ordered home to England to recuperate and regain his strength. But even as his ship was preparing to hoist anchors he was having second thoughts about leaving. 'Do not think me unselfish when I tell you I regret being obliged to leave India,' he wrote to his mother. 'War may be declared with the Sikhs any day. Only fancy my wasting my time in England when I should be on horseback! And what can I do? Fortune does not favour me.'

However, fortune did favour the two friends Chamberlain had made in Afghanistan. Joe Lumsden and John Nicholson had spent two quiet years with their respective regiments, the former at Ludhiana, where he took every opportunity to indulge his passion for shikar, often going off alone or with a companion on shooting trips that took him deep into Sikh country. These trips proved invaluable: Lumsden became a first-class Punjabi speaker and, more importantly, learned to be at ease among the native peoples of the Punjab, whether Sikh, Hindu or Muslim.

John Nicholson, by contrast, kept to himself and made no new friends. He spent two stultifying years at Moradabad, where he performed his military duties in an exemplary manner and passed his evenings studying Urdu. Having lost all his effects in Afghanistan, he had been forced to borrow heavily in order to re-equip himself. Only after his promotion to adjutant of his regiment was he again able to send money home to Lisburn – to pay for the education of his brother Charles at Addiscombe, so that he too could make a military career in India. Yet John's own feelings for the country were unequivocal: 'I dislike India and its inhabitants more every day,' he wrote to his mother, 'and would rather go home on £200 a year than live like a prince here.'

In November 1845 Nicholson passed the language examination which qualified him for a staff appointment. He immediately applied for a posting to the commissariat department of a field force being raised at Delhi under the Commander-in-Chief, Sir Hugh Gough – and, once again, obtained it through the influence of Uncle Hogg. The timing could hardly have been better. In the sonorous words of the Indian Army's great chronicler, Sir John Kaye, 'the Punjab was in a state of extraordinary commotion . . . the army had waxed stronger and more insolent, until at last the military power thoroughly overbore the State. That in this condition of affairs the lawless praetorian bands . . . would some day cross the Sutlej . . . had now become almost a certainty. The British and Sikh powers were about to come into collision.' In mid December 1845, and for no discernible reason – it may have been intended as a cross-border raid, or as a pre-emptive strike to destroy the gathering British forces – the Khalsa Dal crossed the Sutlej and advanced into British territory.

In the seven weeks that followed, the best of Henry Lawrence's Young Men won their spurs. For three of them – Lieutenants Herbert Edwardes, William Hodson and Reynell Taylor – the blooding began at Mudki on 18 December, a battle that established the pattern of the fighting thereafter. Sir Hugh Gough commanded the British forces. This most gallant and loved Irish campaigner had been commissioned at fourteen, had fought engagements as far afield as Surinam and Nangking, and had led his regiment from Talavera to Vittoria in the Peninsular War. Still under sixty, and so a young man as British generals went, he was a brave but utterly unimaginative commander, whose only tactic consisted in closing on the enemy at all speed and then applying 'cold steel' by frontal advance. After an exhausting thirty-mile march, he arrived at the village of Mudki to find the Sikhs in a strong defensive position, all their guns deployed. He immediately ordered an assault. Well-directed and rapid fire from the Sikh artillery caused fearful casualties among the infantry, which included Hodson's grenadiers.

Aged twenty-four, William Hodson was the rawest of the three Young-Men-to-be. He had been in India barely four months, only two of them with his regiment, the 2nd Bengal Grenadiers, when he found himself marching at the head of a company of sepoys into a barrage of grape. Characteristically, he thoroughly enjoyed his first battle, afterwards writing enthusiastically to his father that he had 'entered into it with great zest'. He had to admit that the British losses had been 'most severe, especially in officers . . . The greatest destruction was among the Governor-General's staff – only two escaped death or severe wounds. They seemed marked for destruction and certainly met it most gallantly.' With typical recklessness, Sir Hugh Gough had followed in close on the heels of his infantry, with predictable results among his staff officers and those of the Governor-General, who had accompanied him. One of their number, struck by a musket-ball in the thigh as he sat mounted on his horse beside the C-in-C, was Herbert Edwardes.

On the face of it, Edwardes and Hodson had much in common. Both were sons of English clergymen and – unusually for military officers – both were university graduates. But there the similarities ended, for in temperament the two were poles apart. They never got on, and in later years each grew to dislike and – certainly in Hodson's case – to despise the other. Both went on to make their mark, but posterity has treated them very differently.

Pink-faced, if not baby-faced, with piercing blue eyes, blond hair and a drooping blond moustache, William Hodson had very quickly established himself as a 'colourful character'. In India he suffered badly from what we would now call migraines, and for this reason wore tinted spectacles to shield his eyes from the glare of the sun, so adding to an already striking appearance. Known in his regiment as the 'Company's blade', as much on account of his mettle as for his exceptional dexterity with the sabre, he possessed a mercurial temper – a great charmer who when things went against him gave way to frightening rages. Even as a schoolboy at Rugby he had been hard to handle. One of his teachers there, the Reverend George Cotton, described him as 'arrogant, brash and domineering' – while adding that his 'impulsive nature won him much affection'. This was the Rugby of Dr Arnold and *Tom Brown's Schooldays*, and it is hard not to see in Hodson as a schoolboy something of the fictional Flashman. In his correspondence he comes across as a young man in a hurry, always speaking his mind, less than thoughtful, appearing never to care a damn about others, or what others might think of him. Yet, for all his faults, he came to inspire enormous devotion not from his brother-officers but from the troops who served under him: a soldier's soldier.

Herbert Edwardes was quite the opposite. He was regarded by his contemporaries as a man of learning, an intellectual and a wit, but there is nothing spontaneous about his writing, which often seems over-contrived in that ponderous Victorian way that makes for a hard read today. His actions were always considered, his thoughts carefully weighed and measured, and indeed – quite unlike the unfortunate Hodson – he rarely put a foot wrong: he was a born diplomat rather than a soldier. In picking him for his personal assistant, Henry Lawrence could hardly have made a wiser choice.

Edwardes, arriving at Calcutta early in 1841, had been posted up-country to Karnaul to join the 1st Bengal Fusiliers, a European regiment made up very largely of Irishmen (it later became the 1st Royal Munster Fusiliers). Here he spent three unadventurous years, giving no outward indication that he was cut out for anything more than a plodding career as a field officer, with the prospect of painfully slow promotion into dead men's shoes and early retirement on half pay as a passed-over major at forty.

He is described at this time by one of his fellow-officers as slight and delicate-looking, a far from soldierly figure who took no part in the sporting life in which the other younger officers revelled; a bit of a prig, in fact, but a prig whose features conveyed 'an expression of bright intelligence'. That intelligence is hard to discern either in a large full-length portrait in oils painted some eight years later, or in a studio photograph taken in London at about the same time. In the painting it is the magnificent oriental robes that catch the eye, while the photograph conveys a caricature of a mid Victorian paterfamilias, stern-eyed, stiff-starched and hugely moustachioed, with absurd mutton-chops. All but lost under the camouflage is a delicate face dominated by a large nose and an intellectual brow. Only the star of a Companion of the Order of the Bath pinned over his heart and the gold medal (struck by order of the Board of Directors of the EICo) hanging by a ribbon round his neck suggest we look a little closer.

One of Edwardes's contemporaries who failed at first to do so was a young subaltern in the Bombay Army named Henry Daly. 'Nothing in his appearance to give the impression of daring – or remarkable in any way,' noted Daly in his journal at their first meeting. 'I suspect he is a greatly overrated man – one who has been made by circumstances, and thrust into a position which he lacks ability to fill. Nous verrons.' And see he did, for a decade later Daly had been forced to revise his opinion:

Colonel Edwardes is palpably a man above the mark in talent . . . He is subdued and somewhat grave; has somewhat the affectation of dignity . . . In early youth he was frolicsome, gay and witty; he seems now to have a puritanical conviction that such things are unbecoming. He is a religious man, careful of forms, and inclined somewhat to give out his opinion on controversial affairs. He is friendly and polite to me, yet I do not *warm* to him. He is somewhat diplomatic and less straightforward than is pleasant. Unlike our noble, high-minded host, whose heart is full of true religion, whose mind is cultivated and generous . . . a rare creature, made for love and honour.

This 'rare creature' was Henry Lawrence, who had by then become patron and master to both Edwardes and Daly.

What first brought Edwardes to Henry Lawrence's notice was a series of squibs that appeared in the *Delhi Gazette* under the title 'Letters of Brahminee Bull in India to his cousin John in England'. This newspaper was read by everyone in the tiny civil and military community of Upper Hindustan, and the Brahminee Bull Letters attracted a lot of attention, not so much for their wit as for the bold political opinions expressed by their author, Lieutenant Herbert Edwardes. Something in these squibs evidently also caught Sir Hugh Gough's imagination, because the C-in-C summoned Edwardes to his Delhi headquarters and offered him a job on his staff. Again the timing was opportune, as the army was about to move against the Sikhs. Thus it came about that within days of reporting to the C-in-C's camp, Edwardes found himself at his chief's side for the opening engagement of the First Sikh War, to be struck down, like almost every other member of the C-in-C's staff, by Sikh gunfire.

Also present at Mudki and subsequent engagements was the new Governor-General, Sir Henry Hardinge. A former soldier himself, invalided out after losing an arm at Quatre-Bras in 1815, Hardinge decided – unwisely, as it turned out – to leave command of the army with the more experienced Gough, accompanying him as his second-in-command. With Hardinge was a squadron of cavalry known as the Governor-General's Body Guard, whose adjutant was a modest and self-effacing twenty-three-year-old Englishman from the Isle of Wight named Reynell Taylor.

It was the cavalry which saved Gough's bacon at Mudki, routing the undisciplined Sikh cavalry and so exposing both flanks of the enemy to further attack. And in its allotted place that day was the Governor-General's Body Guard. In a letter to his father dated 1 January 1846 Reynell Taylor set down a stirring account of what it was like to be part of a massed charge:

Conceive a brigade or column of troops galloping through a thick thorn jungle enveloped in clouds of dust so dense that the standard of my squadron was the only landmark I could recognise, approaching nearer and nearer to the thundering batteries of the enemy and the yelling crowd protecting them. Above all the din I heard the word passed to wheel into line; it was merely a left turn for each individual; and on we rushed at the same pace. Loud shouts of friend and foe arose on our right as our gallant dragoons dashed in, clearing all before them, and in another second we were in a mass of bloody-minded Sikh horse and foot, but chiefly the former. I need not give you the details of such work. I believe the men we were opposed to were, or thought themselves to be, cut off from escape by the dragoons, and they fought most furiously. I was personally engaged with five men at different times, and after a tussle of some seven or eight minutes in which our adversaries were all cut down, shot, or driven off, I found myself wounded in three different places, my reins cut and my horse 'Pickle' severely wounded by a sabre.

Many years later Taylor provided a more detailed account of the battle for his old commanding officer – a grim picture of hand-to-hand fighting which shows the gentle Reynell Taylor to have been as valiant a swordsman as any:

I remember stopping the blow of the first man I met and giving him a return blow across the face. Another fellow rode at me with a lance, and I turned it off with my sword when close to my breast; and I believe it was while making a return cut at him that another man, who had come up on my bridle-hand, administered a severe 'smeller' in the face, as poor Fisher would have called it, which, cutting through my shako peak, split my nose like a pea, and deluged my left eye with blood. Another man whom I met rode close up to my sword-hand, and with his teeth set, standing in his stirrups, gave a downright cut at my head, which I stopped; and the sword, a Wilkinson, bears the notch to this day in the thick part near the hilt; the metal, being as hard as a diamond, is yet cut into like lead! In the mêlée I received a severe cut on the shoulder, but by whom given I never clearly made out. It cut through my jacket and two shirts which I had put on for the bitter cold, having been on picket the night before, and cut a great piece out of the deltoid muscle as well. I had also another wound on my left wrist, the sword having been stopped by the bone, but this was not deep. My curb rein was cut, and my horse Pickle received a severe cut in his left flank. The last thing I remember was sparring with a foot-man, trying to get a cut at him. He had his sword lifted high and was just going to make a sweeping cut at my horse's neck when a bullet struck his sword close to the hilt and snapped it off; on which the fellow sank down, shamming dead.

Horse-lovers will be pleased to know that the gallant charger Pickle survived his wounds and continued as Taylor's 'constant companion' for another eight years. Taylor himself was listed on the casualty roll as 'very severely wounded' and took no further part in the war. More than thirty years later he was sitting in a railway carriage when an older gentleman got in and, after peering at his scarred face, muttered to himself, 'Yes, I'm sure it is the same nose. Well, I did make a capital job of that, certainly.' It was the surgeon who had stitched Taylor together after the battle.

The success of Gough's cavalry forced the Sikhs to fall back some twenty miles to Ferozshah. The British army followed up and three days later a second and even bloodier confrontation took place, in which the fighting went on for a day and a night and then a second day, until nightfall. Gough's infantry and cavalry were directed time after time to charge into a wall of round-shot and grape, until they were either destroyed or exhausted. One of the survivors was a bruised, bloody and very angry William Hodson:

In the most dense dust and smoke, and under an unprecedented fire of grape, our Sepoys again gave way and broke. It was a fearful crisis, but the bravery of the English regiments saved us. The Colonel, the greater part of my brother officers, and myself, were left with the colours and about thirty men immediately in front of the batteries! . . . A ball (from a shell, I fancy) struck my leg below the knee, but happily spared the bone, and only inflicted a flesh wound. I was also knocked down twice — once by a shell burst so close to me as to kill the men behind me, and once by the explosion of a mine . . . They returned again to the charge as often as we gained any advantage, and it was evening before they were finally disposed of by a charge of our dragoons, *and our ammunition was exhausted!* – so near are we in our most triumphant successes to a destruction as complete!

Unknown to Hodson, this pyrrhic victory was won only by the quite inexplicable failure of fresh Sikh reinforcements to attack the weakened British troops. On being informed that the Sikhs were withdrawing and that the field was his, Sir Henry Hardinge was heard to mutter, 'Another such victory and we are undone!'

We hear nothing of these first two engagements from John Nicholson. As a commissariat officer, concerned with keeping Gough's army supplied with victuals and ammunition, he is unlikely to have participated in the battle of Ferozshah or the subsequent engagements. However, we do know that he was distressed by the death of a particular hero of his, Major George Broadfoot, torn apart by a cannonball. During the Afghan débâcle it was Broadfoot who, as garrison engineer, had built up the defences of the little fort at Jalalabad, and animated its defenders through the long siege. He had then joined with another junior officer, Henry Havelock, to dissuade the garrison commander and a majority of senior officers from capitulating to the Afghans, as Nicholson's CO had done at Ghazni. To Nicholson he was the very model of the man of action who led from the front, took bold decisions – and never surrendered. In later years he was often heard to remark in times of crisis, 'Let us think how Broadfoot would have acted in the present case'.

Broadfoot had just been appointed Agent to the Governor-General (AGG) for the Affairs of the Punjab and the North-West Frontier, the previous AGG having been killed at Mudki. The Governor-General now had to cast around urgently for another replacement. The most obvious candidate was Captain Frederick Mackeson, the political agent who had done wonders in opening the Khyber for General Pollock's avenging army in 1841. According to a colleague, Mackeson was 'an excellent officer, a first-rate linguist, a man of such temper as no native would disturb, and of untiring energy. His life was spent in discoursing night and day with false Sikhs and false Khyberees at Peshawur, on treading almost alone, or attended by Afghan escort, the paths of the Khyber. A road that Avitabile would not have crossed with a brigade, was probably traversed 50 times by Mackeson with a few Afghan horsemen.'

But Frederick Mackeson did not enjoy the confidence of the Governor-General, who turned instead to a man who was, by comparison, far less qualified – Captain Henry Lawrence, author of the tribute to Mackeson quoted above.

When the terse summons came – 'Broadfoot is killed and you are required forthwith' – Henry Lawrence was marooned in the British Residency in Kathmandu, where he and his wife Honoria had passed two lonely years. Apart from his two years as a civil officer in the Cis-Sutlej region of Ferozepore and his brief spell in Peshawar as a political officer working with the Sikhs, Henry Lawrence's Frontier experience was slight, set against Mackeson's. But it was his views on the Punjab and the Sikhs that proved the deciding factor. These, set out in a series of articles for the *Calcutta*

Review written during his exile in Nepal, had caught the attention of the new Governor-General, who concluded that their author not only knew what he was talking about but could provide wise political advice.

Pausing only briefly in Delhi – where his younger brother John was now making his mark as the Commissioner – to transfer his baggage from post-carriage to camels, Henry Lawrence hurried up the Mughal road by way of Ambala and Ludhiana to join the Governor-General at the Commander-in-Chief's camp near Ferozepore. Sir Henry Hardinge was then sixty, Henry Lawrence at thirty-nine very much his junior, but both were of a type – open, warm-hearted and down-to-earth – and they hit if off at once. Despite his military background, Hardinge was not in favour of any further annexation of Indian territory – and Henry Lawrence's views matched his own. The two men saw eye to eye, so much so that Lawrence very soon became the Governor-General's right-hand man and policy-maker on all matters affecting the Punjab.

Five weeks after Ferozshah the opposing armies met again beside the banks of the Sutlej, at Sobraon. Yet again, Gough threw his troops forward in a series of frontal assaults against massed artillery well dug-in in a strong defensive position – although on this occasion the attack was preceded by a three-hour artillery duel.

Fearing that he would miss the next round of the conflict, William Hodson had just – on the evening of 9 February – secured a transfer from his disgraced 2nd Grenadiers to the 16th BNI. Within hours his new regiment received the order to advance on the Sikh position, a series of entrenchments in front of a bend in the river. 'On we went as usual in the teeth of a dreadful fire of guns and musketry,' he wrote afterwards. Again he was lucky to come through more or less unscathed – 'except that a bullet took a fancy to my little finger and cut the skin off the top of it – a mere pin scratch, though it spoiled a buckskin glove.'

Not quite so fortunate was Harry Lumsden, his future commander, who now re-enters the story as commander of a company of the 59th BNI, part of the storming division on Gough's left flank ordered to lead the assault. His regiment had been present at the earlier battles, but this was to be its greatest test. 'The instant we moved out of our cover in the nullah [dry river bed] we were saluted with an awful discharge of well-directed shot, which did great mischief in our line,' he wrote to his father. 'This sort of amusement the enemy kept up for us with great effect until we reached within 800 yards of their batteries, when . . . the Infantry closed up their half-broken line, and once more moved forward to the charge. The enemy now changed their round shot for quilted grape [grape shot in canvas sacks], which caused even greater loss than the former but could not stop our men, who were by this time driven half mad with seeing so many of their companions killed around them.'

The regiment held its fire until it had closed to within two hundred yards of the Sikh entrenchments. Then, continues Lumsden, 'We gave the Seikhs the benefit of a round of musketry from the whole line, and with three cheers, regularly raced into the trenches with the bayonet, killing all the gunners on the spot, and driving the whole line of the Seikh infantry from the right of their entrenchment into the river, where they were shot down like so many ducks. We now cut away two of the centre boats from their bridge across the Sutlej, thereby cutting off all hope from the rest of the enemy. The enemy had just succeeded in repelling an attack made on them in front by our European regiment and two Goorkah battalions, which they almost cut to pieces with grape, when, to their horror, they saw the whole of our division drawn up inside their own second line of entrenchments exactly in their rear.'

The Sikh army was now trapped between the river and Gough's army advancing on both flanks. First the gunners, attempting to escape by their left flank, were 'instantly charged in front and rear at the same time, and bayonetted almost to a man'. Then the infantry was dealt with: 'Some five or six regiments reached the river, but finding the bridge cut were obliged to try the ford, under a fire of two troops of Horse Artillery and about ten regiments of Infantry, and, as you may fancy, were rather roughly handled.' Finally, it was the turn of the Sikh cavalry, who also attempted to escape by the bridge and were similarly dealt with. At this point Joe Lumsden received a wound to the foot that was to leave him with a slight but permanent limp for the rest of his life: 'I was so excited at the time that I scarcely knew I was hit, and sat on my charger, who was also shot through the leg about the same time, until the Cavalry were driven into the river, after which I felt very sick, and would have fallen off my horse had not an officer of the 10th Foot, seeing that I was wounded, given me a glass of brandy, which refreshed me very much and enabled me to do my duty until the action was over.'

In writing to his father, Lumsden made light of the wound with his usual good humour. 'A musket ball had entered on the top of the little toe and come out half way down the foot. I was obliged to have the wound opened from end to end, and all sorts of queer-looking little bones taken out. This, I was told, was the only chance of saving the foot, so I was obliged to submit, like a good boy . . . I shall now be able to put on a much more fashionable boot. If you hear of an old boy wishing for a cure for corns, just recommend him to have a musket shot sent through them.'

The battle of Sobraon, fought on 10 February 1846, was a turning-point in the fortunes of the British and the Sikhs. 'We took and destroyed in this action seventy-two guns of all sizes,' concluded Joe Lumsden, 'and so utterly ruined all the aspirations of the Seikhs, that in three days we were in Lahore, with the Union Jack flying over the fallen empire of the proud Seikhs.'

Sobraon also marks a first conjunction of Henry Lawrence and his Young Men, though Neville Chamberlain, as we know, was absent in England, still recovering from his infected leg wound, and Reynell Taylor was similarly *hors de combat* in the military hospital at Ferozepore. But present on the battlefield and soon afterwards summoned by Henry Lawrence were John Nicholson, William Hodson, Harry Lumsden and Herbert Edwardes, now recovered from his wound. Also present and already at Lawrence's side was the first of his disciples, twenty-four-year-old Patrick Vans Agnew, formerly political assistant to the late George Broadfoot and now working for a new master. All seven would surely have agreed with the sentiments expressed by Hodson in a letter in the immediate aftermath of Sobraon, that 'a campaign is a wonderful dispeller of false notions and young imaginations. I have indeed much to be thankful for, and I hope I shall not forget the lesson.'

Barely a month later, however, Hodson was already regretting the swift return to peace: 'We must really have a natural taste for fighting highly developed, for I catch myself wishing and "asking for more", and grumbling at the speedy settlement of things and the prospect of cantonments instead of field service. Is it not marvellous, as if one had not had a surfeit of killing? But the truth is, that is not the motive, but a sort of undefined ambition.'

Hodson's talk of 'undefined ambition' would have struck chords with every one of the seven. They were doubtless always thereafter aware of the high cost at which the Punjab had been purchased, and this surely made them the more determined, in thought if not in word, that what had been so hard-won should not be relinquished.

The destruction of the Sikh army at Sobraon forced the Khalsa to sue for peace. In Lahore Maharaja Dalip Singh, eight-year-old boy-sovereign of the Punjab, was required to kneel in submission to the Governor-General under the walls of the fort. However, complete annexation was not on the cards. Henry Lawrence counselled a reconstruction of the Sikh government, albeit 'fenced in and fortified by British bayonets', and the Governor-General concurred. So the young maharaja was allowed to perch uneasily on Ranjit Singh's golden throne while a Sikh Council of Regency, the Durbar, was set up to govern the Punjab in his name. A British Resident was now required to 'control and guide' this Durbar and, effectively, to rule the Punjab. The obvious choice was the newly-promoted Colonel Henry Lawrence.

It had long been Henry Lawrence's habit to keep an eye out for young officers who might one day serve as his assistants. He always carried a leather-bound notebook, and whenever the name of some promising military officer came up in conversation he would jot it down, together with a note or two. As a result, he came to Lahore and to the new British Residency at the Tomb of Anarkali with a 'wish list' of potential political assistants at the ready in his breast pocket. Heading that list were the names of his elder brother George and his younger brother John. The first he appointed Political Agent in Peshawar, the second he made his deputy and Commissioner of the Trans-Sutlej Jullunder Doab, the land between the Sutlej and Beas rivers.

Few accounts of the contrasting characters of the brothers are as perceptive as that penned by the ill-fated Lieutenant William Anderson. It comes from a letter written to his close friend Henry Daly in March 1848, just weeks before Anderson's murder in Multan, and helps to explain how it was that all three Lawrences, and Henry in particular, inspired such hero-worship in their lieutenants. 'One kind of greatness', wrote Anderson, 'is common to all the three brothers – decision of character, unsurpassable and dauntless courage.' George he describes as 'brisk, jolly, less solid than John and the Colonel [Henry Lawrence], but capable of great deeds in a crisis by his pluck, talent, honesty, and decision.' Anderson did not like John at first, but later found him to be 'a splendid creature . . . original, plain-spoken, playful and even prantic in conversation; he is one of the first civil servants in India; knows natives like ABC; notes humbug, pulls out your most secret wishes by an apparent artlessness; is fond of billiards and cigars; writes splendid reports and letters; does immense naukri [service], and has a very nice wife.' But it was Henry Lawrence whom he most admired: 'The Colonel surpasses the brothers by having all their decision, all their experience, but with a refined sensitive nature . . . The shyness of vanity is unknown to him; but the shyness of modesty, which sits well, though not very elegantly, on a great man, is his failing, his demon . . . He surpasses . . . all men I have seen as a perfect knower of men.'

It would have made sense for this 'perfect knower of men' to draw on the experience of older officers who knew something of the Punjab – officers such as Frederick Mackeson. But relations between Lawrence and the now twice-disappointed Mackeson had become strained, so it was perhaps as well that the Governor-General intervened to appoint the latter Superintendent of the Cis-Sutlej territory (east of the Sutlej river, and thus outside Henry Lawrence's domain). One equally experienced political agent was, however, brought in: Captain James Abbott, aged thirty-eight. These two – Mackeson and Abbott – are, if not quite the forgotten men of this period, then certainly the most neglected by their countrymen. They had the misfortune to be not only contemporaries of the Lawrences – James Abbott and Henry Lawrence were at Addiscombe together – but mistrusted by them.

As far as the Lawrences were concerned, they were 'difficult', men who liked to plough their own furrows without others peering over their shoulders. For their part, Abbott and Mackeson could not adjust to Henry Lawrence's casual style of messing, whereby he worked, ate and slept in his quarters at Anarkali's tomb cheek-by-jowl with half a dozen of his assistants. Yet what should one make of the fact that, of all those early political assistants, it is these two, both known locally as 'uncle' – '*Kaka* Abbott' and 'Kishin *Kaka*' ('Kishin' being a corruption of the locally unpronounceable 'Mackeson') – whose names have survived the longest on the Frontier itself?

The historian Sir John Kaye describes James Abbott as 'one of those men whose lot in life it is never to be believed, never to be appreciated, never to be rewarded; of the true salt of the earth, but of an unrecognised savour, chivalrous, heroic, but somehow or other never thoroughly emerging from the shade.' Yet Abbott had made his mark before ever he came to the Punjab. He was the third of four brothers all at that time busy marking out careers for themselves as field officers in the Bengal Army: Augustus, a gunner officer who distinguished himself in the Afghan War; Frederick, a sapper who played a major role in both the Afghan and First Sikh Wars; and Saunders, who fought as an infantryman through the First Sikh War and went on to become an administrator in the Punjab. James first came to general notice with the publication of his *Narrative of a Journey from Heraut to Khiva, Moscow, and St Petersburgh, during the late Russian Invasion of Khiva*, a personal account of an extraordinary mercy-mission that had taken him through Afghanistan to Turkestan and on to Russia to secure the release of some Russian captives. The business turned sour, costing Abbott two fingers on his sword-hand, but he came back to England, by way of the Caspian and St Petersburg, something of a hero. A water-colour portrait of modest size painted while he was in England shows him in the robes he wore on his mission to the Khan of Khiva: a plain Afghan shirt and sheepskin *poshteen* with a long, brightly-coloured turban wrapped round his head. The face is that of a handsome young man in his prime, his untrimmed black beard clashing with a generous brown moustache. It dates from 1841; by the time of his summons to Lahore in the spring of

1846 he had aged greatly, shattered by the death of his much-loved young wife while giving birth to a daughter when they were out in camp. Leaving his baby with friends in Calcutta, Abbott had returned to his political work as assistant to the British Resident in Indore. His posting to the completely unknown district of Hazara, a tract of hilly country bounded by the Jhelum and the Indus north of Rawalpindi, proved a quite unexpected new lease of life. Asked in later years for the secret of his good relations with the people of Hazara, Abbott was apt to reply simply that he 'spoke to them as to gentlemen'.

Frederick Mackeson remains an enigma. Apart from the Governor-General's official eulogy at the time of his death, very little survives to show how his colleagues regarded him or related to him. Unlike Abbott, who left several volumes of manuscript notes about his early years in Hazara, Mackeson left nothing. In his book *The Pathans*, Sir Olaf Caröe writes that 'no portrait of Mackeson has come down; his stature, his features, the look in his eye, are unknown to us today'. Fortunately, Caröe is wrong: a portrait *does* exist, a simple pen-and-ink sketch of Mackeson in profile, tucked away in an album of papers gathered by George Pearse, who had a spell as Frederick Mackeson's political assistant. The first thing that strikes one about this sketch is the absence of the usual bushy beard of the political officer, and the presence of a very elegantly curled moustache; the second is the short curly hair. Commissioner Mackeson comes across as a snappy dresser, a man who cares for appearances. Set beside the sketch are a few lines in Pearse's handwriting: 'Colonel Frederick Mackeson, CB. Commissioner of Peshawar and Hazara. Was assassinated in 1853. This sketch was done by Andrew Blackall. Mackeson was a most grand fellow.'

With his two brothers now at his side, Mackeson in the Cis-Sutlej and Abbott allotted to Hazara, Henry Lawrence's next step was to go through his notebook. The first to be plucked from the Bengal Army and offered a temporary transfer as political assistant was Herbert Edwardes. Originally it was planned that he should go on to join John Lawrence in Jallandar, but after the two had worked together in Lahore for a week Henry decided that Edwardes should stay with him as his personal assistant. The manner of his promotion was truly Lawrencian in style. Without looking up from the letter he was writing, the older man addressed the younger: 'How would you like to be my personal assistant? I think you and I could work very well together.' The younger replied with alacrity that he would like that very much indeed. 'Very well. That's settled.' And Lawrence went back to his writing. However, some moments later Lawrence put down his pen and addressed Edwardes directly: 'There's only one thing I wish you to remember. If I say or do anything that hurts or vexes you, don't brood over it. Just out with it; and we shall come to an understanding at once.' Thus was the informal, intimate and highly unconventional tone of the Henry Lawrence regime set.

Hard on Edwardes's heels came Nicholson, Hodson, Lumsden and Taylor. The last seems to have drawn the short straw, possibly because he remained on the sick-list for some time, and despite the Governor-General's backing his plea to be given 'something in the Political line' in the Punjab went unanswered. The best the Governor-General could do for him was an appointment as a political assistant in Rajasthan, where he chafed for almost a year before receiving his letter of summons from Henry Lawrence.

John Nicholson fared a little better. Although he had been stuck in the commissariat, his hard work had somehow caught the eye of Henry Lawrence, and he was despatched to the hill-country of Jammu to help modernise the army of its ruler, Maharaja Gulab Singh, with the promise of 'something better' in the political field when that was done.

The real winners in this first round of appointments were Hodson and Lumsden. In early March 1846 we find Hodson writing to thank an influential family friend, James Thomason, Lieutenant-Governor of the North-West Provinces, for putting his name forward to Henry Lawrence, 'from whom I have received every sort of attention and kindness. I have been very much struck by his superiority, and freedom from diplomatic solemnity and mystery.' Very soon afterwards he was working as a general dogsbody in Henry Lawrence's office, initially in Simla, the Hot Weather seat of government in the foothills of the Himalayas, and then in Lahore at the start of the Cold Weather. 'I am now writing in his room with the incessant entrances and exits of natives – rajahs, princes, vakeels [attorneys], etc. etc., and officers civil and military,' William Hodson told his father in September 1846, and went on to draw a revealing picture of the Lawrence school of political instruction. Because Herbert Edwardes was ill, Hodson was acting as Lawrence's personal assistant:

I should hardly like staying with Colonel Lawrence (especially as I live day and night in the same room with him and his papers, regularly camp fashion), but that he wishes it, and I manage to give him a slight helping hand by making precis of his letters, and copying confidential papers. He is amazingly kind, and tells me all that is going on, initiating me into the mysteries of 'polit-ical' business, and thus giving me more knowledge of things and persons Indian than I should learn in a year of ordinary life; ay, or in three years either . . . He makes me work at Hindoostanee, and has given me a lesson or two in the use of the theodolite, and other surveying instruments, to the end that I may get employed in the Surveying Department, after two years of which, he says, 'I shall be fit for a Political'.

Dating from this same period is a letter from Hodson's mentor con-taining more sound advice: 'Favour and partiality do occasionally give a man a lift, but depend upon it that *his* is the best chance in the long run who helps himself. So far you have done this manfully . . . Don't, however, be too proud. Learn your duties thoroughly. Continue to study two to three hours a day; not to pass in a hurry, but that you may do so two or three years hence with éclat.'

With the arrival of Honoria Lawrence from Simla in October, Lawrence's young assistant gained a mother-figure who shared her husband's disregard for the conventions and whose informality and Irish wit quickly set every visitor at ease. 'She was not beautiful in the ordinary acceptance of the term,' wrote one of them, Herbert Edwardes, 'but a harmony, fervour and intelligence breathed in her expression.' Although she had her own private parlour in the Tomb it was always open to any assistant who felt like dropping in, and in the evenings often became a rallying-point for the household. The price she paid was a loss of privacy, and of the intimacy she and her husband had formerly enjoyed. As she complained privately to a friend, she now 'hardly ever' saw her husband 'quietly', and the constant stream of visitors was like 'keeping a table d'hôte without being paid for it'.

Joe Lumsden's claims for selection as a political assistant were probably enhanced by Henry Lawrence's long-standing friendship with his father, a fellow-artilleryman, who had asked Lawrence to keep an eye on him. However, Lumsden himself always claimed that what first brought him to the great man's attention was an incident that had occurred a year or two earlier, when he and another subaltern were briefly taken prisoner by a band of robbers preying on travellers on the road between Ludhiana and Ferozepore. They had been on a shooting expedition when they were seized by this band, taken to a nearby fort and locked up. A quick-thinking servant was able to smuggle them a pencil and a scrap of paper on which they scribbled a few lines calling for help. Later that same night the cavalry arrived, in the person of Major Lawrence and an escort of twenty sowars. Lumsden was mightily impressed, not just by the speed of his rescue but by the efficiency Lawrence displayed in arresting the malefactors, obtaining depositions from witnesses and bringing the whole matter to a conclusion in Ferozepore the next day.

Lumsden was initially despatched to Kangra, up in the hills east of Lahore, where he passed the Hot Weather of 1846 in charge of the district. It was 'as hard work as any Christian could well be called upon to get through, having to work from morning until after dark in kutcherry [office] to keep the business of the office from falling into arrears, and after dinner to make up rather heavy treasury accounts. None of the English clerks appointed to the office had arrived, so I was left to my own wits and resources.' This was not the sort of job he wanted and he was soon writing to his father with the admission that 'office work and confinement within doors is not my speciality; I would always rather ride twenty miles than write a note.'

His drudgery was ended by a summons from Lawrence, ordering him to hurry down to Lahore to help fill the gap left by Edwardes's illness. 'I am quite delighted,' he wrote. 'In case of a row with the Khalsa-Jee [Honoured Khalsa] I shall be in just the right box to see everything, and may with a little luck contrive to draw a prize.'

Henry Lawrence's first concern was to restore stability to the Punjab, which for years had lacked any form of ordered government. The mangled but still troublesome Khalsa Dal must be reduced still further in size, a legal code based on both local custom and justice drawn up, and land revenues collected on the basis of objective rather than arbitrary assessment, only to be arrived at by a painstaking process of on-site inspection of holdings and documents, known to the British as 'settlement'. It was Lawrence's view that wherever possible existing local institutions should be respected and employed, rather than imposing alien customs. 'It has been our aim to get as many natives of the Punjab as possible into office,' he later explained. 'We wish to make the basis of our rule a light and equable assessment; and strong and vigorous, through uninterfering police, and a quiet hearing in all civil and other cases.'

This same emphasis on respecting local institutions while providing a just administration was relayed to Henry Lawrence's British officers. We get a clear picture of what Lawrence required of them from the letter of instruction sent to Neville Chamberlain on his appointment as assistant commissioner in Rawalpindi in December 1849 – a standard letter despatched by Lawrence, with minor variations, to all his young men. For more than a century his advice remained the model which district officers in India and Pakistan were urged to follow in the execution of their duties: 'He is the best officer who best manages the following two items – interfere with the people *as little as possible*, and be prompt as you can in disposing of cases. Keep the peace, and collect the revenues, and Utopia will be gained . . . Our assessment should be so light as to require no compulsion in the collection, and we should rather be protectors in the land than tax-masters.'

This was all very well in principle, but the reality was that reform of the civil administration in the Punjab required the approval of a 'venal and selfish Durbar', whose Sikh members resisted Lawrence at every step, while at the same time intriguing against each other. An amusing if prejudiced picture of the Durbar – dominated by the young Maharaja's powerful mother, Maharani Jindan, and her reputed lover, Lal Singh – comes from the pen of Joe Lumsden, newly arrived in Lahore in September 1846:

1. Attock Fort and the bridge of boats across the Indus: engraving from *The Graphic*, 26 October 1878. The mountain battery seen crossing the bridge was on its way to the Second Afghan War, but the scene had not changed since the First Afghan War

2. Street and bazaar in Peshawar, from a drawing by William Carpenter: engraving from the *Illustrated London News*, 1857

3. 'Wild Afreedees and Khyberees', Frontier Pakhtuns gathered under the walls of Fort Jamrud at the gateway to the Khyber Pass: engraving from the *Illustrated London News*, 18 June 1870

4. 'The Fort of Ali Musjeed, Camp of the 4th Brigade of Major-General Pollock's Force, April 1842': water-colour by Lieutenant Alfred Croley

5. 'The Sacking of the Great Bazaar at Caubul, March 1842': water-colour by Lieutenant Alfred Croley

6. Sir Henry Lawrence: a miniature on ivory probably painted at Delhi in about 1847 by an unknown Indian artist

7. Herbert Edwardes resplendent in Afghan dress: oils on canvas, painted by Henry Mosely during Edwardes's home leave in 1850. In the background is the mosque at Multan

8. James Abbott in Afghan dress: a small water-colour painted in London by B. Baldwin in 1841 following Abbott's adventures in Afghanistan and Russia

9. 'Glen at Nara Huzara. Bivouak of my armed levies in 1848': a pen-and-ink sketch by James Abbott showing the defile which he made his base during his guerrilla campaign against the Sikhs

10. John Nicholson: a portrait in chalk drawn by William Carpenter in Peshawar in 1854

11. Major-General Sir Neville Chamberlain, about three years before his retirement from India in 1881 at the age of 61. He was made a Field Marshal in 1900, two years before his death

I was initiated into the mysteries of Grand Durbars and the like, introduced to Lal Sing, the Prime Minister, young Dulip Sing [Maharaja Dalip Singh], and a large bundle of clothes, placed on a chair and called the Maharanee, out of which, now and then, might be seen a pair of feet and a remarkably pretty little hand. When the bundle was addressed, even in the most flowery Persian, the reply was always in a grinding sort of sound, strongly resembling that produced in the process of grinding coffee. However, the bundle, although she will not show her eyes, evidently has good ones, and shows her taste in the choice of her wazir [chief minister], Lal Sing. I have seldom seen a better looking man than Lal Sing. He is, I should say, about thirty years of age, strongly built, tall, and very soldier-like, though as cunning as a fox; talks in a bland, kind tone, which could not hurt a fly, though he would just as soon cut a man's windpipe as look at him. Every one of the sirdars [leaders of misls] hate him, and make no secret of their dislike, but say with the greatest coolness that Lal Sing's life is not worth two hours' purchase after the withdrawal of the British troops from Lahore . . . There is not one of them who is not looking out anxiously for the time when, with our withdrawal from the scene, he may seize the opportunity of opening his neighbour's throat.

Lumsden's view – shared by most of his colleagues, though not by his chief – was that the answer to all this bickering among the Sikhs was annexation: 'I cannot help thinking how much better it would be for all parties if we could only, for the sake of humanity, divest ourselves of a little of that mock modesty the political assumes when acting towards other states, and tell the local authorities at once, that if they cannot undertake to keep all quiet, we must assume the government.'

Added to these difficulties with the Durbar was the problem of how the EICo was to collect a large indemnity placed on the Sikhs for the cost of the war. At the recommendation of Henry Lawrence, Lord Hardinge (he had been created a viscount after the Peace of Lahore in 1845) agreed to a solution that apparently flew in the face of all Lawrence's high-minded ideals and was to have dire consequences for the future stability of the region: to sell the

Afghan province of Kashmir, with its largely Muslim population, to a Hindu. The much-coveted Vale of Kashmir had been conquered by the Sikhs in 1819 but left in the hands of a Muslim governor, Sheikh Imam-ud-Din. In neighbouring Jammu the Hindu ruler, Gulab Singh, had survived the encroachments of Ranjit Singh and remained on the sidelines during the Anglo-Sikh war; he now offered to pay two-thirds of the Sikh war indemnity in return for the title deeds to Kashmir – an offer that was quickly accepted. In consequence, in July 1846 John Nicholson found himself in the curious role of escort commander as he accompanied Maharaja Gulab Singh over the mountains from Jammu to Srinagar to claim his new kingdom.

It very soon became clear to Nicholson that the Maharaja was not wanted in Kashmir: 'We had not been many days in the city before we learnt that the governor had made up his mind to drive Gulab Singh's small force out of the valley and seize us. We had great difficulty in effecting our escape, which we did just in time to avoid capture.' These few words cover the rout of Maharaja Gulab Singh's Dogra troops and a fast and undignified retreat over a mountain pass and back to Jammu.

The British now had no option but to secure Kashmir themselves, in Maharaja Gulab Singh's name, and this meant despatching a military force of ten thousand men from Lahore to remove Sheik Imam-ud-Din. Henry Lawrence took charge of the expedition personally, with Patrick Vans Agnew, Nicholson, Lumsden, and Hodson acting as his lieutenants. The men they commanded were almost all Sikhs, men of the Khalsa Dal who only six months earlier had fought against them. The venture thus had all the potential for a repeat of the Afghan catastrophe in miniature: it was a hazardous and thoroughly unworthy business which Lawrence later described as 'half a dozen foreigners taking up a lately subdued mutinous army through as difficult a country as there is in the world to put the chief, formerly their commander, now in their minds a rebel, in possession of the brightest gem of their land'.

In the event, the Sikh sepoys behaved like lambs. Open battle was avoided by the peaceful submission of Sheikh Imam-ud-Din to Herbert Edwardes, now fully recovered and acting temporarily as political adviser to Maharaja Gulab Singh in Jammu. Lawrence's defence was that his actions relieved the Kashmiris of a tyrant who was milking their land dry; the reality is that he replaced the 'tyrant' with a ruler whom even the kind-hearted Edwardes regarded as 'the worst native' he had 'ever come in contact with . . . a bad king, a miser, and a liar, and the dirtiest fellow in all India'. William Hodson was equally blunt about the enterprise: 'We seem bound to see him established on the throne we carved out for him, and it is our only chance of keeping peace and order; though he is such a villain, and so detested, that I imagine it will be a sorry state of quietness.' The new ruler of Kashmir he describes as 'a fine, tall, portly man, with a splendid expressive face, and most gentlemanly, pleasing manner, and fine-toned voice – altogether the most pleasing Asiatic I have seen – to all appearance, the gentlest of the gentle . . . To us, however, his fondness for flaying men alive, cutting off their noses and ears and hands, etc., savours *rather* of the inexcusable. He was accused of having flayed 12,000 men, which he indignantly asserted was a monstrous calumny, as he only skinned *three*; afterwards he confessed to *three hundred*!'

Once the Maharaja was safely installed in Srinagar, Lawrence returned to Lahore with Hodson and the bulk of the Sikh force, leaving behind Patrick Vans Agnew and John Nicholson to keep an eye on things. Joe Lumsden was given his own task: to take a force of three thousand Sikh infantry, together with six light guns carried on elephants, and reconnoitre the hill country of Hazara, bordering Kashmir to the west.

This was a delightful challenge. The hillmen of Hazara were notorious for their hostility towards intruders; they had resisted every attempt made by the Sikhs to govern their country and had won several famous victories against Sikh armies sent to subdue them. Lumsden had no doubts, even when he discovered that his Sikh soldiers carried no more than twenty-five rounds of ammunition per man – and that a force of some seven thousand *Hazarawals* (people of Hazara) had gathered to oppose his entry into their land. 'You may fancy my feelings', he wrote to his father some three months later, 'on finding myself – a griff of a lieutenant – suddenly placed in the position of a general officer, without any officer to consult, and with troops in whose company I have never been before, except as an enemy. However, I was determined to do my best for the Government, and, if possible, show that I was not unworthy of Lawrence's patronage and trust.'

His first setback occurred when he found that his Sikh troops were 'in the habit of swallowing concoctions of opium, made into pills, daily', and refused to advance into Hazara until their stocks had been replenished: 'It seems that these grand old veterans of Runjeet Sing's army can do nothing without opium, and really become so dejected that you might have wapped them with a big stick. It took several weeks to rectify all this.'

Despite their fondness for opium, the Sikh sepoys turned out to be excellent soldiers – 'first-rate men, ready for any work, always in the best of humours, fond of their officers, and just as obedient to orders as our own troops, and not giving one-quarter the trouble that the latter do'. Lumsden very quickly took to them, as indeed did the Sikhs to him. 'Is it not strange,' he wrote, 'that two of these very regiments, only just a year ago, were fighting against us, and repulsed two assaults of Gilbert's Division at Sobraon? The men and officers often talked over the whole business with me in the most friendly way. These regiments were commanded by Colonel Bhoop Singh, and are the very corps which I mentioned as retiring in a mass through the river Sutlej, after Sobraon, without breaking their ranks. The little colonel had two horses shot under him, and is proud as a peacock of the whole affair. He is a great pet of mine, and always accompanies me shooting.'

What Joe Lumsden experienced in Hazara was to be echoed elsewhere in the Punjab by the Lawrence brothers and many others. Politically the British and the Sikhs would never see eye-to-eye, but on the military level there was enormous respect and fellow-feeling, which were to have far-reaching consequences for the fortunes of both parties in years to come.

Lumsden's first obstacle was the river marking the boundary between Kashmir and Hazara. Finding the Hazarawals massed on the far bank, he resorted to subterfuge: he camped his army beside the obvious crossing-point, drawing the enemy, then in the middle of the night quietly moved out seven hundred men and a boat, crossing the river unopposed a mile downstream. The Hazarawals still held the high ground, however, so Lumsden's men now had to skirmish their way forward to try to take that position. The Sikhs were soon pinned down, with 'a heavy fire of musketry playing on them', unable to advance and unwilling to retire. Only the accurate firing of their own six artillery pieces – 'I never saw such rifle shooting as the Seikh artillery made with their six-pounders. They literally prevented the enemy from raising their heads' – saved the infantry from a massacre. Fortunately, the Hazarawals withdrew at nightfall to a new position along the summit of a high ridge, taking their wounded with them but leaving behind thirty-three dead.

Faced with the task of clearing the Hazarawals from this new and seemingly impregnable position, Lumsden displayed for the first time the extraordinary resourcefulness that would mark him out not simply as a first-rate military leader but as a master of irregular warfare. At the heart of his success were the two key factors of surprise and good intelligence. Instead of ordering an attack on the Hazarawal position, as most commanders of the day would have done, he camped by the river and waited. Within a few days local villagers were approaching his camp to trade, and he talked to them through interpreters. It emerged that the Hazarawal tribesman occupying the summit above were in the habit of making a brief descent from their ridge every evening to some springs, where they cooked their food and rested for the night before returning before dawn to their mountain-top.

Based on this information, Lumsden devised a very simple ruse involving just one member of his force: 'I sent for some herdsmen of the district, and showing them a handful of gold coins, promised to give them if the men would take up a bugler and some odds and ends that they must carry with them to the top of the hill after the enemy had retired from the heights for the night. A bargain was made.' The only hiccough was a disagreement over the selection of the bugler; Lumdsen wanted him to be a volunteer, while the senior Sikh officer wanted to select him himself: 'Let me pick you out a haramzada [base-born, thus low-caste], and it will not matter if he is killed.'

That evening a party consisting of the selected bugler and three shepherds set off for the mountain-top, each carrying a number of earthenware pots filled with gunpowder, with fuses attached. When a signal rocket was fired from the camp they were to light the fuses, and the bugler was to blow all the calls he knew. At nine o'clock Lumsden gave the order to fire the rocket, which shot up into a cloudless sky:

> Bang, bang, bang went the powder pots, the sound of their bursting reverberating through the hills, in the still night air, like salvos of artillery, while the shepherds – who had that day lost some sheep, carried off, it was supposed, by the enemy – sent some large stones bounding down the side of the hill. The enemy, who had just retired for the night, rushed to their match-locks, and concluding that the whole of our forces had by some mysterious agency been conveyed up the hill behind them, instantly took to flight, those in front firing back on later starters, and each little party thinking his neighbour a pursuing Seikh. We in camp were too much convulsed in merriment at the complete success of our stratagem to attempt to follow them.

In Lumsden's words, this little wheeze 'settled the whole business and brought the Kaghan Saiuds to their senses'. The Saiads, a powerful tribe of northern Hazara who were leading the defence against this latest Sikh invasion, now sent in envoys to sue for peace, to 'ask for pardon for the past and with every security for their future good conduct'. Lumsden was now permitted to pass south through the Hazara country without further resistance. 'What think you, as an Artillery officer,' he crowed to his father, 'of my light artillery?' So ended Joe Lumsden's 'first attempt at an independent command', for which he received the thanks of the Government and – 'what I prize more' – the approbation of Henry Lawrence.

In Kashmir, things were not going quite so well for John Nicholson. By November 1846 the Maharaja's position was considered secure enough for Patrick Vans Agnew to be recalled to Lahore, leaving Nicholson 'quite alone'. With the mountains surrounding the Vale of Kashmir now covered in winter snow and the passes closed, he felt trapped as well as isolated; Srinagar and its picturesque Dal Lake was 'anything but a terrestrial Paradise'. His third brother Charles had now arrived in India, as an infantry ensign, and received a letter from John which could hardly be described as welcoming, dwelling as it did on the discomforts he was now suffering:

My fingers are so cold that I can scarcely hold the pen . . . I have suffered so much from ill-health within the last eight months that unless some improvement takes place I fear I shall be obliged to go out of India somewhere on sick certificate before long . . . I sometimes fear that my constitution is going. Nothing brings 'home' to a man's mind more readily in India than illness; he then thinks of the nursing and grateful acts of attention he would receive were he among his own friends. Here I have not even the sight of a white face to cheer me. May you be never in a like predicament!

This was the lowest point in Nicholson's Indian career. In December 1847 he turned twenty-five. He had taken a cut in salary in hope of advancement, but now found himself 'an exile from the civilised world . . . with no duties of any kind to perform', all too aware that Maharaja Gulab Singh required his presence at the Durbar merely to demonstrate to his own court 'the terms of intimacy he was on with the British Government'. He was on the point of quitting – either to return to commissariat work with the army, or to take extended sick-leave – when he received word from Henry Lawrence to return to Lahore. In February 1847 he dug his way through eight and a half feet of snow to cross the Punch Pass, and hurried down to the Punjab plains.

4

'I am to have the making of this regiment'

HARRY LUMSDEN AND PESHAWAR, 1847

> When spring-time flushes the desert grass,
> Our kafilas wind through the Khyber Pass,
> Lean are the camels but fat the frails,
> Light are the purses but heavy the bales,
> When the snowbound trade of the North comes down
> To the market square of Peshawur town.
>
> Rudyard Kiping, 'The Ballad of the King's Jest'

ONCE THE threat of insurrection in Kashmir had receded, Henry Lawrence turned his attention to the 'trans-Indus', the lands between the Indus and the mountains of Afghanistan, focusing on the city of Peshawar and the surrounding plain – known to the British in these early days as Yusufzai, after the strongest Pakhtun tribe of the area, the Yusufzai or Sons of Joseph. Henry's younger brother George was the man appointed to the task. He entered the city on 20 February 1847 as the British Resident, and was gratified to find himself hailed as a liberator from Sikh oppression by Peshawar's predominantly Afghan population. 'The whole city poured out to meet me,' he wrote later in his memoirs, 'and loud were the complaints of the poor people and their demands for justice, many of them carrying fire on their heads as illustrative of their extreme misery and grief . . . I began to

foresee that I had no easy task before me in endeavouring to intro-
duce justice and order, after years of rapine, violence and misrule. I
had also to discipline a mutinous soldiery and police [composed of
Sikhs], and while strictly enforcing the just demands of the
government, to put a stop to all exaction and oppression on the
part of the durbar officials.'

George Lawrence and his military escort were initially quartered in an old Mughal caravanserai known as the Ghor Khatri,
the Tomb of Khatri, a walled enclave which had its origins in a
Buddhist tower built many centuries earlier. It had been the headquarters of the notorious General Avitabile who, ruling Peshawar
on behalf of Ranjit Singh with a rod of iron, had lined the walls
of the Ghor Khatri with the spiked heads of malefactors. But sited
as it was in the very heart of the city, the Ghor Khatri was totally
unsuited to Lawrence's needs, not least because it was a favourite
target of Afridi marauders, who climbed over or burrowed
through its mud walls at night to steal horses and arms. So new
quarters were found, outside the city walls but within comfortable range of the guns on the ramparts of the Bala Hissar,
Peshawar's ancient fort, which Ranjit Singh had pulled down and
then partially rebuilt twenty years before. Ranjit Singh had also
found the time to despoil the magnificent Mughal gardens which
Mountstuart Elphinstone had admired, during his mission of
1809, for their ornamental fountains, roses and fruit trees. In the
midst of the remains of these gardens, laid out by Emperor Babur
in the open country below the fort, was a walled enclosure, once
the country estate of an Afghan governor named Ali Mardan.
Known as Ali Mardan Bagh, Ali Mardan's Garden, it had served as
Elphinstone's quarters before being commandeered by the Sikhs
for use as their Residency; it now became the site for the British
Residency.

Soon after moving in, George Lawrence was joined in Peshawar
by his first political assistant, Lieutenant Harry Lumsden, fresh
from the little triumph of his expedition through Hazara. His
reward for this was a unique double role, as a civil administrator
alongside George Lawrence, and as a military commander. In the
first capacity he was to take charge of the Yusufzai district – most
of the Vale of Peshawar, extending as far east as the Indus and as far

north as the mountains of Swat, an area of some 3,000 square miles – with 'a roving commission to make myself acquainted with the people, the roads, fords, ferries, and forts within and beyond the frontier'. At the same time, he was to raise and lead a special force of mixed cavalry and infantry irregulars, to be known as the Corps of Guides.

The two main difficulties George Lawrence had to overcome in Peshawar were, as elsewhere in the Punjab, the complete breakdown of the civil administration, and the continuing presence of a powerful military machine. Peshawar was no isolated up-country district lending itself readily to government along British lines, but a large city ruled by a Sikh governor who controlled both a corrupt and inefficient Sikh administration and a well-trained, well-armed Sikh military force – and whose priorities were very different from Lawrence's own.

As Harry Lumsden explained much later in a letter to the first historian of the Corps of Guides, there were at this time no British or EICo troops stationed anywhere in the Punjab other than at Lahore: 'All the military duties were performed by the old Seikh army, one division of which was at Peshawar under its own General and staff officers, but at the disposal of Colonel George Lawrence. While the Seikh sirdars carried on the administration of the country, a brigade used to be sent out to the Yousafzai district to collect the government revenue, and according to the custom of the country, collected not only what was the fixed revenue but quite as much more for the benefit of the influential officers of the expedition. These exactions were, as a matter of course, strenuously resisted by most of the tribes, and seldom collected without a fight and destruction of villages.'

Before any revenue was collected under his administration, George Lawrence considered it imperative that a fair assessment of land holdings should be made, which would require the co-operation of the tribal elders – the *khans* who headed the various clans and the *maliks* who were the village chiefs. His first public action was therefore to issue a proclamation ordering all the chiefs in the Vale of Peshawar to return to their villages, on pain of forfeiting their lands and rights, so that equitable rates could be fixed on all their holdings. He and Lumsden then made a start on the exacting process of settlement, by which every patch of cultivated land in the area was assessed for its worth, and a rate of land tax 'settled' on it: 'I marched', explained Lawrence, 'for some days through different parts of the country which, from the small amount of cultivation, was admirably adapted for the movement of troops and field exercise. I succeeded in making satisfactory arrangements, far beyond my expectations, for the payment of the revenue, with several chiefs. All supplies were paid for, a most unusual thing, and no trespass of any sort committed by the troops on the crops of villagers. The cultivators were surprised and delighted at the change.'

These cultivators were all Muslims, mostly drawn from the tribe of Pakhtuns known as the Yusufzai which had conquered and colonised much of the Vale some four centuries earlier. Their hostility towards the Sikhs made it imperative that George Lawrence should have at his command a body of troops who were not Sikhs; who were, as he put it, 'trustworthy men who could at a moment's notice act as guides to troops in the field, and collect intelligence beyond as well as within the border'. Hence the need for a Corps of Guides.

The selection of Joe Lumsden for the task of raising such a corps, fortuitous as it was, could hardly have been more appropriate. Tall, strong, and as keen a marksman, swordsman or horseman as anyone in the Punjab, he was the epitome of the *beau sabreur* – just the kind of man that frontier tribesmen could respect. A friend (the political agent Sir Richard Pollock) described him in later years as 'a singular mixture of shrewdness and simplicity, absolutely free from selfishness and self-seeking, with great originality, a perfect temper, and a keen sense of humour . . . He disliked civil routine intensely which made him turn down offers of civil employment, so affecting his advance.' Bluff, cheery, outgoing and always down-to-earth, here was a young man whose personality was ideally suited to the task of recruiting, training and leading some of the most unpromising soldier-material it is possible to imagine – men who regarded themselves as warriors through and through, but who looked upon any sort of authority with contempt.

Joe Lumsden was just the type to understand such free spirits – in large part, he was one himself. Something of his character can be judged from his nickname, 'Cease firing'. He habitually carried an Irish shillelagh, ostensibly to ward off the dogs which ran at his horse whenever he approached a village, but also used it liberally on the firing range, whacking any soldier who continued to fire after 'Cease firing' had been sounded on the bugle. Lumsden hung this shillelagh on the back of the door at his headquarters, where it quickly became a regimental totem, commanding so much respect that some of his men saluted it as they would the regimental colours.

Early in 1847 a delighted Lumsden was writing to tell his father that he had been given 'the finest appointment in the country, being the right hand of the army and the left hand of the political. I am to have the making of this regiment all to myself. The arming and dressing is to be according to my own fancy . . . I am to recruit my new corps there (Peshawar), which in the first place is to consist of 1 Resaldar, 1 Resaidar, 2 Jemadars, 2 kote duffadars, 12 duffadars, a trumpeter and 80 sabres in the cavalry, with 2 Subadars, 2 Jemadars, 18 havildars, 18 naiks, 4 buglers, and 146 Infantry Sepoys.' Lumsden *père* was asked to send out 'the very best telescope you can set your hands on. I do not mind . . . paying the price for it, so long as it is good enough for the officer command-ing "the Guides".'

According to his younger brother Peter (who joined him in the Guides in 1851, and many years later wrote his brother's biogra-phy), Joe Lumsden established his first regimental headquarters in a picturesque ruin known as the Burj, or watch-tower. This had been built in the seventeenth century by Said Khan, a wazir of the Mughal empire, and here he held court and dispensed justice to the local Afghan tribes. Like George Lawrence's Residency, it too was outside the city walls of Peshawar, but on the south-western side. It consisted of a walled rectangular area with a high, circular watch-tower at one corner, the burj itself, and at its centre an octagonal, domed mausoleum dating from the time of Emperor Shah Jehan – built to be the last resting-place of Said Khan, but never used for that purpose. Like the tomb occupied by Henry Lawrence in Lahore, Lumsden's mausoleum had a central octagonal hall opening out onto a wide surrounding veranda, which served as a mess and regimental office. The tower also appears to have been converted by Lumsden and an upstairs floor added, which he used for his own sleeping quarters. With its immensely thick walls and tower, the Burj complex provided a strong defensive position – although insufficient, it seems, to deter the Zhaka-Khel Afridi, who were masters of breaking, sapping and entering. Sentries had to be posted day and night, and it was a standing order for officers to carry side-arms at all times.

The Burj is the one monument to the early days of John Company still standing in Peshawar. To find it you must cross the bridge leading out of the cantonment area behind Sudder Bazaar, over the railway marshalling yards and into the Railway Colony, where the railway's Eurasian employees used to live in the days of the Raj. Working your way north in the direction of the city bazaar, after some four hundred yards you will see on your right the walls of a medical centre, identified by a discreet noticeboard as the 'CMS Hospital'. This is the Church Missionary Society's Afghan Mission, founded in 1853, largely at the behest of Herbert Edwardes. Although the original surrounding wall and the round tower have been pulled down, the central mausoleum still stands, and today serves as the mission hospital's chapel. A plaque on an inside wall states that the Corps of Guides was raised here on 14 December 1846 by Lieutenant H.B. Lumsden, 'who used this Burj (tower) as his headquarters both in his Military capacity and Civil capacity during the years 1847–1851'.

George Lawrence's Residency was long ago pulled down to make room for the offices and bungalow of the Deputy Commissioner of Peshawar. Two years after his arrival in Peshawar, British military engineers began to lay out a military camp. Ali Mardan Bagh was cut in half and the Residency building became the south-east corner of a defensive square. This was at the instruction of the garrison commander, Brigadier Colin Campbell, who 'crowded the troops, European and Native, into as small a space as possible in order that the station might be more easily protected from the raids of the Afridis and other robber tribes . . . the result of this overcrowding was what it always is, especially in a tropical climate like that of India, and for long years Peshawar was a name of terror to the British soldier from its proverbial unhealthiness'.

This first British military camp was squeezed into a rectangle about 1,200 yards in length and 800 in breadth, outlined today by four roads: the Khyber Road on the north, the Mall on the south, Sahibzada Abdul Qayyum Road on the east, and Michni Road on the west. The southern sector of this square, divided from the rest by Fort Road, made up the civil lines, where the first British civil administrators lived and worked. North of Fort Road and subdivided by a number of lanes running north and south were the military lines: the first block on the east was occupied by the cavalry, followed by a block of Native Infantry lines, two blocks occupied by the artillery, and then finally, on the western side, another block of Native Infantry. The name 'Fort Road' commemorates a nine-sided 'New Fort' intended to replace the first camp but never built. Instead, the cantonment area was extended diagonally outwards from the original square block in a south–westerly direction. A large market area to service the cantonment was then laid out between the cantonment and the city: Sudder Bazaar is still a thriving area of narrow lanes packed with small market stalls.

The absence of a protective fort round the cantonment meant that its inhabitants were always vulnerable to infiltration and assault from the tribesmen in the nearby mountains. 'To resist these marauders,' wrote an early visitor to Peshawar, 'it was necessary to place guards all round the cantonment . . . In addition to the cordon of sentries round the cantonment, strong piquets were posted on all the principal roads leading towards the hills; and every house had to be guarded by a chokidar, or watchman, belonging to one of the robber tribes. The maintaining of this watchman was a sort of blackmail, without consenting to which no one's horses or other property were safe . . . No one was allowed to venture beyond the line of sentries when the sun had set, and even in broad daylight it was not safe to go any distance from the station.' This early visitor to Peshawar was a young subaltern named Frederick Roberts, later to become Field Marshal Lord Roberts.

With the Burj as his base, Lumsden's first months as commander of the Corps of Guides were spent criss-crossing the Vale of Peshawar with a small mounted escort, making himself better-known to the local elders: 'As I had by this time collected some fifty horsemen and twenty infantry, chiefly down-countrymen and Persians, I got orders to set to work at once on a rough revenue settlement, which naturally brought me into contact with the heads of villages, from among whose younger sons and relations I soon selected a score of first-class Pathan recruits for the Guides.'

These early recruits were drawn mostly from the three largest Pakhtun tribes settled in the Vale of Peshawar, the Yusufzai, Khatak and Muhammadzai. An early authority on these tribes was Henry Bellew, who spent more than a decade living and working among them as the first surgeon of the Corps of Guides. What Bellew has to say (in his pioneering monograph *A General Report on the Yusufzais*, published in 1864) on the character of the Yusufzais can be applied equally to any of the other Pakhtun tribes who supplied the Corps of Guides not only with the bulk of its recruits, but also with its principal enemies in the scores of military engagements in which it has participated from 1847 to the present day. 'Like the rest of the Afghan nation generally,' writes Bellew, 'the Yusufzai view themselves as a peculiar and favoured people. The most notable traits in their character are unbounded superstition, pride, cupidity and a most revengeful character . . . They eternally boast of their descent, their prowess in arms, and their independence, and cap all by "Am I not a Pukhtun?" They despise all other races; and, even amongst themselves, each man considers himself equal to, if not better than, his neighbour. Hence most of the bickerings and jealousies so rife in every family throughout the tribe.'

The Yusufzai were guided in their actions by the social code known as *Pakhtunwali*, the 'way of the Pakhtuns'. This included a number of 'distinctive laws', all of which revolved in one way or another around the concept of *nang* or honour: 'The most remarkable illustration of the pride of the Yusufzais is their exaggerated notion of their own honour, *Nang i Pukhtana*, as it is termed, any slight or insult to which is instantly resented.' This code of honour required the strictest obedience to various laws, of which three were key components: *nanawati*, *badal* and *melmastia*. By the first, 'the Pukhtun is expected, at the sacrifice of his own life and property, if necessary, to shelter and protect any one who in extremity may flee to his threshold and seek an asylum under his roof. This applies even to the protector's own enemies.' By the second,

'Badal, or retaliation, must be exacted for every and the slightest personal injury or insult, or for damage to property.' By the third law, every Pakhtun was bound 'to feed and shelter any traveller arriving at his house and demanding them'. Of the three laws, the one most strictly observed was *badal*, governing revenge, which, taken to its limits, had created a state of violent near-anarchy as blood-feuds continued to be waged from generation to generation, often on a tribal scale:

> When undisturbed from without, the several tribes are always opposed to each other; feuds, estrangements and affrays are of constant occurrence; the public roads and private property are alike unsafe. The men, although wearing arms as regularly as others do clothes, seldom or never move beyond the limits of their own lands except disguised as beggars or priests. Everywhere family is arrayed against family, and tribe against tribe, in fact one way and another every man's hand is against his neighbour. Feuds are settled and truces patched up but they break out afresh at the smallest provocation.

Yet at the same time, the wishes of the individual always had to take second place to the interests of the tribe or the clan. Communities were governed by maliks who were in turn subordinate to the tribal chief, or khan. But the powers of both khans and maliks were restricted by a remarkably democratic system of decision-making based on the institution of the *jirga* or council: 'In matters affecting the welfare or interests of the tribe or clan, they cannot act in opposition to the wishes of the general community. These are ascertained through the maliks by jirgah, or council, of the "elders" of each clan, and its sectional khails, separately first, and collectively afterwards. Each clan is a separate democracy. Their members are guided in their views by the grey-beards or elders, the patriarchs of the different families, who, in concert with the malik, decide all matters relating to their own society.'

Some idea of the character of the men Joe Lumsden had to contend with in his capacity as an administrator is given in two stories told by Lumsden himself in later years. The first concerns a chief named Rahmut Khan, clan leader of the Orakzai branch of the Afridi. He had particular influence among the Aka-Khel, Basi-Khel and other local sub-groups among the Afridi occupying the lands south-west of Peshawar, including the southern flanks of the Khyber mountains and the Kohat region. It was very much in George Lawrence's and the Durbar's interests to be on good terms with Rahmut Khan, and in consequence Lumsden made a point of getting to know him well. Once a degree of mutual confidence had been built up, Rahmut Khan confided in Lumsden the manner in which he had become undisputed leader of the Orakzai. For years a long-standing and bloody power struggle between himself and his elder brother had divided the clan and cost many lives. Eventually it was agreed that the dispute should be settled by a jirga. The decision of the jirga went against him, but Rahmut Khan gave out that he would abide by it and renounce all his claims. He then gave a feast of reconciliation, to which he invited his elder brother as guest of honour, together with all his male relatives. 'The supper was given in his own residence, under which he had carefully lodged a heavy charge of gunpowder,' relates Lumsden. 'When all had feasted and were in great spirits, Rahmut Khan duly presented the pipe of peace. It was passed round, and whilst the curling smoke ascended, he quietly slipped out the door, lighted a match, and ran for his life, whilst an explosion blew his brother, home, and relatives into eternity. He told me this little tale himself, remarking, "I had but little trouble after that".'

Another elder, a malik of the Zhaka-Khel clan of the Afridi, used to call regularly at the Burj to pay his respects to Lumsden; he disappeared for some months, and when he reappeared Lumsden asked what had kept him away. After some equivocation the malik replied: ' "Well, sahib, the last time I was here, after visiting you I returned to sleep for the night in the town of Peshawar. There I met a number of young lads of my clan who were bent on stealing officers' horses in the cantonment . . . I could not resist the temptation to see how these youngsters did their work. So I went down with them and the first stable they commenced to cut the wall of was that of the Topkhana [artillery adjutant]. Well, the boys were not quiet enough, and made a noise which disturbed the adjutant sahib; but, will you believe it, the fool of a fellow instead of firing at them fired at me!"' The malik then lifted his cloak to show Lumsden a bare chest peppered with shot marks.

Despite their appetite for violence, many traits in the Pakhtun nature struck a chord in Joe Lumsden. One was a love of shikar; Bellew writes of the Yusufzai's 'natural fondness for field sports, such as hawking, hunting with dogs, and shooting', adding that 'frequently they combine with these pleasures the more exciting business of highway robbery, cattle-lifting and burglary'. Another was their ability to relax and enjoy themselves in company. 'At home,' says Bellew, 'the Yusufzais are of a lively and merry disposition, and are fond of music and poetry; to enjoy these they have frequent social gatherings at their hujrahs [village guest houses] . . . Their music, though noisy, and the result of vigorous performance, is not without its own peculiar merits, to judge from its exciting effects on a Yusufzai audience.'

This audience was, of course, composed exclusively of men, for Pakhtun society was male-dominated – as indeed was the military world inhabited by Joe Lumsden and his brother-officers, if for very different reasons. No Pakhtun woman ever appeared in public unless covered head to toe in the all-enveloping *burqua*. The Pakhtuns, states Bellew, regarded their women as so much property and showed them little respect, yet at the same time were 'most suspicious and jealous of them. It is quite enough for a man to see his wife speaking to a stranger to arouse his passion. He at once suspects her of infidelity, and straightway maltreats or murders her . . . The abuse or slander of a man's female relations is only to be wiped out in the blood of the slanderer and not infrequently the slandered one, whether the calumny be deserved or not, is murdered to begin with.'

From a nucleus of volunteers drawn from the Yusufzai plain the Corps of Guides expanded its recruiting base to include 'men from every wild and warlike tribe'. Years later Henry Daly recalled that by the time he came to the Guides as a temporary commander its ranks included 'Afridis and Goorkhas, Sikhs and Hazaras, Waziris, Pathans of every class, and even Kaffirs, speaking all the tongues of the border – Persian, Pushtu, etc., dialects unknown to the men of the plains. In many cases the Guides had a camp-language or patois of their own.' Only men considered to be of low caste were refused, on the grounds that they would be psychologically unable to take on the so-called warrior castes in combat.

In recruiting his Guides, Lumsden deliberately sought out men who knew how to look after themselves – who were, in Henry Daly's words, 'notorious for desperate deeds, leaders in forays, who kept the passes into the hills . . . On the border and in the ranks of the Guides, tales abundant in humour were told of Lumsden's interviews with men who had defied all authority, and had never been seen in the plains but for murder and plunder.' One such, Dilawar Khan, a Khattak from a village on the Kabul river near its junction with the Indus, was a brigand who specialised in kidnapping rich Hindu bankers and traders, holding them in Yusufzai country until ransoms were paid. Lumsden put a price of two thousand rupees on his head and then, having hunted him without success for many months, issued Dilawar Khan an invitation to visit him in his camp, under promise of a safe return. Rather to everyone's surprise, the brigand turned up. Lumsden received him with great courtesy, then explained to him that life on the frontier was changing fast, and that he would soon have to give up his occupation or be hanged – so why not become a Guide instead? Dilawar laughed and took his leave. However, six weeks later he reappeared, to say that he was prepared to join the Guides so long as he was not required to march in step. Lumsden held firm, and Dilawar Khan finally submitted to drill. In time he grew to be one of the best of Lumsden's men, rising to become a much-decorated subedar (a Native Officer who acted as a company commander). Years later, Dilawar Khan confessed to Lumsden that he had only joined the Guides to learn as much as he could about them; he then intended to desert, and use the Guides' own tactics to outwit them. However, he had been won over by the battalion's *esprit*, and by what he called the 'straightness' of men like Lumsden – and then found it impossible to betray them. He met a tragic end: some years after Harry Lumsden had left the Guides for a higher army command, Dilawar Khan Khattak was sent on a spying mission into the remote mountain kingdom of Chitral. According to Lumsden, he was 'basely betrayed' and murdered – and Lumsden never forgave those officers he held responsible for his old friend's death.

Another early recruit was a Kuki Khel named Gulbaz Khan who had been forced to flee from his village in the mountains after accidentally killing his uncle, the malik. He became one of Lumsden's most trusted Native Officers and fought with the Guides at Delhi in 1857. A tradition of family service soon grew to be a feature of the Guides as it was of other regiments of the Indian Army, but few families can boast of a stronger connection than that of Gulbaz Khan. Of two sons who followed him into the Guides, one died at the Guides' famous last stand at the Kabul residency in 1879. In the third generation, Mogunbaz Khan became a political agent in the Khyber in the 1920s. His son, Major-General Jehan Zeb Khan, the first member of the family to be commissioned, commanded the Guides' Cavalry in the 1960s and is now retired from the Pakistan army and living in Peshawar. His son represents the fifth generation, and has hopes of commanding the Guides' Cavalry himself in the near future.

Within months of its formation, Lumsden's Corps of Guides had a waiting-list. Groups of young bloods hanging around the back of the cavalry lines became a familiar sight, aspirants to the next vacancy to come up. This was after 1851, when the corps' headquarters had been moved from the Burj outside Peshawar to the village of Hoti Mardan, about forty miles north-east of Peshawar on the Yusufzai plain and about the same distance north-east of the bridge of boats over the Indus at Attock. A 'rude fort' in the shape of a five-pointed star was built here and became the depot of the Corps of Guides. It remained the Corps' home for almost ninety years, and now serves as the headquarters of the Punjab Regiment.

Here at Hoti Mardan Joe Lumsden built up his mixed cavalry and infantry irregulars into a fighting force which in his lifetime gained a mystique that made it the most famous unit in the Indian Army, with the same aura of invincibility which today surrounds the British Army's Special Air Service Regiment, the SAS. Lumsden himself soon came to inspire in his men a degree of devotion bordering on idolatry. The story is told of the occasion in the mid 1860s when the Corps was subjected to a formal inspection by John Lawrence – by then Sir John Lawrence, Bt, Viceroy of India – who found something not to his liking and spoke of it in somewhat testy tones to their commander in front of his men. Immediately after the parade Lumsden was approached by his orderly, who told him of the regiment's disgust that he should have been so addressed: 'It is not right and proper that we should allow our Colonel Sahib to be harshly spoken to by anyone. There is, therefore, this alternative: the Lat Sahib [Sir John Lawrence] has arranged to leave by the straight road tomorrow morning for Peshawar, but with Your Honour's permission and by the grace of God, there is no reason whatever why he should ever reach it.'

The reason for this loyalty is not hard to find. Lumsden could match his men in everything they did: he practically lived in the saddle, and liked nothing more than to go out in the evening with a falcon on his wrist and a group of like-minded Pakhtuns riding beside him; he was a first-rate shot; and as a swordsman he was considered among the élite – that he was left-handed was an asset. He demanded the best from his officers, too, who in addition to their military skills were expected to be familiar with every equine ailment, and able to shoe a horse. Like Hodson and Nicholson, Lumsden always led from the front.

In the first summer of the Corps' existence Lumsden was asked by George Lawrence to check on the movements of a gang of raiders who had their base in a mountain fastness called Gundgurh, on the right bank of the Indus in Hazara country. Lumsden took it into his head that to approach the area by floating down the Kabul river during the night would be far cooler than riding forty miles on horseback. He had a raft made from a *charpoy* bed-frame fastened over two blown-up bullock hides or *mussaks*, which he and one of his sowars then boarded. They were pushed off and sent on their way down-river, both smoking cigars. When they had gone some distance, one of the floats exploded 'with a report like that of an eighteen-pounder', hurling Lumsden into the water. After much kicking and splashing he managed to rid himself of his boots and his breeches – or, as he himself worded it in writing to his father, his 'inexpressibles, which, however elegant in a drawing-room, are a great nuisance when one has to kick for life'. He then swam downstream after what was left of the raft, to rescue his sowar: 'I found my unfortunate Guide in the last extremities, unable to swim for fear, and too tired to hold on by the remaining skin. Luckily for him, riding on a mussuck was an old achievement of mine, so climbing up, without more ado I cut the charpoy adrift by undoing the string, and, taking the Guide's pugree [turban] off his head, passed it round his chest under his arms with the two ends round my waist, and thus after nearly two hours in the water, with God's assistance made my way to the bank.'

The problem now was Lumsden's lack of clothes: 'After much laughing and consultation it was agreed that I should take the Guide's pugree around me and sit like Patience on a monument, smiling at Grief, while the Guide went out and told our story, and borrowed a suit and a pair of shoes. He succeeded in his mission, and shortly afterwards out came your eldest son, in a blue loongee [waist-cloth] for a pugree, round his head, a pair of pyjamas wide enough to make the mainsail of a seventy-four, and a flash blue chupkin [waistcoat].'

Seven months after its inception the Corps, still in its infancy, was camped out in the fields when Lumsden received a message from George Lawrence asking him to support a troop of Sikh cavalry in an assault on a hostile village on the edge of the Peshawar plain. The Guides marched through the night to arrive shortly before daylight at the mouth of a narrow, mile-long defile which led directly to the hostile village. Here they made a rendez-vous with the Sikh contingent, whose commander then announced that it was unsafe to proceed any further. Lumsden immediately put himself at the head of his cavalry troop and gal-loped down the ravine and into the village, filling it with his men before its occupants had had time to do more than rouse them-selves from their charpoys. The village malik was seized, together with three hundred head of cattle in lieu of taxes, and not a shot was fired.

The unit's first taste of powder came that autumn when George Lawrence asked for the Guides' assistance in reducing a village called Babuzai, on the Bunner frontier. Babuzai had become notorious on the frontier for repulsing a whole brigade of Sikhs and never afterwards paying a rupee in tax. 'The Seikhs attacked the village in front,' wrote Lumsden, 'while the Guides stole up to the crest of the ridge and dropped down in rear of the enemy, turning all their breastworks and rendering them untenable. Away went the defenders with my men in pursuit, so close on their heels that Futteh Khan, then a trooper in the cavalry, got blown up cutting down a man who happened to be carrying a bag of powder in one hand and a lighted matchlock in the other.'

The success of this raid against a position hitherto deemed impregnable had a very salutary effect, not only on the maliks of Babuzai village, who quickly made their submissions, but throughout the Vale of Peshawar. When the expeditionary force returned to Peshawar, the inhabitants of the city surged out in large numbers to welcome them, and in his address to the faithful at Friday prayers the head mullah of the city's largest mosque spoke of his satisfaction at the new order: 'I have for years prayed that oppression should cease and justice be administered in this unhappy country. My prayers have now been granted, and do you yourselves all offer up prayers that this state of things may continue.'

The Corps of Guides, as an irregular force, operated outside the military system followed by the Bengal Army, doing things in ways that owed as much to local as to British military custom. The greatest difference was to be found in the Guides' Cavalry, where the equivalent of the cavalry troop was the *risalah* formed around a malik or (if he was a Sikh) a sirdar, who brought with him a batch of his own retainers, mounted and equipped at his own expense – and whom he led. Alternatively, a sowar might bring his own horse and weapons with him, for which he expected to receive enhanced pay and status. The weakness of this system was that a lot rested on the quality of the individual leaders of the risalahs, known as *risaldars* or *risaidars*, who exercised a great deal of authority over their own men: it worked in the Guides only because Lumsden was able to command absolute loyalty from his silladars. Over a period of time these men rose to all the usual ranks taken by the Native Officers of the EICo's armies – as risaldars, risaidars and jemadars in the cavalry and as subedars and jemadars in the infantry. However, in an irregular corps like the Guides these Native Officers exercised far more authority than did their peers in the regulars. A British commander with one other British officer to act as adjutant was thought sufficient – in the early years, at least. In the Guides it was a case of Joe Lumsden commanding the Guides' Cavalry and his second-in-command the Guides' Infantry.

A more obvious way in which such an irregular corps showed its difference was in its appearance. For most of the first year of their existence the Guides' sowars and sepoys dressed like other frontier tribesmen, with a long cotton turban wrapped round the head, sandals on the feet, a loose smock for a shirt, baggy pantaloons and a cotton waist-cloth wrapped round the middle – plus a woollen cloak draped over the shoulder or a sheepskin *poshteen*, according to the season. An identifying uniform was required, but Henry Lawrence, enthusiastically supported by Lumsden, took the view that the corps could better carry out its scouting role if it avoided the distinctive semi-European dress then being worn by other units of the EICo's armies. According to Colonel George Younghusband, 'Sir Henry evolved the startling heresy that to get the best work out of troops, and to enable them to undertake great exertions, it was necessary that the soldier should be loosely, comfortably, and suitably clad, that something more substantial than a pill-box with a handkerchief wrapped round it was required as protection from the tropical sun, and that footgear must be made for marching, and not for parading round a band-stand.' Scarlet uniform was to be abandoned in favour of a uniform which would make the Guides 'invisible in a land of dust'.

Towards the end of 1847 a unique compromise was arrived at by which the standard mufti of smock and pyjama trousers was treated with a dye made from a local dwarf palm to produce a drab, pale yellow-green uniform – a colour known in Hindustani as *khaki* or 'dust-coloured'. The Corps continued to dye its own uniforms right up to 1904, by which time 'khaki' had been adopted as standard non-ceremonial service or tropical dress throughout the Indian and British Armies.

The man who saw these changes in uniform through was William Hodson. Like Lumsden he hated office-work, and it had become plain to Lawrence that he had little aptitude for civil administration, however hard he tried. Yet Henry Lawrence clearly had a soft spot for the young man: in October 1847, ignoring the doubts expressed by his personal assistant, he awarded Hodson the appointment he had long been angling for – to be

Harry Lumsden's number two and adjutant of the Corps of Guides. As well as drilling and instructing the men, he was given responsibility for building the fort and new headquarters at Hoti Mardan and equipping the Corps. For the latter he turned to his brother in England, the Reverend George Hodson. 'This was the first of a series of commissions connected with clothing and arming the Guides Corps which was left in my brother's hands,' George Hodson wrote later. Although it was 'scarcely a clerical business', brother George sent out 'drab' cotton clothing for nine hundred men, three hundred rifled carbines, and a number of 'Prussian-style' helmets. These last were a disaster, and quickly abandoned in favour of indigo blue turbans for the Guides' Cavalry and khaki turbans for the Infantry. Thus did the most colourful – and, arguably, the most distinguished – unit in the Indian Army come to be the least colourful on parade.

5

'Connection with us is political death'

HERBERT EDWARDES AND BANNU, 1847–1848

> All our history shows that sooner or later connection with us
> is political death. The sunshine is not more fatal to a dew-
> drop than our friendship or alliance to an Asiatic kingdom.
> Lieutenant William Hodson, in a letter to his brother

ONE OF the first matters to be drawn to the attention of the newly-appointed British Resident by the Sikh Durbar in Lahore was the 'outstanding revenue' owed by a distant corner of the Sikh Empire known as Bannu. Henry Lawrence was informed by the Durbar that the custom was to allow the revenue payments to fall into arrears for two or three seasons, then to send in an army to collect it; that was the Sikh way and, he was assured, the only way that worked, since the local people had 'peculiarly barbarous ideas of freedom' and fiercely resisted all attempts to bring them into the Sikh fold.

Lawrence's brief was to maintain the existing frontiers of the Sikh kingdom, and to assist the Durbar in the collection of revenue. However, he drew the line at allowing a large Sikh army to be sent into Bannu to ravage the country. The Durbar was authorised to despatch a Sikh force – to be made up of fifteen hundred irregular horse, one regiment of cavalry and five of infantry, together with two troops of artillery – but it was to be accompanied by one of Lawrence's political assistants. Lieutenant Nicholson was too heavily committed in Kashmir to be spared, as initially intended, and so Herbert Edwardes was selected to take his place – 'an accident', Edwardes later explained with due modesty, 'to which I am indebted for the many opportunities and honours which would have fallen more happily on my friend'.

The story of what followed on this expedition is recounted with great gusto and good humour by Herbert Edwardes in the two volumes of his *Year on the Punjab Frontier* (1851). As well as being the precursor of scores of personal narratives of war and peace on the North-West Frontier, it is also one of the best, and made Edwardes's name. It has never been reprinted, although a most curious volume published in 1885, edited by John Ruskin and entitled *A Knight's Faith*, carried extracts from Edwardes's book, presented so as to highlight the virtues of its author, whom Ruskin saw not simply as a Christian paladin but as a militant missionary: 'officially a soldier, practically a bishop'.

As he himself asserts in a preface, with some pride and no false modesty, Edwardes's motive in publishing his book was 'to put on record a victory which I myself remember with more satisfaction than any I helped to gain before Mooltan – the bloodless conquest of the wild valley of Bunnoo'. This was quite a claim, but one fully supported by the story he had to tell, of a victory all the more remarkable because it was won by a man who at the age of twenty-nine had never commanded his own troops in the field, let alone those of another power. Edwardes was in no doubt as to how it had been achieved. For him, the political officer was a man charged with a mission: 'to be a pioneer of Christian civilisation in lands where Idolatry too often occupies the Temple, Corruption the Tribunal, and Tyranny the Throne'. It was this Christian mission, he claimed, that had made it possible for 'a barbarous people' to be 'brought peacefully within the place of civilisation, without a struggle, a conquest that the fanatic Sikh nation had vainly attempted, with fire and sword, for five-and-twenty years.' Here, shoulder-to-shoulder, stand two dominant elements in the Edwardes character: the intolerant evangelical zeal which so endeared him to Ruskin, and a self-belief bordering on arrogance.

The district of Bannu, otherwise known as North Derajat, lies west of the river Indus and south of Kohat and Peshawar, extending west as far as the foothills of the first mountain ranges of Afghanistan. Herbert Edwardes describes it as 'a lovely country of Eastern Afghanistan', a bowl bounded by mountains on three sides and irrigated by two rivers, the Kurram and Tochi. To his eyes the land was a veritable Garden of Eden:

Crops never fail in Bunnoo. The rudest and idlest agriculture is overpaid with corn, sugar, turmeric, and almost all the Indian grains in abundance. In spring it is a vegetable emerald; and in winter its many-coloured harvests look as if Ceres had stumbled against the great Salt Range, and spilt half her cornucopia in the favoured vale. As if to make the landscape perfect, a graceful variety of the shee-shum-tree [*Dalbergia sissoo*], whose boughs droop like the willow, is found here, and here alone; while along streams, and round the villages, the thick mulberry, festooned with the wild vine, throws a fragrant shade, beneath which well-fed Syuds [holy men of supposed Arab extraction] look exquisitely happy, sleeping midway through their beads. Roses, too, without which Englishmen have learned from the East to think no scenery complete, abound in the upper parts, at the close of spring. Most of the fruits of Cabul are found wild, and culture would bring them to perfection; as it is, the limes, mulberries, and melons are delicious.

The problem with this Garden of Eden, as Edwardes saw it, was that the serpent had entered it, in the form of its inhabitants: 'Nature has so smiled on Bunnoo, that the stranger thinks it a paradise; and when he turns to the people, wonders how such spirits of evil ever found admittance.' They fell into four main groups: 'The mongrel and vicious Bunnoochee peasantry, ill-ruled by Mullicks, and ill-righted by factions; the greedy Syuds, and other religious mendicants, sucking the blood of the superstitious people; the mean Hindoo traders, enduring a life of degradation, that they may cheat their Muhommudan employers; and the Vizeeree [Waziri] interlopers, half pastoral, half agricultural, wholly without law, but neither destitute of honour or virtue.'

Edwardes seems not merely to have disliked the unfortunate Bannuchi, but to have loathed them wholeheartedly – in part because they were 'mongrels', rather than of pure Pakhtun stock:

They have all the vices of Pathans rankly luxuriant, the virtues stunted. Except in Sindh, I have never met such a degraded people. Although forming a distinct race in themselves, easily recognisable, at first sight, from any other tribe along the Indus, they are not of pure descent from any common stock, and able, like the neighbouring people, to trace their lineage back to the founder of the family; but are descended from many Afghan tribes, representing the ebb and flow of might, right, possession, and spoilation, in a corner of the Cabul empire whose remoteness and fertility offered to outlaws and vagabonds a secure asylum against both law and labour. The introduction of Indian cultivators from the Punjab, and the settlement of numerous low Hindoos in the valley, from sheer love of money, and the hope of peacefully plundering by trade their ignorant Muhommudan master, have contributed, by intermarriage, slave-dealing, and vice, to complete the mongrel character of the Bunnoo people.

The Bannuchi's vices were compounded in Edwardes's view by what he saw as their gullibility: 'A more utterly ignorant and superstitious people than the Bannoochees I never saw. The vilest jargon was to them pure Arabic from the blessed Koran, the clumsiest imposture a miracle, and the fattest fakeer a saint.' This credulity combined with a deep attachment to their faith to make them easy prey for the many *mullahs, sayads, kajis, pirs, hajis* and 'holy vagabonds' which together were classed as *uluma* – religious personages. When he had conducted his first survey of the land, Edwardes was astonished to find that two-thirds was in the hands of mortgagees, of whom the sayads made up by far the largest number:

The Moollah and the Kazee, the Peer and the Syud, descended on the smiling vale, armed with a panoply of spectacles and owl-like looks, miraculous rosaries, infallible amulets, and tables of descent from Muhommud. Each newcomer, like St Peter, held the keys of heaven; and the whole, like Irish beggars, were equally prepared to bless or curse to all eternity him who gave or who withheld. These were 'air-drawn daggers', against which the Bunnoochee peasant had no defence. For him the whistle of a far-thrown bullet, or the nearer sheen of his enemy's 'shumsher' [sword], had no terrors; blood was simply a red fluid; and to remove a neighbour's head at the shoulder, as easy as cutting cucumbers. But to be cursed in Arabic, or anything that sounded like it; to be told that the blessed Prophet had put a black mark against his soul, for not giving his best field to one of the Prophet's own posterity; to have the saliva of a disappointed saint left in anger on his doorpost; or behold a Hajee, who had gone three times to Mecca, deliberately sit down and enchant his camels with the itch, and his sheep with the rot: these were things which made the dagger drop out of the hand of the awe-stricken savage, his knees knock together, his liver to turn to water, and his parched tongue to be scarce able to articulate a full and complete concession of the blasphemous demand.

Edwardes's contempt for the Bannuchi took little account of the vicissitudes they had suffered. Each of the several Pakhtun groups found in Bannu represented a wave of invaders from the west, of whom the most recent and the strongest were the Waziri, Edwardes's 'Vizeerees', the only group in Bannu for whom he had any time. 'Stout, fierce, and fearless of man or beast', these Waziri were the most powerful and most feared of all the Pakhtun tribes. 'It is the peculiarity of the great Vizeeree tribe that they are enemies of the whole world,' writes Edwardes. 'Of the Vizeeree it is literally true, that "his hand is against every man, and every man's hand against him" . . . If you ask where their country is, they point to the far-off horizon, where the azure sky is pierced by the snowy peaks of "Sufed Koh" or the White Mountain, and which in their Pashto tongue they call Spinghar; but that great mountain is only their citadel, at the head of a long line of fastnesses, extending from the frontier at Tank, less than a hundred miles from Derah Ismail Khan on the Indus, to within fifty miles of Jelalabad.'

The Waziri were the most numerous of the Pakhtun tribes and were divided into three main groups: the Utmanzai and Ahmadzai, and their cousins the Mahsud. While the Utmanzai and Mahsud had for the most part remained in the mountains of Afghanistan with their herds of sheep and goats, the Ahmadzai had in recent years begun to encroach upon the plains of India in ever-increasing numbers: 'Again and again the winter brought them back, and in occasional collisions between the savage of the plain and the savage of the mountain, the Vizeeree roved ever the savagest, and became a name of fear and hatred in Bunnoo . . . So he proceeded in his rough way to occupy what he wanted.'

The Ahmadzai Waziri had settled in the mountains north, west and south of Bannu, but descended into the plains every winter to graze their livestock – 'flocks of broad-tailed sheep and goats, and strings of woolly camels and curved-eared horses' – and to plunder the Bannuchi. The 'smiling vale' of Bannu, in consequence, had become a melting-pot of many racial groups, coexisting in anything but a state of harmony: 'Let the reader take this people, and arm them to the teeth; then throwing them down in the beautiful country I have described, bid them scramble for its fat meads and fertilizing waters, its fruits and flowers; and he will have a good idea of the state of landed property and laws of tenure, as I found them in 1847.'

Like other Pakhtun tribes on the frontier, the Bannuchi had fought hard to remain independent of Kabul and Lahore, as well as of the Waziri. 'In the face of armies and devastations, they succeeded in maintaining their new-gained independence,' Edwardes explains. 'Owning no external allegiance, let us see what internal government this impatient race submitted to: in truth, none. Freed from a king [their former allegiance to Kabul], they could not agree upon a chief; but every village threw a wall around its limits, chose its own Mullick [malik or chief], and went to war with its neighbours.' Edwards then calls upon the reader to imagine the different groups behind their high walls: 'The Vizeerees on the outside, the Bannoochees and Sayads, with their Hindoo agents, in the heart of Bunnoo Proper, all watching each other with vigilant ill-will, and so divided by class interests as to be unable to appreciate the danger approaching all alike from without.'

The extent of this anarchy was brought home to Edwardes when, as he prepared to set out for Bannu early in March 1847, he was presented with a map of the region drawn up for him by one of his native agents. It appeared to consist entirely of hundreds of tiny squares: ' "Why, Nizamooddeen," I said, "what is this?" "That?" he said triumphantly. "Why, that's Bunoo!" "And what are these squares?" "Oh! those are the forts." A pleasing prospect for the individual to whom the subjugation of Bunnoo had been confided.' Nevertheless, it was precisely this internal division that allowed Edwardes to proceed with his subjugation.

Edwardes's first incursion into Bannu was really no more than a swift reconnaissance – 'We entered Bunnoo on the 15th of March, and were burnt out of it by the sun on the 1st of May' – but it set the style of what was to come after. Edwardes had left Lahore with a strict injunction from Henry Lawrence that no plundering was to be tolerated – but his Sikh troops regarded plunder as one of their perks. It took two weeks to march westwards across the Punjab to the banks of the Indus, and Edwardes used the time to educate his soldiery in the different standards expected of them under the new administration. 'I had full employment,' he writes. 'On the line of march, in the morning, I did nothing but detect, stay, reprove, chase, overtake, and imprison plunderers, horse and foot; and all the rest of the day my tent was besieged by the people of the country bewailing their damaged fields, and calling on me to punish the offenders. Long indulged in military licence, the Sikh soldiers could not believe that they were no longer to be allowed to help themselves.'

He gives one example of how offenders were treated. Accompanying the expedition were a number of elephants used to draw the guns. One of these was employed by its *mahout* or elephant driver to rough up a farmer whose wheat-field he had raided for fodder. On Edwardes's orders the man was apprehended and the entire force paraded to witness his punishment: 'The troops formed into a hollow square, and in spite of the entreaties of his master, the Mahout was tied up on the triangles and flogged – then passed with bare back down the ranks of his comrades.' This object-lesson was followed by a harangue from Edwardes, in which he warned the assembled Sikhs that if they continued to plunder the countryside as they advanced, they would become the targets of night attacks and ambushes.

This very public enforcement of discipline paid remarkable dividends once they had crossed the Indus and entered Bannu. The Bannuchi, to Edwardes's very great satisfaction, 'instead of flying bodily to the mountains as usual . . . flocked to our camp, and bought and sold with the soldiers, and sat and talked in our assemblies, as friends instead of enemies. The great question of issue between us – the Lahore tribute money – was mutually referred to argument, instead of the sword . . . many were won over to our side, and friendships formed, which afterwards stood us in good stead . . . The bloodthirsty and revengeful tribes of Bunnoo, and the army of their Sikh masters had, for the first time, met in something resembling friendship . . . The small end of the wedge of civilized intercourse had at last been attained.'

It soon became clear to Edwards that the greatest danger he faced in Bannu came not from the divided Bannuchis but from their oppressors, the Ahmadzai Waziri. In writing about these most feared of Pakhtun tribes, Edwardes found much to admire as well as deplore: 'Proud, patriotic, and united among themselves; austere and simple in their own manners, but hospitable to the stranger, and true to their guest against force and corruption, the Ahmadzais stood aloof from the people they oppressed, and looked on in contempt at their cowardly submission, their disunited efforts against the Sikh invader.'

Here we have Edwardes giving early expression to what was to become one of the more paradoxical leitmotifs of the British administrator or soldier throughout the years of the Raj: admiration for the manly, martial qualities of the aggressor, coupled with contempt for the effete servility of those he oppressed. Edwardes's prejudices are neatly summed up in one short paragraph: 'Vizeeree manners! Swahn Kahn [Sawan Khan, a Waziri] asked today for a few days' leave, to go home and sleep with his wife. Bunnoochee manners! Ursulla Khan [a Bannuchi] begged to be allowed to sit on the carpet and contemplate me, as he had fallen in love with me!'

These prejudices were shared by his colleague Reynell Taylor, who followed Edwardes into Bannu: while the Waziri were 'a fine race of men, prone to plunder, and careless about blood-shedding it may be, but bold, plain-spoken, true to their friends and not unusually treacherous', the Bannuchi were full of vices, including a positive addiction to assassination: 'A Bunnoochee idea of a successful field is, time – midnight – and the long-sought rival, or enemy, asleep under his vine in the open air; no witness but the moon, and leisure given for three well-planted blows with the small broad-backed knife, under which a man may linger long enough to drink the full bitterness contained in the knowledge of his enemy's triumph.'

Edwardes's good opinion of the Ahmadzai Waziri was in part a result of his encounter on this first foray into Bannu with one of their most able chiefs, the above-mentioned Sawan Khan, clan leader of the Ahmadzai. An Assistant's Report entered in the Lahore Political Diaries for 1847 contains a memorable description by Herbert Edwardes of this redoubtable leader:

He is a powerful chief, and his country boasts that it never paid tribute to any sovereign, but exacted it in the shape of plunder from all tribes alike. Swahn Khan is just what one might picture the leader of such a people: an enormous man, with a head like a lion, and a hand like a polar bear. He had on thick boots with thongs and rings, and trod my carpets like a lord. The Hindostanee servants were struck dumb and expected the earth to open. With his dirty cotton clothes, half redeemed by a pink loongee over his broad breast, and a rich dark shawl intertwined into locks that had never known a comb, a more splendid specimen of human nature in the rough I never saw. He made no bow, but with a simple 'Salaam aleikoom' [Greetings, good day] took his seat.

Edwardes had invited the khan to his camp to explain to him that, while the Lahore Durbar had no quarrel with the Waziri who stayed up in the mountains, those who came down to occupy land in the plains of Bannu would have to pay for the privilege. This was not something Sawan Khan could accept; Edwardes should look upon the matter as if the Ahmadzai had paid the Bannuchi for the land they had taken from them, so that it was the Bannuchi who should pay to the Durbar whatever was due. 'Is that the case?'

challenged Edwards. 'Am I a liar?' demanded the khan – to which Edwardes replied diplomatically, 'No, you are a Vizeeree, and Vizeerees never lie.' He went on to propose a compromise that would allow Sawan Khan to preserve *nang*, his honour: Edwardes would return to Bannu in the Cold Weather to inspect the lands encroached upon by the Waziri and hear what all parties had to say: ' "I will come and see the lands, and hear both sides of the question, and then tell you what I think of it. After that, if you say it is justice that you should pay, I will make you pay; and if you say it is justice that you should *not* pay, I will give you a *sunnud* [certificate] of exemption. But you are to be on your honour as a Vizeeree!" Swahn Khan hereupon stretched out his tremendous arm, grappled my hand, and shook it till he nearly dislocated my shoulder. "Agreed – agreed: that is *insaf*, justice!" he roared.'

This was the first occasion on which Edwardes was called upon to exercise his diplomatic skills on a large stage: in a crisis the Ahmadzai could probably muster a *lashkar* or tribal army numbering some 50,000 jezailchis, and the Waziri altogether treble that number. They were the power-brokers of Bannu and their acquiescence was essential if Edwardes was to make any progress. Although in temperament about as far removed from a Pakhtun as could possibly be imagined, Edwardes nevertheless had a quite extraordinary flair for handling and resolving sensitive political issues, whether it was a quarrel among colleagues, or statesmen. On such occasions he was able to curb his tongue and turn his sharp wits to fathoming and bringing out the best in them. For all his narrow-minded prejudices, and for all that he regarded them as credulous savages, he was able to admire men like Sawan Khan for their innate nobility, and seems to have been able instinctively to understand the way their minds worked. How else can one explain the degree of trust he inspired in powerful figures like Sawan Khan and, a decade later, Dost Mohammad Khan of Kabul?

The success of this first foray into Bannu encouraged Henry Lawrence to send Edwardes back in the autumn of 1847 on a second mission, with a brief to reconcile the Bannuchi to Sikh rule. He was 'to subdue them by a peaceful and just treaty; and reduce the nominal revenue, which was never paid, to a moderate tribute in acknowledgment of sovereignty'.

This time it was a two-pronged entry: Herbert Edwardes followed his previous route into the country from the south-east, while a second political agent brought in another military column from the north, starting from Peshawar. This was Lieutenant Reynell Taylor, whom we left the year before a disappointed man, making his way out of the Punjab to take up a political appointment in Indore. Here he had chafed for some seven months, until the letter of summons came from Henry Lawrence. In fact, the letter was in three parts on a single sheet of rough foolscap: a brief note at the top from Henry Lawrence, congratulating him on his new appointment; below it a more formal letter from George Lawrence, warning Taylor that he would probably be joining him in Peshawar; and scribbled at the bottom another congratulatory note, in Herbert Edwardes's handwriting. This last reads in part: 'The wind of future events blows from the north. Business at present is frightful, but as things settle and *zealous assistants* come to the rescue (!), I hope we shall have a little respite.'

Taylor arrived in Peshawar at the start of the Hot Weather of 1847 to find his new chief, George Lawrence, laid low with the first of a series of bouts of 'Peshawar fever' (probably recurrences of malaria contracted elsewhere), and in consequence spent much of the summer 'acting' as the *hakim-i-wukt* or ruler of Peshawar in George Lawrence's place – quite a baptism for an inexperienced political assistant of twenty-five. But by the start of the Cold Weather Lawrence was well enough to resume his duties, leaving Taylor free to lead the supporting column of troops which was to combine with Edwardes's main column in the heart of Bannu.

If Reynell Taylor is the least glamorous of Lawrence's Young Men, his accomplishments overshadowed by the more dramatic actions of Edwardes, Nicholson and the rest, he was nevertheless the first British officer to enter the Afridi stronghold of Kohat, the country between Peshawar and Bannu, since Elphinstone's embassy a quarter of a century before. To judge from the entries in his diary, he was much given to introspection and self-doubt, and had grave misgivings about an enterprise which he considered to be 'altogether very risky work'.

As George Lawrence had learned from his previous experiences on the Khyber, the only way to be sure of safe passage through tribal areas was to secure the agreement of the tribes concerned beforehand. By the laws of Pakhtunwali each tribe was then bound to provide an armed escort, known as a *badragga*, which offered protection up to its borders but not a step beyond. In this instance, George Lawrence had secured the good offices of two tribal chiefs – Sultan Mahommad Khan, the most powerful of the Afridi maliks of Kohat, and the notorious Rahmut Khan, chief of the Orakzai, he who had regaled Harry Lumsden with the tale of how he had blown up his elder brother and his family – but their presence at the head of his column of Sikh soldiery, together with their badraggas, appears to have done little to set Taylor's mind at rest.

The bridle trail south from Peshawar runs through the home territory of the Adam Khel clan of the Afridi and the village of Darra. This takes its name from the *darra* or pass over the ridge above it, which every traveller has to cross to enter Kohat and the country of the Orakzai. It was a very nervous young man who rode up to that spectacular saddle with its commanding views north and south (and which today is surmounted by the famous arch of dressed stone known as the Handyside Gate):

My anxieties made me think that the Afreedees and Oorruckzyes looked more numerous and impudent than usual, and old Rehmut Khan Ooruckzye regaled me with accounts of the number of Sikhs that had died in that pass, and told me, too, that it was only my Iqbal [prestige or status] that prevented the Pathans from falling on my baggage . . . I sat down to my disconsolate dinner, and had hardly taken two mouthfuls before I was informed that some men had been wounded near the foot of the pass and robbed. These individuals accordingly appeared, and asserted that they had been attacked by the very men who were affecting to protect the baggage; and I confess I do not think this improbable, for I have felt very suspicious of our strange, wild assistants, with their hungry-looking knives and tulwars [curved sabres], their long guns and general thievish appearance.

Despite Taylor's fears, the column reached Kohat without further incident. Here Taylor, still wary, was fed and entertained by the khan in his country garden, concluding with a warriors' dance that was not at all to his taste: 'They first executed a sort of mummery and dance with naked swords, the whole party crowded together and the gesticulations most violent; and yet, strange to say, nothing approaching an accident occurred. A singular part of the performance was a mode they had of first walking round in a circle, and, either with the hilt of the sword or the hand, making a motion as if enticing some one to come to them, and this accompanied by the blandest and most amiable smiles and gestures. Then all of a sudden this was exchanged for a scene of the wildest confusion, swords, arms, legs, and heads were tossed about in the most frantic manner, and the expression of the face changed to one of fierce malevolence.' For Taylor, these gestures were a reflection of his hosts' duplicitous character: 'I could not help thinking that the first performance might represent the insidious way in which the too confiding were enticed into their Golgothic valleys, and the second their consequent fate.'

From Kohat Taylor marched south with his column over a low range of mountains forming a natural barrier between Kohat and Bannu. These, an extension of the Salt Range, barren hills made up of raw, exposed pink rock marked with streaks of white crystal, give way to a broad plain watered by two rivers running down from the Safed Koh range, the snow-capped 'white mountain', the Kurram and then the Gumbila, a tributary of the Tochi. Taylor was encamped with his column north of the first of these rivers when Edwardes showed up quite unexpectedly. 'When I was writing after breakfast,' he notes in his diary on 6 December 1847, 'I was suddenly surprised by a man rushing into my tent and saying that a saheb had arrived. On going out, who should I find but Edwardes, the other general, who had ridden over from his camp about thirty miles off!'

Two days later the columns met and camped together in a Waziri-dominated area of open pasture north of the Kurram river which they named 'The Wells'. Taylor's part in the business was now over. He had been offered the job Edwardes was now taking on, but had turned it down – perhaps wisely: it is hard to see how he could have inspired in the maliks of Bannu the same degree of confidence. Leaving the greater part of his force behind with Edwardes, he marched back to Peshawar with a small escort.

Just as Taylor had enjoyed, albeit ungratefully, the protection of the Afridi chief Mahommad Khan in Kohat, so Edwardes now had the protection of the Ahmadzai Waziri Sawan Khan: 'It was he whose presence in our camp made us as secure in the winter pasture grounds of the Vizeerees as though we had been in the citadel of Lahore.' He was beginning to appreciate the high value his host placed on *melmastia*, the third law of Pakhtunwali, which required him to provide shelter without hope of payment or return of favours – even when, as in this case, it was not in his interests. He was also given the opportunity to learn how seriously Pakhtuns took the second law of Pakhtunwali, *badal* – the duty to always avenge a wrong done to oneself or one's family – when he received a visit from the sixteen-year-old son of one of the Bannuchi maliks: 'Ursulla Khan, a fine young lad . . . came in to impart to me his own and his father's uneasiness about past murders. "What", he asked, "is to be the law?" I asked him, jokingly, "What does it signify to a lad like you?" He replied modestly, "Oh, I've only killed four, but father has killed eighty!" One gets accustomed to this state of society; but in England what monsters of cruelty would this father and son be considered!'

These maliks and khans had in most cases earned rather than inherited their titles: 'Either he became so by being the greatest landowner, or the wisest in council, or the most terrible in fight. In short, he owed his chieftainship to influence, not blood or right, and his sons after him succeeded only to the same privileges on the same conditions.' With the title came power and privileges, but also responsibilities. From tithes paid over to him by the local landowners, the malik was required to maintain a public fund: 'Out of it the high mud walls around the fortified villages were repaired, the canals and water-courses kept open, arms and ammunition purchased, the pilgrim feasted on his holy progress, the neighbour, saint, or stranger hospitably entertained, the beggar relieved, and the song of the wandering minstrel rewarded. At the end of the year, if there was any surplus left, it became the chief's private property; but if there were any deficiency, he was expected to defray it out of his own resources.'

Every malik in Bannu exercised control over a *tappah*, a confederacy of fortified villages, its size depending on how powerful he might be: 'Petty aggressions were continual, and the power of every Mullick was liable to constant fluctuation from the decrease or increase of his influence among the landowners of his own Tappah . . . the result was that several years had come and gone, and still seen the twenty rich Tappahs of Bunnoo equally divided among seventeen or eighteen chiefs.'

It was to bring order to this state of near anarchy that Edwardes now summoned the elders of both the Waziri and the Bannuchi to attend him at his camp beside the Kurram River for the public council known throughout the frontier regions as the *jirga*. He had earlier sent ahead of him a proclamation addressed to 'the Mullicks and people of Bunnoo', which set out in clear terms exactly what he proposed to do in Bannu: 'I told you last spring, that if you did not accept the easy terms which I offered you, and pay up your arrears, I should come to collect the balance in winter, build a fort, establish a Sikh garrison, and put your fertile land under a Kardar [government agent and collector of taxes], like any other part of the Punjab kingdom. I am now on my way to keep my word . . . If you wish for peace and kindness, therefore, and to be good subjects of the Maharajuh, let the Mullicks present themselves in my camp without delay, and the people stay quietly in their houses.'

As the maliks began to arrive at Edwardes's camp he found that the growing reputation of the conquerors of the Sikhs had preceded him: 'One chief wanted to know whether it was true that English people could not tell lies; and appeared, from his look of commiseration, to attribute it to some cruel malformation of our mouths. Another enquired whether it was really true that when I was young I had read books for twelve years uninterruptedly, without sleeping?'

With the powerful Waziri khan at his shoulder, Edwardes was able to go to the Bannuchi with a carrot and stick. 'Assist me,' he told the assembled chiefs, 'and ten per cent of your assessments shall be each year divided amongst you . . . [but] if you do not, I shall depose you and confiscate your estates.' The Bannuchi maliks had much to gain by coming under the protection of the new regime in Lahore, and the majority were easily won over. But for the Waziri it was a very different matter. Earlier, Sawan Khan had observed Edwardes going over the ground with surveying instruments, and on learning their purpose had made it plain that the Waziri did not and would not pay taxes: 'The measurements were doubtless a very nice idea, but if it was done with any intention of taking revenue, it might as well be dispensed with, as such a thing was altogether visionary, and could certainly never come to pass.'

Nevertheless, Sawan Khan was bound by his earlier promise to put his case and hear out Edwardes. Accordingly, he and the other elders of the Ahmadzai assembled outside his tent, where a large carpet had been laid out under an awning. They sat themselves down cross-legged in a circle and listened attentively as Edwardes spoke to them in Persian, his words then being translated into Pushtu by an interpreter. For all his polite turns of phrase, Edwardes did not mince his words. 'If you do not like laws and paying revenue,' he declared, 'you are quite at liberty to give up your lands to the Bunnoochees, from whom you took them, and return to those happy hills where there is no revenue to give and no corn to eat. Of one thing be assured; that I will either make you pay revenue like the Bunnoochees or expel you from Bunnoo. I have troops enough to destroy your whole tribe. I do not believe, however, that you will be fools enough to forsake in a day the lands which you have been thirty years in conquering, or forgo the whole of your rich harvests, rather than pay a part.'

This was bitter medicine for the Ahmadzai, long used to having everything their own way. They asked to be given time to debate Edwardes's ultimatum. For a week their elders met in daily jirga, at which every man present was given time to have his say. A protracted and stormy debate ensued, with many angry voices raised to denounce Sawan Khan as a traitor, some even supporting the call of a local ulema for a *jihad* or holy war to be declared against the infidel Sikhs and their British allies. But by the end of the week passion had given way to realism, and the assembled maliks finally agreed to put their marks of affirmation to Edwardes's treaty paper. 'I caused each chief to sign the terms,' Edwardes writes, 'or rather to make a scratch where he was told; and as none of them had ever had a pen in their hands before, much laughter was occasioned by this approach to the slavery of civilisation; and the assembly broke up in good humour, to which I further contributed by a feast in honour of the alliance.'

Edwardes's next step was to put his Sikh troops to work building a stronghold, 'the inner fort to be one hundred yards square, its walls twenty feet high and nine feet thick, surrounded by a deep dry ditch . . . the outer fort or cantonment, eighty yards from the inner one, to have walls ten feet high and six feet thick'. Its site was chosen after several days spent surveying the country: 'I found that the source of all influence, power, and wealth in Bunnoo was the River Khoorrum; and one chief was described to be powerful, because his fort was uppermost on its banks; while another attributed all his misfortunes to his estate being low down inland. It seemed therefore, that a fort placed at the head of the Khoorrum, might command the valley by commanding the irrigation.'

Edwardes finally settled on an area of high ground on the right bank of the river and not far from a settlement known simply as the Bazaar or market. The fort was to be named, somewhat insensitively, Duleepgarh, in honour of the Sikh boy-ruler of the Punjab, Maharaja Dalip Singh, and later became the kernel of the town of Bannu. As soon as its potential size and strength became apparent, opposition to Edwardes's occupation began to make itself felt: stragglers outside the walls were ambushed, and potshots were loosed off under cover of darkness. An attempt on Edwardes's life was foiled by the alertness of his guards, who seized the would-be assassin before he could deliver the fatal blow.

These opponents were right to be alarmed, because no sooner had the walls of Fort Duleepgarh reached a safe height than Edwardes put out an order that throughout Bannu every watchtower and every outer wall surrounding a village must be pulled down by its inhabitants. 'Where just laws are in force, every fakeer's hut is a castle, because no one dare enter it to injure him,' was his argument. 'You are hereby ordered, therefore, to throw down to the ground the walls of every fort and enclosed village within the boundaries of Bunnoo; and I hold the mullicks responsible for the carrying out of this order within fifteen days.'

The news was received by the Bannuchi with astonishment and dismay, since in effect it meant rendering their villages defenceless and open to the depredations of their enemies. Yet, equally astonishingly, the walls were taken down – with great reluctance at first but then, as it became apparent that the order was being carried out on all sides, with enthusiasm, so that within one month every one of Bannu's hundreds of forts had been levelled.

Reynell Taylor had not been back in Peshawar for long before he heard of the attempt on Edwardes's life. Ashamed by what he saw as his own lack of courage, in not staying on in Bannu to support his colleague, he immediately petitioned John Lawrence (then deputising for his sick brother) to be allowed to return. As soon as permission came through he rode down through Kohat with an escort, rejoining Edwardes in Bannu in early February 1848. The transformation that Edwardes had brought about astonished him. 'It really is wonderful what Edwardes has accomplished,' he enthused in his diary on 11 February. 'The whole of the fortified villages, amounting to 400, have been knocked down by the people themselves, and in their places the walls of the new fort of Dhuleepgarh, surrounded by a cantonment wall, have arisen . . . A military road has been marked out between this and Lukkee in Murwat, and about two koss [three to four miles] of it have been made.' That was the plus side: 'On the other hand, the fear of assassination is still rife, and we are obliged to go and sit well armed, even among our attendants, Edwardes's adventure having shown that it is useless to depend for safety on either guards or attendants.'

By early spring the region was settled well enough for Edwardes to feel that he could leave Reynell Taylor to continue with the first rough revenue survey already begun, while he himself began to explore the southern portion of the country, a region known, after the chief people settled there, as Marwat. Although Pakhtun in origin, the Marwati were one of the tribes which had been pushed east by later waves of Afghan migrants from the mountains. In the process they had adopted the Punjabi language as well as some of the plains customs, as Edwardes noted with amusement:

At every village there has been a 'demonstration' of women got up to induce me to let their husbands off from paying the revenue which the crop-measurers were bribed to suppress; and very severe actions have I had to fight with these Marwat amazons, but all in good humour; for they break their way through the escort, seize my horse by the bridle, and taking me regularly prisoner, commence a kind of deprecatory glee, made up of a fractional part of the simple burden, *Arzlarri!* (I have a petition) . . . The effect of it rising A sharp from the throats of at least two hundred women, half of them laughing while the other half scream, must be left to an imaginative ear . . . In the end I have to watch an opportunity to bolt, followed by all my horsemen, and the loud laughter of the unsuccessful petitioners . . . This custom of allowing their women to be seen is a trait worthy of remark as quite peculiar to Marwat, and contrary to one of the strongest prejudices of Afghans, who jealously shut up their females. Even in low-bred and vicious Bannu the women shun observation . . . The enlightened ladies of Marwat, therefore, drew down from the Afghans in my train unqualified expressions of blame and astonishment; and no sooner did we approach a village, and catch sight of the blue-petticoated crowd outside, than '*Tobah! Tobah!*' (Shame! Shame!) burst from every mouth.

From Marwat country Edwards crossed the range of hills which formed the southern boundary of Bannu and continued on to Tank, where he had the satisfaction of meeting an old acquaintance, Shah Niwaz Khan. This remarkable friendship had started with a chance encounter two years earlier in Jammu, when Edwardes helped two strangers in distress by giving them a small sum of money. What followed from that was like something out of the *Arabian Nights*: a year later, as Edwardes set out on his first reconnaissance of Bannu, these same two Pakhtuns reappeared and asked to accompany him. On the march Edwardes, in asking some locals about the country ahead of them, happened to mention Tank: 'One of the two Pathans modestly lifted up his head and said, "My father was once king of it"!' He had been deposed by the Sikhs. Edwardes then discovered that this exiled prince and his companion had not eaten for two days, having long since sold off the last of their possessions. He fed them and loaned them 500 rupees from his treasury. Later, at his recommendation, Henry Lawrence installed Shah Niwaz Khan as the ruler of Tank, in succession to his father.

And now, a year on, Edwardes was able to see the consequences of his good deed. 'Shah Niwaz Khan of Tank arrived in camp, and gives a modest but satisfactory account of his country,' Edwardes wrote in his diary on 4 March. 'His best report, however, is in the mouths of the common people of the districts round, who already compare him to his wise grandfather, Surwar Khan . . . I cannot say what a happiness it is to me to have had it in my power at once to restore him to his home, and to recover a whole people from ruin. It is, perhaps, the best thing I have done on this frontier; yet it was only a happy hit – a thought that it would do – a recommendation to Lawrence – his order – and it was done! Talk of conjuring trees with singing birds out of a mere cherry-stone – why, here is a populous country conjured up, in a waste, by a scratch of a pen.'

From Tank Edwardes moved on southwards again, to the town of Kulachi, where it soon became evident that all was not well. 'There is hardly a vestige of cultivation to be seen in the land,' he wrote in his diary on 6 March. 'The rain fell too late. Waste, waste – waste on every side. On arriving in the city the whole population moved out in a body, and raising their hands in the air, cried with one voice, "*Furyad, Sahib log! Furyad!*" (Complaint, masters! Complaint!) I felt it to be a powerful appeal, and by the help of God will, before I leave, lighten the burdens of the poor.'

While he was working on land settlement at Kulachi, news reached Edwardes that a local chieftain named Shahzad Khan was hiding up in the hills just sixteen miles away to the west, together with a large number of men from his tribe, the Nassur. Shahzad Khan, who had opposed any deals with the Lahore Government, first refused Edwardes's invitation to come down and talk, then ignored an order to do so – or leave Sikh territory. Edwardes felt he could not afford to let this flouting of his authority go unpunished. 'I was quite determined to clear the account,' he wrote, 'for the man who hopes to rule a barbarous country must first make his orders law, else the barbarians will very soon rule *him.*'

Acting without delay, Edwards set out at nightfall with his force of three hundred men. Just before daybreak the next morning his guides pointed out Shahzad Khan's camp fires twinkling in the shadow of a great mountain called Solomon's Throne. 'I called a halt', Edwardes wrote, 'under the shelter of a ravine to look at it, breathe the horses, and let the stragglers close up.' But as dawn broke it became clear to Edwardes that there *were* no stragglers: the greater part of his force had taken advantage of the darkness to 'lose their way'. He had now to decide whether to press on and risk defeat, or turn back and lose much of the *iqbal* which his recent actions in Bannu had won him. What followed was a mixture of farce and near-tragedy.

'With a heart not over-high', Edwardes led his remaining force of some eighty cavalry sowars at a brisk trot towards an encampment which had now been roused by the furious barking of its dogs, then circled round to its rear so as to prevent Shahzad Khan's people from escaping into the mountains. A call to surrender was met by a volley of shots from the Afghans' jezails, so Edwardes drew his sword and ordered his men to charge. But as he galloped full tilt into the camp, he realised to his horror that no more than a dozen of his men were charging with him:

> The dozen were composed of Muhommud Alim Khan (I think I see him now with his blue-and-gold shawl turban all knocked about his ears), Kaloo Khan and Lumsden's Duffadar of Guides; each backed by a few faithful henchmen. The only officer non-inventus was the Sikh russuldar . . . How we ever got out of it is unaccountable; but we did, after cutting our way from one end to the other of the Nassur camp. Somewhere about the middle of it a tall ruffian, whom I was told afterwards was Shahzad's brother, walked deliberately at me with his jezail, and sticking it into my stomach, so that the muzzle almost pushed me out of the saddle, fired! The priming flashed in the pan, and as he drew back the jezail I cut him full over the head; but I might as well have hit a cannon-ball – the sword turned in my hand; and the Nassur, without even resettling his turban, commenced repriming his jezail, an operation which I did not stay to see completed . . . I have always looked back to the moment when that jezail missed fire as one of all my life when I looked death closest in the face.

Despite the botched action and the scare, as far as Edwardes was concerned the outcome was entirely satisfactory: Shahzad Khan retreated deep into Afghanistan with his people, and Edwardes's point was made: 'Nor was I ever again told by any other Cabul merchant in the province under my charge that he would not come when he was called, or would not obey the laws of the Sikh territory in which he lived or bought or sold.'

Edwardes had now done everything he had set out to do, and more. As he began to lay plans to return to Lahore, he could reflect with considerable satisfaction that his six months in Bannu and points south had made a manifest impact on the frontier. Though it was perhaps 'not quite the thing' to have made them in so many words, the claims he later aired in the preface to his *Year on the Punjab Frontier* were hardly exaggerated. He had indeed achieved a 'bloodless conquest of the wild valley of Bunnoo', a conquest effected 'simply by balancing two races and two creeds. For fear of a Sikh army, two warlike and independent Muhommudan tribes levelled to the ground, at my bidding, the four hundred forts which constituted the strength of their country; and for fear of those same Muhommudan tribes, the same Sikh army, at my bidding, constructed a fortress for the Crown, which completed the subjugation of the valley.' While some of these were to prove but short-term achievements, one was to have long-lasting consequences: Edwardes awakened the frontier tribes to the fact that the power he represented thought and acted very differently from the Sikhs. A new image of the British began to take shape, one far removed from the tarnished reputation that two occupying armies had left behind in Afghanistan, and one which entered into the equation when, a decade on, these same frontier tribes found themselves having to choose sides.

6

'Power to the omnipotent Sahibs'

JAMES ABBOTT AND HAZARA, 1846–1848

> *Khalk-i-Khuda*
> *Malk-i-Sirkar*
> *Hakm-i-Sahiban alishan.*

> Mankind to God
> Land to the Government
> Power to the omnipotent Sahibs.
> Nineteenth-century Urdu proverb

O F ALL the districts of the NWFP, Hazara is perhaps the least glamorous in terms of confrontations and bloodshed. In part this is because it is the furthest from the Afghan border, and therefore the most 'settled' – to use a term beloved of British administrators; but it could be argued that it is the most settled because of James Abbott.

Hazara is physically separated from the other Frontier districts by being on the other side of the Indus, a wedge of territory lodged like a tent-peg between Swat on the west and Kashmir and Jammu on the east: 'The country now called Huzara, but Abisara when Alexander visited it, is a triangular tract of rugged mountains and fertile valleys, with a northerly apex, lying between the Indus and the Jelum; in length, north and south, about a hundred miles, with a longitudinal breadth at base of about fifty miles. The noble flood of the Indus laves its western limits, and the river Jelum (the Hydraspes of older times), a noble river, also forms its eastern limit.'

These words were written by James Abbott, and they come from one of two manuscript volumes of pasted-together scraps, part narrative and part polemic, entitled 'Huzara and Its Place in the Second Sikh War', which he assembled some years after being ejected from Hazara. As well as his popular *Narrative of a Journey from Heraut to Khiva, Moscow, and St Petersburgh, during the late Russian Invasion of Khiva*, Abbott wrote several works of fiction and a number of poems – none with any obvious merit, and few of them published. On the page his handwriting is the scrawl of an untidy schoolboy for whom the task of putting words down on paper is a chore rather than a pleasure, an impression reinforced by most curious punctuation. It is as though he had left Addiscombe College believing that punctuation was best achieved by sprinkling colons more or less at random. This eccentricity is part and parcel of Abbott's undoubted charm, but for clarity's sake I have taken the necessary liberty of repunctuating his text wherever I have quoted it. It does not make his story any less extraordinary.

The measure of this most open-hearted of men is revealed in the opening lines of the preface to a text which he intended to publish, but never did:

> That portion of the narrative having special relation to myself is so embarrassed with the records of defeat, painful to narrate, though shared with the dauntless Nicholson, that I had difficulty in deciding to pursue it, and can scarcely yet resolve to publish it. But, standing as I now stand on the verge of the shadowy world, I feel myself to be debtor to the Public for a Narrative of sorts, vindicating the noble character and conduct of the people of Huzara, to whose affectionate devotion I owed life and liberty, when my fortunes seemed desperate, and to whom I cannot but attribute a very important share in arresting the peril which threatened our control of the Punjab in 1848/49.

It is no exaggeration to say that Abbott's high regard for the people of Hazara, the Hazarawals, was reciprocated. To this day, villagers in those areas most closely associated with Abbott will assert with absolute conviction that *Kaka* Abbott prayed in the local mosque and was a pious Muslim. In one village they say that he first came there as a young stranger named Bati, and for some years served as a humble water-carrier, bringing water up to the mosque from the streams below. Then he went away, and when the villagers next saw him it was as Abbott Saheb, dressed in uniform and riding on a horse as the Deputy Commissioner of Hazara. Whatever local legend asserts, the official record has it that James Abbott first went to Hazara in December 1846, charged by Henry Lawrence with settling the border between the Sikh Punjab and the new kingdom of Kashmir and Jammu. He very soon took it upon himself to extend his brief: 'As that line seemed to cut across one of the most important mountains of Huzara, I determined to enter that District, believing that I might not only gain there the information I was seeking, but be also of service in reconciling discords.' His Sikh military escort was not at all happy with these plans: 'Huzara was at that time a name of terror to the Sikhs . . . the suite of the Lahore Commissioner, my compeer, related the most absurd stories of the ferocity of its inhabitants: carefully concealing their own disgrace in the complicity of the Sikh Army with them. The country was at that time in open rebellion, for when the British victory at Sobraon had been announced in Huzara the people had risen with one accord upon their oppressors, and had expelled the Sikh Field Force and the garrisons of their numerous castles and towers from the country.'

The reason for the ferocity of the Hazarawals towards the Sikhs soon became apparent to Abbott: over the previous thirty years, the Sikhs had made repeated efforts to conquer them. The more than twenty Muslim tribes who populated this hill country had managed on a number of occasions to ambush and defeat Sikh armies, but in the end their disunity had allowed the Sikhs to build and garrison a number of strong forts at strategic points, and so subdue them. They had then governed Hazara in the most oppressive fashion. 'The Governor of Huzara', according to Abbott, 'held unlimited power to plunder, slay or dishonour any Muhummedan.

The garrisons of the forty castles and towers, scattered over the country, lived chiefly on plunder. Labour was never paid for by more than the day's food for the labourer. Two thirds of the actual produce of the fields were required of the husbandmen. All this tyranny had been instituted and exercised by the Sikh Governors and had been suddenly annulled by the British. This I mention not as adjudicating against the Sikhs, who were only retaliating the persecution they had suffered from Muhummedans, but as explaining the impossibility of speedily establishing confidence between the two Races.'

Having more or less expelled the Sikhs, the Hazarawals now found that under the terms of the British treaty with Maharaja Gulab Singh their territory had become part of the new kingdom of Kashmir and Jammu. Abbott was thus entering Hazara as a representative of their former oppressors, escorted by Sikh soldiers, and with instructions to set the seal on a treaty that bound them to a Hindu ruler – who, as it happened, had himself only recently been their oppressor on behalf of the Sikhs. Abbott's approach from the south coincided with Harry Lumsden's incursion from the east, but whereas Lumsden's intention was to skirt the interior, Abbott was set on reaching Haripur, the town established by Ranjit Singh's general Hari Singh as the administrative centre of Hazara. He advanced on the back of a large elephant, with Sikh outriders on either side, a column of Sikh infantry before and a troop of elephant-drawn Sikh artillery following behind. 'On my march,' he later wrote, 'I was much interested with the aspect of a country which I little knew then was to become my residence for six years. On my right hand rose Mt Serrh to the height of about 1500 feet above the valley, a pyramidal isolated rock of limestone, at whose base stood one of the prettiest and best preserved of the topes [Buddhist stupa or monument]. On my left was the long mountain ridge of Gundgurh, the terror of the Sikhs, still at open defiance with the Government. In front, mountain rose above mountain, in long succession, the farthest capped with snow. I found, still smoking from its ashes, the village of Moti, burnt by the chief of Gundgurh.'

Here, to his surprise, Abbott was met by a deputation of maliks, armed to the teeth but come 'to implore the British Government to accept the allegiance of Huzara, dwelling on the cruel oppression of the Sikhs, which had been at its height when Raja Gulab Singh had been their deputy, and announcing their resolution to shed the last drop of their blood rather than submit to the tyrant to whom we had now consigned them'.

As he progressed deeper into Hazara territory, Abbott began to learn more about the different hill tribes who made up its inhabitants. The majority were Pakhtuns, such as the Jadun, Swathi and Sayyid clans who were linked to the Yusufzai tribes of Mardan and Swat and who had migrated across the Indus in the early seventeenth century. Other groups such as the Tanoli and Mashwani belonged to earlier waves of migrants from Afghanistan, the nomadic Gujar probably the oldest of them all. Some of the elders of these tribes were still hostile and remained in the hills, but others made determined efforts to put their views across to the visiting Feranghi at every opportunity. One of the first to impress him was Mir Jeman Khan, 'by race a Yoosufzye, by clan an Oothmanzye, by family a Sydukhani'. He was a young man of striking presence – and, it transpired, an outlaw:

> His frame gave promise of great power; but a character better
> suited to the saddle than the hillside . . . His countenance was
> massive, the nose aquiline, the brow broad, the eye well opened,
> large, fearless and inviting confidence; he wore a strong mous-
> tache and a close black beard. His face was shadowed by an
> immense black turban of blue-black cotton cloth, the ends
> sparkling with gold thread . . . Accustomed from childhood to
> be hunted as the wolf, or bayed as the lion, the voice of kindness
> was a strange novelty to him, and seemed to penetrate his
> inmost soul. His eyes met mine with a confidence not to be
> mistaken, as he gave a rapid sketch of the misery which he and
> others had endured under the Sikh Tyranny; and more espe-
> cially when their tyrant was that Raja Goolab Singh to whose
> tender mercies we had again consigned them. He reiterated the
> earnest desire of the whole people of Huzara to become British
> subjects or, if that could not be, to be at least retained as subjects
> of Lahore, where their dearest rights would be protected by the
> British Agency.

A few more meetings with tribal leaders like Mir Jeman Khan, and Abbott was won over. He extended his progress through the country from weeks to months, but long before it was over had reached a fateful decision, concluding that 'a painful and prolonged misery to thousands must result from the transfer of their district to Cashmere'. Accordingly, he wrote to Henry Lawrence in Lahore setting out the facts and explaining how much better it would be for all parties if Hazara did not go to Maharaja Gulab Singh. Abbott gained an ally in Patrick Vans Agnew, who was following in his wake, and the end result was that an exchange of territory was made, and Hazara remained part of Sikh Punjab. This quite remarkable political coup understandably gained Abbott prodigious *iqbal* among the Hazarawals, never to be forfeited despite all the tribulations of the later years.

The transfer of sovereignty back to Lahore allowed Abbott to return to Hazara in the summer of 1847 as its first British Deputy Commissioner. As a servant of the Lahore Durbar, he was nominally under the instruction of the Sikh Governor of Hazara, Sirdar Chatar Singh, and of his Deputy, Jundial Singh, both newly appointed like himself. However, as far as Abbott was concerned he had only one master, and that was Henry Lawrence, the British Resident in Lahore. He would consult with the Governor but act as he, not the Sikhs, thought best. This of course was precisely what Henry Lawrence was doing, on a far grander scale, with the Sikh Durbar; inevitably British and Sikhs, both in Hazara and Lahore, found themselves on a collision course.

In Hazara James Abbott's first action was to establish an administrative base for himself and his co-rulers, Chatar Singh and Jundial Singh, who were to join him in Haripur as soon as he had restored law and order. Haripur, like Peshawar on a smaller scale, stands at the centre of a bowl of hills, almost entirely surrounded by mountains. In the recent uprising against the Sikhs, the town had been sacked and fired. Abbott rebuilt the four towers that had stood at each corner of the town's walls and turned one into a residence-cum-office for himself, making over the other three to Sirdar Chatar Singh and his Sikh officials. The nearby fort of Govindgurh, on a hillside just above the town, was reoccupied by a large garrison of Chatar Singh's Sikh regiments. 'The officers came to pay their respects to me,' writes Abbott in his narrative. 'I had only one chair, which I myself occupied; but I was ashamed (being only a Captain) to see standing around me, Colonels, Lieutenant-Colonels and Majors. I begged them to be seated on the carpet. They bowed but continued standing.' Never one to stand on ceremony, Abbott continued to insist that the Sikh officers make themselves comfortable on the carpet in the local manner, only to learn after much whispering that the reason for their reluctance was that their 'red satin nether-garments' were too tight to allow them to bend their knees. Another source of embarrassment was the guard and its accompanying band at Govindgurh, which insisted on turning out to salute him whenever he appeared anywhere near the fort:

I tried always, by waving my hand and accelerating the pace of my horse, to quash the proceedings. But the zealous Sikh Officer-on-Guard would take no denial. He shouted to his men to fall in; and his shout brought scuttling in, from all parts of the compass, his scattered myrmidons, some pausing on the road to get into their breeches, which they occupied only on grand occasions; others attempting the like feat on the run; some hopping along with one leg in, while the other was lunging desperately at its scabbard; and the two or three warriors who were so happy as to have reached the ranks, presenting arms amid all these demonstrations, at word of command; while the Band played up, in execrable tune and time, its own especial variation of 'Home! Sweet Home!'

As Harry Lumsden had discovered during his own Hazara venture, the Sikh officers commanding the troops in Govindgurh were thoroughly professional soldiers. Abbott found them good company, but soon became aware that these pleasant men were the chief instruments of an extremely repressive regime that had banned all public expressions of faith among the Muslim population: 'Any Moosulman praying in public was liable to be slain on the spot by any armed Sikh . . . The calls to worship and attendance at the musjid [mosque] were alike forbidden, while the slaughter of a cow or of a bullock was punished by death.' Within days of Abbott's arrival these practices began to be challenged, tentatively at first and then with growing confidence: 'One morning early I heard the "Bahng" or early call to prayer of Muhummedans, cautiously and timidly, near my tent. And, as my presence prevented any violence to the sounder from the Sikh troops of my escort, it was repeated again and again. And, gradually, the evening and the midnight calls succeeded; but still, only where my presence secured immunity. I then represented strongly the hardship of the case; and Sir Henry Lawrence, who, no doubt, had like representations from other district officers, interfered; and, not without much persuasion, procured the removal of the more offensive and intolerable restrictions.'

Nothing could be more calculated to enhance Abbott's popularity among a people whose devotion to their faith is absolute than this lifting of the ban on public worship – although Abbott himself makes the point that the Sikhs had imposed these bans as a tit-for-tat retaliation for the atrocities perpetrated on the Sikhs by the Afghans in earlier years. Guru Nanak, the founder of the Sikh religion, had preached universal tolerance, but Muslim persecution had 'converted his harmless followers into a nation of warriors filled with hatred of their oppressors'. Now the hatred was ingrained and mutual, and was to bedevil the subcontinent for generations to come.

Abbott's first official duty was to begin what was termed a 'rough settlement', by making personal inspections and checking deeds of land-ownership, so that revenue could be collected. This meant that he spent most of his days 'touring' – that is to say, trekking, on foot, in the saddle or in the howdah – and his nights in camp. It was a slow process, made infinitely slower by the scores of disputes over land rights: 'In every step I met returning exiles, thousands having been banished for defending their rights, or to enrich, by their disinheritance, the favourites of the local governors. I was afterwards, for six years, occupied incessantly in finding room for these unfortunates, without altogether dispossessing those who had enjoyed their lands during the banishment of their owners.' Many of these petitioners were outlaws with a price on their head, brigands who claimed to have been driven into lives of crime by the tyrannical actions of the Sikh governors and who now sought amnesty: 'These men appeared suddenly before me in my rides along the wild frontier, and trusting their fate to my honour besought me to intercede for the restoration of a portion of the lands from which they had been expelled by Sikh rapacity. They were mostly petty Rajas and chiefs of the ancient family of the Gukkurs [Gakkar], whose miserable remains of once kingly professions had lately been wrested from them by the Sikhs.'

The most notorious of these outlaws was 'Raja Shahwulli Khan of the Gukkur race', who had kidnapped Chatar Singh's chief revenue collector and held him in the hills until a ransom of £150 had been paid. Abbott listened sympathetically to Shahwali Khan's protestations of innocence, and came to the view that he and others like him were, for the most part, 'robbers of necessity'. He pleaded on his behalf with Henry Lawrence, who granted him the return of a small part of his hereditary lands. As might be expected, this went down very badly with the Sikh governor, who took 'exceeding umbrage' and complained that 'in a British court of law no difference was made between the Sofaid-push [wearers of white, thus the rich] and Seeah-push [wearers of black, the poor]; between the noble and the scum of the earth'. To rub salt in the wound, the pardoned Gakkar chief then took to parading ostentatiously up and down on horseback in full view of the governor's residence on land outside the town of Haripur which he claimed was his, 'riding hawk-on-wrist, the most picturesque of figures, over the lands once his lawful possessions and but lately underlying the terror of his raids'.

Shahwali Khan was one of those larger-than-life characters that Abbott found it impossible not to admire, made easier in his case by Abbott's belief that the Gakkar were descendents of Alexander the Great's Greek soldiery who had settled in these parts:

Shahwulli Khan in physiognomy might well have personated a Greek. He was a man of few words and no professions, true to his pledge and sensitive upon the point of honour. A year or two subsequent to his amnesty I had occasion to censure his gallant but unfortunate son, Raja Nadir Khan, for a somewhat serious fault. The old man thought my censure touched the honour of his son. He rose and laid at my feet his own sword and shield. 'Take them,' he said. 'You bestowed them and they are yours, but leave us our honour unblemished.' I was deeply touched. I soothed and reassured him, but I have never forgotten that scene. He was at that time engaged in a violent quarrel with the son aforesaid, so that no fondness prompted the action.

Another equally notorious outlaw was less easy to admire – 'Jafir of the Dagger Hand', a petty landowner whose sword-hand had been struck off as punishment for a murder. After the loss of his hand and the confiscation of his lands Jafir had fled to the Margalla Hills south of Hazara, where he 'became so terrible for his highway robberies that the Margalla pass, which he haunted, deserved its name of "cut throat" in more senses than one'.

Abbott encountered Jafir of the Dagger Hand while out on tour, and never forgot his first meeting with 'this strange ruffian [who] never laid aside his wild attire, even when free from apprehension . . . He was a man of large stature, powerfully though lightly built, and very athletic. His features were well-formed, but his eye was full of treachery. He had a great name for courage, which after-knowledge of him led me somewhat to doubt.' However, what really made Jafir stand out was his novel weaponry:

He had somewhat more than supplied the place of his forfeited right hand by attaching to the stump with splints and bands of steel a short, double-edged dagger and a hook. With the hook he held the reins of his horse, gathered into a knot, according to eastern custom. With his forearm, which with its splints and bands of steel was sword-proof, he could guard his head; whilst his left hand was free to wield the sabre, and with the dagger he could stab any unwary adversary. And, as this dagger was always ready-grasped and generally held in contact with his sword hand, he could in one moment remove the sheath and insert the blade between the ribs of anyone so unwary as to parley with him.

Jafir's case was not difficult to pronounce on. A previous Sikh governor had persuaded him to stop his banditry by restoring his *jagir* or land-holding. However, following a change of governor this agreement had been declared null and void, so that Jafir of the

Dagger Hand had been forced once more to take to the hills. 'As his offences had been condoned by the local ruler when he was reinstated in his jaghir,' Abbott decided, 'it seemed to me there could be but one honest opinion. This I stated, and "Jafir of the Dagger Hand" became a peaceful zemindar [landowner].'

These early successes among the Hazarawals were largely confined to the plains area in the south of the region. Few among the tribes who occupied the surrounding higher ground were prepared to accept Abbott's presence so readily. The strongest resistance against the Sikhs in the recent past had come from the two tribes who occupied the mountain range which Abbott had passed on his left as he first entered Hazara: the Gandgar Hills. The Tarkheli occupied the southern half of the range, the Mashwani the north. Both were still extremely hostile, as were the powerful Tanoli in the Tanawal mountains to the north, the Swati who occupied the fertile plains beyond them, and the Dhund to the far east.

To help Abbott win over these various tribes Henry Lawrence now sent up two junior assistants on temporary loan: Patrick Vans Agnew and John Nicholson. Vans Agnew, the more experienced, led a column of Sikhs into Tanoli country, due north of Haripur, while Abbott took Nicholson with him to work on the Tarkheli at the southern end of the supposedly insurmountable Gandgar Hills. Guided by a tribesman from the rival Mashwani clan, they led a small force of infantry right up to the Salam Khand, the highest point of the mountain, at dead of night. As with Lumsden's little *coup de guerre* the year before, the unexpected appearance of their enemy on the summit above them so shocked the assembled Tarkheli men that they fled without firing a shot. The ripples from this bloodless victory spread far and wide in Hazara, and the chiefs of some half dozen tribes hastened down to Haripur to make their peace with the Deputy Commissioner: 'The Kurral Chiefs of Suttara were the first to submit. Then Hussun Ali Khan, chief of the senior or eastern branch of that tribe, occupying wild and very strong mountains on which the Sikhs had experienced some signal defeats . . . The mullicks or village heads of the Dhoonds of Dunna (being the Western half of that Tribe) now made their submission and were followed, beyond hope, by the Syuds of Khagan, the remotest of all the tribes subject to the Ruler of Huzara, theirs being the deep, wild glen of the Nyusook River.'

Of all the tribal chiefs of Hazara, the most powerful was said to be Jehandad Khan of the Tanoli, whose land straddled both banks of the Indus and whose fellow-tribesmen were 'brave and hardy and accounted the best swordsmen in Huzara'. There was a long history of conflict between Jehandad Khan's family and the Sikhs, and the name of his father, Painda Khan, was said to be as 'magic to the ears of the people of Huzara' because of the struggles he had fought on behalf of his 'poor and circumscribed and rugged principality' against the Sikhs. Abbott was aware that before his death Painda Khan had made his son swear never to trust his safety to any ruler, so that the prospect of Jehandad Khan giving in without a fight seemed faint. Patrick Vans Agnew, sent to parley with him, returned without success. Abbott then conveyed a personal appeal to the young khan, warning him that 'he must decide whether to be treated as a loyal chief or a rebel'.

Much to Abbott's surprise, Jehandad Khan responded by sending a messenger from his castle at Amb on the far bank of the Indus to say that he was on his way to present himself before the Deputy Commissioner. Determined that the submission of this most influential of chiefs should be stage-managed for maximum effect, Abbott set up an open-air durbar to receive Jehandad Khan with as much ceremony as he could muster. What he could not foresee was that the unexpected intervention of a member of his own entourage would nearly wreck the proceedings.

Among the Sikhs it was customary to treat dwarfs as good-luck symbols; every notable had such a dwarf in attendance as a sort of court jester, and one had wished himself on to James Abbott: 'A very ugly half-witted dwarf, who was fed by the bounty of the Kazi, was in attendance. He was dressed in scarlet, wore a huge turban, a shield of buffalo hide bossed with stars and crescents slung over his back, a sabre in his girdle. He delighted to strut in front of my horse when I rode. He had an idea that it was his especial duty to protect my person and, in the year following when the Sikh army rose upon us, he insisted upon sleeping, armed cap-à-pied, at my tent door.' Jehandad Khan – 'a good looking young man of 26 years, tall and slender, with remarkably large and fine eyes' – rode into Abbott's encampment surrounded by an escort of horsemen clad in 'shirts of mail and steel skull-caps, handsomely mounted and equipped, who made a most picturesque display'. As he dismounted, Abbott's dwarf dashed forward and grabbed the khan's cloak: 'Pointing at his face, he exclaimed, "Here he is, my Lord, this is he who commits all the murders in the country and burns our villages." The bystanders, who regarded the Chief with great awe, were thunderstruck; and, though the dwarf was instantly rebuked and led away, his imbecility being well known to all, my apologies for his rude speech and gesture could not at once restore the Chief's equanimity.' To Abbott's relief, the young khan subsequently calmed down, and duly made his submission to the Lahore Durbar.

Now only two tribes, the Eastern Dhund on the south-western border of Hazara and the Swati, occupying a fertile bowl of country known as the Pakli Plain in the very heart of Hazara, remained defiant. The most determined of the two proved to be the Dhund, 'dwelling upon the Jelum [the river Jhelum] in the shadow of the stupendous mountain Maachpoora'. Patrick Vans Agnew was sent to parley with them, but reported upon his return that they were 'intractable' and 'conceited beyond measure'.

The start of the Cold Weather of 1847 found the Dhund still obstinately clinging to their independence. Abbott now felt he had no option but to mount a full-scale military expedition against them, a course of action that troubled him greatly. 'As in the course of this narrative', he writes, 'it cannot but appear that I admire and sympathise with the struggle of free tribes for their liberty, it may be asked how I reconciled myself to the office of an invader . . . The reader must judge whether I decided rightly or deluded myself into a course inconsistent with such professions.' This was to be but the first of some hundreds of such punitive expeditions to be despatched under British orders into the tribal areas of the North-West Frontier between 1847 and 1947 to bring a hostile tribe, clan or village to heel. It was made up of two columns, each with two Sikh infantry regiments and four field guns borne on elephants. The reserve column was commanded by Jundial Singh, the newly-arrived Deputy Governor, with orders to keep as far as possible to the valley floor, while the main column under Abbott followed the higher paths along mountain ridges. After successfully surmounting some unexpectedly difficult terrain, Abbott and his troops arrived on the highest point of a ridge thickly wooded with tall cedars and commanding magnificent views south across the Punjab plains and eastward across the valley of the Jhelum to the mountain ranges of Kashmir and the Western Himalayas. He set up camp at a site called Muri which, anglicised into Murree, became the first British hill-station of the Punjab. 'I was probably the first Englishman that had ever set foot upon it,' muses Abbott with a founder's pride. 'I saw here for the first time the magnificent mass of Mount Maachpoora [Muckshapuri, 2817 metres above sea level], of which I had heard and dreamed so much, presenting toward the River Jelum a stupendous surface of precipice. Its summit is densely covered with cedar forests and is the resort of Jogies and alchemysts from India, who hold watch there by night expecting, by dint of certain incantations and ceremonies, to discern the spirits which alight as flames of fire upon plants professing alchemical properties.'

Of the hostile Dhund there was nothing to be seen, since they had dispersed before his advance. So Abbott sat and waited for them to come forward and parley. However, winter was now fast closing in: 'On 18 November a heavy fog overspread the mountains, which the people of the country assured me denoted a fall of snow.' This greatly alarmed his Sikh officers, who begged him to forbid the sounding of bugles because these would cause the snow to fall. He responded to their pleas, but even without the intervention of bugles it began to snow heavily, forcing them to retreat from the ridge to a less exposed camping ground. Despite their apprehensions, the Sikh soldiery took the novel phenomenon in their stride, but not so a small party of high-caste Hindu sappers, a detachment from the Bengal Army's Sappers and Miners who had been brought along to widen and strengthen the trail for their elephants: 'The Sappers were the hardiest and most handy of our British Sipahis [sepoys] but the snow quite paralysed their vegetable fibre and congealed their vegetable juices . . . their tent, frozen to the consistence of a deal plank, slid through their nerveless hands and just before they reached the camping ground it had slipped from the mule's back into a deep hollow filled with snow, and nothing could encourage them to dig it out. As their caste prevented them from fraternising with the Sikh soldiery, their predicament was not known until nightfall. I had the choice of inviting them to shelter in my own nutshell of a tent, or seeing them perish.' Never one to stand on rank or ceremony, Abbott invited them to share his tent: 'As the space did not admit of their reclining, it was necessary to keep a woodfire lighted, night and day, to the torture of my eyes.'

The snow also created severe problems for a small contingent of Sikh cavalrymen accompanying the column, who were fearful of losing their horses to the cold. Finding a nearby Dhund village occupied only by the tribe's women and children, the sowars ejected the occupants and installed themselves and their horses in their place. This did not find favour with Abbott, who knew how important it was to win the goodwill of the Dhund. Ignoring the appeals of his Sikh officers, he ordered the sowars out and restored the homes to their owners: 'The horse being the property of its rider and his principal means of subsistence, and the chance of its perishing outside being very great, it was necessary to harden my heart, by reflecting on the far wider evil of allowing the Dhoonds to believe that British troopers may stable their chargers in the bedchambers of the wives and daughters of their allies.'

The continued refusal of the Dhund to fight or to parley forced Abbott to try more subtle tactics. Handing over command of the field force to Jhunda Singh, with instructions to rebuild a number of Sikh forts in the Dhund country and to install garrisons in each, he himself started on a rough settlement of the region. In the course of that work he discovered – or so he claimed – that the land assessments set by previous Sikh governors were far too high: 'On visiting their arable land and observing how very small an area was available for each plough, and how many mouths each plough must feed, it became evident to me that the grain produced was barely adequate to the subsistence of the people, and that the Government should demand of the people little more than a nominal rent. I therefore stretched my authority to reduce to the utmost the assessment of these tracts.' Once the news of these revised assessments reached the Dhund tribesmen lurking in the hills, the issue was more or less settled. Their chiefs and maliks lost little time in abandoning their extremely chilly hideouts and appearing before Abbott to take the salt of the Lahore Durbar.

The submission of the Eastern Dhund meant that the whole of Hazara was now secured for the Sikh government. Abbott felt he had every reason to be proud of what he had achieved: 'In June 1847 I had commenced the duty entrusted to me of coercing the wild mountaineers of Huzara and of making a revenue settlement suitable to the capability of the land. On Christmas Day the same year I found my task completed as I descended from the last mountains of the District into the plains at their feet . . . For my own part I marvelled to find my task accomplished so speedily and without bloodshed . . . The name of Englishman had been my passport to the hearts of the people. Where I had apprehended the necessity of shedding the blood of brave men fighting for their dearest rights, the levelled matchlock had been thrown aside and I was free to deal with them as with men returning to their allegiance.'

Abbott had also succeeded in building up a close rapport with the Sikh officers who had escorted him on all his duties: 'Their obedience was so prompt and implicit, their behaviour in camp and quarters and on the march so exemplary, that it shamed the conduct of our own Native Troops.' This rapport did not, however, extend to Sirdar Chatar Singh, the Sikh Governor of Hazara, and his deputy. While outwardly cordial, their relations with Abbott had become increasingly strained with every week that passed after their first arrival in Haripur in November 1847. Abbott claims in his narrative that he always showed Chatar Singh the respect that was due to him – 'I will venture to say that no British Officer ever treated Native Gentlemen with more consideration than was evinced by me for the Governor and Deputy Governor of Huzara' – but the fact of the matter is that he was following his own agenda. Whether out of deliberate but unwritten policy, or by political instinct, Abbott's methods were such as to cause the people of Hazara increasingly to rely upon the Deputy Commissioner, representing the British, rather than Chatar Singh, representing the Sikh Government of the Punjab. Abbott's argument was that, 'having entered Huzara a year before the Sirdars [in fact it was only six months], my influence with a people who detested the Sikhs had been established previous to the arrival of the Sirdars . . . The people had thus become accustomed to resort to me in all their difficulties and it was impossible suddenly to divert their resort from my own to the Sirdar's judgement seat on his arrival as Nazim [Governor].'

James Abbott was fast making Chatar Singh's position as Governor of Hazara untenable – just as Henry Lawrence in Lahore, in the higher interests of good government, was effectively undermining and whittling away at the authority of the young Maharaja Dalip Singh and his Sikh Durbar. Convinced that Dalip Singh's mother, Rani Jindan, was fomenting opposition to the British, Lawrence had her placed under house arrest in October 1847. To every thinking Sikh sirdar the conclusion must have been inescapable: what was held in the name of the Sikhs today would, unless the process could be halted, be in the 'name of Englishman' tomorrow. Many must have shared the Rani's convictions, expressed in an angry letter from her place of confinement to Henry Lawrence: 'Why do you take possession of the kingdom by underhand means? Why do you not do it openly? On the one hand you make a show of friendship and on the other you have put us in prison. Do justice to me or I shall appeal to the London headquarters.'

Two surviving portraits of Henry Lawrence dating from this time, both miniatures painted on ivory by a Delhi artist in the EICo style, show a man lean as a greyhound, with gaunt, sunken cheeks; the hard, calculating eyes and pursed, mean mouth suggest a man of Machiavellian cunning. No doubt this is how many besides the artist saw him, but it must be remembered that Henry Lawrence had suffered months of poor health and, after fifteen hard years in India, was about to take a long-overdue furlough.

On Christmas Day 1847 James Abbott was joined in his camp on the edge of the plains below Murree by the young man he was now pleased to call his friend, John Nicholson. Together they rejoiced in the news that although their chief had temporarily vacated his post as Resident to go home to England, he had handed over to his 'able, energetic and fearless Brother, Mr John Lawrence'. The Punjab, as far as they were concerned, would remain in a safe pair of hands.

In January 1848 Henry Lawrence took ship for England in the company of his friend and ally Lord Hardinge, the departing Governor-General. Although well aware that there was still wide-spread unrest among the Sikhs, both were satisfied that much progress had been achieved in the Punjab. But no sooner had their vessel left the Hoogly for the open seas than the new Governor-General, Lord Dalhousie, on the grounds that his predecessor had shown too much favour to the Lawrences, acted to remove John Lawrence from the post of Acting Resident and Chief of the Council of Regency. In Lawrence's place he nominated Sir Frederick Currie, a member of the Governor-General's Council, whose chief qualification for a position demanding 'the highest capacities of the soldier and the statesman' was that he had drawn up the 1846 treaty with the Sikhs. So it came about that an inexperienced office-wallah from Calcutta, appointed by an equally inexperienced Governor-General, was placed upon the hottest political seat in India. Ignoring the advice of the men on the ground, they turned instead to a blinkered, obstinate Commander-in-Chief, the recently-created Baron Gough of Ching-keangfoo, Maharajpur and Sutlej. Together, this dire triumvirate proceeded to propel the Punjab into the Second Sikh War.

The ancient city of Multan, lying some two hundred miles south-west of Lahore on the western extremity of the Punjab, had been seized from the Afghans by Ranjit Singh in 1818. Since then it and the surrounding province had been ruled by Hindu governors appointed by Ranjit Singh, first Sawan Mal, then his son Mulraj. Both had been allowed to govern as semi-independent rulers, on payment of generous tribute to the Sikhs. Over a period of almost twenty years Dewan Mulraj had grown both immensely rich, and accustomed to the idea of ruling more or less as he pleased. He was, in John Lawrence's opinion, a 'ruler of the old school, and so long as he paid his revenues he considered the province his own to make the best of'. However, the death of Ranjit Singh encouraged Dewan Mulraj to hold back those revenues. When the Lahore Durbar called upon him to pay what was due he temporised, saying that he wished to step down and hand over the governorship to his son. John Lawrence had been instructed by his brother to take no new initiatives, so that when Dewan Mulraj informed him of his wish to resign, John asked him to defer his decision until Sir Frederick Currie should have arrived in Lahore, in early March 1848, to take over from him.

In John Lawrence's words, Currie very soon proved himself 'a regular Pecksniff', alienating his new staff as soon as he arrived by ordering them to move out of the Residency building and find accommodation elsewhere. Under the Lawrences it had become customary for the junior political assistants serving in Lahore to quarter themselves somewhere in that curious mausoleum, even if it meant doubling and trebling up. Henry Lawrence himself had been quite happy to share a room with Herbert Edwardes, and with Edwardes's immediate successor. The man from Calcutta put a stop to all this chumminess. 'In yours and my time there was neither privacy nor comfort,' wrote John to his brother in England. 'Now there will perhaps be too much of both.' More seriously, Currie also curtailed the Lawrence brothers' practice of following native tradition in making their office open to petitioners, and of hearing anyone who called on them. 'With you we contest and badger and dispute,' John Lawrence quotes a Sikh notable as saying to him. 'You are one of our own. But what can we do with Currie Sahib?'

Currie made no effort to find out what lay behind Dewan Mulraj's machinations. He accepted Mulraj's resignation at its face value and decided to replace him with a Sikh governor from Lahore, Sirdar Khan Singh. At the same time, he made it known that he would be disbanding some of the Dewan's local troops and replacing them with new regiments, also from Lahore. The first of these would accompany Sirdar Khan Singh as his escort, together with a British political agent and a British military commander. William Hodson was expecting to be given the political post but, to his disgust, Currie selected Lieutenant Patrick Vans Agnew. With Vans Agnew went Lieutenant William Anderson, a young infantry officer of the Bombay Army who knew the Multan province well and had previously accompanied Vans Agnew on a political mission to Gilgit.

For reasons unknown, these two officers chose to make their way to Multan by sailing in comfort down the Ravi, while Sirdar Khan Singh and his escort marched overland. As a result, these troops, consisting of five hundred Gurkha infantrymen bolstered by a troop of cavalry and eighty artillerymen, reached Multan without getting to know either of the British officers. Nor did these two seem to be aware that they might be viewed by Dewan Mulraj and the Multanis as the agents of unwelcome change. 'We do not yet know precisely what our duties are to be,' wrote Anderson, *en voyage* downriver, to an old friend from his regiment, Henry Daly, 'but I fancy I shall be obliged to disband some 3000 or 4000 irregular troops of Mulraj, the late jaradar [tax-collector] . . . My other duties will be to help Agnew as much as possible in his revenue and magisterial transactions. To say that I am a lucky fellow, Daly, is less than the truth.'

They joined the military column at Multan on 18 April, and were received by Dewan Mulraj with every sign of friendliness. On the following day the two British officers, together with a small escort of mounted horse, accompanied Sirdar Khan Singh as he was taken by Dewan Mulraj on a tour of Multan's fort, which crowned the centre of the city. Mulraj ceremonially handed over the keys to Sirdar Khan Singh, and they then turned about and began to ride out of the fort. However, as the two British officers were crossing the bridge over the moat a sentry pushed his way past their mounted escort, stabbed Vans Agnew with a spear and then slashed at his arm with his sword. This appeared to be the signal for a concerted attack on the two Britons; Anderson was immediately surrounded by a mob of Multani irregulars, pulled from his horse and set upon. Rallying the mounted escort, Sirdar Khan Singh rescued Anderson and Vans Agnew from the crowd and carried them to the Idgah, a Muslim place of worship a short distance outside the walls of the city, where they had encamped the night before. Here Vans Agnew dictated a few lines addressed to Sir Frederick Currie in Lahore and handed them to a despatch rider. A second horseman was given a copy and ordered to cross the Chenab and the Indus and ride towards Bannu.

Unknown to Vans Agnew, an ally was less than sixty miles away. In the late afternoon of 22 April, Herbert Edwardes was camped beside the river Indus at Dera Futteh Khan, hearing evidence in a court case, his tent packed with Baluchi tribesmen, when an exhausted rider galloped into his camp. He carried a letter which he had been ordered to deliver to the senior British officer in Bannu. From the messenger's agitated manner Edwardes deduced, as did everyone else present, that this was no ordinary letter. He opened it and read the copy of Patrick Vans Agnew's desperate appeal for help, written in the clear copperplate handwriting of a Company munshi:

> My dear Sir Frederick,
> You will be sorry to hear that, as Anderson and I were coming out of the fort gate, after having received charge of the fort by Dewan Moolraj, we were attacked by a couple of soldiers, who, taking us unawares, succeeded in wounding us both pretty sharply. Anderson is worse off, poor fellow. He has a severe wound on the thigh, another on the shoulder, one on the back of the neck, and one in the face. I think it most necessary that a doctor should be sent down, though I hope not to need one myself. I have a smart gash in the left shoulder, and other in the same arm. The whole Mooltan troops have mutinied, but we hope to get them round. They have turned our two companies out of the fort.
> Yours in haste,
> Lt P.A. Vans Agnew

To this was added a few lines scribbled in pencil in Vans Agnew's own handwriting:

> My dear Sir,
> You have been ordered to send one regiment here. Pray let it march instantly, or, if gone, hasten it to top-speed. If you can spare another, pray send it also. I am responsible for the measure. I am cut up a little, and on my back. Lieutenant Anderson is much worse. He has five sword wounds. I have two in my left arm from warding sabre cuts and a poke in the ribs with a spear. I don't think Moolraj has anything to do with it. I was riding with him when we were attacked. He rode off, but is now said to be in the hands of the soldiery. Khan Singh and his people all right.
> Yours in haste,
> P.A. Vans Agnew
> 19th 2 p.m.

Shocked, Edwardes read and reread the letter, conscious that all eyes in the courtroom were on him: 'No one spoke, not a pen moved, and there was that kind of hush which comes over an assembly under some infinite feeling of alarm. I never remember in my life being more moved, or feeling more painfully the necessity of betraying no emotion.' Finally, Edwardes looked up and told the messenger he would attend to him shortly. Then, in an admirable display of English sang-froid, he resumed the trial: 'Turning to the gaping *moonshees* I bade them "go on with the evidence", and the disappointed crowd once more bent their attention to the witnesses. But from that moment I heard no more. My eyes, indeed, were fixed mechanically on the speakers, but my thoughts were at Multan with my wounded countrymen.'

Once the trial was over Edwardes, knowing that he was the nearest to hand, at once began to put together a relieving force. His own escort was too small to attempt a rescue, so he sent messengers out to every chief in the area, calling on them to show their support for him by immediately despatching as many men and arms as they could spare. The response was more than he could have hoped for, and within thirty-six hours he had mustered a scratch army of some three thousand 'bold villains ready to risk their own throats and cut those of anyone else', with promises of more to come. Edwardes wrote later with enormous affection of his 'bold villains': 'The officers I learned to know well – their characters, their circumstances, and their wants; and, by living the same life as they did, wearing the same dress, talking the same language, and sharing with them all dangers and fatigues, they became attached to me and I to them.' One in particular, Kowrah Khan Khosh, a chief of the Khostwal Pakhtuns – 'brave, so humble, so hot in fight, so cool in council' – became a greatly admired friend.

No sooner had Edwardes crossed the Indus on 24 April than he heard that Vans Agnew and Anderson were dead. Once in the Idgah, Sirdar Khan Singh had tried to organise their defences; but the open-sided building was indefensible. During the night of 19 April most of the troops slipped away, and by dawn on the following morning a mere handful remained. This is the only instance in the course of the long relationship between the British and the

Gurkhas in which Gurkha troops (albeit in the service of the Sikh Durbar) deserted their British officers – and it is an episode few historians of the alliance have cared to mention. What happened thereafter was later pieced together by Herbert Edwardes from talking to Sirdar Khan Singh and a number of other eye-witnesses:

> An indistinct and distant murmur reached the ears of the few remaining inmates of the Idgah . . . Louder and louder it grew, until it became a cry – the cry of a multitude for blood . . . A Company of Mulraj's Mazbis – outcasts, turned Sikh – led the mob. It was an appalling sight, and Sirdar Khan Singh begged of Vans Agnew to be allowed to wave a sheet and sue for mercy. Through weak in body from loss of blood, Vans Agnew's heart failed him not. He replied: 'The time for mercy is gone; let none be asked for. They can kill us two if they like; but we are not the last of the English: thousands of Englishmen will come down here when we are gone, and annihilate Moolraj and his soldiers and his fort.'

The crowd poured into the building, pushed aside Khan Singh and surrounded the two wounded officers. Vans Agnew was sitting by Anderson's bedside, holding his hand and speaking words of comfort to him, when he received several blows from a tulwar which finally took off his head. Anderson was hacked to death where he lay. There is no evidence that Mulraj was party to the original conspiracy, but the deaths of Vans Agnew and Anderson left him no option but to become leader of what was principally, at this point, a Sikh sepoys' revolt. At his durbar on the following day he taunted Sirdar Khan Singh, presenting him with Vans Agnew's head in a sack and telling him to return to Lahore with 'the head of the youth he had brought down to govern at Mooltan'.

On the basis of further intelligence received from Multan, Edwardes concluded that Dewan Mulraj was now seeking to widen a local revolt into a Sikh uprising that would oust the British from the Punjab. He sent despatches to Sir Frederick Currie in Lahore and to Lord Gough in Simla, urging them to lose no time in sending whatever troops they could muster to Multan. John Lawrence, now returned to his post as Commissioner of the Trans-

Sutlej Jullunder Doab, did the same; informing Currie that he himself could summon brigades from Ferozepore and Jullunder and march on Multan without delay, he added: 'I see great objections to this course but even greater ones in delay.'

Abbott, in Hazara, shared John Lawrence's belief that an immediate response was vital if the Multan uprising was not to spread to other parts of the Punjab. Indeed, the revolt merely confirmed what he had already suspected: that a long-planned Sikh conspiracy was being put into action. He had by now built up a highly effective network of what he termed 'voluntary collectors of intelligence' among the tribal population of his district: 'My intimate relations with the people of Huzara, who had access to me at all hours, even during my meals or when I rode out to breathe the fresh air . . . afforded unusual opportunities of gathering and collecting intelligence.' Some months earlier one of these spies or informants had brought him what he regarded as clear evidence of a Sikh conspiracy: an angry Sikh soldier had been heard to boast that the British were to be ousted from the Punjab at the end of the month of April. Abbott, writing to warn Lahore, had been assured by Currie that such a plot was out of the question. Then, only a few days before the Multan killings, while he was out on tour, Abbott received an urgent summons from the Sikh governor, Chatar Singh, urging him to return to Haripur. Here he was regaled with a confused story about raiders from Swat having crossed the Indus into Hazara territory; but when he at once set his foot back in the stirrup and announced that he was off to investigate, he was held back by Chatar Singh, who claimed there was no need, because the raiders had been dealt with. Though he could not guess why, Abbott immediately suspected that the Governor had deliberately lured him back to Haripur and was now seeking to detain him there. When within days Chatar Singh brought him the news of the Multan killings, these suspicions seemed to be confirmed.

Like his colleagues, Abbott's first action was to write to Lahore urging Currie to take prompt action. Some weeks later he received a devastating reply: the Hot Weather was now upon them and, that being so, the Commander-in-Chief had decided that he would not risk marching British troops over the Indian plains. He therefore declined to send any into the Punjab 'until the close of the Summer and Rainy seasons' – in effect, not for another six months.

For Abbott, as for George Lawrence and John Nicholson in Peshawar, and Herbert Edwardes and Reynell Taylor in the wilds of Derajat and Bannu – all, it should be remembered, deeply shocked by the murder of their colleagues – there was only one conclusion to be drawn: they were on their own. 'As we learned from Lahore that no army would advance for the next six months,' writes Abbott, 'it was manifest that upon the district officers lay the onus of preventing the threatened chaos.'

For his part, Abbott began to bombard the Resident with a succession of outspoken letters that grew increasingly intemperate as the weeks passed. They scuppered his career prospects – but, as Abbott says in his own justification, he felt he had no option but to let Currie know 'the opinion entertained by *all* his District Officers, upon the feeble and unEnglish policy of deferring to punish an outrage so atrocious upon British honour . . . My letters can be defended by the consideration alone of the extremity of the case. I hoped that, if they failed to convince the Resident, they would open the eyes of the Governor General to the necessity of interference.'

Abbott's colleagues felt equally strongly, but behaved more diplomatically. We can gauge Herbert Edwardes's feelings from a private letter sent to William Hodson at the Lahore Residency on 24 May. For a month Edwardes had been firing off letters to Currie begging him to send troops to his assistance, and had had not a single reply. In the absence of any response from Lahore, he had begun to take on Mulraj with his own small army of irregulars. Having gained an important ally in the person of the Nawab of Bahawalpur, a powerful chieftain of Arab origin whose ancestors had won large tracts of land east of the Indus from the Rajputs, he had, with help from a Baluchi chieftain, attacked and captured the strategic fort at Dera Ghazi Khan: 'The success should be followed up by Bahawal Khan [the Nawab of Bahawalpur] crossing the Sutlej, my crossing the Indus, and driving all Mulraj's troops into the fort [at Multan], after which you might wait as many months as you chose with both safety and dignity until you were ready with a siege. Every post I urge this to the Resident, and I am quite sick of every post bringing no reply!'

Edwardes was furious with Currie for yielding to Gough's wish to postpone hostilities till the autumn. 'Postpone a rebellion!' he writes in his letter to Hodson, 'Was ever such a thing heard of in any government? Postpone avenging the blood of two British officers! *Should* such a thing be ever heard of in British Asia? I read in the papers of enormous military preparations. Editors puff the advancing columns. You tell me of a future 25,000 men, fifty siege guns etc., etc., and all for what? Forsooth, to do nothing for five months! It is a burlesque upon politics, war, and government. Give me two of all these prophesied brigades, and Bahawal Khan and I will fight the campaign for you while you are perspiring behind tatties [sun-screens] in Lahore and bottling up your British "indignation" at the slaughter of our countrymen. Action, action, action! Promptitude! These are the watchwords which constitute iqbal.'

Too politic to speak his mind outright to Sir Frederick Currie, Edwardes vented his anger on the unfortunate Hodson:

Some extraordinary infatuation rests upon you all in Lahore. You talk quite coolly and at ease: 'Send away the queen' [Maharaja Dalip Singh's mother, Rani Jindan] and 'breathe again'; 'trust I am now getting over the worst' – and argue yourselves into the belief that 'Mulraj is in a bad way', 'at a standstill' and, in fact, on the eve of submission! Clearly you are under the thumb of some awful traitor whose interest it is to keep you in the dark. Mulraj is daily adding to his means of resistance; digging up and mounting long-buried guns; enlisting on an average 100 men per diem, collecting revenue etc. etc. Is this the sort of 'standstill' you all contemplate for five months? . . . While I write this the rebels are firing a salvo on the opposite side of the river, and have already fired nearly 100 rounds!

In suggesting that Hodson was in Currie's camp, Edwardes was doing him less than justice. Hodson and his commanding officer, Joe Lumsden, had spent the greater part of the last month in the saddle with detachments of the Guides' Cavalry and Infantry, chasing from one hot-spot to another in an increasingly futile attempt to quell outbreaks of rebellion among the regular Sikh regiments quartered in the larger towns of the eastern Punjab, stronghold of the old Khalsa Dal. What had begun as a trickle of desertions of regular Sikh troops was now becoming a flood, and their example spurred hundreds of former sepoys and sowars of Sikh regiments disbanded after the war to take up arms once more. 'We are surrounded here with treachery,' Hodson wrote to his father on 7 May. 'No man can say who is implicated, or how far the treason has spread. The life of no British officer, away from Lahore, is worth a week's purchase. It is a pleasant sort of government to prop up, when their head men conspire against you and their troops desert you on the slightest temptation.'

It now became imperative that all the strategic forts still garrisoned by Sikh regulars should be taken over by EICo troops before these too went over to the rebels. One of the most important was Govindgarh, outside the Sikh holy city of Amritsar. The task of securing it was given to Lumsden's Guides, but since Joe Lumsden and the bulk of the Guides' Cavalry were already committed elsewhere, it was his second-in-command who took up the challenge. To seize what he describes as 'Ranjit Singh's treasure-fort', Hodson despatched a platoon of Guides' Infantry under the command of a young subadar named Rasul Khan, with orders to gain entrance to the fort by subterfuge and to hold it until the main force commanded by Sir Frederick Currie arrived.

It was a typical Guides coup. A few days later Hodson wrote to his father describing how his men had 'covered themselves with glory (and dust) by the way in which they got into, and took possession of, the famed fort of Govindgarh. A hundred of my men, under a native officer – a fine lad of about twenty, whom I have petted a good deal – went up quietly to the gates on pretence of escorting four State prisoners whom I had put in irons for the occasion, were allowed to get in, and then threw up their caps and took possession of the gateway, despite the scowls, and threats, and all but open resistance of the Sikh garrison. A day afterwards a regiment marched from Lahore and went into garrison there.'

On 8 June, having just learned that another regiment of Sikh cavalry had joined the rebels at Multan, Edwardes wrote one more of his polite but pointed missives to the Resident in Lahore: 'This event is most unfortunate and commences a new crisis . . . It is painful to think what the consequences may be to Lieutenant Taylor in Bunnoo, Major Lawrence and Lieutenant Nicholson in Peshawar, and Captain Abbott in Huzara . . . In the territory of which I have charge, I conceive it to be my immediate duty to extricate my junior and assistant, Lieutenant Taylor, from the meshes of the army in Bunnoo.'

Reynell Taylor had sent the greater part of the troops garrisoned at Duleepgurh south to support Edwardes and, as a result, had left himself vulnerable to attack by the remainder still at Bannu, mostly Sikh infantry and artillerymen. In accordance with Edwardes's instructions, he now handed over charge of the fort of Duleepgurh to a Tiwana malik named Fatteh Khan and rode north to join George Lawrence in Peshawar. In delegating this responsibility to Fatteh Khan Edwardes had made one of the hardest decisions of his life, knowing as he did that he had effectively signed the malik's death-warrant. Fatteh Khan was an old friend of Edwardes, a man whom he had helped set free from the clutches of Maharaja Gulab Singh of Kashmir and Jammu the year before. He was, in Edwardes's opinion, 'of all others the man for desperate times', but also much hated by the Sikhs. Having been selected, Fatteh Khan, had no option, according to the code of honour of his people, but to do as Edwardes wished: 'I shall never forget the ghastly smile with which he replied, clasping me by the knees, "I would have wished to go with you to Mooltan; but as there is work to do in Bunnoo, I will go. I owe you both life and honour, and as there is a God in heaven I will pay the debt!"'

The inevitable followed: very soon after Taylor's departure the Sikhs in the garrison rose against Fatteh Khan, seizing the guns and forcing him and the Pakhtun irregulars with him to retreat into the inner citadel of the fort. When their water ran out Fatteh Khan's followers urged him to make terms with the besieging Sikhs, but this he refused to do, on the grounds that he had given his word to Reynell Taylor that he would not surrender. He then took up his tulwar and shield and ordered the gates of the fort to be opened. If Edwardes's account of his death is to be believed, Fatteh Khan then advanced on the enemy shouting out a challenge: 'I am Mullick Fatteh Khan, Towannuh! Do not shoot me like a dog; but if there be any two among you equal to a man, come on!' He immediately went down in a fusillade of musket-balls.

Herbert Edwardes's own day of glory came soon afterwards at the long-forgotten battle of Kineyri, fought on 18 June, celebrated throughout Britain at that time as 'Waterloo Day'. Edwardes's Waterloo in 1848 was, in its own way, equally decisive. By now his little army of Muslim irregulars had been reinforced by the Nawab of Bahawalpur's troops and two regiments of Sikh infantry, together with some field guns, under the command of Colonel Van Cortlandt, an officer of mixed race who had served under Ranjit Singh as a free-lance commander. Telling himself that 'no Englishman could be beaten on the 18th of June', Edwardes crossed the Chenab River at daybreak on a ferry-boat at the head of his Pakhtun irregulars and immediately came under fire from Mulraj's cannon. Remembering what he had witnessed at Mudki and Sobraon, Edwardes resisted the temptation to advance on the enemy's position before Van Cortlandt's guns could be brought to bear. But Van Cortlandt was caught up in the laborious process of ferrying 1,500 men, together with those guns, across the river; sending him a note to come up with all speed, Edwardes ordered his men to lie down behind whatever cover they could find, and wait.

To do nothing but lie on the ground while being bombarded by Sikh artillery was not something his allies could countenance indefinitely, however. After seven hours they had had enough, and demanded that Edwardes give the order to attack. 'Every one', complains Edwardes, 'thought he was a general, and if I would only listen to *him* (pulling me by the sleeve to interrupt my rebuke of someone else) the battle would be mine.'

This arguing very soon stopped when the Sikhs were seen to be leaving their positions and advancing, preceded by a mass of horse many times greater than Edwardes had under command. Knowing that his infantry were too few to withstand a cavalry charge, Edwardes had no option but to order his own mounted irregulars, hidden in cover to one side of his position, to charge the enemy's cavalry on the flank: 'Spreading their hands to heaven, the noble band solemnly repeated the creed of their religion as though it were their last act on earth, then passed their hands over their beards with the haughtiness of martyrs, and drawing their swords, dashed out of the jungle into the ranks of the enemy's horse who, wholly taken by surprise, turned round and fled, pursued by Foujdar Khan and his companions to within a few hundred yards of the rebel line.'

The charge threw the enemy's cavalry into confusion, but failed to halt the advance of Mulraj's infantry. Under cover of a heavy discharge of round-shot they marched forward in well-ordered columns until they were within six hundred yards of Edwardes's position and then, to the command of drumbeats, wheeled into extended line. At this most desperate juncture a bugle call from the rear of Edwardes's position suddenly and dramatically announced the approach of Van Cortlandt's two regiments of regular infantry – and his battery of guns. To buy time for these to take up their positions, Edwardes ordered his Pakhtun maliks to form a defensive line between the advancing enemy and his own reinforcements: 'Standards were shaken in the wind, ranks closed, swords grasped, and matches blown, and the long line waved backwards and forwards with agitation as it stood between the coming friend and the coming foe.' In the very nick of time, as the Sikh infantry were about to discharge their first volleys, Van Cortlandt's guns appeared; the ranks of the Pakhtun line parted to let them through, and Edwardes's little army now assumed the offensive.

The first volley of Van Cortlandt's six-pounders, firing grape over open sights, tore through the massed Sikh infantry with devastating effect. Taken completely by surprise, the blue and white lines halted, wavered, then broke apart. Seizing the moment, Edwardes called for his men to charge. 'Away they went,' he writes, 'Soobhan Khan himself, a stout heavy soldier, leading them on and leaping over bushes like a boy.' It now became a race to see whether they could get to the Sikh guns before the rebel infantry could regroup to defend them. Through the confusion Edwardes saw half a dozen horsemen detach themselves from his Pakhtun cavalry, gallop through his own advancing infantry and hurl themselves on the nearest Sikh guns: 'Their leader received a ball full in the face, and fell over the "cannon's mouth". It was Shah Niwaz Khan of Esaukheyl, whose family I had recalled from exile to rule over his own country. The regiment followed and carried at the point of the bayonet the only gun which awaited their assault . . . Our whole force now advanced over the contested ground, the men shouting as they passed the captured gun.'

Back once more behind their original breastworks, Mulraj's guns began to fire again. But Van Cortlandt had brought his dozen six-pounders forward, and as soon as they were in position Edwardes called for a second charge:

Now I gave the word for the whole line of wild Puthans to be let loose upon the enemy. One volley from our battery, and they plunged into the smoke-filled space between the armies with a yell that had been gathering malice through hours of impatient suffering . . . In vain the rebels tried to rally and reply. Our infantry was on them, and another and another gun was abandoned in the flight . . . Thus, without a General, without order, and without hope, the rebels were beaten back upon Noonar; and having placed its sheltering heights between them and their pursuers for a moment, they threw aside shame and arms, and fled, without once halting, to Mooltan.

So ended the battle of Kineyri, where Dewan Mulraj's army left five hundred dead on the battlefield, together with six artillery pieces and their ammunition: a victory won in large part by undisciplined, irregular levies commanded by a twenty-nine-year-old lieutenant. A second encounter, hard on the heels of the first, forced Mulraj's troops back to the safety of Multan – where they remained. The city and its fortress were too strong and too well defended to be assaulted without siege batteries, so Edwardes had to content himself with containing Mulraj in the city – 'like a terrier barking at a tiger' – until a proper army could be sent to relieve him.

It appears entirely in character for Sir Frederick Currie, having declined to take any responsibility for the events that led to the deaths of Vans Agnew and Anderson and turned a deaf ear to the appeals of his subordinates, to now claim credit for Edwardes's remarkable campaign – just as he later claimed to have heeded Abbott's warnings of a Sikh conspiracy led by Chatar Singh. Currie's continuing refusal to see things as they really were led

John Nicholson, in a rare expression of wit, to confer on him the title of 'the Rosy One'. Writing from Peshawar to James Abbott on 1 July, Nicholson commiserated with him over the Resident's refusal to heed his warnings of unrest among the Sikh regiments still in Hazara. 'It is impossible ever to fathom the Rosy One's real intentions,' he went on to say. 'We are without further news from Multan or Lahore, save that the Resident talks of the success of *his* "Muhammaden combination" and the way in which *he* "humbugged the Khalsa". I imagine he will make a favourable report of E. [Edwardes] for so well carrying out his plans and instructions. I will get [George] Lawrence to send you a letter he had from him yesterday – an amusing but disgusting production.'

As the days became weeks and the weeks first one month and then a second, and still the Government was seen to be doing nothing to oppose Mulraj in Multan, so, in John Lawrence's artlessly mixed metaphor, 'like the waves of the sea, step by step the rebellion spread'. In the rarefied heights of Simla, Lord Gough remained obdurate, and Lord Dalhousie with him; but down below in the Hot Weather furnace of Lahore the 'Rosy One' at last gave way before the deluge of letters from his political assistants – although not until he had safely tucked away in his pocket a note from the Governor-General giving him a free hand. In late July 1848 the Acting Resident despatched an army to Multan, but an army devoid of British troops or British officers and made up largely of Sikhs led by Sikh officers. Its overall command was given to Raja Sher Singh, son of Chatar Singh, the Governor of Hazara; and it was to be reinforced by additional Sikh regiments sent from Hazara under the command of the Deputy-Governor of Hazara, Jundial Singh. It seems not to have entered Currie's head that this might be a fateful combination.

In Hazara, Abbott's delight over Currie's decision to send an army to Multan turned to dismay when details of its composition reached him, convinced as he now was that Chatar Singh, Jundial Singh, Sher Singh and Mulraj were ringleaders in a plot to revive the Sikh Khalsa and throw the British out of the Punjab. He had now learned from one of his spies that shortly before his mysterious recall to Haripur a secret meeting of Sikh sirdars drawn from all corners of the Punjab had taken place in Chatar Singh's house.

He suspected that the army now being sent to invest Mulraj at Multan would, sooner or later, switch sides.

Over the preceding year many of the Sikh officers attached to Jundial Singh's contingent had become Abbott's friends. When the time came for them to march south with their regiments to join Sher Singh's army, Abbott was filled with the deepest foreboding, believing them to be marching to their destruction. Many of the officers shared his disquiet. 'Several of them were in tears,' he later recalled. 'My own heart was sad enough, for it seemed to me probable that we should never again meet as friends, and that they were marching to ruin, worse than death. Old Colonel Boodh Singh, commander of the celebrated Cherunjeet Cavalry Corps, came to me in tears, and made me place his hand in that of Sirdar Jundial Singh. It was his corps that first broke into open rebellion, soon after this leave-taking. So we parted with heavy hearts; and I never met with any of them again.'

As Abbott feared, and as Sir Frederick Currie should have anticipated, Sher Singh's army, having marched to Multan, there changed sides to become the mainstay of the Sikh revolt.

7

'Huzara and its part in the Second Sikh War'

JAMES ABBOTT AND HAZARA, 1848–1849

> I despise the man who does not guide his life by honour.
> The very word drives me mad.
> And when a man is mad, what does he care if he wins or
> loses a fortune?

> Khushul Khan Khattak (1613–1691),
> Warrior-poet of the Pakhtuns

EVEN BEFORE the Hazara contingent had joined up with Sher Singh's army, Hazara's Deputy Commissioner had taken to the hills. Abandoning his headquarters in Haripur, James Abbott decamped to a small house he had had built for himself as a 'summer residence' on a knoll above Shirwan, a remote mountain village about twenty-four miles north of Haripur. Here he stayed, in defiance of Sir Frederick Currie's order to return at once to Haripur and apologise to Chatar Singh for his lack of trust in him. 'In Huzara I was a state Prisoner to the Sikh troops and garrison,' Abbott argued. 'To change my residence was imperative if I was to remain master of Huzara.'

Towards the end of July 1848 Abbott received news that a full brigade of Sikhs stationed in the plain of Pakli to the north of him was on the move. The village maliks of the area reported that the Sikh troops had 'sold off their supplies, broken up their bazaar, recalled their marching cattle from graze, and . . . given out that they were about to march on 1st August.' It was plain to Abbott that their intention was to join forces with Chatar Singh in Haripur. This he was determined to prevent.

To reach Haripur the Pakli brigade would have to break through the intervening hills by way of the Mangali Pass, so Abbott at once turned for help to 'the best and bravest of the petty chiefs of the villages near the Manghal Pass, Peer Khan by name. Him I now despatched with all secrecy, well provided with money to collect together in the pass and supply with ammunition a body of peasantry sufficient to man the pass, promising to join him as soon as the actual march should be signalled by beacon.'

News of the blocking of the pass reached the Sikhs of the Pakli brigade, and they stayed put. However, less than a week later Abbott received an alarming message from Haripur. It was from an American soldier of fortune named Kennedy, who taken service in Ranjit Singh's army as an artillery officer and now, under the *nom de guerre* of 'Colonel Canara', commanded Chatar Singh's artillery. His message was that he had been ordered by Chatar Singh to move his guns out of the town and park them under the walls of the nearby fort; he had refused to act without Abbott's approval, and now feared the worst because Chatar Singh had summoned to Haripur a Sikh regiment based outside his jurisdiction, at Hasan Abdal. What, he asked, should he do? Abbott had scarcely finished reading this when a second messenger arrived with the news that Colonel Canara was dead. Abbott relates the event thus in his memoir:

Chattur Singh would not hear of any delay. He commanded instant compliance. This Canara declined. Chattur Singh then sent two of his companies of infantry to storm the guns. Canara ordered his trembling gun crews to double charge the guns with grape. When the infantry advanced, he ordered his men to fire. The men trembled and hesitated. Canara seized a linstock [the staff holding the match] and applied it to the vent of one of the guns. It burned priming [the gunpowder on the firing pan]. He applied the match to the second gun. That, too, burned priming. Whether through treachery or fear, they had probably not been loaded. A servant of Chattur Singh creeping behind Canara, as with sword and pistol he stood singly opposed to a host, shot him through the back, and carrying his head to Chattur Singh, was rewarded by that chief with one hundred pounds for that dastardly murder.

The killing of Colonel Canara should have ended once and for all Sir Frederick Currie's belief that Sirdar Chatar Singh was what he professed to be: a loyal servant of the Durbar. But Abbott, by isolating himself in the mountains north of Haripur, had made it easy for Chatar Singh to cut his lines of communication with Lahore; his mail was intercepted, so that the first accounts of Canara's murder received by the Acting Resident in Lahore came from the Sikh Governor himself, who was able to convince Currie that this unfortunate event had been the result of an act of mutiny on Canara's part, inspired by James Abbott. Astonishing as it now seems, Currie 'readily adopted that account and transmitted it in triumph to the Governor General'.

Fortunately, not all Abbott's mail was sabotaged. One messenger from Shirwan evaded Chatar Singh's guards and reached George Lawrence in Peshawar, providing him with a detailed account of events in Hazara. Abbott ended with a plea that immediate steps be taken to secure the highway linking Peshawar with Rawalpindi and Lahore, so as to isolate Chatar Singh from the rest of the Punjab. Going immediately to Nicholson's bungalow, George Lawrence found his assistant on his bed, laid low by a bout of fever. Nevertheless, having listened in silence to what his chief had to say, Nicholson asked at once what he could do. Emphasising the absolute necessity of securing the fort at Attock, Lawrence added: 'Had you been fit for the work I should have wished to send you; but that is out of the question. Herbert or Bowie must go in your place.' As Lieutenants Herbert and Bowie were both newcomers to the Punjab, the mere idea was enough to make Nicholson tumble from his bed with the remark, 'Never mind the fever; I will start tonight.'

At sunset that evening Nicholson climbed into the saddle to ride out of Peshawar at the head of a troop of sixty Pakhtun irregulars, together with two companies of newly-recruited Muslim matchlockmen. Only three of the sixty horsemen were known to him before he set out, yet they stuck with him, which says a great deal about both Pakhtun character and the man they followed. They rode through the night and arrived at the banks of the Indus just after first light, having covered a distance of some fifty miles. Only half the irregulars had been able to sustain Nicholson's pace, but with these thirty he crossed the bridge of boats at Attock and rode up and into the fort. His sudden appearance at this early hour gave Nicholson an advantage which he exploited to the full. Calling out to the startled guards at the main gate to gather their weapons and follow him, he rode on to secure the inner citadel of the fort. When the sentries at a third gate raised their weapons against him he leaped from his horse, wrenched the musket from the hands of the man nearest him and, in a furious voice, ordered the others to arrest their guard commander. Deprived of their officers, still half-asleep and unable to grasp what was afoot, the Sikh regulars who made up the bulk of the garrison meekly obeyed. On Nicholson's further instructions they turned out on parade, grounded their arms on command and then, to his further command, marched out of the fort. Within a matter of minutes and without a shot having been fired, the entire fort was his. 'That I was able to effect this', wrote Nicholson to George Lawrence later, with characteristic understatement, 'is owing to the staunchness of the irregulars, whom I harangued with happy effect, notwithstanding the efforts of the regulars to mislead them.'

The coup at Attock sowed the first seed of the 'Nikal Seyn' legend among the Sikh soldiery, and to look at what followed from a Sikh perspective is to begin to understand how and why that legend so swiftly took such firm hold.

With the arrival of Nicholson's two companies of infantry, Attock was safely secured. His next priority was to prevent Chatar Singh leaving the Hazara region, so early the next morning he handed over command of the fort to a Muslim subordinate and led his band of irregular horse on to Hasan Abdal, a small town about thirty miles down the Rawalpindi road and about the same distance from Haripur. Here they ran into a party of Sikh cavalry bivouacked by the roadside, mutineers who had turned against their colonel and were now on their way to join Chatar Singh.

As at Attock, Nicholson imposed his will instantly and decisively. 'I paraded the party and dismissed and confined the ringleaders on the spot,' he wrote in a report to Currie. 'The remainder begged forgiveness, and having some reason to believe them sincere, and wishing to show that I was not without confidence in Sikhs, I granted it. I shall, of course, keep a sharp look-out on them in future.' He could not resist closing his report with a restatement of the obvious: 'Everything, if I may offer an opinion, depends on promptly sending up troops . . . A single brigade with a nine-pounder battery would be ample, with the aid which Captain Abbott and myself would be able to render. Delay will have a bad effect in every way.'

Currie's response was entirely predictable: no troops would be sent, because the Governor-General and the Commander-in-Chief did not feel it would be right to despatch a force in any one particular direction. To Nicholson's dismay, Currie's letter also contained new orders: he was to act as peace-maker in what the Acting Resident still believed was a clash of personalities between Chatar Singh and James Abbott, precipitated by the latter's 'discourtesy' in not trusting the former. 'I consider the restoration of amicable arrangements a matter of no difficulty,' Nicholson wrote back with heavy irony, 'if the sirdar's [i.e., Chatar Singh's] conduct in tampering with the troops throughout the country, cutting off Captain Abbott's daks [mail couriers], sending agents to raise the labouring population of this and the neighbouring districts, ordering kardars [government agents] out of his jurisdiction to send him their treasuries, and writing to Maharajah Gulab Singh for armed aid, can be overlooked; for all this can be proved against him.'

Within an hour of despatching this reply Nicholson got news that more Sikh regulars were on their way to join forces with Sirdar Chatar Singh – an infantry regiment, now camped near Rawalpindi, about forty-five miles to the east. Roughly half-way between Hasan Abdal and Rawalpindi the road cuts through the east-facing limestone escarpment known as the Margalla Hills by way of the Margalla Pass, and commanding that pass was a small *burj*, a tower built on the summit of a steep-sided knoll. Nicholson believed that by taking the tower he could block the advance of the Sikh regiment. With him went his sixty horse, now supported by five hundred 'matchlockmen' send down by Abbott from Hazara, as well as a smaller group of local tribesmen.

One of these was a chieftain named Hassan Karam Khan, whose tribe, the Khattar, had entered India in the eleventh century as part of an Afghan invasion force and was now settled in the Attock and Fatehjang areas of the Punjab. Hassan Karam Khan's family home was in the village of Wah, which stands back a little from the road between the Margalla ridge and the town of Hasan Abdal and takes its name from 'Wah!', a common exclamation of delight among Punjabis, said to have been uttered at this spot by the Mughal emperor Shah Jehan. The story is that the Emperor, stopping here in 1645 on his way to Kabul, caused a garden to be made, and its appearance so pleased him that he made the exclamation which gave the staging-post its name. Hassan Karam Khan and his half-brother Fatteh Khan were the two biggest landowners in the area – and bitter rivals. While Hassan Karam Khan came to Nicholson's aid with his own body of horse and foot, Fatteh Khan held himself aloof.

The stone tower at the Margalla Pass was taken over and the high ground on either side lined with Nicholson's men, in a strong defensive position. However, when the Sikh regiment appeared two days later it halted some distance short of the pass, setting up camp inside the walls of a Muslim cemetery. Seeing that the Sikhs had failed to walk into his trap, Nicholson brought his men down from their positions in the dead of night and led them forward to a patch of jungle beside the Sikh camp. Soon after sunrise he rode up to within hailing distance and called for the colonel to come forward to parley. Within earshot of the Sikh troops Nicholson then set out for him what he declared to be their last chance: if the men returned to their duty they would be forgiven, but if they failed to do so he would consider them mutineers, and punish them accordingly. By Abbott's account, he then sat back, 'drew out his watch, and bade the Colonel observe the time. "Now!" he said. "I give you, your Regiment and guns, just one hour to commence your march back to Rawalpindi. If within that space the march be not commenced, I will destroy you, to a man."'

The debate between those among the Sikh sepoys who wished to fight and those who were now having second thoughts was, in

Nicholson's spare description, a 'stormy one'. It was conducted in full view of the tall, full-bearded figure of 'Nikal Seyn' himself, seated silent and motionless on his horse; and something about his brooding presence appears to have had a decisive effect. Just before the hour was up the Sikh colonel threw in the towel: 'He came out, begged pardon on his own behalf and that of his men, and declared their willingness to march whithersoever I directed them. I accordingly saw them en route to Rawal Pindi before leaving the ground.' For the third time in six days Nicholson's bluff had worked – and another seed had been sown.

For the next few weeks Nicholson spent up to sixteen hours a day in the saddle, riding from one spot to another with the hardiest of his Pakhtuns and Afghans in a desperate balancing act – strengthening or redeploying his levies in scattered outposts; scouting for news of armed Sikhs attempting to combine with Chatar Singh; breaking up such bodies of troops whenever they were found; and dissuading others who might be wavering from switching their allegiance. A short note he sent to James Abbott from Hasan Abdal at this time gives some idea of the pressure he was under: 'I intended writing you . . . but sleep overpowered me before the writing materials came. My fine chestnut died during the night of the effect of a gallop to Margalla and back again.' To strengthen his alliance with Abbott, Nicholson sent him a party of Khattar tribesmen under the command of the son of his new ally Hassan Karam Khan, a young lad named Muhammad Hayat Khan.

Just before the end of August 1848 Chatar Singh finally came out into the open. Proclaiming that he was 'devoting his head to the gods and his arms to the Khalsa', he declared war on the EICo and called for all loyal Sikhs to rally to his banners. James Abbott's response was to call on all loyal Hazarawals to gather under his flag at Shirwan. The first to do so were the maliks of the Mashwani tribe, who held the northern half of the Gandgar Hills – an act of faith that placed them first in Abbott's affections forever after. He describes them as a 'rugged looking race, ugly and not gracefully built, whose clothing is of cotton cloth, dyed indigo black. But they are among the truest and staunchest defenders of a hillside that the world can boast, and are good shots with their clumsy smooth-bore matchlocks.' Although few in numbers, the Mashwani came to form the central core of Abbott's irregulars, strengthened by other volunteers who came and went as the occasion demanded. Among them were Swati from the western bank of the Indus: 'Whenever an attack was expected they flocked to my standard, clad, like the Mushwanees, in black and speaking only the Pushtoo tongue. The mail worn by these men consisted of a skull cap of steel having a cowl of fine chainwork, and shirt of chain mail, the usual buckler of buffalo-hide being slung upon the back.'

More usefully, Abbott also gained the support of two hundred foot-soldiers from the Suttri tribe in Kashmir who had served as regular infantrymen under Maharaja Gulab Singh: 'They formed a Band of much use to me, because they understood and would obey orders promptly, held together on the march instead of scattering over the country like the undrilled levies, and obeyed the bugle, which the others did not comprehend. Unfortunately I could neither procure nor make them bayonets, for their firelocks.' With the addition of the Suttri, his force at times amounted to more than eighteen hundred men – never enough to take on Chatar Singh in open battle, but sufficient to harry him and prevent him from moving his army south to link up with his son Sher Singh.

The support of the Mashwani encouraged Abbott to move down from his eyrie at Shirwan and set up a new base in Mashwani territory, in a narrow ravine close to the deserted village of Nara, less than nine miles from Haripur. From here he could watch Chatar Singh's every move, and act to forestall him if he tried to march south towards Hassan Abdal or Rawalpindi. As his account makes plain, Abbott and his fellow guerrillas were forced to rough it:

I had no roofs, no tents for the shelter of my picturesque bands. Each shifted for himself, amongst the ravines, the rocks and bushes. It was the rainy season, but happily for us, no rain actually fell. The favourite bivouac was a deep ravine, south of the ruined village. The spring there wells forth from the base of the cliff, the only water procurable within an area of several miles. Here natural excavations in the cliff sheltered some, trees, shrubs and rocks others, and nearly the whole of the men crowded there. Being clad in the black cotton garb of the Pathans of the Indus, the effect was truly wild and savage. The standards varied, according to the taste of each chief. Our only martial music was the harsh clarinet of the mountains, which, as played by the natives, resembled the bagpipe or hurdy gurdy; a dolorous strain, well calculated to fill an enemy with the blue-devils. Such was the state of my Camp.

Chatar Singh's first move took Abbott by surprise: he sent an infantry regiment and two guns marching north out of Haripur, as if to relieve his Sikh brigade trapped in Pakli. Abbott's response was to take his levies on a forced march eastwards over the mountains to the Salhad Pass, midway between Haripur and Mansehra – only to learn that they had been outwitted:

I had reached the village of Sulhud, wearied with a march of thirty miles, under the scorching sun of August – a march in which one of my men died of thirst. Released for a few hours from the sultry and oppressive atmosphere of Nara, I had inhaled with delight the pure, cold breeze rushing down that cleft of the mountains where I had halted, had dined luxuriously upon the fresh bread and milk which the peasant of Huzara readily shares with travellers, and after posting my matchlockmen in the pass, had fallen asleep in the open air as I watched the beautiful stars tracing their circles in the Heaven. Suddenly I awoke at the sound of my name and found standing over me a huge turbaned figure whom I at once recognised as 'Jafir of the Dagger Hand'. My own hand stole at once to the dagger beneath my pillow for, if Jafir was famous for prowess, he was still more infamous for murder. In answer to my inquiry, he said that Nicholson had dispatched him post-haste to summon me to his assistance . . . having unexpectedly encountered Chattur Singh and his forces at the Moti ravine.

The Governor of Hazara, having tricked Abbott into moving his forces out of the way, had then marched south with the rest of his men to join his former deputy, Jundial Singh, and this enlarged force had been advancing down the Indus valley towards Hasan

Abdal when it was spotted by a band of Nicholson's scouts from Margalla.

At first Abbott refused to believe Jafir's story, and demanded that he produce a note from Nicholson to support it. But Nicholson had, it seemed, been caught without writing paper; instead, he had given Jafir an umbrella lent him by Abbott at their last encounter. Abbott recognised his umbrella, which had a pointed head carved by himself on its handle, but still found himself torn between his distrust of Jafir and his desire to help Nicholson: 'Jafir was, I knew, much trusted by Nicholson, a circumstance that often caused me uneasiness, for he was a desperate and unscrupulous ruffian . . . Nor could he be ignorant that the Nazim [Chatar Singh], who had given one hundred pounds for Canara's head, would give three times that sum, at least, for Nicholson's. The umbrella gave some air of probability to his tale. But, as he usually carried Nicholson's umbrella when not in use, he might have ridden off with it, unsanctioned.'

For all his suspicions, however, Abbott felt he had no option but to take Jafir at his word: 'The bugle, therefore, was sounded and men were sent to gather from the pass my scattered levies. And in an hour I was in full march for the Moti ravine, where the two hostile forces were said to be confronted.' This second march began just after midnight on 21 August, and ended twenty hours later: they had covered some forty miles while 'the fiery sun of August rose and set upon us again'. This double march was all the more remarkable for having been undertaken by men who, with the possible exception of Abbott himself, did not eat or drink during the hours of daylight, because it was the month of the fast of Ramadan, 'so strictly observed in Huzara that men die rather than taste even water between sunrise and sunset'.

En route they had been met by a malik named Jullal Khan, of Lungra – 'a landowner of decayed fortune, a gentlemanly fellow and a friend' – with the good news that Nicholson had been able to halt Chatar Singh, not by force of arms but by the power of his personality: ' "The Nazim," he said, "had been in full march, with his whole force, when Nicholson Sahib had encountered him and had said to him, 'If you presume to cross the Moti ravine, I will destroy you.' And Nicholson Sahib had pinned the Nazim to the spot with his eye; and there sits the Nazim still, trembling and cowering, like a sparrow in the presence of a dragon."' More precisely, Chatar Singh's force – made up of three regiments of regular infantry, five hundred horse, eight guns drawn by elephants and thirty swivel-guns mounted on camels – had been halted by the unexpected blocking of a vulnerable section of the road by an unknown number of hostile tribesmen. Keeping to the high ground, Abbott and his men skirted the Sikh camp to take up strong positions scarcely a mile from where Nicholson and his men had established themselves above the Moti ravine. Together they now effectively blocked Chatar Singh's progress south.

The Governor's response was to play for time. He wrote to Currie, pleading that his actions had yet again been misunderstood. He also sent his old lieutenant, Jundial Singh, to Nicholson with a request that he should pull back his troops as a gesture of goodwill; he felt threatened by Abbott's levies, and wished to negotiate in a less hostile atmosphere. Less familiar than his senior partner with Chatar Singh's methods, Nicholson agreed, leaving Abbott no alternative but to move his own troops back from the ravine. No sooner had they completed their withdrawal than the Sikhs brought up their eight guns and began firing on them, while the infantry ran forward to secure the positions just vacated.

The Moti ravine was the last obstacle on the road to Hasan Abdal. It marked the point at which the foothills gave way to the plains, where Abbott's tribal foot-soldiers would always be at the mercy of Chatar Singh's cavalry and guns. They now found themselves powerless to prevent Chatar Singh marching on to rendezvous with his son and the main Sikh army. And just to drive home the folly of showing mercy to an enemy in one's power – a mistake no Pakhtun would have made, and which Nicholson himself never made again – it was now learned that the Sikh regiment met below the Margalla Pass two weeks before, and ordered back to Rawalpindi, was closing in on them from the rear, having made a long detour around the Margalla Hills. This time, when Nicholson tried to repeat his earlier tactics, they were in no mood to be cowed: 'The Corps, which had then been a lamb, had since Jhunda Singh's arrival became a lion. Nicholson's commands were answered by the fire of their two guns, which killed two of his horsemen and obliged him to retire.'

Having failed to stop Chatar Singh leaving Hazara, Abbott and Nicholson were left with no option but to fall back. Abbott returned to Hazara to regroup his exhausted levies, while Nicholson returned to Attock with his Pakhtun horse. Had Chatar Singh seized his moment and continued his march, the history of the Punjab might have been very different. Unaccountably, however, he halted his advance on Hasan Abdal. A second regiment of disaffected Sikh infantry had been marking time in Rawalpindi, and it may be that Chatar Singh was waiting for them to come up before committing his army to the plains – where he too would be vulnerable.

This delay, whatever the reason behind it, provided Nicholson with a second chance, and once again, it seemed to him, the key was the Margalla Pass. He had entrusted the guardianship of that all-important *burj* – 'a rude tower of undrest stone cemented with clay' – to a Gakkar outlaw named Ata Ali Khan, a man of unpredictable mood whom Abbott thought mentally unstable. When Nicholson rode up from Attock to reclaim the tower from Ata Ali Khan, he found it held against him: angered by what he believed to be an insult inflicted on him by Abbott, Ata Ali Khan had gone over to the Sikhs.

With the Khattar chief Hassan Karam Khan and his irregulars at his side, as well as some of Abbott's Hazarawal levies, Nicholson felt that a show of force would be enough to turn Ata Ali Khan and his men out of the tower. According to Abbott, he 'judged that if he led the attack, shame would prevent his men from holding back. His levies took just the reverse view of the question, arguing that he, being ahead, could not possibly see who misbehaved. Of eight hundred matchlockmen, not one could be induced to follow him, against a handful of men posted in a small tower.' Apparently unaware that only Hassan Karam Khan and a few of his men were indeed following him, Nicholson scrambled up the steep hillside to the base of the Margalla tower – where the 'Nikal Seyn' legend was nearly stifled in its infancy.

Nicholson himself, in a letter to his mother, confesses to no more than 'a slight hurt from a stone in a skirmish in the hills . . . I have often had a worse one, however, when a boy at school, and I only mention this because a friend wrote me from Lahore that it was reported I had been seriously hurt, and I fear lest the rumour should reach and cause you anxiety.' More details come from James Abbott, probably based on what Nicholson told him. 'The Margalla Tower was built without a door,' he explains, 'being ascended by a ladder to the roof, the ladder bring drawn up by the defenders. Only Nicholson and a handful of chiefs reached the tower, under a hot fire of matchlocks, but could effect no entrance. He endeavoured in vain to tear the stones out of the uncemented wall. When close to the walls the assailants found some respite from the fire of the garrison . . . but large stones were hurled down upon their heads, and still Nicholson's dastard levies held aloof from their commander . . . He received a severe contusion to the head and two of his chiefs were slain . . . The Sikh troops sent for the relief of the tower being now close at hand, he was obliged to retire without having effected anything.'

Neither version explains how Nicholson, wounded as he was, managed to extricate himself; nor is there any account of the reason why Nicholson thereafter became so intimately bound up with the family of the Khattar chieftain Hassan Karam Khan. A chance find in an album of photographs in the Oriental and India Office Collection at the British Library adds some detail, however, and provides a much better explanation for John Nicholson's interest in Hassan Karam Khan's young son than some modern interpretations. The photographs, collected by Sir Donald Macnabb, Commissioner of Rawalpindi and Peshawar in the late 1870s and early 1880s, include two groups taken outside the Deputy Commissioner's bungalow in Kohat. Seated beside the DC in each is his political adviser on tribal affairs, Nawab Muhammad Hayat Khan, CSI, and attached to the photographs is a short note in Sir Donald's handwriting:

Muhammad Hyatt Khan was Nicholson's orderly. His father Hassan Khan, headman of Hassan Abdal, was a friend of Nicholson's after the fight at the Margalla Pass. When Nicholson joined the British Army before Chillianwalla he heard that Hassan Khan had been murdered. He sent a message to Fatteh Khan Dreg, another notable of Hassan Abdal whom he suspected of being in some way privy to the murder: 'If I get through this I'll hang you for being privy to the murder of Hassan Khan, unless you revenge him by killing the murderer.' When Fatteh Khan got the message he acted. Riding from Wah to Hassan Abdal, one of Fatteh Khan's men came up behind the murderer and shot him! Nicholson took charge of Hassan Khan's son and brought him up.

This note helps to make sense of a story of Abbott's in which he states that one of the chiefs killed at the Margalla *burj* 'left a young son, upon whom Nicholson lavished much care and attention'. Abbott wrongly calls this chief 'Futteh Khan', but he was almost certainly Fatteh Khan's half-brother Hassan Karam Khan Khattar whose son was Muhammad Hayat Khan. Abbott continues:

The boy, when about seven years old, presuming upon his influence, said one day to Nicholson: 'Sahib, I have a favour to ask. Will you promise to grant it?' Nicholson, supposing it related to some trifle, had nearly acquiesced. Happily, he determined to hear first the nature of the request. 'You must first', he said, 'tell me what you want.' 'Only, Sahib,' replied the urchin, 'your permission to kill my cousins, the children of your and of my deadly enemy Futteh Khan (another of that name).' 'To kill your cousins!' exclaimed Nicholson, doubting the evidence of his ears. 'Yes, Sahib, to kill all the boys while they are young. It's quite easy now.' 'You little monster!' said Nicholson, scarcely believing the child could be in earnest, 'would you murder your own cousins?' 'Yes, Sahib, for if I don't they will certainly murder me.'

There is no reason to doubt the substance of this story, but the boy must have been older than Abbott's account allows, because he was recognised as at least the titular head of a group of his father's men sent to join Abbott at his refuge at Nara, as noted earlier. Ten or twelve would be a more realistic estimation, since Muhammad Hayat Khan is known, nine years later, to have been playing an active soldiering role as Nicholson's right-hand man. The word 'orderly' used by Sir Donald Macnabb also needs to be corrected, suggesting as it does that he was little more than Nicholson's servant. Many of the village and clan chiefs who in these early days joined irregular corps raised by British political officers were locally powerful men who brought their own retainers with them and led them as troop-leaders. Muhammad Hayat Khan falls into this category. He rode at Nicholson's side as a medieval squire might have ridden beside his liege lord, and he often fought at his side. Similarly, Harry Lumsden had Fatteh Khan Khattak (not to be confused with Hassan Karam Khan's half-brother Fatteh Khan Khattar) at his side, as William Hodson had Sirdar Man Singh when he raised Hodson's Horse. To call such a man an orderly is to demean a very special breed. Nor should anything unhealthy be read into Nicholson having 'lavished much care and attention' on Muhammad Hayat Khan after his father's murder; he was, after all, the son of a man who was quite probably killed because of his support for Nicholson.

After the reverses suffered at the Moti and Margalla passes Abbott and Nicholson once more united their forces in an effort to thwart Chatar Singh and prevent the Sikhs from gathering in strength, but now suffered a third disappointment. At Damtour, just east of the present garrison town of Abbottabad in the heart of Hazara, they attempted to prevent Chatar Singh's army marching north from Haripur, through the Dor Valley, to link up with the Pakli brigade in Mansehra. Overtaking Chatar Singh's columns as they advanced up the Dor, they brought their levies down from the surrounding mountains and disposed them in ambush at the head of the valley to await the arrival of the enemy.

One of Abbott's chiefs had warned him that he should never run or gallop from one position to another, because such haste would be misconstrued as flight by his men. But no one had thought to offer Nicholson this same good advice. He had taken up a commanding position among the advance piquets, from which he could watch the Sikh regiments as they advanced up the valley, while Abbott stayed back with their main defensive line. As the leading column of Sikh infantry wheeled into line to attack his first piquets, Nicholson decided that reinforcements were needed. Leaving his position, he jumped onto his horse to gallop back to Abbott's line. From his own position a mile away, Abbott had to watch what ensued without being able to do a thing to stop it:

> The sight of the fearless Nicholson in what they supposed full flight terrified the whole of the levies, and was the signal for their instant flight. When Nicholson reached the nearest of our positions, whence he had hoped to gather reinforcements, not a man was there . . . The spur of the mountain-root which I occupied jutted out into the valley through which the Sikh columns were swarming. It was a sea of heads . . . As Nicholson galloped back for reinforcements and as the picket on the hilltop fled, my head turned, insensibly, in that direction to see what welcome our people would give the enemy. I looked. The whole line had vanished. Not a living thing appeared on all that ridge of hill, so lately thronged with life. I rubbed my eyes. I hoped I was dreaming; then hoped the fellows might only be crouching to avoid the enemy's fire. I hoped their matchlocks would speak in volleys as the Sikh columns came in range. But there was not a matchlock to speak. All had vanished the instant they had seen Nicholson galloping back for reinforcements.

The intended ambush became a rout as Nicholson, Abbott and their maliks sought in vain to rally their troops. Abbott was furious, but blamed himself as much as his junior. 'Certainly Nicholson and myself should not have advanced, even to reconnoitre,' he admits. 'Had our main force fired even a shot . . . we would have tried again and again the battle with Chattur Singh. But such an affair as this served only to disparage the British cause with both friend and foes.'

Thoroughly discomfited, they gathered together what remained of their allies, and conferred. It seemed pointless to continue the struggle, so they dispersed, Nicholson retiring once again to Hasan Abdal, Abbott to his ravine above Nara. 'We parted,' says Abbott, 'little expecting ever to meet again.'

For the remainder of the Hot Weather of 1848 and through the Rains that followed – a period of some six to eight weeks – John Nicholson concentrated his efforts in an area of the Punjab where he was more in his element, patrolling the open Doab country lying between the Indus and the Jhelum rivers, where his fast-moving squadrons of irregular horse could harry and punish almost at will. And this is where the 'Nikal Seyn' legend, after its brief setback at the Margalla *burj*, took firm hold – so much so that in later years Sikh mothers scolded naughty children with the warning that if they did not behave, Nikal Seyn would surely come and take them away. Here, so Abbott records in a magnificently purple passage of his memoirs, 'his fiery ardour and noble self-devotion rebuked the miserable spirit of despondence and procrastination which had so nearly sentenced to inaction a magnificent army . . . Cowardice shrunk from his presence and courage caught inspiration from his glance. And the Sikhs are not very blameable for their legend, ascribing to Nicholsyne Sahib all the glory of that campaign.' In the mountains of Hazara, however, James Abbott could at first do little but skulk in his Nara hideout and bide his time, while his scouts kept watch over Chatar Singh's movements.

In mid September 1848 the Sikh army commanded by Chatar Singh's son Sher Singh, sent by Sir Frederick Currie to reduce Multan, at last came out in open rebellion against the EICo and began a slow progress north-eastwards to combine with Chatar Singh. Until that moment the Governor of Hazara had, as we have seen, done little to advance the Sikh cause beyond marching up and down like the Grand Old Duke of York, making threatening noises. The prospect of alliance with his son now emboldened him to move his army out of Hazara once again, towards Hasan Abdal – only to turn his army about, just as before.

In the meantime James Abbott had issued a fresh call to arms, and the hill tribesmen of Hazara once again rallied to him. Greatly encouraged, he placed himself and his levies between the Sikh army, now inexplicably on its way back to Hazara again, and the hill-fort of Salamkhand, which stood isolated on a small plateau in the Gandgar Hills. Chatar Singh had left behind a large garrison of Sikhs in the fort, and it may be that he had decided to add their numbers to his force before finally marching south. In any event, Abbott got wind of Chatar Singh's movements and determined to use the opportunity to draw the Sikhs into a position where his tribesmen would have the upper hand. A mixed force of local Tarkheli and Mashwani was deployed around the fort, while Abbott's levies were placed in concealed positions on high ground south of it. Some eight hundred of the best of Abbott's matchlockmen he positioned at the top of a cliff called the Rutta Bunna or 'Red Boundary', which gave them a commanding view over the narrow valley up which the Sikhs would have to advance to reach the fort. Here was what in modern military parlance would be called the 'killing field'.

On the evening of 17 October 1848 James Abbott watched through his telescope as the Sikhs set up camp in the valley below and lit their cooking-fires. From their dispositions he judged they would begin their assault on his own positions the following morning. Despite Chatar Singh's advantages in infantry and artillery, Abbott was confident that he could stop him in his tracks so long as his own troops kept their nerve. He was well aware that these were tribesmen to whom the western military tactic of defeating the enemy by concentrated and tightly regulated firepower was unknown, whose own tactics were largely based on the principles of 'shoot and scoot', and of never taking on an enemy except when he was at a clear disadvantage – ideally, unsuspecting and asleep. He knew, too, that success was dependent on the loyalty of the Mashwani, 'to whom appertained the Northern portion of Mt Gundgurh, and upon whose presumed good faith rested all my hope of repulsing the enemy'. What he did *not* know was that about a third of the Mashwani present had done a deal with the advancing Sikhs: provided their villages and crops, lying immediately below the Rutta Bunna cliff, were spared, they would not open fire.

'Oct. 18 1848. I arose at two o'clock thoroughly refreshed and gazed upon the distant Sikh camp, already brilliant with fires': so begins James Abbott's journal on what was to prove the most fateful day of his life. 'As the day broke I perceived through my glass their batteries forming up into two columns . . . Then the two columns marched (as my spies had forewarned me) by two distinct routes.' The left column approached Salamkhand Fort up a ravine while the right, commanded by Chatar Singh himself, marched across the base of the mountain in a flanking movement.

At a distance of about twelve hundred yards Chatar Singh's four eight-pounders were unlimbered from their elephants, primed, loaded and fired. Their aim was good, Abbott noted, 'but the shot generally [fell] just short of my feet'. His maliks having begged him to stay in one place during the battle, he had deliberately sought out a position on a high promontory, where he could be seen by all his men, and set himself up with a chair, table and umbrella: 'I sometimes have fancied that the Artillery men spared me intentionally,' he notes in his Narrative. 'The majority certainly were unwilling rebels and I was a conspicuous mark.' Abbott gazed intently through his spyglass as the Sikh left column approached the Rutta Bunna cliff, about two miles distant, then entered his 'killing field':

I watched them through my telescope in breathless expectation. Now they seemed to be parallel with the cliff, yet not a matchlock spoke . . . now they were halted under the cliff. I expected every moment a cloud of grey smoke to tell of the fire of the defenders . . . Three Regiments stood in the ravine, close packed in column. On a high cliff immediately above them lay 800 steady shots, with their matchlocks levelled at them. Had those matchlocks fired, nearly every one must have brought down its man . . . Even if the Mishawanis, to save their crops from destruction, should refuse to fire, I felt sure that Kullunder Khan [a malik of the Tarkheli] would have no scruples, and his three hundred men, so posted, should have made great havoc of the Sikh ranks by their fire . . . For more than half an hour the forces lay thus confronted. Then the enemy resumed their march up the ravine, yet not a matchlock spoke, and I felt a sickness stealing over my heart in this proof that the men I had most trusted were faithless.

Abbott was given little time to brood over this betrayal, as Chatar Singh's infantry were now advancing forward on his right flank. Here they were first opposed by a small force of Tarkheli under Ata Muhammad Khan. Because of their limited numbers, the Tarkheli had been ordered to do no more than impede the advance, and to fall back slowly if pressed; 'the ardour of their

Chief got the better of his obedience,' however, 'and whenever the enemy's skirmishers ventured within their reach they were driven back'. Soon the main column of Chatar Singh's infantry was within matchlock range of his front line, and Abbott had to watch his men abandon one position after another, firing scarcely a shot, while the Sikhs 'stormed in succession each ledge of the terraced ascent'. The failure of the Mashwani on the Rutta Bunna cliff to open fire had 'damped the spirits of all and the enemy's vast superiority in numbers discouraged them. They thought more of lying close under the fringe of shrubs which formed their cover, than of firing rapidly.' His telescope allowed Abbott to observe events in dramatic and depressing close-up: 'The distances separating parties lying in the same line with my eye could not of course be more than guessed, but sometimes the faces of the hostile parties seemed almost in contact, the defender being above, under partial cover, and the assailant beneath, exposed at full length to his opponent's fire, and when at such times our matchlocks were silent my disappointment was very keen. The enemy, supported by their two Howitzers, steadily advanced towards the post which, with a reserve of two hundred matchlocks, I occupied, while Chattur Singh's four guns kept up a fire of round shot over their heads.'

Just as it seemed they would be overwhelmed in this last position, the Tarkheli malik Kullunder Khan and the vanguard of his three hundred men quite unexpectedly made their appearance, together with a number of Mashwani from Sirikot. Having been prevented from opening fire at the Rutta Bunna cliffs by the disloyal Mashwani, who had levelled their jezails at them, they had withdrawn and then circled round along the top of the ridge to reach Abbott's position from the rear. Their arrival turned the tide: the firepower of the defenders suddenly doubled, and then trebled, as the waverers in Abbott's ranks gained new heart. As more and more men were either hit or pinned down by accurate fire, the Sikh advance slowed – and then halted altogether. As Abbott watched, a section of Chatar Singh's Sikhs suddenly began to waver and retreat: 'Ata Muhammad Khan, excited at seeing his ancient enemies in force in his village, had charged sword in hand upon a dense mass of Sikh Infantry and had created among them a momentary panic. Had he been well seconded by his own men, the slaughter had been great . . . but the days of "derring do" from Huzara were past, and the bulk of his people hung back . . . Only five or six of them accompanied him in the charge and he and they were cut to pieces while fighting like heroes.'

Throughout the attack Abbott had observed men streaming out of the fort of Salamkhand. Now its powder magazine exploded with a terrific bang that momentarily halted the battle: 'The castle had been standing silent and grim amid the fire which rallied round it and had formed the foreground to a wide view over and down the River Indus and the plains of the Yousufzye. Suddenly, it burst forth in flames and volumes of smoke and dust, which rose curling to the skies. Then shot up a column higher than the rest which unfolded its contents upon the winds and distilled its reservoirs of dust in jets, which streamed back slowly to the Earth.'

The explosion seemed to signal the end of the battle: 'The Nazim, perceiving the hopelessness of dislodging me, far less of winning that day access to Sirikote at the mountain summit, recalled his left wing, which retired by alternate sections, with perfect order and regularity.' Buoyed up by this sudden improvement in his fortunes, Abbott was all for charging the retiring columns, but his chiefs were against it: 'As the desertion of our levies at Margalla, Moti and Dunitour had made me resolved to be guided, throughout the affair, by the advice of those who had experience of their mode of fighting (of which Nicholson and myself evidently knew nothing), I abandoned the attempt.'

For two days the opponents maintained their positions, Abbott and his Hazarawals holding the mountain and the Sikhs camped below. Then, on the third day, Abbott and his allies had the satisfaction of seeing Chatar Singh's forces strike their tents and march back towards Hasan Abdul. They were never to return to Hazara. He had the disappointment of missing a chance to secure what he believed could have been a famous victory, but Abbott and his men had driven the Sikhs out of his beloved Hazara – and he could take considerable comfort from his enemy's losses: one hundred and fifty killed for twenty of his own men. 'It showed ill beside the exploits of the peasants of Huzara in days gone by,' he writes in the closing pages of his 'Huzara and Its Place in the Second Sikh War'. 'It was however to be remembered that . . . the men of the country were no longer fighting for the honour of wives, daughters and sisters but in defence of a man of different faith, whom they had known little more than a year.'

This was scarcely more than a preliminary sideshow of the Second Sikh War, but for James Abbott and the people of Hazara it was their finest hour. It seems somewhat ungenerous to note that, while they won their final battle against Chatar Singh and drove the hated Sikhs from their land, they failed to halt them. Those same Sikhs now marched south to join their countrymen, and to begin in earnest their second crusade against the British.

8

'Sometimes pleasure, sometimes pain'

THE SECOND SIKH WAR AND ANNEXATION, 1848–1849

Kabhi sukh aur kabhi dukh
Angrez ka naukar.

Sometimes pleasure, sometimes pain
In service of the English.

Indian Army proverb

WHEN SHER Singh and his Sikh army switched sides in October 1848, Herbert Edwardes's hopes of taking Mulraj's fort and the city of Multan appeared to have been dashed. However, Sher Singh was less concerned to relieve Dewan Mulraj than to combine with his father Chatar Singh and other Sikh dissidents: he withdrew from Multan, and began a slow march back towards Lahore. In the meantime, Edwardes and his native allies investing Multan had now been joined by a contingent of EICo troops from the Bombay Army, under General Whish, which had been hauled in barges up the Indus by steamers. With the arrival of a second flotilla carrying a battery of heavy guns, they could begin the siege in earnest. Equally welcome, from Edwardes's point of view, was the arrival of Joe Lumsden at the head of a troop of his Guides' Cavalry. A handful of Guides sowars had accompanied Edwardes through Bannu as his personal bodyguards and scouts, and had already proved their value as intelligence-gatherers, but here in Multan they excelled themselves. 'To the Guides', wrote Edwardes admiringly, 'it was a perfect game, a lark, to disguise themselves and take service with Mulraj, and come out of the fort with Mulraj's men to fight against their own masters, and to have to run away when Mulraj ran away; and then towards the close of the siege to come out and join their own side and help take the place.' One even managed to pass himself off as one of Mulraj's personal orderlies, to eavesdrop on the Dewan's councils.

'My Guides have gained for themselves and for me a good name in the British camp,' Joe Lumsden wrote to his father on 14 October. 'Only think, when I was on duty elsewhere one day sixty-six of my men rode slap through and through ten times their number in the hope of recovering some camels which the Seikhs had driven off from General Whish's camp. They did not get the camels, but covered themselves with glory.' The sixty-six, under Risaidar Fatteh Khan's command, had chased after the marauders, only to run slap into the entire strength of Mulraj's cavalry. They had no time to do more than spur their horses and charge, forcing their way through the enemy horse, reforming on the other side, turning about and hacking their way back through again. Seeing the enemy in a state of confusion, they then rallied and reformed for a third charge, whereupon the Sikh cavalry turned and fled, with Fatteh Khan's men in close pursuit right up to the walls of Multan.

There now remained in the whole of the Punjab only one substantial body of troops which had not come out openly for the old Sikh khalsa: the twelve regiments at Peshawar. They bided their time, waiting to see how things went for their compatriots in the rest of the Punjab. In the meantime, the seeming incapacity of the British Government proved too much for the Amir of Kabul, Dost Mohammad Khan, who still coveted the former Afghan territory west of the Indus and now sought to do a deal with Chatar Singh in exchange for its return. Seeing how the wind was blowing, George Lawrence arranged for his wife and their two small boys to be conveyed by way of Kohat to Lahore, under the escort of the brother of Dost Mohammad Khan. Since Henry Lawrence had helped to set this gentleman free from imprisonment, and had restored him to his jaghirs in Kohat, George Lawrence was entitled to feel that his family would be safe under such protection. However, the Dost's renewed interest in 'the place of his father's sepulchres' exerted too great a strain on his brother's loyalties: he turned his party about and took them back to his home in Kohat. A plea for help from Mrs Lawrence reached John Nicholson in Hasan Abdal, but he found the roads blocked and the passes guarded, and was forced to turn back. Much of the country was now in open revolt, with thousands of veterans of the Khalsa Dal converging on Sher Singh's camp from every corner of the land of the five rivers, while the Muslim population lay low, waiting to see what the future would bring. With Chatar Singh's army now firmly in possession of the land between Attock and Rawalpindi, Nicholson retreated south across the Jhelum and Chenab with eighty horsemen. On 21 October he reported to Currie that the advance guard of Sher Singh's army was closing on Gujranwala, fifty miles north of Lahore. 'The non-advance of our troops', he added, 'has disheartened all our well-wishers (and they were few enough), and proportionately inspirited our many secret enemies.'

Five days later, in the late afternoon, the guns on the parapets of the Bala Hissar in Peshawar began firing on the British Residency, 'throwing in a torrent of round shot and grape, by which many of the defenders were killed or wounded'. The firing slackened off as darkness fell, but it was obvious to George Lawrence that the Residency could not be defended. Under the cover of darkness, he and surviving members of his staff and escort led their horses out through the back of the Residency compound and away from Peshawar. Making a wide detour to skirt the city, they rode up to Darra and then over the Kohat Pass unmolested. Arriving at Kohat next morning, George Lawrence was reunited with his wife and children but found himself, for the second time in his life, a prisoner of the Afghans. Here he learned of Dost Mohammad Khan's agreement to ally himself with Chatar Singh in exchange for the lands stolen by Ranjit Singh, and that he was now bent on reclaiming the Vale of Peshawar and all lands on his side of the Indus.

The entry of the Afghans onto the stage dramatically raised the stakes in the Sikh insurrection in the Punjab, for up to that point the

British had counted on the hostility of the bulk of the Muslim community towards the Sikhs, and on their support in any confrontation. The Punjab crisis was now transformed from a Sikh insurrection into a war that seriously threatened the British position in India; the military intervention that had been so long postponed could be delayed no longer. Choosing a ball at Simla at which to make his declaration of war, Governor-General Dalhousie at last announced that the gloves were off. 'Unwarned by precedent, uninfluenced by example,' he is reported to have declaimed to the assembled dancers, 'the Sikhs have called for war; and on my word, sirs, they shall have it with a vengeance.' With the Cold Weather now officially begun, the Commander-in-Chief descended from the Olympian heights of Simla to inspect the Grand Army of the Punjab, now assembled in the plains at Ferozepore.

After reporting for duty in Lahore, John Nicholson was ordered to Ferozepore to assist Colonel Frederick Mackeson in his role as Political Agent in the Field. However, he very soon antagonised his superiors with his increasingly vociferous protests about the plundering of local villages by the troops of the Grand Army and its thousands of camp-followers. Not only was this pillaging widespread – it was also, in his opinion, encouraged by many British officers. His campaign against 'the moral wrong of plundering like so many bandits' made him extremely unpopular in camp, but he persisted nevertheless, demanding of the Commander-in-Chief the powers of a provost-marshal, so that he might hang on the spot anyone he caught looting or plundering: 'If I get them, rely on my bringing the army to its senses in two days.' Lord Gough evidently had more pressing things on his mind, because no such powers were granted.

However, Nicholson was not entirely without friends in the Grand Army. To his great joy, his second brother, Charles, not seen since he was a boy of twelve, rode into camp with the 31st BNI. Now as tall as his older brother, Charles had also something of his commanding presence – a pale, stern face, dark eyes and hair and, above all, a proud carriage. He is said to have shared John's haughty manner of holding himself, later described by Lady Edwardes as 'that grand lifting of the head which all who knew John Nicholson can remember in him'. Also in camp were Henry Lawrence, knighted in April 1847, on his arrival in England, and Nicholson's old friend from Afghanistan days, Neville Chamberlain, both returned from sick-leave, the one to resume command of the Lahore Residency, so unwisely exercised by Sir Frederick Currie, the other as brigade-major of the 4th Cavalry Brigade. And here, too, were Joe Lumsden and William Hodson, Lumsden fresh from the fighting at Multan and now appointed head of the Commander-in-Chief's intelligence department, charged with keeping the Grand Army informed of every move the enemy made.

Anxious to avoid battle until his army was at full strength, Sher Singh made every effort to prevent Gough's forces from closing on him. As the opposing armies manoeuvred and counter-marched in their efforts to out-guess and turn each other's flank, Lumsden and Nicholson kept their irregulars fully occupied: maintaining communications between the Grand Army and Lahore, escorting the trains of bullock-carts bringing up supplies and ammunition, and constantly patrolling the rough country of ravines and scrub that made up much of the no-man's-land between the armies.

Early in December 1848 Gough's cavalry commander, General Sir Joseph Thackwell, aged sixty-eight, made the first strike. Learning that the Sikhs were camped on the far side of the Chenab, he crossed the river with a large force of cavalry in a bid to fall on Sher Singh's left flank. Nicholson's Pakhtuns had found an unguarded crossing and seized a number of boats, which enabled the entire force to be ferried across the river without being spotted by Sher Singh's scouts. While this flanking movement was in progress Lord Gough brought the main body of the Grand Army forward to the banks of the Chenab in front of the Sikh camp, where it came under fire from artillery well concealed on the opposite bank. The firing very soon slackened off, and then died out altogether. Suspecting that this was a ruse intended to draw his troops forward, the Commander-in-Chief turned to his staff and called for a scout to be sent across the river. Neville Chamberlain, who had always felt himself singularly unlucky to have missed the first Sikh War and was determined not to be left out of the second, had deliberately cut short his sick leave in order to hurry back to India. Seeing in Lord Gough's words a golden opportunity to distinguish himself, he immediately volunteered to swim across. The Chenab was then in full flood, so it was a long, hard swim; but, fortunately for Chamberlain, when he reached the far bank he discovered that the Sikhs had pulled back their guns and withdrawn.

Had General Thackwell's flanking movement been carried out as planned, the Sikhs would have been trapped between the two halves of the Grand Army. However, he had halted for twenty-four hours to allow his guns to catch up, giving Sher Singh time to extricate his army from the trap without any great loss. Nicholson was highly critical of what he saw as a promising chance thrown away, and when he heard that the Commander-in-Chief was playing it up as a significant victory, he made his contempt widely known. This earned him a private but firm rebuke from his old chief: 'My dear Nicholson,' wrote Sir Henry Lawrence, 'Let me advise you, as a friend, to curb your temper . . . Don't think it necessary to say all you think to every one. The world would be a mass of tumult if we all gave candid opinions of each other. I admire your sincerity as much as any man can do, but say this much as a general warning. Don't think I allude to any specific act; on the contrary, from what I saw in camp, I think you have done much towards conquering yourself; and I hope to see the conquest completed.'

Nicholson's response to this warning was characteristically uncompromising:

I am not ignorant of the faults of my temper, and you are right in supposing that I do endeavour to overcome them – I hope with increasing success. On one point however, I still think I am excusable for the plain speaking which, I am aware, made me very unpopular with a large portion of the officers of the Army of the Punjab. I mean with reference to the plundering of the unfortunate people of the country, which generally prevailed throughout the campaign, and which was, for the most part, winked at, if not absolutely sanctioned, by the great majority of officers. I knew from the first that I was giving great offence by speaking my mind strongly on this subject; but I felt I should be greatly wanting in my duty, both to the people and the army, if I did not, to the best of my ability, raise my voice against so crying an evil.

With the start of 1849, the situation in the Punjab reached crisis-point. Lieutenant Herbert, the youngest of George Lawrence's political assistants in Peshawar, had been deputed to take charge of the Mughal fort at Attock, which now became the key defensive point as some 3,500 Afghan horsemen swept down through the Khyber and across the Vale of Peshawar to converge on the bridge of boats at the Attock crossing. Since Nicholson's dramatic seizure of the fort, a new batch of Sikh troops had joined the garrison. With Chatar Singh's forces close at hand on their side of the river and the Afghans advancing on the other, they had been growing ever more hostile, to the point where Herbert's position became untenable. With him were a British Army sergeant and a corporal, together with a dozen Hazarawals sent to him by James Abbott. On the night of 3 January this small party slipped out of the fort by a postern and carried two rafts down to the river. The first, bearing the sergeant and half the Hazarawals, was badly launched and immediately struck a rock. All its occupants were thrown into the water and swept to their deaths. The corporal, already semi-delirious with fever, became hysterical and refused to climb aboard the second raft. Fearing the noise would alert the sentries, Herbert decided to stay with the soldier, ordering the remaining Hazarawals to push off without them. The two were soon found by the Sikhs, and taken prisoner. Attock fort now fell into Chatar Singh's hands; handing it over to Dost Mohammad Khan, he at once began to march south with all speed, to join his son beside the Jhelum.

In Hazara, James Abbott now found himself totally isolated. He was, as he saw it, 'the only remaining British officer upon that frontier', so he decided to send a placatory message to Amir Dost Mohammad Khan, expressing friendship and inviting him to join with the British in crushing the Sikh rebellion. For this attempt at international diplomacy he was reprimanded by the Governor-General, who declared him to be 'an incorrigible'.

If the Company was to have any future in Northern India, it was imperative that Sher Singh's army be destroyed before he was joined by Chatar Singh and the Afghans. Lord Gough now did his best to avert this conjunction, while the Sikhs sought to avoid battle until it had been effected. All the feints, advances and wheelings of what Lord Gough was pleased to call his 'extensive combinations' finally ended at the battle of Chilianwala on 13 January 1848. On that afternoon the Grand Army closed on Sher Singh's forces a few miles south of the Jhelum. The Sikhs, with their usual military thoroughness, had dug themselves in in a strong defensive position made up of a series of entrenchments, their artillery fronted by a mile-deep band of thorn-covered open ground. Rather than rush straight in, the C-in-C disposed his infantry and cavalry with care, and then waited for his artillery to come up. He had been warned by Lord Dalhousie against repeating the tactics of Ferozshah, and as he waited he assured the Governor-General that he would only commence operations the next morning, when all his guns were in position. And yet, with quite incredible stupidity, Gough now re-enacted the folly of Ferozshah – with even bloodier consequences. His excuse was that the Sikhs had fired upon him: 'They put my Irish blood up, and I attacked them.' It is highly probable that Sher Singh's commanders had prepared their position as a deliberate trap based on an understanding of Gough's character. It may have been a sense of this that prompted Colonel Mackeson to beg the C-in-C to wait, and thereby make use of his advantage in firepower – ninety-two guns against the Sikhs' sixty-two; he also pointed out that the cotton trousers of the sepoys would give no protection against thorns. But to no avail. 'I am the Commander-in-Chief,' Mackeson was told, 'and I desire you to be silent.'

It is a well-understood military maxim that one never attacks a defensive position without a ratio of numerical superiority of at least two to one: Gough threw sixteen thousand foot-soldiers and cavalry against twice that number. The front lines of the cavalry became entangled in the thorn-thickets, which tore the bellies of the horses and brought their advance to a halt, so that they became sitting ducks as the Sikh artillery ranged in on them. Riders lost control as their terrified mounts bucked, kicked and ran amok, desperate to escape the pain of the thorns. Seeing what was happening in front, the sowars in the cavalry regiments following behind ignored their officers' commands and galloped back through their artillery, spreading panic and confusion. It was left to the infantry, hacking its way through that mile of waist-high thorn-bushes under the most concentrated barrage since Waterloo, to save the day, at a cost of more than two thousand dead. In one regiment alone – the 24th Foot – the bodies of thirteen officers and the Regimental Sergeant Major were laid on tables in their mess tent the following day. But by nightfall the Grand Army of the Punjab had captured forty Sikh guns. Having broken the back of the Sikhs' defence and driven them from their trenches at the point of the bayonet, the infantry was ordered to halt, and then to fall back on the village of Chilianwala. This allowed the Sikhs to return under cover of darkness and reclaim no fewer than twenty-eight of those forty guns, at the same time finishing off several hundred of the British wounded who had been left on the battlefield. 'I treat it as a great victory,' wrote Lord Dalhousie to his friend Lord Wellington in England, 'but writing confidentially to you, I do not hesitate to say that I consider my position grave.' To another friend he admitted that 'one and all, Generals of Division, officers, soldiers, sepoys, publicly attribute this great loss and small results to the total incompetence of the Commander-in-Chief, and justly so. They have totally lost confidence in him.'

There is nothing from Nicholson about this bloody affair, in which he acted as one of Gough's aides-de-camp. However, he was seen by one British officer to grab the shoulders of another, who was hanging back behind his advancing men, and propel him with a series of kicks up the backside into the hottest of the artillery fire. Chamberlain, Lumsden and Hodson also missed the fight, being engaged in other duties. Writing to his sister Harriet after the battle, Neville Chamberlain made it plain that the Sikhs were given every advantage: 'They outnumbered us six or seven times, outflanked us, chose their own position, and had to be attacked in a jungle which it was impossible to reconnoitre . . . No field in India has, I believe, ever been more severely contested.' Yet he refused to pass judgement on his Commander-in-Chief, although there were rumours of a possible drum-head court martial: 'That we were handled to the greatest advantage is not for me to decide, but I hope that Lord Gough's life may be spared, for a braver man never sat on a horse.' William Hodson, however, had no such qualms. 'Our loss has been severe, and the mismanagement very disgraceful; yet it will be called a victory and lauded accordingly,' he wrote to his father. He had his own views as to where the fault lay:

At the age at which officers become colonels and majors, not one in fifty is able to stand the wear and tear of Indian service. They become still more worn in mind than in body. All elasticity is gone; all energy and enterprise worn out; they become, after a fortnight's campaign, a burden to themselves, an annoyance to those under them, and a terror to every one but the enemy. The officer who commanded the cavalry brigade which so disgraced the service at Chilianwala was not able to mount a horse without the assistance of two men. A brigadier of infantry, under which I served during the three most critical days . . . could not see his regiment when I led his horse by the bridle until its nose touched the bayonets; and even then he said faintly, 'Pray, which way are the men facing, Mr Hodson?' This is no exaggeration, I assure you. Can you wonder that our troops have to recover by desperate fighting, and with heavy loss, the advantage thrown away by the want of heads and eyes to lead them?

Chilianwala is generally accounted a draw, since Gough's Grand Army failed to break the Sikhs, who were able to extricate themselves with most of their guns. Three days later their losses were more than made good when Chatar Singh's forces finally marched into Sher Singh's camp to a grand *feu-de-joie* of guns and muskets, thereby enlarging the Sikhs to approximately sixty thousand strong. Fortunately for Gough, less than a week after this enlargement of the Sikh army, Multan fell to the EICo's Bombay Army, allowing valuable reinforcements to be hurried across the Punjab to bolster the Grand Army.

Among these reinforcements was the Adjutant of the 1st Bombay Fusiliers, twenty-eight-year-old Lieutenant Henry Daly. He will be remembered as the bosom friend of William Anderson, whose wounding and subsequent killing at Multan was the spark that set off the Second Sikh War. Not yet selected by Henry Lawrence, he is the last of the Young Men to be introduced to this story. Determined to avenge his friend's death, Daly had contrived to get himself accepted as a member of the force under General Whish which steamed up the Indus from Karachi in late August 1848 to invest Multan. He had played an active role in the battering and final assault of the city and its fort, and before marching on to Lahore had watched with grim satisfaction as the remains of Anderson and Vans Agnew, recovered from the ditch into which they had been thrown, were taken in procession by a bearer-party of the Bombay Fusiliers over the drawbridge where they were first wounded, to be reinterred inside Dewan Mulraj's citadel.

His duty to his friend discharged, the young Irishman from Connaught turned his eyes eastwards to Lahore, and managed to join Herbert Edwardes as he escorted Mulraj in chains to Lahore. Here the former governor was put on trial and, despite a lack of credible evidence, found guilty of the murders of Vans Agnew and Anderson. He was sentenced to be hanged, but at Sir Henry Lawrence's pleading this was commuted to life imprisonment. Is it possible that Dewan Mulraj was the grizzled old prisoner from the Sikh Wars locked up in Lahore fort around whom the young Rudyard Kipling wove his delightful story of a young Englishman bewitched and duped by the charms of a Muslim courtesan, *On the City Wall*?

The two armies met again on 21 February 1849, before the town of Gujrat. Ten days earlier Sher Singh had staged a brilliant deception, moving his entire force round Gough's right wing during the night, with the intention of crossing the Chenab and striking at him from the rear. Warning of this move had been sent to Gough's camp, but arrived too late to be of any value; it would probably have been discounted in any event, since its source was James Abbott, more than a hundred miles away in Hazara.

The entry of the Afghans into the war had added greatly to Abbott's problems. Hitherto the Hazarawals had been happy to support him, on the ancient Pakhtun principle of 'my enemy's enemy is my friend'. Now, they had no reason but loyalty – and every reason to throw in their lot with their former countrymen.

The first to do so were two of his most important allies, Khan-i-Zaman, khan of the Tarkheli clan, and Ghulam Khan, chief of the Tarin. Knowing that others would follow their example unless he acted, Abbott called a *jirga* of all the clan and village chiefs in Hazara. They gathered on the steep hillside above Nara and listened in silence as Abbott made a heartfelt plea for their support: 'There I set before them the question, "Should I stand my ground, or should I fall back? Was my presence regarded as a boon, or the contrary? If a boon, I would remain, but in that case they must aid me heart and hand."'

The khans and maliks heard Abbott out, and then conferred amongst themselves. When every man present had had the opportunity to speak his mind, the *jirga* made its decision and called Abbott back to hear its verdict. To Abbott's dismay, the *jirga's* spokesman proved to be none other than Khan-i-Zaman, the leading defector. However, he then confounded Abbott by declaring that one sentiment was common to them all: 'That my presence had been beneficial to them and that their honour and safety were concerned in my dwelling among them. I thanked them for their confidence and then consulted with them on the measures to be pursued.' His faith restored, Abbott enacted a ceremony which, whether spontaneous or carefully calculated, demonstrated that he had every confidence in Khan-i-Zaman: 'Before dismissing the assembly I solemnly invested Khan i Jeman Khan, Tarkhaili, with the Turban as Chief of Gundgurh, a ceremony of very old usage, dating back at least two thousand years but which had not been previously observed, owing to his having been an outlaw.' Cynics may interpret this vote of confidence in Abbott as but an expression of the Hazarawals' obligation to honour the Pakhtun code relating to hospitality and shelter. Others may prefer to see it as a remarkable tribute to the little man who had done so much to restore the *iqbal* of the Hazarawals.

The Nara *jirga* marked a turning-point in Abbott's fortunes. He was gratified to find that the attempts of the remaining dissident, Ghulam Khan of the Tarin, to gather other tribal leaders to his banner were being treated with contempt: 'While Goolam Khan the loyal was Goolam Khan the Nawaub, Goolam Khan the traitor was Goolam Khan the outcast'. Indeed, he even gained an unexpected ally: 'Nawaub Khan of Shingari, finding that his mortal enemy Goolam Khan had left my standard, posted to me in high glee. He allowed, on examination, that he had taken a solemn oath on the Koran to follow Goolam Khan's example, but he volunteered to take two oaths, each twice as solemn, to be true to me, now that his enemy had quitted my camp. As I considered that he might, at any future time, take three such oaths to betray me, I accepted his allegiance but dispensed with his oaths of loyalty.'

Soon after the Nara *jirga*, Abbott received a most curious message from a friendly *pir* from the neighbouring Yusufzai territory, a Muslim holy man whom he describes as 'father confessor of all the Notables of the Yousufzye'. This 'Right Reverend friend' reported that he had received a vision in which he saw the Sikh army 'stealing to the rear of the British Force, confronting them and threatening them with great disaster'. Abbott took this to be a genuine warning 'couched under the symbol of a vision', and immediately sent a messenger to carry the intelligence to Colonel Mackeson in Lord Gough's camp. Travelling on foot, this unnamed messenger covered a distance of about a hundred and twenty miles in four days, and reached Mackeson on 13 February – the morning *after* the Sikh army had made its night march to reach the banks of the Chenab at Wazirabad undetected.

Two chance encounters combined to rob the Sikhs of their last prospect of victory. The first involved Lieutenant Lake, a young engineer officer who had earlier fought beside Herbert Edwardes as commander of the Nawab of Bahawalpur's troops and who had just returned to political duties in the Doab under John Lawrence. Coming across an advance party of Sikh irregular horse about to cross an unguarded ford, he hurriedly assembled a scratch force of local infantry and two guns, and opposed the crossing. Unaware of how small this force was, the Sikhs turned back and rode off to a second crossing-point – where they ran straight into the Guides' Cavalry.

Harry Lumsden and William Hodson had now once more combined their cavalry and infantry as one unit, with the cavalry under Lumsden scouting on ahead and the infantry following up behind. 'We had just arrived on the banks of the river,' related Lumsden, 'when we suddenly came on a large detachment of

Goorchurries [Sikh cavalry] who had forded the stream close to Wazeerabad, and [who] were quite as much taken aback at seeing us as we were at finding them on our side of the stream. Without hesitation we went straight at them, and drove the lot helter-skelter through a deep ford, and dismounting, set to work to make a breastwork, commanding the passage to be occupied by our Guides infantry as soon as they came up. They arrived at 4 p.m. and I instantly posted Hodson off to report what I had done to Headquarters.' Lake's little force and the Guides between them had halted the Sikh vanguard at the Chenab, but – as is the way of these things – it was the brigade commander summoned by Hodson who received all the plaudits. 'The poor Guides', says Lumsden, 'got scant credit for their share in this business.'

Gough's Grand Army caught up with the Sikhs seven days later, at Gujrat. Gough knew by now that he was to be replaced by General Sir Charles Napier, the conqueror of Sind, as soon as was practicable, and the prospect of being sent home in disgrace seems to have concentrated his mind – here at Gujrat, for the first and last time, he made full use of his artillery. It was, wrote Harry Lumsden, 'an artillery action throughout, and much more like a grand review than a day which was to settle the destiny of the Punjab', a day that began with a concentrated three-hour artillery barrage in which every one of Gough's heavy guns was brought to bear on the Sikh defences. This was followed by a textbook deployment of his horse artillery:

A more beautiful sight could not have been on earth than the steady advance of upward of one hundred guns – horse artillery going to the front at a gallop and then 'Left about!' 'Action front!' supported by our cavalry, the heavy guns all the while smashing away at the Seikh artillery, and breaking their masses of infantry and cavalry. Three times did the Seikh infantry form line to advance and charge at our horse artillery, who coolly watched them until they came within the range of grape, and gave them a shower of such rain as had never come within the range of their conception. Their lines at first halted, shook backwards and forwards like a field of wheat in a heavy wind, and at last broke and bolted like a flock of wild sheep, the horse artillery following at a gallop, and keeping up a murderous fire on them for miles. Our cavalry took up the pursuit when the horse artillery left off, and finished as pretty a day's work as any army in India ever got through.

The Sikhs fought with the desperation of cornered lions. They had never given quarter and, in view of what had been done to the British wounded at Chilianwala, none was granted them. The pursuit continued for four hours, and eventually became a slaughter. 'In these encounters,' wrote the cavalry commander, Brigadier Hearsey, 'Neville Chamberlain of the Irregulars particularly distinguished himself by the number of the enemy he slew.' Both the Chamberlain brothers, Neville and Crawford, wrote accounts of the battle, but neither has survived. However, a letter Neville Chamberlain wrote to his mother two weeks later gives details of the reward his services had earned him: 'The day after the battle, the Commander-in-Chief sent for me, and told me that he was much indebted to me for my services. The old gentleman likewise told me that, did his own brother stand in my way, I should have the first regiment in his gift, and I told him . . . that my ambition was to be sent to Peshawar. Brigadier Hearsey is to command the cavalry going to Peshawar, and on his staff I shall have an opportunity of seeing everything.' At last he had made his mark.

Preceded by a series of wild rumours, news of the victory reached Hazara, now assailed by bands of maurauding Afghan horsemen. On 18 February Abbott heard that the Sikh army had outwitted the British and was marching on Lahore. 'I could only laugh outright,' he records in his narrative. 'Our game now seemed to be up and I remained in hourly expectation of disastrous intelligence from the seat of war.' Six days later, however, he was far happier: 'I saw the chief of my intelligence department, Kazi Abdool Gofar (a man unrivalled in procuring and transmitting intelligence), enter my Durbar with a beaming countenance. On enquiry he said, "The whole Doorani [Afghan] Force has bolted suddenly from Huzara. No one knows wherefore. They were all busy cooking their food. A courier from the [Sikh] Army arrived. They dropt their food as if scalding hot, mounted their horses and were off."' The following day another of Abbott's intelligence gatherers arrived to report that an Afghan soldier seeking water from a well had told the assembled villagers that the Sikh army had been destroyed. To illustrate his point, he had raised a handful of dust to his lips and blown it to the winds.

Abbott now received a letter from Mrs George Lawrence, smuggled out of Chatar Singh's camp near Rawalpindi: Chatar Singh was holding all the British prisoners there, but planned to take them back across the Indus as hostages. Could he stop them by seizing the Margalla Pass? In less than an hour Abbott was on the march. Reaching the pass early next morning, he and a mixed band of Hazarawals took by surprise a party of Afghan horse, who galloped off in the direction of Attock in a cloud of dust. Looking eastwards from the top of the stone *burj* towards Rawalpindi, Abbott saw the remnants of the Sikh army spread out across the plain, 'still a vast multitude but destitute of tents'. Expecting them to retire as the British army came on, he determined to use his men to deny them an escape route. So he deployed his small force along the heights of the pass, and waited.

Fortunately for Abbott and his Hazarawals, no gallant last stand was required of them, for on 12 March Sher Singh and Chatar Singh surrendered, together with their armies. Henry Daly was on hand with his 1st Bombay Fusiliers to see the two generals arrive to give themselves up before the gathered ranks of the Grand Army: 'Father and son rode side by side. The Sher's face is of an oval form; his eyes dark and deep set; a black beard surrounds all. The countenance is expressive of determination and devilry, for there is something sinister about it . . . nothing of the ease-loving, luxurious Easterner. The father's features are fine; he looks a noble. He appeared sorrowful and worn, his head was almost concealed. Not so the son, who keenly eyed the soldiers who thronged the banks to see them pass.'

On the 13th Daly watched some ten thousand Sikh horsemen surrender their arms: 'They formed up and rode by in twos and threes, every man depositing his arms as he passed. Before night a mass of matchlocks, firelocks, swords, shields, and spears was collected, covering 20 square yards, and rising 8 or 10 feet high. A similar deposit took place at our yesterday's ground. Every fellow after thus laying down his arms is allowed to go free; poor devils, they seem starved. I must tell you that we pay every one a rupee. They are allowed to carry off their horses . . . though they are abject and broken even to starvation, still I incline to the opinion that dismounting them would have been wise.'

John Nicholson and Neville Chamberlain watched this scene with similarly mixed emotions, having learned to admire and respect the Sikhs as fellow soldiers as well as enemies. Recognising a veteran as he laid down his sword, Nicholson asked him how it had come to this: 'Did you not say you would drive us into the sea? Your guru should have advised you better.' To which the Sikh replied ruefully: 'Ah, sahib, there's no striving against Fate. There's no fighting upon a diet of cabbages. Just try it yourself, sahib.' Neville Chamberlain records an equally poignant incident: 'One old fellow I noticed in particular; he stood for a long time looking wistfully at his arms and the pile before him, and evidently could not make up his mind to give them up. At last the officer on duty came and touched him on the shoulder and ordered him to move on; he then threw down his sword and matchlock with a crash, and turned away with tears in his eyes saying, "All my work is done now."'

The victory at Gujrat salvaged Gough's reputation and left him a hero. Mightily relieved, Lord Dalhousie, whose own fate was closely bound up with that of his army commander, was able to write home of his hearty rejoicing in the fact 'that the Old Chief has been able to close his career with this crowning glory'. Gujrat destroyed the Sikh Khalsa Dal, and with it all hopes of a revived Sikh nation. Had the Sikhs governed the Punjab half as well as they organised their artillery and infantry, they would have been unbeatable; but then, had the Grand Army of the Punjab been fielded sooner, a second war against the Sikhs might not have been required.

While the surrender of the Khalsa Dal was taking place, strenuous efforts were being made to chase the retreating Afghans. The Guides were deputed to find the Lawrence family and the other prisoners and bring them back to the British camp at Rawalpindi, which was speedily and safely accomplished. Joe Lumsden and thirty of his sowars then joined with John Nicholson and the best-mounted of his Pakhtuns to make a dash for Attock, with the aim of seizing the bridge of boats before it could be cut loose or burned by the Afghans. With them as their commander rode 'the flying general', the elderly but dashing General Sir Walter Gilbert, a man known throughout British India for his horsemanship. By the painful expedient of having each man run between two riders while hanging on to their stirrups, they also carried with them thirty Guides' infantrymen. In this manner the party reached Attock just as the last of the Afghans was retreating over the bridge. The Guides sowars immediately opened fire with their rifles and drove the Afghans off the bridge of boats, but were too late to prevent them cutting away the ropes securing it to the far bank. Before dawn next morning two boat-loads of Guides had crossed the Indus and taken possession of the little fort at Khairabad, so that the twenty or so boats making up the bridge could be re-assembled and made fast – but already most of the Afghan army was heading for the safety of the mountains. A party of horse that included John Nicholson and Neville Chamberlain chased the stragglers to the mouth of the Khyber Pass, that very gateway from which both had emerged in such low circumstances seven years earlier. On the same day, Joe Lumsden re-entered the city of Peshawar at the head of his Guides' Cavalry.

On 30 March 1849 the young Maharaja Dalip Singh held his last Durbar in the citadel of Lahore and signed away all claims on behalf of himself, his heirs and his successors to the sovereignty of the Punjab. A proclamation issued by the Governor-General was then read aloud; it declared that the Kingdom of the Punjab was at an end, and that 'all the territories of the Maharajah Duleep Singh are now and henceforth a portion of the British Empire in India'. The Punjab was annexed, adding another eighty thousand square miles to Britain's dominions and advancing British India's north-western boundaries to the mountains of Afghanistan and Kashmir. Lord Dalhousie's inherited earldom was augmented to a marquess-ate, and he wrote home to crow: 'It is not every day that an officer of their Government adds four million of subjects to the British Empire, and places the historical jewel of the Mogul Empire [the Koh-i-Noor diamond] in the crown of his sovereign. This I have done.' Lord Gough was also advanced in the peerage, to become Viscount Gough of Gujerat and Limerick.

Support for the annexation was widespread. John Nicholson spoke for every one of Sir Henry Lawrence's Young Men when he wrote that he was 'not surprised to hear that the country is to be annexed. No fear of any one in this quarter getting up a row about it. All regard it as annexed already.' The one opponent had been Sir Henry Lawrence himself, who considered annexation to be against the better interests of the people of the Punjab. This had not endeared him to the Governor-General who, while accepting that Sir Henry's return to the Punjab was necessary for a smooth transition of government, now saw to it that his powers were curbed. A three-man Board of Administration was set up comprising Sir Henry as the President, with his brother John and another civilian as the Board's two other Members. Initially the third was Charles Mansel, replaced in 1851 by Robert Montgomery, a contemporary of the Lawrences and a fellow-Ulsterman who later gave John Lawrence significant support, first as Commissioner of Lahore and subsequently as Lieutenant-Governor of the Punjab (his grandson was 'Monty' of El Alamein). The powers of the three members were to be shared, but each had special responsibilities: John Lawrence for finance, Mansel for the magistracy, and Sir Henry for political, diplomatic and military affairs.

The new Province of the Punjab was now parcelled into ten administrative Divisions, each to be presided over by a Commissioner. Every Division was further subdivided into three or four Districts, each in the charge of a Deputy Commissioner, supported by an Assistant or two and a small staff of locally-recruited native officials. The five trans-Sutlej districts running westwards and south from Peshawar as far as Dera Ghazi Khan, together with the most northerly of the cis-Indus districts, Hazara, now became the Frontier Districts of the new province. Lahore remained the provincial capital, but Peshawar assumed greater importance as the local seat of government for these Frontier Districts, under the direction of its own Commissioner – the genesis of the North-West Frontier, and of today's North-West Frontier Province.

Of Sir Henry's prime tier of political assistants, nearly all returned to their previous areas, but with the new title of Deputy

Commissioner, and extended powers. George Lawrence went back to Peshawar, with Joe Lumsden as his Assistant Deputy Commissioner in charge of Yusufzai District, Reynell Taylor returned to Bannu, and John Nicholson to Rawalpindi. As his chief political assistant, Herbert Edwardes once again took up his place at Sir Henry Lawrence's side, where he helped to oversee a number of newcomers to what was now much more a civil than a political administration.

James Abbott was Deputy Commissioner for Hazara; for him, it was merely a matter of striking camp, to march the few miles from the Margalla Pass to the border of the territory which, uniquely among all those who served John Company in the Punjab frontier, he could claim never to have abandoned. He returned to Hazara as its undisputed master, and to the continuing benefit and happiness of its people. There he was to remain for four years, years which merely strengthened the reputation he had already acquired, and which must be distilled here into four brief portraits, each containing some measure of *Kaka* Abbott.

The first comes from the pen of Lady Lawrence, the redoubtable Honoria, who kept a daily journal intended for the eyes of her young children far away in England. To her it seemed that James Abbott had by this time much of the Old Testament prophet about him: 'He is about forty, small make with eager black eyes and well marked features. I suppose it is many years since shears or razor approached him, and his hair and beard are silver white. A broad-brimmed white hat, coat and trousers made after the taste of a Hazara tailor, a spiked staff about seven foot long, and the whole man alive with energy, a remarkably sweet and gentle voice.' She goes on to describe him living 'as a patriarch' among his people: 'It is delightful to see a British officer loved and respected as he is. I do not mean that he is perfect, for he has some failings that make it difficult to deal with him officially, and he gives papa more trouble than many a man of not a tenth part the merit. The more so because papa has so high a regard for him. Abbott is morbidly sensitive, and he has lived so long without coming into contact with other educated minds that he cannot apprehend any view other than his own.'

'Papa' had to put up with Abbott's cussedness for six years in all, yet could still speak of him as 'a true Knight errant'. Here was a man who could be both 'gentle as a girl in thought and word and deed, overflowing with warm affections', and at the same time 'a scientific, courageous and energetic soldier with peculiar power of attaching others, especially Asiatics, to his person'.

Herbert Edwardes, who succeeded Abbott in Hazara in 1853, echoes Honoria Lawrence when describing his relationship with the Hazarawals: 'He had literally lived among them as their patriarch – an out of door, under tree life. Every man, woman and child in the country knew him personally, and hastened from their occupations to salute him as he came their way. The children especially were his favourites. They used to go to "Kaka Abbott" whenever their mouths watered for fruit or sugar plums. He spent all his substance on the people.'

Lastly, a brief and cryptic note from one of his juniors, Lieutenant (later General) G.G. Pearse, who was his assistant in Hazara in 1851 and wrote that he 'lived in a world of plots and . . . kept many spies'.

Opinionated, hyper-sensitive eccentrics in the Abbott mould will always rile those who go by the rules and never step out of line. Such men – the Curries of this world – move effortlessly up the promotion ladder in every large organisation; they can find no place in their official reports for the human factor, but are quick to note irregularities when things go wrong. And it was just such an irregularity, coupled with long memories of Abbott's earlier obduracies, that finally brought him down.

Honoria Lawrence's portrait of Abbott was set down early in February 1852 during a visit to Haripur. She was there because her husband was in Hazara to enquire into the deaths of two British civilians who belonged to the Punjab Government's Salt Department. 'Papa was busy upon the murders of Mr Cain and Mr Trapp and trying to apprehend the murderers,' she writes in her journal:

Papa summoned Jehan Dad Khan, the head of the clan, and his minister Boostan Khan . . . a bold ruffianly looking fellow who came in, knowing himself charged for his life, with the air of a prince, sat down on the ground and answered all Papa's questions in an easy off hand way that looked very much like innocence. I confess I was glad when the examination was over and the men let go, for they had a following of five or six hundred men, all stalwart fellows who had accompanied their chief and would have enjoyed exceedingly a good scrimmage with the chance of plunder . . . Papa ended by saying to the elders of the tribe, 'If you give up the murderers they will be hanged, but your hostages will be released with honour and gifts. If you refuse to give up the murderers, the hostages will be taken to Lahore, perhaps to Hindustan, and I will come with an army to burn your villages and give your country to another.' The old fellows folded their hands and said with some fun, 'We should consider your presence an honour, but our country is rather a difficult one for your army.'

Abbott has left no record of his own about this business, but the fact that the President of the Board of Administration found it necessary to go to Hazara to conduct such an enquiry in person signified a growing impatience in Lahore and Peshawar over the way Abbott was running his little patriarchy. Things finally came to a head in the autumn of that same year, 1852, when Abbott was accused of having acted despotically in apprehending the most important of the Saiad maliks in the far north of the country, in response to complaints of oppression from their Gujar tenants. He was ordered by Lahore to release the malik – but by this time the Saiad clan was up in arms. An expeditionary force was assembled under the command of Colonel Frederick Mackeson, now Commissioner of Peshawar, and thus Abbott's senior. It advanced up the Kaghan Valley, and the Saiad duly made their submissions. All might have been well had Mackeson and Abbott not then quarrelled over how best to control the Saiad country. One was for building a road and then putting up a fort, the other wanted the fort first, with a road to follow after. It was a trivial dispute, arising as much as anything from Abbott's resentment of Mackeson's intrusion into his fiefdom, but Abbott went over Mackeson's head to complain to Lahore in his usual intemperate language. The Board of Administration decided it had had enough of Abbott. Mackeson was supported, and Abbott was sacked – or, rather, transferred back to the Bengal Army, his special services 'no longer required'. Something about the affair smacks of a fix. The official papers give nothing away, but it seems possible that at the heart of his removal lay an ever-growing concern in Lahore that here was an official with divided loyalties. Sir Henry Lawrence and Herbert Edwardes had both seen at first hand how the 'patriarch' lived, and how he governed, and neither accorded with their view of how a DC should comport himself. *Kaka* Abbott had, in the late nineteenth-century phrase, 'gone native' – and so he had to be removed altogether.

At the close of the Second Sikh War Lord Dalhousie had publicly expressed 'special thanks' for the 'gallant stand' made by Abbott in the hills of Hazara, to which had been added the thanks of both Houses of Parliament. But Abbott's final reward for what he described as eighteen years' separation from civilised society, of which every hour had been 'devoted to the service of Government and to the promotion of the happiness of the thousands committed by Government to my care', was to be posted to the other end of the country, in charge of a government gunpowder factory in Calcutta. He remained on the Indian Army List for many years, was made a Companion of the Order of the Bath in 1873 and retired as a general in 1879. In 1894, two years before his death, he finally received a belated knighthood.

Abbott's dismissal may have been summary, but there was nothing remotely cursory about his leave-taking of Hazara. His last public act was to send messages to every corner of the district, inviting each and every one of its citizens to join him as his guest at a farewell feast on the Nara Hill, the scene of his most glorious days. He is said to have spent everything he had saved, bar one month's pay, on providing the food and other refreshments for this extraordinary party, the greatest public gathering Hazara had ever known. 'And there for three days and nights', says his replacement, Herbert Edwardes, 'he might be seen walking among the groups of guests and hecatombs of pots and cauldrons – the kind and courteous host of a whole people.' When the feasting was done, Abbott handed over his official papers to Edwardes, packed the few belongings he had accumulated over the years, and rode down to the border, escorted all the way by a 'weeping and lamenting' crowd of Hazarawals.

Of all the Young Men of the 1840s and 1850s it is James Abbott whose name has weathered the best, both in folk-memory and in place-names. The new district capital of Hazara was named 'Abbottabad' at Edwardes's suggestion, and remains 'Abbottabad' today. In the 1930s Sir Olaf Caröe, encountering a Yusufzai from Hazara who had recently celebrated his hundredth year, asked him if he had ever met *Kaka* Abbott. The old man replied that he remembered him well. 'He was a little man with bristly hair on his face and kind eyes, and we loved him,' Caröe quotes the old man as saying. 'I was in the *jirga* when he was asking us if we would stand and fight the Sikhs if he stood by us. We swore we would, and there were tears in our eyes, and a tear in Abbott Sahib's eye too. And we did! He was our father, and we were his children. There are no Angrez like Abbott Sahib now.'

9

'Every man a fair hearing'

Consolidating the Frontier, 1849–1853

> No man who has ever read a page of Indian history will ever
> prophesy about the Frontier.
>
> Lord Curzon, Viceroy of India, 1899–1904

WITH THE annexation of the Punjab in March 1849, William
Hodson found himself relieved of the civil duties he had
continued to carry out while attached to the Corps of Guides as
its second-in-command. He had anticipated and wished for the
annexation, but had not thought through its consequences: 'I did
not expect that it would be carried out so suddenly and so
sweepingly as it has been. I have been *annexed* as well as the
Punjab. My "occupation's gone".' His worries were shared by Joe
Lumsden, who became so depressed at the prospect of civilians
taking over a service hitherto dominated by military officers that
he seriously considered giving up his dual role as commandant of
the Guides and ADC Yusufzai to return to full-time soldiering
with the Bengal Army. However, the return of Sir Henry
Lawrence and the revelation of new plans for the policing of the
Frontier soon persuaded him otherwise. Having proved its worth
many times over, the Corps of Guides was now to be enlarged, to
become the spearhead of a new force of irregulars raised

specifically to police the five frontier districts and the Trans-Sutlej. This, to be known as the Punjab Irregular Force, would initially consist of the Guides, together with two new corps, one of cavalry and one of infantry.

The command of the new cavalry corps was offered to Neville Chamberlain – the prize, arguably the most exciting cavalry command in India, promised by Lord Gough after the battle of Gujrat. It was more than he could possibly have hoped for – yet he turned it down. His reason for doing so appears almost mundane. In a letter to his father Chamberlain says he refused the command 'on account of the wholly insufficient pay offered to the men', and it may indeed have been as simple as that. Chamberlain came from a regular cavalry background in which every sowar's mount was provided and paid for by the army – a very different system from that followed by irregular cavalry units, where each man was expected to provide and support his own horse as his own property, with the constant risk that if he lost his horse in the course of his duties he lost also his livelihood as a soldier. Perhaps Chamberlain hoped that by making a stand he could persuade the Army Council to reform the system. Another less worthy possibility is that he had expected to be offered the vacant command of the Bengal Army's 1st Irregular Cavalry, also known as Skinner's Horse or the 'Yellow Boys' (later the 1st Bengal Cavalry), and was playing for time. In the event, he was not: the 1st Irregular Cavalry went to his younger brother Crawford, and the new cavalry corps to a hitherto unnoticed young officer.

In a letter written from the military cantonment of Amballa on 17 May, Neville Chamberlain tried to make light of a disastrous decision: 'To thus have been forced to throw up what of all other things I most coveted, was very annoying, but although I often think how much happier I should have been had I remained in our new province, instead of returning to the dull routine of canton-ment life, still I have the pleasure of feeling that my decision was the right one, and that the motives which caused me to sacrifice my own interest were based on the higher ground of hoping thereby to benefit the public service. My stubborn principles have cost me a vast amount of happiness, and some four or five hundred rupees a month.'

So one man's misfortune became the good fortune of another – in this instance, Lieutenant Henry Daly of the Bombay Army, who has so far done no more than flit in and out of this narrative as observer rather than participant. This young officer had been born in Western India in Kirkee, where his father was serving in the Bombay Army. Although from an old Irish family – Protestant, of course; no Catholics could then gain officers' commissions – he was brought up by an uncle on the Isle of Wight before returning at eighteen to the land of his birth, to follow his father's footsteps. Daly had, it might be said, the luck of the Irish, an uncanny knack of always being in the right place at the right time. He comes across as a good, steady soldier displaying no obvious signs of out-standing leadership or hunger for advancement – yet one juicy appointment after another dropped into his lap. He was relaxing in Peshawar after the excitements of the chase after the Afghans when he received two tempting offers: a safe seat in Bombay as Assistant to the Adjutant-General of the Bombay Army, and the post of second-in-command of the new Punjab irregular cavalry corps under Chamberlain. His instinct was to stay with what he knew best and take the staff post in Bombay, but before making up his mind he called at the Deputy Commissioner's bungalow to seek George Lawrence's advice. To his astonishment, Lawrence topped both, offering him the plum Neville Chamberlain had just turned down – the job of raising and commanding what became the 1st Punjab Cavalry, also known subsequently as Daly's Horse (later the 21st Prince Albert Victor's Own Cavalry (Daly's Horse) and, later still, the 11th Prince Albert Victor's Own Cavalry (Frontier Force), following a merger with the 2nd and 3rd Punjab Cavalry).

A year later, Henry Daly was writing home from his headquar-ters in Kohat to describe, with justifiable pride, how he had recruited, raised and equipped a cavalry corps, 'unshackled by a bank, unaided by the Government advance'. There is no question as to whose it is: 'My regiment consists of 4 British officers and 6 troops, each with its complement of native officers nearly 100 men, so that the corps is almost 600 strong . . . In my regiment each presidency has furnished an officer. A strange combination. A lieutenant, Bombay Army, commandant; a captain, Madras Army,

2nd in command; and a cornet of Bengal Cavalry, adjutant.' The fourth officer was the surgeon, the equivalent of today's Medical Officer.

Unlike other EICo regiments, which belonged to the armies of one or other of the three Presidencies of Bengal, Bombay and Madras, the new Punjab Irregular Force came under the direct control of the President of the Board of the Punjab, Sir Henry Lawrence. As Daly explained to his father, the three corps that initially made up the Punjab Irregulars followed their own system of recruitment and remuneration – that difference which, presumably, lay at the heart of Chamberlain's concerns about pay:

Here a native of good birth and character was [sic] to command his troop, in which, of course, a number of his own dependants and followers would be. His pay is nearly £300. He is allowed to mount a certain number of his friends and followers on his own horses, otherwise the horse must be the property of the rider, who draws pay from the Government for the service and support of himself and his horse. The men arm, dress, and mount themselves under the orders and responsibility of their commandants. Government provide *nothing* but pay and ammunition. The drill and discipline are the same as in the line. In almost every one of these corps are men of noble birth, whose fathers in former times were chiefs and rulers. I have several and more gallant soldiers no army contains.

The young commander had a high opinion of his men: 'A native gentleman of birth and position can scarcely be excelled in the dignity of his deportment. Personally he is devotedly brave, and, as a body, with a British officer or two at their head in whom they have confidence, no troops could be finer.' Most of those recruited to Daly's corps were Yusufzai, the remaining two-fifths made up of Sikhs and Dogras. At first, however, he had had great difficulty recruiting anybody, for reasons which shed further light on Chamberlain's decision: 'I deemed it highly desirable to enrol a considerable number of the Pathans of Eusafzai and of the hills around, Sikhs and the so-called Multanis, men of the Derajat . . . They were invited to enter a service in which the pay was no more than they then received, and in which they considered discipline and duty alike severe, for rumour had invested our regulations with great severity; in addition, they were to provide themselves with arms, clothing and good horses. These were not great inducements for them to quit employment about Kohat and Bannu, where their pay was the same, though they owned only a 20-rupee pony and a family matchlock. I regretted this failure, for they are gallant soldiers.' In time, however, the 'strong notions prejudicial to our service' were overcome, and the recruits developed into first-class soldiers: 'They are quick to appreciate the benefit of order, and being good horsemen, soon master every detail of drill. This accomplished, they are proud of their *aieen* [regulations].'

As in Lumsden's Corps of Guides, some of the best of Daly's native officers had chequered pasts. One of these, Risaldar Sundil Khan, had come to Daly and told him plainly that he had been a resaidar in the Bengal Army's 14th Irregular Cavalry until he was court-martialled for a breach of discipline and dismissed. Daly decided to make enquiries:

It happened that Hodson of the Guides was living at the Residency with me when this occurred. Hodson was well acquainted with Sundil Khan, had seen him on service, was aware of his former position. From him I heard all. Hodson is not a man to form a wrong estimate of character. His testimony was stout in Sundil Khan's favour; from this and other enquiries I came to the conclusion that, although the offence against discipline required his dismissal from the 14th Irregular Cavalry, it was not of such a nature as to stain the good character to which so many had testified . . . I appointed him a resaidar . . . Most amply has he redeemed his promises . . . In August 1849 he was promoted to resaldar . . . he is now stretched upon his bed suffering from a sword-cut wound, received in a gallant charge he headed at Bahadur Khel in February last.

To fund provision of their modern rifled carbines and other essential items of good-quality equipment, Daly was forced to make stoppages from his men's pay: 'These I regularly continued until the whole amount was received from the sowars. It was well and often explained for what purpose these stoppages were made, and, although it was long before they saw the result, I never heard a murmur at their continuance. A sowar with his carbine, accoutrements, alkalik [saltpetre for gunpowder], and sound horse-gear, stands to pay Rs 63.' That was one side of the coin – having to deal personally with almost every single aspect of regimental logistics. The other was brighter: 'The raising of a regiment gives one a great advantage in this respect; I know every man personally, who he is, and whence he came. Seeing that I have enlisted the corps, they look to me and not beyond, and so invest their commandant with all power.'

Side by side with the 1st Punjab Cavalry was formed the 1st Punjab Infantry. Also known as Coke's Rifles, this was the first of eight regiments to be raised as Punjab Irregulars. In time they, together with the Guides' Infantry and Cavalry, became known as the Punjab Frontier Force, the famous 'Piffers'. Although originally intended for policing duties rather than fighting, the Piffers very quickly became supreme exponents of mountain warfare.

Coke's Rifles was the only Punjab Irregular Force corps regiment not to adopt the khaki uniform introduced by the Guides and soon taken up by Daly's Horse. Instead, both officers and men wore a blue-black indigo-dyed drill coat, trousers and *pagri*, very similar to the so-called rifle green then worn by the sharpshooters of the British Army's Rifle Corps. This earned the unit the name of '*Siah post*' (black coats), and rendered its men notoriously conspicuous against the dun-coloured hills of the Frontier; not until 1891, under pressure from Lord Roberts, did the regiment accept khaki for service dress.

The man responsible both for raising the regiment and for the choice of uniform was Colonel John Coke, who formed the 1st Punjab Infantry in Kohat in 1849 and commanded it for a decade. He belonged to the Lawrence brothers' generation, born in the same year as Henry Lawrence and, like so many EICo officers, the son of a clergyman. Big and broad-shouldered, with black hair and beard – a beard was all but *de rigueur* for any self-respecting frontiersman at this time – he was a down-to-earth, no-nonsense infantryman. He, Joe Lumsden and Henry Daly inevitably spent a great deal of time together, on and off duty, and the last describes him as 'a particularly fine, high-minded fellow; and man of good family and sound notions. A *gallant* soldier, with reading and information not often met with. A more agreeable companion I could hardly have *selected*.' However, it is worth noting John Coke's favourite maxim, that the way to deal with the Pakhtun was to 'first knock him down, then pick him up', which suggests he was closer to the Nicholson mould than any other of his contemporaries.

Coke, Daly and Lumsden all had the distinction of administering districts as Assistant or Acting District Commissioners from time to time, besides commanding their corps. In this respect Coke proved almost as headstrong as Abbott, frequently threatening to resign when his decisions were queried or countermanded by Sir Henry Lawrence in Lahore. Joe Lumsden's brother Peter tells of the time his elder brother rode over the pass from his district in Yusufzai to confer with Coke in neighbouring Kohat. Coke met him at the foot of the Kohat Pass and asked if he was in good health. 'Yes,' replied Lumsden, 'but no thanks to you. At Shirukki, as I passed, out came one of your Afridi friends, blowing at the match of his matchlock, and vociferously enquiring whether I was Coke! Nothing but my being able to assure him that I was Lumsden, not Coke, saved my skin.'

Where these three pioneered, others followed. The men selected to command the other Punjab Irregular Force regiments subsequently raised were the pick of the bunch, all young officers who had shown themselves to be 'thrusters' – and nearly every one hand-picked by Henry Lawrence. Their names will be familiar to anyone who knows anything of the Indian Army. They included 'Sam' Browne, VC (commander of the 2nd Punjab Cavalry, 'Sam Browne's Cavalry', who lost an arm and won his Victoria Cross in the Mutiny), Dighton Probyn, VC (who took over command of the 1st Sikh Irregular Cavalry – originally 'Wade's Horse', later renamed 'Probyn's Horse' – after Captain Wade's death in 1858, and also won his VC in the Mutiny), Charles Brownlow (2nd Punjab Infantry, 'Brownlow's Punjabis'), Alfred Wilde (4th Punjab Infantry, 'Wilde's Rifles') and John Vaughan (5th Punjab Infantry, 'Vaughan's Rifles').

★

Within months of their formation, the Punjab Irregular Force regiments, cavalry and infantry alike, had become irreplaceable tools in the Deputy Commmissioner's armoury, nowhere more so than in Bannu (officially known from April 1849 onwards as the District of Northern Derajat). Reynell Taylor had returned to Bannu to become its first DC and remained in that lonely outpost for almost four years, administering as best he could an area that extended along an exposed border for nearly a hundred and fifty miles from north to south, embraced ten thousand three hundred square miles of country, and contained a population estimated at seven hundred thousand.

Herbert Edwardes, it will be recalled, had only the year before 'subjugated' the Bannu's warring inhabitants and brought a barbarous people 'within the pale of civilisation', knocking down four hundred forts in the process. But while Edwardes was being lionised in England, collecting orders, medals, honorary degrees, fellowships and testimonial dinners, and publishing his achievements in *A Year on the Punjab Frontier*, it was left to his more modest former assistant to put the lasting worth of those achievements to the test. The *Punjab Reports* for 1849–51, covering the first two years of Taylor's administration, show very clearly that the *Pax Edwardesiana* had in fact achieved little beyond leaving the now fortless Bannuchi at the mercy of the Waziri. 'Major Taylor', reads the most loaded sentence in the *Reports*, 'was so much absorbed with the defence of the frontier and the superintendence of the military details, all of which for the first two years fell to his lot, that he found it impracticable to assess the land tax.' A year later he was given an Assistant and the situation improved marginally, but continuing complaints from Lahore about incomplete accounts, delayed reports and other deficiencies show that he was still having a hard time of it.

Because Taylor is sandwiched between two great men – Edwardes who preceded him and Nicholson who followed – he has been represented as a weak link in the chain, someone who was altogether too soft on the belligerent Waziri, treating them as 'an indulgent father does his wayward children'. It was bad luck for Taylor, and for his reputation, that he omitted to tell his side of the story, as Edwardes did for himself and as others did for Nicholson.

In truth, he had an almost pathological dislike of 'showing-off', and hated to hear others boast about what they had done. He was once heard to remark in mild reproof to someone he felt was dwelling excessively on his own exploits, 'I should not say too much about it if I were you. You did your duty as best you could and that's enough.' Virtue, as far as this most devout of Christians was concerned, carried its own reward.

Whatever the official records may indicate, there is written evidence from his sometime Assistants in Bannu, Lieutenants Holled Coxe and Richard Pollock, to show that Taylor did a good job in very difficult circumstances. To start with, the means placed at his disposal were, in Holled Coxe's opinion, 'ludicrously inadequate': an office staff consisting of two untrained clerks, whose only acknowledged skill lay in copying letters but who were somehow expected to produce revenue accounts from scratch. In any case, office and court work had often to be set to one side in the face of constant raiding by the Waziri. Matters first came to a head in December 1849, when a long-simmering quarrel over unpaid revenues between a Bannuchi malik named Bazid Khan and some chiefs from the Umarzai clan of the Ahmadzai Waziri boiled over into open warfare. The Umarzai retired into the hills, gathered together a force some two thousand strong, and returned in the night to sack and torch not only Bazid Khan's village but fourteen others. The raid marked the start of a series of attacks, ambushes and robberies that kept a large sector of the outlying sub-districts in turmoil for more than two years. Taylor's military resources consisted of detachments of irregulars drawn from Daly's Horse, Coke's Rifles and Lumsden's Guides, together with two police battalions and a battery of artillery – hardly sufficient to police a 150-mile frontier.

Matters soon grew so serious that permission had to be given to rebuild some of the village forts knocked down on Edwardes's orders, and to distribute arms to the villagers for their self-defence. To keep the new road open, a series of fortified posts had also to be built at regular intervals and manned by detachments of armed police. According to Coxe, 'Rockets were distributed at the outposts to be fired at the first indication of danger; the old native custom of beating a drum at a threatened point, from whence it

was taken up by the neighbouring villages in succession, was util-
ised; details of horse and foot were held ready to turn out at the
first alarm; and when there was any considerable gathering of
Wuzeerees on the neighbouring hills, the roads and the river bed
were patrolled all night.'

Relief from the raiding always came with the start of the Hot
Weather, when the Waziri withdrew to the hills, only to begin
again as soon as the cooler winds began to blow in the autumn.
From October through to May Taylor and his military escort were
either on stand-by or on the move, often riding thirty or forty
miles in a night in response to alarms. Throughout all this time the
District still had to be administered, so that during daylight hours
Taylor spent most of his time stuck behind his desk. In this respect,
too, the degree of civil unrest meant he had to concentrate on
judicial matters, in his capacity as a civil magistrate – hearing and
deciding on criminal, civil and revenue cases – to the neglect of
settlement. And here appears what was probably Reynell Taylor's
major weakness. Richard Pollock considered him to be 'a saint on
earth', whose leading concern was the welfare of the people under
his charge: 'Duty and religion were stamped on all he did, from
hour to hour and day to day.' But even the loyal Pollock has to
admit that his chief was hopelessly cautious in his deliberations:
'Taylor worked slowly and over-conscientiously . . . [he] could
never satisfy himself as to his work, and such a feeling makes quick
work impossible, and *only* quick work enables one in a place like
India to get through all that has to be done in a day . . . His over-
conscientiousness now and again caused injustice by delays that
might have been avoided, and in criminal cases, especially where a
life or lives hung on his decision, he quite tortured himself to get at
all possible details and circumstances before taking the responsibility of acquitting or condemning.'

Add to this over-deliberation Taylor's determination to give
time to every visitor who called at his office or sat down on his
veranda, and one begins to understand his negligence in the matter
of the late (or non-) delivery of returns, reports and accounts. In
his first years in India Taylor had been an enthusiastic sportsman
and *shikari*, but in Bannu he very rarely took time off from his
work. 'He would allow himself no recreation,' remarks Coxe.

'During the many years that I passed in intimate association with him I could never induce him to join our shooting parties, or even to take the occasional recreation of a game of cricket or rackets.' The only exercise he allowed himself was a brief constitutional gallop at sundown. This became such a settled habit that a standing joke among the other officers who worked with him was 'Here comes Taylor, as usual, with the bats.'

Every one of the Young Men had emerged from the Second Sikh War with a heightened reputation. But John Nicholson's was very much a local one, among the Punjabis rather than the British, and he was able to exploit it, when he returned to Rawalpindi as its District Commissioner, in imposing his own style of local govern-ment. Three stories are told of him at this period. The first con-cerns his treatment of a local robber chieftain who had such a strong network of supporters in the area that none of the local maliks would help in his capture. Nicholson began by putting a price on his head, and then doubling it. When this failed to produce any result he turned to direct action, riding alone into the freebooter's village. By a great stroke of luck, the first person Nicholson encountered when he entered the village was his quarry. When the man refused to surrender, Nicholson ran him through with his sword, then cut off his head. This was placed upon his desk (or in a corner of his office – accounts differ), and he then invited every headman in the district to call on him. As each malik entered, he was asked whether he recognised the owner of the head, and advised to ponder his fate.

The second story portrays Nicholson off-duty. The Punjab countryside at this time was still largely uncultivated scrubland abounding in deer and wildfowl, a paradise for the *shikari*. But Nicholson, characteristically, went for the bigger sort of game which preyed on the lesser. His method of killing tigers almost defies belief – but for the fact that it is known to have been employed by the Mughal princes in their great lion and tiger hunts of former days. Once the tiger had been located and isolated in long grass, Nicholson would ride his horse at a gallop round and round the beast, never allowing it a still target to charge at. Without slackening his speed for a moment, he would gradually contract the circle, all the while forcing the tiger to keep turning to face him, until eventually the wretched beast grew so disoriented that he was able to dash in and administer the *coup de grâce* with his sabre. To call it highly dangerous is an understatement. The first strike had to be accurate and powerful enough to kill outright, because with a tiger there was no second chance.

The third tale concerns the Nikkalseynis, the curious religious sect which developed a cult round his person. One of several accounts comes from an engineer officer named Alexander Taylor, who later went on to great deeds at Delhi Ridge in 1857. In 1849 Lieutenant Taylor was supervising the construction of what was to be the Grand Trunk Road from Lahore up to Peshawar. He was sitting in the newly-built *dak* or government post-house bungalow at Hasan Abdal when a group of about twenty men in saffron robes entered, saluted, and then sat down cross-legged before him. After a long silence Taylor asked them their business, and was told by their leader that they were worshippers of Nikal Seyn, and had come to pay their respects to him as a member of Nikal Seyn's race. They had deified John Nicholson, and were on their way to meet the object of their adoration – who, as Taylor later heard, had them flogged and thrown out. Predictably, not a word about the Nikalseynis is heard from the deity himself, who was revolted and enormously irritated by the whole business. However, there is a diverting sidelight in an Appendix attached to James Abbott's Hazara manuscript, a delightful story which so nicely illuminates both John Nicholson and its author, and the way they lived, that it deserves to be quoted in full:

Some months subsequent to the annexation of the Punjaub to British India, there sprang up a Sect styling themselves Nicholsynie, and whose creed seemed to consist in worship of Major John Nicholson as the latest incarnation or Avatar of their Godhead. The founder, who was a Hindoo Fuqueer (apparently a Gosyne), and those who followed him, five or six in number, dressed like Gosynes in garments of the colour of faded leaves, wandered about the Punjaub but seemed to have their chief habitat at Hussun Abdal, a spot very interesting to Nicholson, where he had resided when holding charge of the Sinde Sagur

Doaba. There a profuse fountain gushes from the rock and becomes at once a rivulet, over which Nicholson was wont to throw a platform of Planks, and pitch his tent, having thus the stream, which he christened 'Bendemeer', flowing through his tent. From thence he paid me occasional visits, and on one occasion my duties allowed of my going to see him there, rejoicing over the current of his 'calm Bendemeer'. The respect which he there won from an opprest population by his rigid justice had been since inflamed into admiration amounting to awe by the fiery courage he had displayed in the Second Sikh War, when everything great or gallant achieved by our arms was ascribed to him. This prompted the Fuqueer aforesaid to enroll his name upon the scroll of the Hindoo Olympus, judging no doubt that Nicholson was a rising sun likely to repay with golden rays his worshippers' devotion. The Sikh and Muhummedan Races he saw crouching at the feet of the British; who could be expected to adore Gods, who could not or would not give victory to the prayers of their worshippers? So the self-constituted Priest, after experiencing several rebuffs from his adopted deity, determined to try his luck with the Deity's old comrade [i.e., James Abbott], and one morning at day-break, while I was engaged as usual in writing in the room which served me as bed-chamber, dining-room and hall of audience, I was disturbed by the chanted prayers of the Nicholsynie Priest, who was squatted opposite my window, and with all the power of his lungs was offering adoration to Nicholsyne Sahib and (though in an inferior degree) to Goonairh [Govinda?] and Huonooman [Hanuman], who acted in his worship as part of the retinue of the chief divinity. I was at first amused by this evidence of Nicholson's high appreciation by the people of the Punjaub, but when this matutinal din became a daily infliction I rather winced under it and tried to persuade the Chief Priest to [the] resorts and Government of his god [i.e., Abbott tried to make the fakir move on to Nicholson's District].

Finding him resolute to remain, I endeavoured to procure him some deserted shed where he might obtain shelter from the weather, but this was no easy matter now, the dispersed population having thronged back the instant British protection had secured the weak from the lawless. And, before I could find him any shelter, an affair took place which showed the fuquir was quite unworthy of protection.

He had for some time past been soliciting me to bestow upon him an old Beaver hat. But, as I professed only one, this was impossible. He would not tell me what he wanted it for, and this mystery regarding a demand which he professed with so much earnestness, gave me a vague suspicion of some ulterior motive. To refuse his request was painful, as he had staked his reputation on the extension of Nicholson's name, so one day when he was pressing very earnestly for the gift of the hat aforesaid, I offered him ten rupees to forgo his request. This, however, he would not accept and after a while I discovered that he had been more successful with some Gentleman at Rawulpindi, who had made him heir to his cast-off Beaver. Some weeks subsequent to this inheritance a shopkeeper rushed into my kucherry [magistrate's office] at Hurripoor to lodge a complaint against the Nicholsynie Priest, whom it seems he had met on the road and who had asked him for alms, and on his refusal had set upon the ground in his path the hat aforesaid, daring him to advance and outrage the 'Sahib log' [master race; thus, the British] by treading upon one of their hats. Rather than do this, the shopkeeper had given in to the fuqueer's demand and had paid him a rupee.

After this exposure of his zeal in the worship of Nicholson, I set my face rigidly against him, and recommended his return to his home, wherever that might be. He obeyed and resorted to Nicholson, who was then in the Deyrajat, and made a second attempt to propitiate his deity. But his God gave him so many more kicks than halfpence that he retired crestfallen to Hussun Ubdal, where with unabated zeal he resumed his worship of his intractable divinity, and when I last heard of the sect it was flourishing and increasing.

By the autumn of 1849 Nicholson had completed ten years' service in India and was entitled to a year's furlough. 'Get married and come back soon,' was Sir Henry Lawrence's parting advice to him, adding that he would have a post waiting for him when he returned. John Nicholson's main concern, however, was not to find a wife but to get back to Lisburn and see his mother, who had recently suffered the loss of a second son in India. This was his third brother, William, who had joined the Bombay Army in Sind in 1847 and was found one morning in June 1849 delirious in his cot, with two of his ribs broken and his body a mass of bruises. The cause of his death was never properly established; it was put out that he had fallen into a ravine while sleepwalking.

In December Nicholson rode down to Lahore and there met Herbert Edwardes, who was also returning home on leave, taking John Lawrence's two small daughters back to England with him. They sailed by leisurely stages down the Sutlej and Indus rivers to Karachi and then on to Bombay, where they caught the next mail steamer to Suez. During these carefree weeks the relations between Ulsterman and Englishman – now aged 29 and 31 respectively – grew from comradeship into the most intimate of friendships. 'They became', as Lady Edwardes put it, 'more than brothers in the tenderness of their whole lives henceforth, and the fame and interests of each other were dearer to them than their own.'

In a foreign land, surrounded by strangers, a close friendship can be a powerful blessing, and should not perhaps be expected to bear intense scrutiny. Lady Edwardes's remarks have been taken to imply a homosexual relationship, but this is to judge the past in the light of our own post-Freudian worldliness, and fails to allow for the importance of religion in the lives of these young exiles, and the inhibitions it placed on them; in this, they were in some respects closer to Islamic fundamentalists like the Taliban than to ourselves. With Nicholson, Herbert Edwardes, Reynell Taylor and others like them, sexual expression was blocked in favour of spiritual. John Nicholson may very well have doted on his mother, and on no other woman but her, but he was also a very shy young man – shy as only an Irish country bachelor can be – and deeply imbued with a Calvinist sense of sin. In Herbert Edwardes, he found someone with the same unswerving resolution and conviction as his own, but possessed of many qualities he himself lacked, such graces as articulacy, sociability, wit, erudition and, above all, that air of unforced self-possession which is the hallmark of the English landed classes – someone he could admire wholeheartedly. 'You must not compare me with Herbert Edwardes,' he once remarked. Sir Henry Lawrence he respected no less, but Sir Henry he looked up to as a father-figure and master; he was not a bosom-friend.

For his part, Herbert Edwardes returned Nicholson's admiration in equal measure, though temperamentally and culturally they were poles apart. Edwardes must have been flattered to know that this rough-edged, volatile, morose giant, before whom others trembled, and who cared nothing for other men's opinions, cared for his; that he, almost alone of all men, had his confidence.

One topic common to the letters of every administrator in the Punjab at this time is ill-health. There are frequent references to being 'laid up' or 'knocked up' by bouts of intermittent or recurrent fever – the notorious 'Punjab head', or the 'Peshawar fever' – which leave the sufferer prostrate for weeks. Malaria was part of the price of conquest. 'I am about again,' writes William Hodson to his father in September 1849, 'but not able to work. Sir H. Lawrence is very unwell: I fear that his constitution is utterly broken down, and that he will either have to go away from India for two years or more, or that another hot season will kill him. He is ten years older in every respect than he was during our Kashmir trip in 1846.' Paintings and photographs bear this out. The young 'Pat' Lawrence, as his contemporaries called him, was ruddy-faced, square-jawed and round-cheeked, like his brother John; before he had reached forty he was prematurely aged, his eyes deep-sunk and shadowed, his cheeks emaciated, his hair thin and fast receding.

Quite apart from his physical ailments, Sir Henry Lawrence had come under increasing emotional strain since the formation of the Lahore Board triumvirate. Much as he loved and admired his younger brother John, he found it difficult to work with him. In the past John had been either directly or indirectly under his authority but now they were equals in a three-cornered partnership. They could agree on most things, but inevitably there were matters on which they disagreed. They also differed in their working methods: Henry was a man for quick decisions, who acted and moved on, leaving the details for his subordinates to sort out and fill in; John, by contrast, was the thorough-going civil servant, who weighed each thought and always presented a carefully-prepared case. It was John's approach which usually won the support of the third member of the Board of Administration whenever there were differences of opinion – and, increasingly, which gained the approval of the Governor-General when matters had to be decided at a higher level.

It soon became clear to Sir Henry that he had lost the confidence of Lord Dalhousie, who referred to him as the man who 'supposes himself King of the Punjab' and more and more often treated him with contempt. 'I am at a loss to understand the Governor-General,' Henry wrote in a letter to John in June 1851 after one particularly brutal put-down. 'Bad enough to snub us when we were wrong, intending to do right; but to be insulted upon tittle-tattle is too bad. The remarks, too, on the last batch of Jaghires, on which we all agreed, are not pleasant. I am heartily sick of this kind of letters. One works oneself to death, and does everything publicly and privately to aid the views of a man who vents his impertinences on us, in a way which would be unbecoming if we were his servants.' Sir Henry's frequent absences from his office as a consequence of ill-health did nothing to help his growing isolation. When Mansel stepped down as the third member of the Punjab Board his place was taken by an old family friend from Ulster, Robert Montgomery, well known to both brothers but a contemporary and school friend of John's. His arrival precipitated their disagreements into an open quarrel which reached the point where the two could hardly bear to speak to each other, or sit at the same table. Montgomery found himself having to act as intermediary and peace-maker, a thankless role which he described as being like 'a tame elephant between two wild bullocks'.

The issue which brought the differences between the brothers to a head was the matter of land-rights. Henry took the view that the Punjab could only be held through and with the support of the largely Sikh feudal aristocracy, which meant allowing them to hold on to their large grants of land (known as *jaghirs*), and to their pensions; this was the traditional Indian way of doing things, and he felt they should not interfere with Indian custom except where absolutely necessary. John took the modernising view: that the jaghirdars' powers should be reduced and their revenues used by the state to improve the lot of the peasantry. In sum, the younger brother stood for change, while the older supported the status quo, fearing that the British were 'too soon putting down the native system, before we were prepared for a better'. This dispute can be seen as the beginning of the power-struggle between two schools of thought within the British civil administration in India that ended only with Independence – between the *gharib parwas* ('protectors of the poor'), who sought social change, and the *amir parwas* ('defenders of the rich'), who believed in working through the established order.

In the case of the Lawrences, the dispute ended with the defeat of the older brother. Henry was outmanoeuvred, and forced by the Governor-General to stand down. As a sop he was appointed Agent to the Governor-General in Rajputana – while John became Chief Commissioner of the Punjab, a new, unified office that Henry himself had argued for and coveted. It was a very bitter blow, not only for Sir Henry Lawrence but also for his Young Men. Herbert Edwardes wept when he heard the news and John Nicholson was equally bereft, at once offering to accompany Henry Lawrence into exile. 'I don't know how I shall ever get on when you are gone,' he wrote despondently to the man whom he had come to love almost as a father. 'If there is any work in Rajputana I am fit for, I wish you would take me with you. I certainly won't stay on the border in your absence. If you can't take me away, I shall apply for some quiet internal district like Shahpur.'

Sir Henry's high-minded response was to tell his former lieutenants that the best way they could support him was by continuing his work in the Punjab. To his victorious brother he wrote: 'If you preserve the peace of the country and make the people happy, high and low, I shall have no regrets that I have vacated the field for you.' To this appeal John Lawrence replied simply: 'I will give every man a fair hearing, and will endeavour to give every man his due. More than this no one should expect.' A new era in the government of the Punjab had begun.

With Sir Henry Lawrence gone, the older generation of administrators in the Punjab was now represented by Major George Lawrence and Colonel Frederick Mackeson. The former continued in office as Deputy Commissioner in Peshawar for another few months only; having grown used to working in harness with Henry, he chose to leave the Punjab to join him in Rajputana as one of his political agents, and here he remained for the rest of his working life, another fourteen years. His place in Peshawar was filled by Frederick Mackeson, now promoted to Commissioner, a position he held for only a matter of weeks.

Late one afternoon in mid September 1853 Mackeson was sitting out on the veranda of his bungalow when he was approached by a petitioner who salaamed and proffered a sheet of paper. There was nothing unusual in this – accessibility, as we have seen, lay at the heart of the Lawrence philosophy, even out of office hours. It would have been more proper for the man to have waited on the veranda of the main building, the Commissioner's cutchetry, which was just across the garden from Mackeson's residence, but the *chaprassis* who controlled the flow of visitors were evidently satisfied that here was a genuine petitioner. He had, after all, been observed earlier in the day saying his prayers outside the house. When the man reached Mackeson, he pulled out a large dagger and stabbed him in the heart.

The assassin was found to have come from Swat, and claimed no other motive than patriotism: he feared that, if they were not stopped, the British would take over Swat just as they had taken over Peshawar, the Yusufzai country, Bannu and Hazara. In the bazaars, however, it was widely rumoured that Mackeson had committed an offence against Islam, so that a religious *fatwa* had been pronounced against him, which his assassin had acted upon. And in Peshawar's cantonment messes it was said that Mackeson died because he had got himself involved with an Afghan woman, so laying himself open to the sub-clause within the Pakhtun code known as *tor* – the requirement to revenge any dishonour done to a woman, only to be effected by killing both the dishonourer and his victim. When word of this last rumour reached Nicholson in Bannu he reacted with typical fury, demanding that Edwardes take action to scotch the *canard* at source: 'I hear', he wrote on 28 September, 'that some of the Mil[itar]y at Peshawar have got up a story that M's murder was owing to his intrigues with women – I have no hesitation in declaring it to be an infamous lie – poor M was fond of women, but he was not the worse public servant on that account, and he was much too right minded & had too much regard for his private & public character to bring discredit on himself & his Govt by intriguing with married women – I am trying to trace the slander to its source & I hope you will do what you can too.'

Whatever his motive, the Swati was tried and hanged. To discourage others from following his example, John Lawrence ordered his body to be sown into a pig's skin, a punishment said to be 'most abhorrent to Muhammadans' because it was believed to block entry to Paradise. And to counter any moves to make a martyr's shrine of his burial place, the murderer's body was cremated in the Hindu manner and the ashes thrown into a river. However, even this did not serve to dissuade other religious fanatics from murdering numerous political officers and Europeans in the years that followed, as the headstones in Peshawar's two surviving Christian graveyards testify. Because of fears that Mackeson's body would be dug up and desecrated he was not interred in the Christian cemetery, which at that time lay just beyond the cantonment's perimeter; instead, he was buried in what was now coming to be called the Company Garden, the *Kampani Bagh*, a last acre of Ali Mardan's Garden in the heart of the cantonment itself. At the instructions of the Governor-General a tall obelisk of black marble was raised over the grave. The inscription upon it read, in part, 'The defiles of the Khyber and the peaks of the Black Mountain alike bear witness to his exploits . . . The loss of Colonel Mackeson's life would have dimmed a victory; to lose him thus is a misfortune of the heaviest gloom for the Government which counted him among its bravest and best.' The vacant Commissionership was filled by Major Herbert Edwardes.

By the time of Sir Henry Lawrence's departure the three commanders of his Punjab Irregulars – Joe Lumsden, Henry Daly and John Coke – were all firmly in the saddle. Not so Neville Chamberlain and William Hodson. In August 1849 the former had received an invitation from Sir Henry to return to the frontier as a member of the Punjab government's civil department: 'Would you be prepared to serve as Assistant under perhaps a young civilian, or an officer junior to yourself?' he had enquired. 'After a year or two's training under a man of civil experience, I should be glad to see you in charge of one of our frontier stations – Hazara, Dera Ishmael Khan, Ghazee-Khan or Peshawar.' Such a move meant a severe cut in pay and might well put an end to Chamberlain's dreams of a glorious military career, so it was only after several weeks of deliberation that he accepted the offer. After six months in Rawalpindi training under John Nicholson's successor, he moved up to Hazara to become James Abbott's Assistant in Haripur. However, for much of the summer of 1850 he was down with fever and no help at all to the DC. 'All I wished for was to be left alone,' he wrote to his mother when he had recovered, 'and if death claimed me, that I might be laid on the top of some wild hill away from the haunts of men.' As soon as he was well enough to study he began to take lessons in Pushtu: 'By October I hope to be sufficiently au fait to carry on a conversation, for it is a great drawback not being able to exchange thoughts as well as bullets with the enemy.'

His first chance to be of use to Abbott came at the end of the year, when the patriarch of Hazara decided to go on an eight-week tour along his northern boundary, leaving Chamberlain in sole charge. 'There is no lack of occupation,' he wrote home, going on to set down a detailed list of the duties of an Acting DC. Even a partial quotation will demonstrate the wide-ranging responsibilities that were part of the job:

1. I am Magistrate, which means I have to seize and try all offenders for every offence which human beings can be guilty of; also control of the Police.

2. As Collector, to manage and look after the revenue in all its branches, and to decide all civil suits, as likewise those cases which in Europe would be tried in ecclesiastical courts.

3. As Superintendent I receive appeals from myself to myself, both in criminal and civil cases; and I have to submit my opinion on heavy cases, such as murder, etc., for the confirmation of the board at Lahore.

4. The charge of the jail.

5. Charge of the treasury, and responsible for all accounts.

6. Physician and Surgeon-General to the troops and population, and keeper of Medical Stores.

7. Executive Engineer and Superintendent of all public works.
8. Postmaster.
9. Superintendent of mule train and bullocks.
10. Commissionary of Ordnance.
11. Commanding 1 regiment of infantry, 2 troops of cavalry, 1 company of artillery, with mountain guns and falconets attached, 1 company of pioneers (irregulars), 1 company of the Utzai tribe, 1 company of the Mathwazi tribe, 1 company of messengers, guides, and spies.

Before his two busy months of 'acting' were up, Chamberlain had received an offer from John Lawrence in Lahore that he could not refuse: a chance to return to a military life, on vastly improved salary, as head of the Punjab Military Police. His official title was to be Military Secretary of the Punjab Board, and his work would include the management of the Punjab Irregular Force. The latter appointment placed him nominally in command of this entire corps but his duties would mainly consist in the raising and management of a force of ten thousand men, mostly Sikh soldiery disbanded after the recent war. Broken down into small units, these would provide each district of the Punjab with its own force of armed militia, which the Deputy Commissioner and his Assistants could draw upon as local peacekeepers. This time Chamberlain had no scruples about accepting the job, even though it fell short of what he had hoped for in the way of command in the field. 'The duties are purely sedentary,' he wrote sadly to his sister in January 1852. 'A pen is my weapon, and as I dislike the labour of committing my thoughts on paper as much as ever, the change has no great advantage in my eyes. I feel as if I had never been intended to be a "pen", and we never like what we cannot excel in.'

This feeling of dissatisfaction evidently remained with him, for when a war with Burma appeared to be in the offing in the spring of 1852 Chamberlain wrote at once to the Governor-General, offering his services in any capacity – which earned him a curt rebuff from Lord Dalhousie's Private Secretary with the information that his lordship had 'a decided objection to officers volunteering on such occasions, especially when the volunteer proposes, under the influence of his military ardour, to abandon important duties in another sphere, to the detriment of the Government he is serving'. We next find Chamberlain writing to his friend William Hodson to see whether he would be willing to exchange appointments; again he was rebuffed.

Hodson was having his own ups and downs, largely as a result of his shortcomings as an administrator. At the close of the war he spent six months as an Acting DC in Amritsar, but failed to come up to Sir Henry Lawrence's exacting standards. 'It seems to me that a year has not lessened the great defect in your character and drawback to your usefulness – viz, impetuosity and excess of self-reliance,' Sir Henry had written: damning but all-too-accurate words. Hodson was then sent back to his previous post as number two in the Corps of Guides. In June 1849 we find him writing to his brother in England, reflecting on the 'absurdity in dropping from the minister of a province into a drill-sergeant'. Once again he was teaching new recruits to the Guides' Infantry how to march: 'Now daily, morning and evening, I may be seen standing on one leg to convince their Afghan mind of the plausibility and elegance of the goose-step. I am quite a sergeant-major just now.'

But only a matter of weeks after rejoining the Guides, Hodson was back in a civil post, having been given a second chance by Sir Henry. He now became Assistant to the Commissioner in Lahore, a position that combined revenue, judicial and police work under the 'stern and hard taskmasters' of the Lahore Secretariat. Not at all surprisingly, Hodson hated it, and very soon he was begging to be allowed to return to the Guides, where under the extremely free rein of Joe Lumsden's command he had at least been allowed to act more or less as he wished. So for the third time William Hodson became the Corps of Guides' adjutant and second-in-command, and so he remained, despite ever-growing impatience, until Lumdsen went home on leave in the spring of 1852. Then, at long last, he became his own master in a office equal to his talents: Commandant of the Corps of Guides and Acting Deputy Commissioner for Yusufzai. It must have seemed to him that his future was secured. He wrote to his brother that he thought himself 'quite the most fortunate man in the service'. He relished his new responsibilities, and threw himself into his work with renewed vigour: 'The natural taste of the Yusufzai Pathans for broken heads, murder and violence, as well as their litigiousness about their lands, keeps me very hard at work.' The same letter provides a glimpse of his packed daily routine:

A daybreak parade or inspection, a gallop across the plain to some outpost, a plunge in the river, and then an early breakfast, occupy your time until 9 a.m. Then come a couple of corpses, whose owners (late) had their heads broken overnight, and consequent investigations and examinations; next a batch of villagers, to say their crops are destroyed by a storm, and no rents forthcoming. Then a scream of woe from a plundered farm on the frontier, and next a grain-dealer to say his camels have been carried off into the hills. Is not this a dainty dish to set before – your brother? Then each of my 900 men considers me bound to listen to any amount of stories he may please to invent or remember of his own private griefs and troubles; and last, not least, there are four young gentlemen who have each his fancy, and who often give more trouble in transacting business than assistance in doing it.

These 'four young gentleman' were junior officers on temporary attachment to the Guides, all subalterns, of whom one – the new adjutant, Ensign Turner – was to prove Hodson's nemesis. From this time his letters begin to carry the occasional allusion or hint suggesting that all is not quite as well in the Guides as he would have their recipients believe. In particular, the Corps accounts are in a mess, and he has to find time to work with Turner and the Guides' chief munshi, Najaf Ali, in sorting them out. 'I am very busy here unravelling the confusion left by Lumsden,' he notes in a letter to his wife in December 1852 – for Hodson was now a married man and a father, his wife a widow from Calcutta whom he had known before her first marriage. He had first met and fell in love with Susan Mitford as a young man in Guernsey. Then he went away to India and after some years Susan married a man twice her age, later accompanying him to Calcutta, where he died. Hodson thereupon rushed down to Calcutta as fast as the *dak* service allowed, and reclaimed her for himself. He returned to the Punjab a married man, to set up house with his bride at the new Guides' depot at Hoti Mardan. With the birth of a daughter, born in January 1852 and christened Olivia, their happiness seemed complete.

A policy for dealing with the predominantly Pakhtun frontier tribes, based on containment rather than full control, was now being slowly and sometimes painfully developed. Tribes or clans which submitted to British rule and paid their taxes were deemed to be 'settled' and were offered protection, together with small subsidies and allowances, usually paid to their maliks. The problems began with tribal groups occupying land regarded as part of British territory who refused to accept the Pax Britannica, either by declining to pay their dues or by violating the peace through raiding, robbery or kidnapping. If the miscreants could not be immediately apprehended, punishment was imposed, initially in the form of collective fines on the village, clan or tribe to which the malefactors belonged. If these fines were not paid, grain or livestock was confiscated, again on a collective basis. And if these measures still failed to bring the perpetrators to heel, the authorities abandoned the Indian Penal Code and invoked *rivaj*, the customary law as followed by the Pakhtun tribes beyond the settled areas. *Rivaj* was based on the principle of tribal rather than individual responsibility: the whole village, clan or tribe was now held responsible, and further pressure was brought to bear through the practice known as *barampta*, by which any male member of that same clan might be taken hostage, no matter where, and held in custody until either the fines were paid or the wrong was put right. The onus was thus firmly on the tribal elders to sort matters out themselves in their own way and find a solution acceptable to the administration. They were fully aware that if they failed to do so, the authorities would proceed to far more drastic steps, either employing *bandish*, the blockading of a tribal area by using troops and friendly tribes to cut off all its trading links with the outside world, or – the ultimate measure – sending in a punitive expedition.

Soon after he took over as Commissioner in Peshawar in the autumn of 1853, Edwardes had occasion to resort to *bandish*. The crime was the waylaying of a government messenger who was taking a small quantity of a most valuable new remedy for malarial fevers made from the cinchona bark – quinine – to a representative of the British EICo in Kabul. As he made his way through the defiles of the Khyber he was jumped by a party of Kuki Khel Afridi and carried off, together with his precious cargo. Edwardes instantly declared that any member of that clan found in British territory was to be seized, offering fifty rupees for every malik and twenty for every tribesman. By nightfall that same day, three hundred rupees' worth of Kuki Khel tribesmen were locked in Peshawar gaol. The following day both messenger and quinine were safely delivered to Edwardes by a deputation of Kuki Khel; the imprisoned hostages were released only after the three hundred rupees expended by the government had been recovered.

Collective responsibility and reliance on the tribal *jirga* to sort things out in its own customary way were elements of Pakhtunwali that the British were happy to incorporate into their dealings with the frontier tribes. But other elements of the Pakhtun code could never accord with British ideas of justice and good government and would always remain a source of discord – most notably *badal*, the requirement to exact revenge as a matter of honour, and *nanawati*, the obligation to offer shelter, even if this meant harbouring and refusing to give up criminals wanted by the authorities. While a local DC could perhaps take revenge killings in his stride, the refusal to surrender law-breakers who had sought and been given asylum was another matter altogether, because it struck at the heart of government. For both sides this was an issue too important for compromise. Virtually every one of the scores of confrontations between Government and tribe that escalated into open conflict in the course of the next century can be traced back to this single issue of principle versus honour.

The first such confrontation took place in the autumn of 1853. For three years the Afridi clans of the Jowakai hills west of Peshawar had been descending from their homes in the mountains between Kohat and the Khyber to raid every village within a radius of thirty miles. Fines had been imposed, goods seized, hostages taken and held in custody, and blockades imposed – all to no effect. Finally, John Lawrence travelled to Peshawar to sort the matter out in person. With Peshawar's Commissioner, Herbert Edwardes, at his side he met the maliks of all the Afridi tribes who lived in and about the Jowakai Pass in *jirga*. He offered to draw a line under the events of the past three years, provided that the tribes agreed to three conditions: to commit no further crimes on British territory; to allow no asylum to malefactors who fled into their lands; and to surrender a number of criminals who were known to have taken refuge in their villages. Not a single Afridi malik could accept the third condition, while one of the eight clans – named in reports as 'the Bori', although no Afridi clan today carries this name – refused all three. Lawrence was left with no option but to mount a full-scale punitive expedition against these so-called 'Bori'. Seeing what was coming, the Bori withdrew up the Bara Valley to their mountain fastness some twenty miles to the north-west of Kohat, while fifteen hundred troops of the Punjab Irregular Force gathered in Kohat itself: Hodson's Corps of Guides and a squadron of Daly's Horse; the 1st, 2nd and 3rd Regiments of the Punjab Infantry; and two field-guns drawn by elephants. The Guides led the advance, taking the military column deep into the mountains, while the hostile Bori abandoned their villages and retreated before them. The later historian of the Guides, Colonel G.J. Younghusband, makes the point that the Afridi's tactics were always to avoid open battle and to fight only when they had the advantage: 'Afridis may be driven all day like mountain sheep, but when the night begins to fall, and their tired pursuers commence of necessity to draw back to lower levels for food and rest, then this redoubtable foe rises with all his strength, and with sword and gun and huge boulder hurls himself like a demon on his retiring enemy.'

This is what the Bori proceeded to do. They allowed their homes to be pulled down, their cattle to be rounded up and their crops to be burned, all without so much as a single *jezail* being loosed off in retaliation. They continued to withdraw ever deeper and higher into the mountains, from dawn right through the day, until just before sunset, when the leading scouts of the Guides' Infantry found themselves at the end of a narrow valley, with a steep slope to their front and crags on either side. Commanding this leading detachment was the Guides' adjutant, Ensign Turner. As he and thirty of his men began to clamber up the mountainside, they suddenly came under intense *jezail* fire from three sides and were pinned down. The rest of the Guides' Infantry moved up in support but within minutes found themselves under such sustained and accurate fire that they too were unable to move. When darkness fell the Bori tribesmen began to skirmish down the mountainside in their hundreds, taking full advantage of the cover provided by rocks and boulders.

Just when it seemed that Turner and his men would be overwhelmed, the Guides' surgeon, Dr Lyell, quite unexpectedly appeared at the head of a company of Gurkhas from the 3rd Punjab Infantry. Their uphill charge and the dramatic increase in rifle fire that followed their arrival was enough to slow the Bori advance, winning the Guides time to withdraw from their exposed positions and dash back down the hillside. The Bori tribesmen then made the classic mistake of following in hot pursuit. Once they had reached more open ground, Hodson gave the order for the Guides' Infantry to form a square and then fire by volleys on the now exposed *jezailchis*. In the meantime, his cavalry sowars had run to where they had left their chargers tethered. Scrambling onto their mounts and hurriedly forming into line, they made a short and somewhat ragged charge after the retreating Bori, driving them back up to the foot of the mountain.

According to Lord Roberts, then an ensign of eighteen, the other Afridi clans took no part in the affair, other than as spectators: 'The tribesmen with whom we had just made friends sat in hundreds on the ridges watching the progress of the fight. It was no doubt a great temptation to them to attack the "infidels" while they were at their mercy, and considerable anxiety was felt by Lawrence and Edwardes as to the part our new allies would play; their relief was proportionate when it was found they intended to maintain a neutral attitude.' Within eighteen hours the operation was over. The Bori elders descended from their mountain stronghold to make their submission, and the military column withdraw to Kohat with its eight dead and thirty-one injured. A fort was built on Bori territory and named Fort Mackeson, to commemorate the recently murdered Commissioner of Peshawar and to ensure that the Bori henceforth kept to the straight and narrow.

★

That same year, 1853, the lives of the Hodsons began to fall apart. To escape the summer heat Susan had taken little Olivia up to the new sanatorium in the Murree Hills, but here the child fell ill and died, so becoming the first of many British children whose tombstones can be found in Murree's small Christian cemetery. 'We seem to have lost everything,' wrote her disconsolate father. 'She had wound her little being round our hearts to an extent which neither of us knew until we woke from the brief dream of beauty and found ourselves childless.' Perhaps in an effort to forget the pain of this loss, Hodson redoubled the energies he devoted to reshaping the Guides, overseeing the completion of the new fort at Hoti Mardan and tightening up what he saw as lax discipline. As far as he was concerned, Joe Lumsden had been far too easygoing, allowing his Native Officers too much leeway in managing the men. What had been acceptable in a small band of soldiers of fortune could not be tolerated in the leading corps of the fast-expanding Punjab Irregular Force.

As early as March 1853, however, some months before the death of Olivia Hodson, John Lawrence had written to the Governor-General to express his growing concern over Hodson's conduct as commander of the Guides: 'Hodson is, I believe, very unpopular, both in the Guides and with military men generally. I don't know exactly why this is . . . He is gallant, zealous and intelligent, and yet few men like him.' Over the following months, as Hodson's drive to smarten up the Guides intensified, an increasing number of his officers, British and Native, turned against him – and, more dangerously, began to speak out against him to others outside the corps. As far as Turner and the other British officers were concerned, Hodson could do nothing, since they were all gazetted to the Bengal Army. But the Native Officers of the corps were a different matter, since they were locally recruited. As their commanding officer he could do with them more or less as he pleased, and he dismissed those whom he regarded as the leading troublemakers. Among them was a notoriously difficult character widely regarded as Joe Lumsden's right-hand man, Risaldar Fatteh Khan Khattak (not to be confused with Fatteh Khan Khattar, mentioned in an earlier chapter, but no doubt related to Dilawar Khan Khattak, the bandit who was 'turned' by Lumsden and became one of his leading subedars). Even John Lawrence admitted that this Fatteh Khan was 'a perfect devil when his blood was up, and that is very often', going on to describe him as a man with 'many and bitter feuds throughout Khuttack . . . grasping and domineering beyond all bounds'. In August 1852 John Lawrence is to be found warning Hodson, in writing, to tread more lightly: 'You may depend on it that neither the European nor the native officers are as razi [content] as they might be. I have heard it from half-a-dozen quarters . . . There may have been faults of their part, and the discipline may not have been all that it ought to have been. But sudden changes are best avoided. The corps got a great name under Lumsden, who was beloved, I may say, even for his very defects, to say nothing of his virtues. If right men go wrong, people will blame you. I don't think that Pathans can bear a very strict system of drill and setting up at any time . . . I heard that you addressed Futteh Khan as Futteh Khan Mazool [dismissed]; this was sufficient to set such a chap all of a blaze.'

Hodson ignored this and subsequent letters. He was now in serious trouble on a number of grounds: despite repeated requests, he had failed to provide adequate accounts both for expenditure on equipment for the Guides and for a journey to Kashmir; it was also being alleged that he had insulted Najaf Ali, the Guides' munshi and senior accountant, who had responded by striking him in the face, and that he was conducting some sort of private vendetta against 'the greater part of his Pathans and Afridis'. 'My dear Hodson,' wrote Lawrence in February 1854, 'Why don't you send a reply to official requisitions? What is to become of you if you will not answer letters? . . . I hear you say that you work day and night, but at what I can't think! A clever fellow like you ought to have little difficulty in getting through business with proper despatch. I want a reply to the reference about native officers being appointed and dismissed by the commandant of the Guides . . . What are you doing with Kader Khan's son in limbo? What has *he* to do with the acts of his father? Why is not Kader Khan brought to trial before the Commissioner?' These last queries related to a Yusufzai chieftain and his son whom Hodson believed to be behind the murder of his close friend Colonel Mackeson as well as a more recent attempt to kill one of the Guides' junior British officers. In his capacity as Deputy Commissioner for Yusufzai, Hodson had locked up both father and son in his fort at Hoti Mardan, infuriating Herbert Edwardes, who wrote to Lawrence to protest at this 'cruel and arbitrary treatment'. Lawrence sent Hodson a final warning in March 1854 – 'This is the last time I shall write on this subject' – and when this failed to produce an adequate response, he asked Herbert Edwardes to act. The outcome was that Hodson was relieved of his responsibilities both as the Acting Deputy Commissioner of Yusufzai and as Officer Commanding the Corps of Guides. On the strength of charges laid against him by the Corps' adjutant, Ensign Turner, and the regimental munshi, Najaf Ali, he was accused of corruption: specifically, of falsifying the regimental accounts over the purchase of a charger.

After a long delay, a military court of enquiry was convened in Peshawar to hear a string of charges ranging from gross negligence to embezzlement of regimental funds. A remarkable number of witnesses, led by Ensign Turner and Najif Ali and supported by a dozen men from the ranks of the Guides, appeared to testify against Hodson. No one, it seems, was summoned to speak in his defence. The charges were eventually whittled down to one central issue, whether or not the regimental accounts under Hodson's supervision had been falsified, and the court found Hodson guilty of both gross negligence and persistent falsification. The findings were sent to Lord Dalhousie, who concluded that Hodson's case was 'as bad as possible'. In view of Hodson's previous distinguished character and record, however, he ordered him – 'with much regret, for he is a gallant soldier and an able man' – to be remanded to his regiment, the 1st Bengal Fusiliers.

The real scandal of the Hodson affair was the manner in which the court of enquiry conducted its business. It was little more than a witch-hunt, with no serious attempt being made to challenge the veracity of the witnesses, or their motives, or to make any independent scrutiny of the regimental accounts as they were presented to the court. Whatever the rights and wrongs of the case, the outcome was the destruction of Hodson's reputation and career. 'My ruin is absolute and complete,' he wrote some time afterwards: 'I was in the most envied position on the frontier – commanding a distinguished regiment which I had helped to raise and form, and which I had myself instructed, and governing an important district; and I was in receipt of a hardly earned (but honourably earned) income of £1,200 a year. I am now a regimental subaltern of £300, or rather £250, a year! And all this without fault of mine, but simply from the bitter enmity of one man whose official position gave him the long-sought opportunity of gratifying his rage.'

No contemporary ever publicly named the man Hodson believed to have been responsible for his downfall, but there can be no doubt that it was Peshawar's Commissioner. Herbert Edwardes had never shared his former patron's liking for Hodson, never understood why Sir Henry, so keen a judge of character, should have petted or indulged him so. Now that he was in charge in Peshawar and his former master exiled in Rajputana, he was not prepared to give Hodson the benefit of the doubt, or even a fair trial when the matter of the supposed fiddling of the Guides' accounts came before him. He set his face firmly against the man, and Peshawar's tightly-knit European community, dominated by the military, followed his lead. One member of that community, however, although well aware of the faults in Hodson's character, took a more impartial and charitable view: 'He was older than almost anyone of his standing in the army,' the chaplain, Mr Sloggett, wrote some years later in a frank letter to Hodson's brother and biographer. 'He was in this way superior to most of his fellows, and being at the same time naturally sarcastic and fearless, he would say and do things which galled men to the quick and made them hate him.' Many stories critical of Hodson's running of the Guides were put about by his junior officers: 'There is no doubt that young Turner talked about all these things very freely in the Peshawar society, and that the stories to Hodson's prejudice were eagerly caught up and circulated because of his general unpopularity . . . Add to this the envy caused by his rapid rise owing to Sir Henry Lawrence's notice of him, and his unpopularity is accounted for.' Mr Sloggett was also highly critical of the way in which the court of enquiry had gone about its business: 'When, then, the committee of enquiry was ordered, and the members of it were at last all collected in Peshawar – some of whom arrived days or weeks before the whole could assemble in those days of slow and tedious travel – these became infected with the prevailing prejudice to such a degree that they believed him guilty before the court assembled at all, and actually took possession of his regimental papers and accounts. Moreover, the native munshi and accountant, true to his national character, joined in and inflamed the stories against the fallen man.'

It says a great deal for Hodson that, despite being brought low by what seems to have been a transparent injustice, he refused to let the event sour his life. 'I trust', he wrote to a friend, 'I am too much of a soldier to permit myself to be subdued by reverses, or to sit down and fret over the irremediable past . . . I do not say, however, that I do not *feel* the reverse most keenly . . . I admit that there are many things in which I might with present experience have acted differently, perhaps more wisely and more well.'

IO

'I have just shot a man who came to kill me'

JOHN NICHOLSON AND BANNU, 1852–1857

> *Te zan ta Nikal Seyn wayay?*
> Who do you think you are? Nicholson?
> Expression of irritation current in Bannu in 1999

WHEN HERBERT EDWARDES returned to Peshawar in October 1853 as the replacement for Colonel Mackeson, he had a wife at his side. At Petersham near Richmond, in July 1850, he had married his childhood sweetheart Emma Sidney, with John Nicholson as his best man. Later, in her two-volume memorial of her late husband's life, Emma Edwardes wrote of the separation that 'long years, weary waiting, and an anxious and prolonged campaign had swept in between him and a long-cherished dream of happiness – the happiness that his noble, pure, true and devoted heart had nursed tenderly in full confidence of hope ever since he was a boy.' Theirs was unquestionably a love-match, and there can be no doubting their devotion to one another throughout the years, many of them spent apart. 'I cannot tell you', Herbert Edwardes himself wrote to Nicholson from Southampton docks as he set sail once more for India, a year after his marriage, 'how good it is for our best purposes to be *helped* by a noble wife, who loves you better than all men and women, but God better than you.'

In the same letter he urged his friend to follow his example: 'If you return a bachelor, this may be in your favour; but if your heart meets one worthy of it, *return not alone.*' But John Nicholson did of course return alone. He had stayed in England ten months longer, spending the greater part of his furlough with his mother and sisters in Lisburn but also travelling extensively on the Continent, taking in a review of his troops by the Tsar in St Petersburg, and coming to the conclusion that without drastic reform, the British Army was incapable of fighting a modern war. He had returned to London armed with a new gun bought in Berlin, a Prussian breech-loader with a rifled barrel capable of rapid fire and of killing at 500 paces. This he had touted unsuccessfully around the War Office, urging that the British Army's smooth-bored Brown Bess be scrapped in favour of this revolutionary new 'needle-gun'.

His last action before leaving London in January 1852 was to have his portrait taken in daguerreotype by a Regent Street photographer, having promised his mother that he would send her a photograph of himself before he returned to India. It shows Nicholson at twenty-nine, ill-at-ease and uncharacteristically smooth-shaven, and is the only known photograph of him. There is no hint in his uncouth, awkward face of the superman who five years later would inspire an army.

On his way back to Lahore Nicholson stopped off to see the Edwardeses in Jullunder, where he was made very welcome by Emma Edwardes, who always spoke and wrote of him thereafter in the same loving tones as her husband. In Lahore he met Neville Chamberlain, now Military Secretary of the Punjab Board of Administration, and from his old chief, Sir Henry Lawrence (this was before the quarrel between the Lawrence brothers that culminated in his exile to Rajputana), learned that Reynell Taylor was anxious to go home on furlough: the post of Deputy Commissioner of Bannu was his if he wanted it.

In April 1852 Nicholson and Taylor met on the boundary between Bannu and Kohat to begin the formalities of the hand-over, Taylor accompanied by his Assistant, Richard Pollock. 'The circumstances of my first meeting with Nicholson quite naturally prejudiced me against him,' Pollock recorded. 'It was difficult to hear the first conversation of these two, as to what had been done and what had to be done, without more or less resenting the confident tone of the new arrival, who unconsciously overrode the explanations of the officer who had toiled so hard with great self-sacrifice, and from the moment of his arrival to take charge could only speak of what he hoped or rather meant to do.'

As soon as he had completed the handover, Taylor travelled down the Indus to Karachi to join Henry Daly, whose health had suffered a complete breakdown after repeated bouts of malaria. The two then made their way by sea to Bombay and there caught a steamer home to England. Both were on the lookout for a wife, and both found one. In October 1852 Daly married Susan Kirkpatrick, a young lady from the Isle of Wight whom he had known from his boyhood, and took her back to his family home at Daly's Grove, near Ballinasloe in Ulster, where they spent a year before travelling out to India towards the end of 1854. Reynell Taylor returned to his family home at Haccombe in Devon in time to be at the bedside of his father, a long-retired John Company general, when he died. In Devon he remained for nearly two years, and in December 1854 married Ann Holdsworth of Widdicombe. He was thirty-two, she just seventeen. Two months later they set sail for India. Reynell Taylor's biographer mentions the marriage in passing, but does not refer to it again: perhaps it was not one made in heaven.

For all Richard Pollock's reservations about John Nicholson, he was soon forced to admit that Bannu's new DC was as good as his words: 'Taylor would in five years have done less than Nicholson did in two; and their methods were absolutely different – one was all action, looking or fighting for quick results; the other over-elaborated.' Indeed, 'all action' was the essence of John Nicholson. No sooner had he established himself in the newly-built DC's bungalow at Bannu – a thick-walled, gloomy building still referred to as 'the Nicholson bungalow' – than he set about stamping his mark on his District, working with an energy that seemed to those who witnessed it or bore its brunt to border on the superhuman. Here was no father-figure, but a despot. The difference between the old order and the new was well expressed by his friend Herbert Edwardes:

I only knocked down the walls of the Bannu *forts*. John Nicholson had since reduced the *people* – the most ignorant, depraved and bloodthirsty in the Punjab – to such a state of good order and respect for the laws, that in the last year of his charge, not only was there no murder, burglary or highway robbery, but not an *attempt* at any of these crimes. The Bannuchis, reflecting on their own metamorphosis in the village gatherings under the vines, by the streams they once delighted to fight for, have come to the conclusion that the good Mohammedans of historic ages must have been just like Nikalsain. They emphatically approve him as every inch a Hakim [master]. And so he is.

Almost Nicholson's first action was to bring a halt to the marauding that had made the streets of the new-laid cantonment at Bannu a 'no-go' area after dark. 'When I first joined at Bannu night thefts in the cantonment were often attempted,' explains Richard Pollock. 'Thieves, well armed, came in from across the border, and we found their common method was to sneak up the dry beds of the irrigation channels.' Nicholson sent out parties of armed police to lie in ambush in these channels: 'They soon had an opportunity of engaging a party of Wazirs, several of whom were wounded or killed. Their leader turned out to be a Waziri Malik, or headman of a village just outside the Gumatti Pass, which held lands inside and beyond the border. By day this man was a respectable, responsible person – by night a thief; he was killed in the fight.' The day following the police ambush happened to be Bannu's Friday market day. Nicholson ordered the body of the malik to be taken to the market place and exposed there 'as a stoat might be on a barn-door'. The night raids very soon stopped. Twelve years after this incident Pollock returned to Bannu as DC, and was told by the townspeople that Nickal Seyn himself had seized this unfortunate malik alive – and had then cut him to pieces in the market place. Thus do legends grow in the telling.

For all the eulogising that followed Nicholson's death, not all his fellow politicals liked him, or approved of his methods. Lewin Bowring, who served in the lower Punjab from 1849 onwards, notes in an unpublished 'memoir of service in India' that Nicholson 'as a civil officer was not so successful, for he could not brook opposition, and was wont to enforce his will with a large black ruler, placed on the table before him, with which he kept his officials in awe, one old moonshee averring that his nose had been broken by this instrument of punishment'. Yet even this critic has to admit that 'notwithstanding Nicholson's stern unbending character, or possibly in consequence of it, he was immensely respected'.

Nicholson was highly critical of what he regarded as the lax control over the district exercised by his predecessor, and was determined to impose new standards. Believing that the local chiefs and maliks had exploited Taylor's gentle, high-minded nature, Nicholson set out very deliberately to awe them into subservience. At an out-of-doors *jirga* held soon after his arrival, a deputation of Afghan chiefs from the trans-border area failed to show him the respect he regarded as his due. 'Their insolence in speech and behaviour was very marked,' states General John Younghusband (father of the explorer Francis), then a junior officer in Chamberlain's Punjàb Military Police. 'Nicholson listened to what they had to say. At last one of them hawked and spat out between himself and Nicholson. This was a dire insult and meant as such.' Nicholson had his orderlies seize the man and force him to kneel. He was then ordered to lick up his spittle from the dust and, once that had been done to Nicholson's satisfaction, bundled out of camp.

Nicholson followed this by publicly humiliating a Muslim mullah. The unfortunate man was sitting quietly outside his village mosque when Nicholson rode past with a few local maliks and his usual escort of mounted police. Instead of salaaming the new *haquim*, the mullah stared at him with what Nicholson interpreted as contempt. As the cavalcade rode on Nicholson called to ask one of his orderlies whether he had observed the mullah's defiant behaviour. 'Yes,' replied the orderly, whereupon he was ordered to bring the mullah to Nicholson's camp. Questioned, the mullah was judged to have been guilty of showing disrespect. His punishment was to have his beard shaved off – a grave offence to pious Muslims. As a public insult to Islam, this might have led at the very least to a *fatwa*, if not a *jihad*. But the Pakhtuns have always placed their own interpretation before orthodox Koranic law, and

Nicholson's action, because it was so clearly related to his honour, aroused as much respect as anger. He had been insulted, and under the clause in Pakhtunwali relating to *nang*, he was bound to make good the insult to his *iqbal*.

With respect came obedience. As a later political – S.S. Thorburn, a settlement officer in Bannu in the 1870s – noted, at first John Nicholson was hated as a 'hard-hearted, self-willed tyrant . . . but by degrees, as his self-abnegation, his wonderful feats of daring, the swift, stern justice which he meted out to all alike, became known, this impression gave way to a feeling of awe and admiration; and the people both within and beyond the border became so cowed that, during Nicholson's last year of office, raids, robberies, and murders were almost unknown – a happy state of things which has never occurred since.'

We know from this same source that Nicholson's ideas of 'swift, stern justice' were very far from the norm, though it could be argued that they were suited to the time and place. He regarded flogging as a great score-settler, a quicker and more effective way of punishing lawbreakers that hauling them into his court to be fined or sentenced to gaol. Thorburn writes that he himself, when faced with a pair of local disputants in his cutcherry and unable to decide 'which party in [the] suit was lying the less', would often let them argue among themselves. As words began to fly, a point would often be reached when one of the parties would say to the other, 'Turn your back to the Sahib, and he will see it still waled from the whipping which Nicholson gave you' – to which the other would retort, 'You need not talk, for your back is scored also.' Nor does Nicholson seem to have had any scruples about extending his flogging regime to those outside his jurisdiction. John Younghusband tells of an incident he witnessed during one of the Punjab Chief Commissioner's tours of inspection of the Trans-Indus frontier district. 'I was walking with John Lawrence,' he relates, 'when Nicholson came striding along with his head well in the air, as it always was when he was very angry. Behind him came his orderly, leading a gold-laced, scarlet-coated jemadar of chuprassies [that is to say, Lawrence's most senior office orderly]. "Lawrence," said Nicholson, "this infernal scoundrel has been taking dasturi [custom, thus bribes or commission] for the supplies brought into camp. I am going to flog him. You have no objection, have you?"' Although put out by this usurpation of his authority, Lawrence could think of no discreet way of countermanding his subordinate, and so the flogging went ahead.

We also have from Thorburn the bizarre story, told him by the elders of one village in Bannu, of Nicholson's Moses-like judgement in the case of a man named Alladad Khan, whom he suspected of cheating an orphaned nephew out of his inheritance. The youth attempted to take his uncle to Nicholson's court to reclaim his land, but so powerful was Alladad Khan in his village that no one dared come forward to speak against him, and Nicholson had to suspend the case. Soon afterwards, his well-known grey mare was found by a villager, grazing on Alladad Khan's land. Alladad Khan was summoned, along with a crowd of other villagers, and they decided the safest thing to do was to drive the horse onto someone else's land. 'They had not gone very far,' relates Thorburn, 'when they saw Nicholson himself, tied to a tree. After the first start of surprise and inclination to run away en masse, some of the bolder spirits advanced with officious hands to release their dread Hakim; but no, Nicholson would not permit it, and demanded wrathfully on whose lands he was standing. No one answered, but all pointed silently to Alladad Khan, who came forward and tremblingly said, "No, no, the land is not mine, but my nephew's."' Nicholson, so Thorburn relates, then had the wicked uncle swear before all the assembled villagers that the land was not his – and the next day in court ordered it to be restored to the nephew. Delightful though it is, however, the story does not match Nicholson's character, but has, rather, the ring of an old folk-tale recycled by a storyteller to add to the Nicholson mystique by placing him among the wise old justice-givers of antiquity.

Nicholson's pacification of Bannu was only achieved by degrees. In his first year of office his main concern was to bring the Umarzai Waziri to heel. Their raiding had tailed off with the advent of the Hot Weather, as it always did, but before they had a chance to resume in the autumn Nicholson set out at the head of a force of fifteen hundred mounted police to assault their strongholds. The Waziri proved impossible to engage, of course. 'Three columns moved against the Umarzai Wazirs,' records Pollock. 'But by reason of the long distances to be traversed, the difficult nature of the country, the trying season etc., but little punishment was inflicted as regards killed and wounded. But the purdah [curtain] had been lifted, and they saw their country was accessible.' The customary razing of the Umarzai villages in the mountains was followed by a blockade which soon forced the clan's elders to came into Bannu under a flag of truce and ask for terms. Nicholson's reply was short and to the point: 'Pay a rupee a head and behave well in future.'

Not every punitive expedition went so well. When a section of the Sheorani tribe staged a cross-border raid and plundered a village in the north of the district, Nicholson rode up to Kohat to arrange with John Coke for the Punjab Irregular Force infantry troops based there to be called out to make a quick retaliatory strike. However, neither man bothered to inform the local brigade commander or the Commissioner in Peshawar – still Colonel Mackeson at that time – which provoked the Governor-General to write to John Lawrence protesting at Nicholson's high-handed behaviour: 'I know that Nicholson is a first-rate guerrilla leader, but we don't want a guerrilla policy.' In the circumstances, the reproof Nicholson received from John Lawrence was very mild indeed. He was ordered to 'report officially all incursions. I shall be in trouble if you don't. The Governor-General insists on knowing all that goes on, and not unreasonably; but I can't tell him this if I don't hear details.' Nicholson was also ordered to hand 'the Sheorani business' over to the Kohat brigade commander who, to Nicholson's great indignation, took weeks to bring his force together and mount a punitive foray into the hills.

If John Lawrence handled this most difficult of his political officers with kid gloves, it was because he valued his abilities, writing to Lord Dalhousie to defend one whom he regarded as 'the best district officer on the frontier. He possesses great courage, much force of character, and is at the same time shrewd and intelligent. He is well worth the wing of a regiment on the border, as his prestige with the people, both on the hills and plains, is very great. He is also a very fair civil officer, and has done a great deal to put things straight in his district.'

For all the attempts of his superiors to bring Nicholson into line, his contempt for red tape and government orders remained undiminished; a visitor to his office saw him kick a bundle of official government papers across the floor with the remark, 'This is the way I treat these things.' However, he did make an effort to respond to Lawrence's pleas to keep him better informed by sending him more reports – even if these communications provided only the barest details. This probably had less to do with any lingering animus against the man who had brought about the downfall of his beloved master than with his dislike of letter-writing. The most striking example of his brevity in communicating with Lawrence is the note in which he reports an attempt on his life. In full it reads: 'Sir, I have the honour to inform you that I have just shot a man who came to kill me. Your Obedient Servant, John Nicholson.'

To only three men did John Nicholson ever trouble to write anything resembling a friendly letter – Edwardes, Lumsden, and Chamberlain – and only to the first did he come near to revealing anything of himself and his feelings. A letter dating from the early days of their relationship begins by warning Edwardes not to 'expect a long letter or any news from me. I have had another very severe attack of fever which lasted eight days & though I have I hope now got rid of it, I am in a deplorable state of weakness.' It closes, however, with what sounds very like a plea for Edwardes's continuing friendship: 'I don't think I can stand another hot weather in the plains. Be a better correspondent to me, than I have been to you of late.' Over the years, as their friendship developed, Nicholson began to lower his guard with Edwardes, revealing an altogether more humane and vulnerable individual than his public persona suggests. One of the longest of the precious few letters that survive, containing a less laconic account of the circumstances of the attempted assassination, is here given in full:

My dear Edwardes, I take up my pen to give you an account of a narrow escape I had from assassination the day before yesterday. I was standing at the gate of my garden at noon with Sladen and Cadell [two junior army officers], and four or five chuprassies, when a man with a sword rushed suddenly up, and called out for me. I had on a long fur pelisse of native make, which I fancy prevented his recognising me at first. This gave time for the only chuprassie who had a sword to get between us, to whom he called out contemptuously to stand aside, saying he had come to kill me, and did not want to hurt a common soldier. The relief sentry for the one in front of my house happened to pass opportunely behind me at this time, I snatched his musket, and, presenting it at the would-be assassin, told him I would fire if he did not put down his sword and surrender. He replied that either he or I must die; so I had no other alternative, and shot him through the heart, the ball passing through a religious book which he had tied to his chest, apparently as a charm. The poor wretch turns out to be a Marwutee, who has been religiously mad for some time. He disposed of all his property in charity the day before he set out for Bannu. I am sorry to say that his spiritual instructor has disappeared mysteriously, and, I am afraid, got into the hills. I believe I owe my safety to the fur chogah, for I should have been helpless had he rushed straight on.

The chuprassie (an orderly from my police battalion) replied to his cry for my blood, 'All our names are Nikal Seyn here', and, I think, would very likely have got the better of him, had I not interfered, but I should not have been justified in allowing the man to risk his life, when I had such a sure weapon as a loaded musket and bayonet in my hand. I am very sorry for this occurrence, but it was quite an exceptional one, and has not at all altered my opinion of the settled peaceful state of this portion of the district. Making out the criminal returns for 1855 the other day, I found that we had not had a single murder or highway robbery, or attempt at either, in Bannu throughout the year. The crime has all gone down to the southern end of the district, where I am not allowed to interfere.

Yours affectionately,

J. Nicholson

Not all Nicholson's surviving letters to Edwardes are serious in tone. A postscript to a run-of-the-mill note surprises by revealing a momentarily tender and compassionate Nicholson, entirely confounding our image of a man without heart or humour, or time for the small, important things. 'If there are any humming-tops,' it begins, 'Jew's harps, or other toys, at Peshawar, which would take with Waziri children, I should be much obliged if you would send me a few. I don't ask for peg-tops, as I suppose I should have to teach how to use them, which would be an undignified proceeding on the part of a district officer.' These toys were wanted for a Waziri boy, brought before Nicholson on a charge of attempted poisoning, who had also been subjected to sexual assault (then, as now, a serious evil in some sections of tribal society, where such practices are a commonplace):

Fancy a wretched little Waziri child, who had been put up to poison food, on my asking him if he knew it was wrong to kill people, saying he knew it was wrong to kill with a knife or a sword. I asked him why and he said *'because the blood left marks'*. It ended in my ordering him to be taken away from his own relatives (who ill-used him as much as they ill-taught him) and made over to some respectable man who would engage to treat and bring him up well. The little chap heard the order given, and called out, 'Oh, there's *such* a good man in the Miri Tappahs, please send me to him.' I asked him how he knew the man was good? And he said 'He never gives any one bread without butter on it.' I found out, on enquiry, that the man in question was a good man in other respects and, he agreeing, I made the little fellow over to him; and I have seldom seen anything more touching than their mutual adoption of each other as father and son, the child clasping the man's beard, and the man with his hands on the child's head. Well, that is a long story for me, and all grown out of a humming top!

A third Nicholson–Edwardes letter of this period sheds interesting light on the religious attitudes of the two men. Soon after Edwardes's arrival Peshawar in October 1853, he and another military officer began collecting funds for a Christian mission. Nicholson's attitude to this was ambivalent. His Assistant in Bannu, Richard Pollock, writes of his chief's 'horror of cant' and his dislike of strict religious observance: 'I have heard him speak rather bitterly of the enforced strictness of his ante-school days, mentioning the dislike it gave him to the Sunday observances of those days.' Nicholson had no great faith in missionaries, but was happy to contribute to Edwardes's project – provided it was not known: 'I wish your mission in Peshawar every success, but you require skillful & practical men as well as good men. As far as my experience of missionaries goes, they are generally selected with infinitely less care than recruits – the most uncouth brute I ever saw in my life I think was a missionary on his way to Jerusalem, of all places . . . I will send you 500 rupees; and as I don't want to get credit from you for better motives than really actuated me, I will tell you the truth, that I give it because I know it will gratify my mother to see my name in the subscription list . . . On second thoughts, I won't have my name in the mission subscription list. Write me down "Anonymous". I will tell my mother it is I.'

It was at this time strictly against the standing rules of the EICo for any officer, civil or military, to promote or be involved in any missionary work in India – but the rules were being broken with ever-increasing flagrancy in these last pre-Mutiny years. Edwardes, as his wife's *Memorials* sets out in detail, was quite happy to break any number when it came to proselytising for the Christian faith in India. St John's Church, the Afghan Hospital and the famous institution of Edwardes College are all testaments to his efforts to Christianise 'one of the most fanatical cities of India'.

Despite the fierce religious zeal of both Edwardes and his wife, with whom the saving of their friend's soul seems to have become a preoccupation, their arrival in Peshawar in October 1853 was a source of great joy to John Nicholson. Reunited after a year's separation, the two men met regularly thereafter. Whenever he could, Nicholson took a couple of days off from his official duties to spend with the Edwardeses in Peshawar; he thought nothing of covering the sixty miles between Bannu and Peshawar in one ride, changing his own horse half-way for a fresh mount sent out to Kohat by Edwardes. Of his two other close friends, Joe Lumsden and Neville Chamberlain, he saw very little at this time. Both had taken home leave, and when they returned Lumsden resumed command of the Corps of Guides at Hoti Mardan while Chamberlain returned to Lahore as Military Secretary and commander of the Punjab Military Police.

Then, early in 1855, two unrelated events occurred which had the effect of poisoning the friendship between Chamberlain and Nicholson. First the command of the Punjab Irregular Force – in which Chamberlain had turned down a command five years before, when that body was first being assembled – fell vacant. Both men applied, each unaware that the other had done so. As soon as Nicholson got wind of Chamberlain's bid, he at once withdrew his own; he also wrote to Chamberlain, acknowledging the superiority of his claims and wishing him every success. Chamberlain never received this letter, and when he arrived in Kohat in February to take up his command, he was puzzled to find that his old friend in the next-door parish avoided him, as well as hurt by Nicholson's failure to acknowledge his promotion. Each man felt slighted by the other: Nicholson because Chamberlain had not thanked him for standing down; Chamberlain because Nicholson had failed to congratulate him, and appeared to be jealous of his appointment. This unhappy breach coincided with a border raid into Bannu by a party of Mahsud Waziri in which one of Nicholson's most trusted lieutenants, Zaman Khan, was killed. The incident took place well to the rear of the frontier posts which had been established in that area, manned by detachments of the Punjab Military Police – the forerunners of today's Frontier Constabulary. Nicholson, upset by the death of his friend and furious at what he saw as negligence on the part of Chamberlain's men, wrote a wild letter to the Chief Commissioner to tell him so. John Lawrence sent a toned-down version of Nicholson's criticisms to Chamberlain for his comments – which elicited an equally intemperate response from Chamberlain in which he defended his force's actions and threatened to resign unless Nicholson apologised.

John Lawrence now found himself in much the same position as that in which he and his brother had placed Montgomery a couple of years earlier. His appeals to both parties fell on deaf ears: neither man was prepared to apologise or to compromise. Lawrence's revelation that Nicholson had indeed written to congratulate him on his appointment shook Chamberlain's resolve, however, and he began to crack. But Nicholson held his ground, as uncompromising as ever, still convinced that he had been slighted, still refusing to drop his charge of negligence. The dispute dragged on for ten wearisome months, until an earnest appeal from John Lawrence to Nicholson enclosing a renewed message of friendship from Neville Chamberlain – 'he has only to come within reach for me to extend both hands towards him' – finally brought the two face to face in Kohat. Only here, it seems, did Nicholson finally learn from Chamberlain that he had never received that first letter withdrawing his bid. He became increasingly agitated in his distress as he listened to Chamberlain's explanations, and finally grabbed Chamberlain's ivory paper-knife from the desk and bit it clean in two. Peace was restored, and their friendship resumed its old course, although they had few opportunities to meet informally thereafter.

The quarrel between Nicholson and Chamberlain was not the only dispute among his officers that Lawrence had to contend with. An equally bitter row raged between John Coke and Edwardes over the by now familiar issue of a District Commissioner's tendency to run his district like a personal fiefdom, ignoring instructions from the Lahore Secretariat – that same 'excess of self-reliance' for which Sir Henry Lawrence had banished William Hodson from civil service and which, more recently, had brought about the downfall of James Abbott. John Lawrence's letters to Coke during the summer of 1855 tell the whole story. It begins with the Chief Commissioner doing his best to mollify Coke and soothe his ego, but as Coke refuses to back down, so Lawrence's patience begins to wear increasingly thin. 'My dear Coke,' he writes on 26 July, 'How can any work go on when a man says that unless he has his own way he will resign? But such is too often the burden of your song . . . If Edwardes was brusque and peremptory, you would consider him a brute; and if he is conciliatory, he is an "oily gammon". Well then, what must they think of you but as "wayward and unreasonable" unless you have your own way? You desire to make war and conclude peace, to do this and modify that, and all off your own bat! Now no Government can stand this. No doubt you are often right, but not always; because, though thinking usually clearly and justly, you look at things too narrowly. You fancy all the world is reduced to the Kohat focus.' It says much for John Lawrence's untiring forbearance that a *modus vivendi* was eventually achieved which allowed all these strong-minded and wilful frontiersmen – Edwardes, Nicholson, Chamberlain and the rest – not only to work together but to respect one another's opinions.

But if there was one single matter which continued to divide the Young Men at this time, it was the question of Afghanistan and what line to take with its ruler, Dost Mohammad Khan, the Amir of Kabul. The Dost had been left severely alone since his last incursion into the Vale of Peshawar and beyond, at the time of the Second Sikh War, but as soon as Herbert Edwardes took up Mackeson's post in Peshawar he began to challenge this policy. His argument was that the peace and security of the Punjab rested on two elements: a clearly established border with Afghanistan that could be defended, and good relations with Afghanistan. The lesson of the Afghan War was that it was military folly to extend British India's borders any deeper into the mountains of Afghanistan; 'Our true military position', he believed, 'is on our side of the passes, just where an army must debouch on the plain.' He further believed that the security of this frontier rested on 'a strong, independent, and friendly Afghanistan'. These goals could only be achieved by arriving at some form of treaty of friendship with the Dost.

Such a policy was anathema to the many officers still serving in the Punjab for whom the Afghan War was much more than a distant memory. Like most of Edwardes's colleagues, John Nicholson was extremely disturbed to hear from his friend in May 1854 that he had begun to treat indirectly, through the Pakhtun chiefs, with 'the enemy' – and wrote to tell him so: 'I hope you will never forget that their *name* is *faithlessness*, even among themselves. What, then, can strangers expect? I have always hopes of a people, however barbarous in their hospitality, who appreciate and practise good faith among themselves – the Waziris, for instance – but in Afghanistan son betrays father, and brother brother, without remorse. I would not take the trouble to tell you all this, which you no doubt know already; but I cannot help remembering how even the most experienced and astute of our political officers, in Afghanistan, were deceived by that winning and imposing frankness of manner which it has pleased Providence to give the Afghans, as it did to the first serpent, for its own purposes.'

John Lawrence was equally hostile, declaring that there was no point in having any sort of peace treaty with the Afghans. 'I have two reasons against it,' he wrote. '(1) that you will never be able to get the Afghans to *make* a treaty; and (2) if they make it, they will not keep it.' Other experienced voices also spoke out against his proposals. But Edwardes pushed ahead, going over Lawrence's head to the Governor-General and winning Lord Dalhousie's cautious support. The outcome, after months of patient negotiation, was a treaty signed at the mouth of the Khyber in March 1855, between John Lawrence on behalf of the EICo, and a son of Dost Mohammad Khan representing his father. It bound the Afghans to be 'friends of our friends and enemies of our enemies', and closed a door on the past by signalling an end to the EICo's ambitions to expand any further westward than its existing frontier.

As far as Lawrence and others were concerned, this was quite enough. But Edwardes was determined to secure the alliance with Afghanistan even more firmly. Again he won the backing of the Governor-General, and again John Lawrence was outmanoeuvred. In January 1857 a supplementary treaty was signed, this time at Fort Jamrud and with the Amir in person. A reluctant John Lawrence was more or less forced to attend by order of the new Governor-General, Lord Canning. John Nicholson had by then moved north from Bannu to become DC Peshawar, so he too should have been present, as the most senior local official. However, he refused absolutely to have truck with the Afghans, declaring that he 'could not trust himself if he met them, and might even be tempted to shoot one'. He rode off to the furthest corner of his new district and there sulked in his tent until the whole business was over and the Afghans had disappeared back up the Khyber. On 26 January 1857, after a final round of negotiations, the Amir put his *firman* to this second treaty of friendship, declaring as he did so that he had made a lasting alliance with the British and that, 'happen what may, I will keep it faithfully till death'.

Ironically, this treaty gained the man who opposed it a knighthood, while the man who had forced it through received no official recognition at all. The new Sir John could, with no loss to his own standing, have set the record straight, but chose not to do so. Herbert Edwardes, equally characteristically, refused to make a fuss. 'Not a finger will I move in the matter,' he wrote resignedly when asked to make public his own leading role in the matter:

> We all think it a defect in John Lawrence that he praises no one. But I acquit him of all mean and selfish motives in it. It is not that he *wishes* to keep the credit for himself, though practically it has that effect. It is a *principle* of his *not* to praise public servants, for fear of its 'putting wind into their heads', as he expresses it! This is, I think, a mistaken argument; for there is a higher necessity – in justice, to praise the good men do, as well as blame the evil. John Lawrence's blame is an ever-impending thunderbolt, but he is a Jupiter Tonans who never smiles upon his world . . . He is emphatically a hard man in public matters, and so all one has to do is to love him in private, and respect him in public.

It was a thoroughly Christian response.

Far sooner than he or anyone else could possibly have imagined, Amir Dost Mohammad Khan was called upon to honour the promise made at Fort Jamrud in January 1857. Within four months of the signing of the supplementary treaty of friendship, the EICo's authority as the ruling power in India came under direct challenge; within six months it had reached a point where any objective observer would have been forced to conclude that the British were finished in India and their military forces on the verge of annihilation. As regiment after regiment of the Bengal Army turned on its officers and marched to join other mutinous corps in Delhi, Cawnpore and a score of other stations across Upper India, while other regiments, regular and irregular, were withdrawn from Peshawar, Nowshera, Kohat, Hoti Mardan and other stations in the Punjab and marched down to join the little British force beleaguered on Delhi Ridge, how tempting it must have been for Amir Dost Mohammad Khan to go back on his word and claim what he and every Afghan believed was his. What deterred him was the greater understanding of the British that he had gained through his negotiations with Edwardes – and, undoubtedly, his sense of honour. He had given his word twice over, and he meant to keep it. And despite all the pressures exerted by his compatriots, despite the deepest forebodings of Lawrence, Nicholson, Chamberlain and others, he remained loyal to his oath.

Before we reach the fateful events of the Hot Weather of 1857, a few moves are yet needed to get all the major players into their places. Sir Henry Lawrence has transferred from Rajputana to Oude and is out of the Punjab frame – his own moment of destiny will come at the Residency in Lucknow; George, the elder brother, remains stuck in Rajputana; their younger brother John is still very much in charge in Lahore as Chief Commissioner; in Peshawar, Sir John's right-hand man, Herbert Edwardes, is Commissioner, joined there late in 1856 by his dearest friend, John Nicholson, as the new DC. This formidable duo is backed up by Neville Chamberlain, based for much of the time just over the ridge in Kohat, where he sits somewhat uncomfortably beside John Coke, nominally his subordinate. Four of the Young Men remain to be accounted for, and they come in pairs, their fortunes intertwined: Joe Lumsden and Henry Daly, Reynell Taylor and William Hodson.

First, the commander of the Corps of Guides. Among the provisions included in the small print of the supplementary treaty of friendship with Afghanistan was one for three British officers to proceed to Kandahar as a military mission, together with a small escort drawn from the Guides. The officers selected were the commanding officer, his younger brother Peter and the new surgeon of the Guides, Dr Bellew. By this little turn of fortune's wheel, which must have appeared to offer so much promise of military adventure, Joe Lumsden lost what he most coveted in life – the chance to lead his beloved Guides to glory. And by that same turn Captain Henry Daly, commandant of the 1st Punjab Cavalry, was in February 1857 promoted acting commander of the Guides, given on a plate, and for the second time in his career, a prize he had never coveted. Two comparative newcomers to the Corps, Lieutenants Quintin Battye and T.G. Kennedy, were made second-in-command and cavalry commander respectively.

Reynell Taylor and William Hodson make as unlikely a pairing as could possibly be imagined, the one stolid, cautious and God-fearing, the other dashing, incautious and still full of self-belief.

What brought them together were Taylor's painstaking efforts to get to the heart of the scandal which had destroyed Hodson's reputation – a man for whom he can have had scant personal regard.

Reynell Taylor returned to India with his very young wife Ann in March 1855. He had barely set foot on Indian soil, at Fort William, when he was handed a letter from the Governor-General asking him to take over the command of the Corps of Guides 'until something else turns up'. His immediate response was to hope that he should 'not have anything to do with Hodson's accounts'. He arrived in Hoti Mardan to find the Corps leaderless (it will be remembered that Lumsden was on home leave and Hodson disgraced) and in great disarray, riven by dissensions among its remaining officers, both British and Native, and seriously reduced in numbers as a result of Hodson's purges. Hodson's main accuser, Ensign Turner, had now also left the regiment, replaced as adjutant by a Lieutenant Godby. In August Taylor's hopes were dashed when he was asked by John Lawrence to take a second look at the Guides' accounts, and at the main charges laid against Hodson relating to their misuse. His absence from the Punjab during the preceeding two years and his limited acquaintance with Hodson made him the ideal man to look at the case dispassionately.

With Godby, Taylor spent four months picking his way through the accounts, and then set about writing his report. Since he combined with the duties of commander of the Guides those of the Deputy Commissioner of Yusufzai, it was another three months before this report was finally presented to John Lawrence. His findings, however, were unambiguous: Hodson had indeed 'made himself disagreeable' to the Corps, but this had nothing to do with the central issue. 'The whole thing', he wrote, 'hinged on the genuineness and trustworthiness of the available regimental records.' He had gone through every scrap of the Corps' accounts and had found them to be in order: 'I may briefly sum up my opinion by saying that I believe it to be an honest and correct record from beginning to end.' He had found no evidence of either negligence or malpractice on Hodson's part. Indeed, he had examined every instance of supposed irregularity and had found 'Lieutenant Hodson's statements borne out by the facts of the case'. The

Corps' accounts had indeed been 'irregularly kept', but Hodson had inherited a highly irregular system of accounting from Lumsden. And in this respect, the court of enquiry had failed to take proper account of what Taylor called the 'ubiquitous service' of the Corps of Guides, 'during which its numerous detachments had been paid by the various officers to whom they had been temporarily attached, causing a constant and most troublesome system of adjustments from the headquarters, which latter were also usually on the move, and the commanding officer obliged to take frequent advances from political or civil treasuries'.

In submitting his report Taylor added his opinion that, since so much notoriety had surrounded the previous proceedings, it would be only fair to Hodson to assemble a second court of enquiry to consider in public the results of his own investigations. However, the authorities thought differently: Taylor was advised that the Commander-in-Chief saw no need for a second enquiry, and that the new Governor-General, Lord Canning, concurred. They were prepared to grant Hodson a 'full acquittance' on all matters relating to the Corps' accounts, and wished thereby to close the chapter on 'this harassing and painful business'. Only later did it emerge that neither the C-in-C nor Lord Canning ever saw Taylor's report: they had acted on the recommendation of a Military Secretary who regarded Taylor's report as undermining the authority of the original military court. The report was thereafter 'filed and put away' and its contents read by only a handful of officers in the military secretariat. Sir John Lawrence and others in the Punjab administration could certainly have made a fuss, had they so wished, but the records are silent on this point. The conclusion must be either that Lawrence had no wish to upset the military establishment, or that he had had enough of Hodson and did not want him back.

With the return of Joe Lumsden to India at the end of 1855 Reynell Taylor returned once more to civil administration, first as DC in Jhelum and then in April 1857 as DC in Kangra, in the Himalayan foothills, with his headquarters at the idyllic little hill-station of Dharmsala. The Taylors, now with two infant children to worry about, were delighted to find themselves in one of the healthiest and most peaceful corners of India. But for the Hodsons there was still no peace. Indeed, William considered his 'full acquittance' worse than useless, because it left him with no real grounds for a public enquiry. He continued to protest his innocence, vociferously but fruitlessly. 'The powerful hostility of the Punjab Government, which provoked and invited the attack upon me, has been too strong to allow the most ordinary justice to be done to me,' he wrote to a friend in July 1856. 'Although the result of the enquiry which I so long demanded in vain into my regimental finance accounts of the Guide Corps was pronounced to be "triumphant", no notice whatever has been taken of it by Government.'

The appointment of a new man, General George Anson, to the post of Commander-in-Chief in the autumn of that year gave Hodson fresh encouragement. In April 1857 he took leave from his regiment and travelled up to Simla with the aim of pleading his case in person before the general. After a great deal of unsuccessful lobbying he finally succeeded in meeting the C-in-C at a dinner-party, and secured a private interview. The general proved thoroughly genial and sympathetic; he was unaware of the contents of Taylor's report, but after hearing Hodson out agreed to call for it and do what he could. 'He would write himself to Lord Canning and try to get justice done me,' wrote Hodson delightedly to his brother immediately after the meeting. 'I do trust the light is breaking through the darkness and that before long I may have good news to send you.' This meeting with Anson took place in the first week of May 1857; at the C-in-C's behest, Hodson returned to his regiment at Dagshai in the plains to wait for news from Calcutta.

Two months before there had occurred a series of disturbances among a number of native regiments of the Bengal Army at Barrackpore and elsewhere in Bengal. Then, on the evening of 10 May, sowars of the 3rd Light Cavalry quartered at the up-country military station of Meerut went on the rampage, killing and looting their way through the military cantonment and civil lines. Despite the presence of two British regiments and several batteries of artillery, an inept divisional commander, General Hewitt, and a traumatised station commander, Colonel Archdale Wilson, failed to react appropriately and so allowed three mutinous regiments to get away into the night. They galloped and marched the thirty-five miles to Delhi, won over the soldiers garrisoning the Red Fort there, and seized control of the city. In the civil lines just north of the city English and Eurasian families were hunted down and killed, the survivors fleeing to a patch of high ground a few miles north of Delhi, a rocky ridge surrounded by thorn trees. Here they gathered beside a signalling tower known as Flagstaff Tower, the highest point on the ridge. A brief message of alarm, tapped out on the telegraph before the lines were cut – 'The sepoys have come in from Meerut and are burning everything – Mr Todd is dead and we hear several Europeans – we must shut up' – carried up and down the country the news that sepoys of the Bengal Army had risen in mutiny to destroy one of the biggest military stations in India and seize the old Mughal capital.

General George Anson – a mere stripling of sixty – acted decisively, giving orders for British troops stationed at Dagshai and two hill-stations nearby to mobilise and gather at Amballa, where he and his staff joined them on 15 May. Evidently he had been impressed by the fair-haired and angry young officer met earlier in the month, for he appointed Hodson assistant quartermaster-general to the force now being raised to retake Delhi. However, the most pressing need was for good intelligence, in particular from Meerut, from where nothing had been heard since the initial outbreak. On 20 May Hodson was asked whether he could re-establish contact with the brigade commander at Meerut, and at once agreed to go. Travelling by way of Karnal, he covered the one hundred and forty miles in two days.

'When day broke in galloped Hodson,' wrote an officer of the Meerut garrison. 'He had left Karnal (76 miles off) at nine the night before with one led horse and an escort of Sikh cavalry and, as I had anticipated, here he was with despatches for Wilson! . . . Hodson rode straight to Wilson, had his interview, a bath, breakfast, and two hours' sleep, and then rode back the seventy-six miles, and had to fight his way back for about thirty miles of the distance.' As Hodson must have hoped, Anson was impressed. 'The pace pleased him, I fancy,' he told a friend laconically, 'for he ordered me to raise a corps of irregular horse, and appointed me commandant.'

So came into being Hodson's Horse (later to become the 10th Bengal Lancers, also known as the Duke of Cambridge's Own), and with it a chance for its commander to restore his name and his fortune. But the good news from Calcutta that he believed would clear his name never came. The matter was not raised with the Governor-General, which suggests that General Anson failed to get around to writing about the case, as he had promised. On the same day on which he gave Hodson his new appointment, 27 May, Anson went down with cholera, and was dead by nightfall. The wags ascribed his death not to cholera but to 'an attack of John Lawrence'.

I I

'Mutiny is like smallpox'

THE SEPOY MUTINY, MAY–JULY 1857

Na Iran, ne kiya, ne Shah Russe ne,
Angrez ko tabah kiya kartoosh ne.

Iran and the Shah of Russia they conquered
But here the English have been overthrown by a simple
cartridge.

Couplet composed by Emperor Bahadur Shah
in June 1857 after his restoration to the
throne of Delhi by the Meerut mutineers

HISTORIANS CONTINUE TO argue over the origins of the sepoy mutiny that became known by the British as the Indian Mutiny. Various contributory factors were involved, such as the issue of cartridges greased with what was said to be beef fat or pig fat or both, and the annexation of the kingdom of Oude on the pretext of misgovernment, but the root cause was a growing unease among both Hindu and Muslim sepoys about the way their traditional way of life was being interfered with, and a real fear that those things which they held most dear – religion and caste – were being actively undermined. The British Government was forcing the pace of change in ways that threatened the customs of centuries, bringing reforms such as the banning of suttee and female infanticide and introducing new technologies such as the telegraph, the steamer and the railway. On a more personal level, ever-increasing numbers of EICo officers, both civil and military, were now taking their cue from moral spokesmen like Bishop Samuel Wilberforce who were telling them it was part of their civilising duty to convey the blessings of Christianity to those under their charge; to 'coerce them into goodness by introducing our faith among them'. This was seen by many Muslim sepoys as an attack on their religion, and by many Hindus as part of a conspiracy to force them to break caste. Quite aside from the real issue of the greased cartridges, the sepoys of the Bengal Army had recently suffered a series of damaging blows to their morale: their foreign allowances for service in Sind and the Punjab had been withdrawn, many had suffered loss of landowners' rights under new land reforms, and under the General Service Enlistment Act of July 1856 Brahmin and Rajput sepoys now risked caste pollution by being sent across the 'black sea' to such places as Burma. Over the last decade, something had also been lost from the relationship that bound officers and men together: more British officers were being allotted to each regiment, with a corresponding loss of responsibility for Native Officers; more of the best officers in the regiment were being drawn off for political or staff postings; and those that remained seemed less willing to learn the language of their men, or to make the effort to understand their concerns. The arrival of the new Governor-General in Calcutta in February 1856 signalled the start of a wave of rumours among the troops of the Bengal Army that grew wilder with every passing month: Lord Canning had been sent by Queen Victoria to convert all her subjects to Christianity; thirty thousand Sikhs from the Punjab were being enlisted to break the power of the Hindus in the Bengal Army; bone-dust was being mixed with the flour supplied to the men, to break their caste. The disturbances at Barrackpore had failed to ease the tension; the grievances remained pent up, so that when the explosion finally came it was both catastrophic and widespread.

As to its course, here we can focus only on the parts played by Henry Lawrence's Young Men, first in the Punjab and then at Delhi. This is not to give them unjustified prominence, for it is no exaggeration to say that the actions of six of the Young Men – Edwardes, Chamberlain and Nicholson at one level and Hodson,

Daly and Coke on another – combined to turn almost certain defeat into victory. Of Henry Lawrence himself no more need be said than that he applied the watchword of Londonderry to Lucknow: for although he died of his wounds on 4 July, early in the epic 172-day siege of the Residency, its defence owed a very great deal to his foresight and his determination to stand and fight.

Up-country in Peshawar the response was no less resolute. On the evening of 11 May Ensign Fred Roberts – 'Little' Roberts then, 'Bobs Bahadur' only much later in his career – was dining in the officers' mess when a telegraph signaller rushed in. The telegram in his hand was the first message from Delhi 'to all stations in the Punjab' with news of the outbreak at Meerut. The senior officer present ran across to the Commissioner's bungalow, where he found Edwardes and Nicholson together at supper: at the start of the year Emma Edwardes had been forced to return to England to recover her health, and since that time Nicholson had taken to living at his friend's bungalow rather than his own. Edwardes immediately summoned the commander of the Peshawar Brigade, a Brigadier Sydney Cotton, and despatched a rider to Kohat with a call to Neville Chamberlain to join them with all speed. Nicholson, meanwhile, made his way over to the officers' mess and cautioned those present to keep the news to themselves. These four – Edwardes, Nicholson, Chamberlain and Cotton – met at daybreak the following morning to hold a council of war. Roberts was asked to take the minutes, and so was a witness to their deliberations.

When he first arrived in Peshawar Roberts had been told all sorts of wild tales about John Nicholson, but had met him for the first time only a few weeks before when he went out into the hills to do some surveying. Returning to his camp one evening, he had found pitched beside his own a second tent, that of the local Deputy Commissioner. That night they dined together. 'Nicholson impressed me more profoundly than any man I had ever met before, or have ever met since,' Roberts later wrote. 'I have never seen anyone like him. He was the beau ideal of a soldier and a gentleman. His appearance was distinguished and commanding, with a sense of power about him which to my mind was the result of his having passed so much of his life among the wild and lawless tribesmen, with whom his authority was supreme. Intercourse with this man amongst men made me more eager than ever to remain on the frontier, and I was seized with ambition to follow in his footsteps.'

At the meeting in the brigadier's bungalow in Peshawar it was John Nicholson who set the agenda. He had long expected just such a mutiny in the Bengal Army, and had no doubts as to its causes. 'Neither greased cartridges, the annexation of Oude, nor the paucity of European officers were the causes,' he declared. 'For years I have watched the army and felt sure they only wanted the opportunity to try their strength with us.' Not only did he have an explanation, he also had a plan prepared. 'Mutiny is like smallpox' was how Nicholson expressed it, here and on subsequent occasions, in what became almost a mantra. 'It spreads quickly and must be crushed as soon as possible.' Any hint of rebellion in the Punjab must be stifled before it had a chance to take hold. For this purpose Nicholson proposed that what he termed a 'movable column' should be formed immediately – a fast-moving strike force of picked troops that could travel by forced marches to wherever trouble seemed to be brewing. At the same time, any of the eight regular regiments of the Bengal Army then stationed in Peshawar whose loyalties were considered questionable must be transferred to outstations where they could do less harm. At this early stage the mutiny appeared to be confined to the predominantly Hindu Brahmin and Rajput soldiery of the Bengal Army, mainly from the Gangetic plains, so Nicholson had every hope of the support of both the Muslim tribal leaders and the Sikh sirdars. He therefore proposed as a third step that new levies of Pakhtun and Sikh irregulars should be raised with all speed from Multan and elsewhere.

The Nicholson plan was put to the elderly and infirm commander of the Peshawar Division, General Reed, more or less as a *fait accompli*. 'The old General', wrote Henry Daly, basing his account of the meeting on what Edwardes told him some days later, 'in his sleeping drawers and slippers, looked puzzled and almost before he knew what had taken place, the proceedings were on paper; orders out for the movement and collection of troops at various dispositions . . . Even at the last, the old General looked bewildered and puzzled . . . presiding in silence while these efforts to save India were manfully and nobly made.' It was agreed that the Movable Column should set off towards Lahore as soon as possible. Its main force would be made up of local irregulars – the Corps of Guides' Cavalry and Infantry from Hoti Mardan, Coke's Rifles and three squadrons of irregular horse from Kohat – the 1st (under Lieutenant Watson), 2nd (under Lieutenant Charles Nicholson, John's brother) and 5th Punjab Cavalry – and one troop of Horse Artillery from Peshawar. They would be joined on the march by three more regiments of Punjab irregulars – the 4th Sikhs, and the 2nd (under Captain Green) and 4th (under Captain Wilde) Punjab Infantry – and two regiments of the Queen's Army – HM 17th Foot from Nowshera and HM 24th from Rawalpindi. Next came the question of who should lead the Column. All present – except possibly the bewildered General Reed – were fully aware that the security of the Punjab would almost certainly rest on his shoulders. 'It was felt', records Roberts, 'that in such a crisis the best man must be selected, irrespective of seniority,' Nicholson made it known that he and Brigadier Cotton would be best employed in Peshawar, so by general consensus Neville Chamberlain was chosen to command. To Robert's delight, Chamberlain made him his staff officer. 'I took with me only just enough kit for a hot-weather march,' he records in his autobiography, 'and left everything standing in my house just as it was, little thinking that I should never return to it.'

Writing some days later to give his mother the news of his appointment, Chamberlain begged her not to be alarmed at the course of events, 'for we are in the hands of the true and only God who rules the whole world and all nations, and the convulsion now going on around us must be intended in the end to advance His glory, and therefore as Christians and soldiers our duty is to meet the storm with calm fortitude.' His faith left him in no doubt as to the eventual outcome: 'Even if every native soldier in the Punjab was to desert us, I think by good management the European troops might be assembled in one place, and bid defiance to the whole population until rescued from England . . . We are pushing on some of our Irregular Infantry from across the Indus, as likely to be staunch; and unless the Mahomedans get up a holy war cry, the Pathans in our ranks are little likely to sympathise with the Hindoos.'

Henry Daly had been in command of the Corps of Guides at Hoti Mardan for barely a fortnight when he first received news of the mutiny. 'Heard at 8 this morning that the 55th Native Infantry had marched from Nowshera at gunfire [the morning gun fired at daybreak] to relieve the Guides at Mardan,' reads his diary for 13 May 1857. 'About an hour afterwards received an order from Colonel Edwardes to move without delay with the corps into Nowshera. A private note explained: open mutiny at Meerut and elsewhere; reliable troops to be collected and moved off towards Jhelum. No more scotching the snake . . . Handed over the fort, and marched at 6 p.m. with about 150 cavalry and 350 infantry. Reached Nowshera at midnight. Two hours after received an "urgent" to proceed forthwith to Attock to relieve the three line companies in charge of the fort, and hold it until the arrival of a detachment from Kohat [the advance party of the Movable Column]. Marched accordingly at daybreak. The men had nothing to eat (the Ramzan) during the previous day, and were much distressed during this burning march.' It was now the hottest month of the Indian calendar, with daily temperatures in the plains regularly exceeding 120 degrees Fahrenheit – and, to cap it all, the month of Ramadan had just begun, when no adult Muslim may eat or allow water to pass his lips between the hours of sunrise and sunset.

Twenty-four hours after the Guides had secured Attock Fort, Neville Chamberlain arrived at the head of the Movable Column, with General Reed in tow. Daly was much struck by the contrast between the two. The general he found to be 'a poor, weak, old gentleman in HMS [Her Majesty's Service; that is to say, the Queen's and not the Company's Army], of a very different temper and style; frivolous in all points, petty, with no grasp, no knowledge; writing little notes to subordinates with much care and little grammar.' Chamberlain he describes as 'neither punctilious nor pedantic; a resolute, thoughtful *soldier*; neither brilliant nor cultivated, but sensible, grave, and solid'.

Daly was now told there had been a change of plan. Instead of staying at Attock he was to take his Guides on to Lahore ahead of the Movable Column, with all speed. They were to march at night and rest wherever they could finder shelter during the heat of the day. For the remainder of that day, 15 May, the men slept in the cooler recesses of the old fort, rousing themselves at sunset. While Daly walked down to the Indus and took a last refreshing swim, the Muslims among his men said their prayers and broke their fast at the convivial shared feast known as *Iftar*. At one in the morning they breakfasted in the dark and an hour later three troops of horse and eight companies of infantrymen assembled in the courtyard of the fort to begin a march which has since entered the annals of military history. Daly's diary for the first three days tells the story:

16th Boran, 32 miles from Attock. Marched at 2 a.m. in the midst of a sweeping, violent dust-storm, after which the air grew cool. Many of the men sore-footed after that hot, long march from Mardan to Attock, but all cheerful and making light of their work. The Punjab is paying back to India all she cost her by sending troops stout and firm to her aid. Bugle at midnight, move off at 1 a.m.

17th Jani-ki-Sang, 32 miles; a pleasant march, reaching our ground about 8 a.m.

18th Started at 1 a.m. Overtaken within 4 or 5 miles of Pindi by Edwardes, travelling down in a buggy to consult Sir John [Lawrence]. I jumped into the buggy and went with him to Sir John's – reached at 5 a.m. Chamberlain in bed at the door. Sir John in bed within, called us and began conversing on affairs with his old frankness and cordiality. Affairs are bad.

The Chief Commissioner's presence in Rawalpindi was entirely fortuitous; he had been on his way to Murree to join his family for a much-needed break in the hills. However, it enabled a second council of war to be held, as informal as the first. Here Chamberlain learned there were no more than twenty-eight thousand British troops in India, their senior commanders already showing all the familiar signs of indecision and time-wasting. The good news was that twelve thousand of those soldiers were in the Punjab. General Reed, as the most senior officer in the province, was their commander – but in name only; all decisions were taken by John Lawrence and executed by his lieutenants, and nearly all of them had first-hand experience of the evils of inaction in a crisis and were determined they should not be repeated. Robert Montgomery, Commissioner in Lahore, had already set the pattern: as soon as the first telegrams reached the city he ordered the European population into the fort and then disarmed the 6,000-strong native garrison. Lawrence, similarly, made his position clear by telegraphing General Anson's successor as Commander-in-Chief, General Sir Henry Barnard, a message that went well beyond frank advice: 'Act at once, march with any body of European troops to the spot, and the danger will disappear. Give it time, and it will flame through the land.'

Henry Daly took part in this second council, and was struck by the high spirits of those present. 'Even amidst all the grave affairs Edwardes' wit and humour sparkle,' he noted in his diary. 'He has named the old General "the Dictator". In the sort of Council of Discussion at Sir John's, the line of operations was fixed on, papers actually written by Edwardes, and then the remark – "Now let us send for the Dictator". Thus, cut-and-dried affairs are put affirmatively to the General . . . Sir John, full of pluck, fearing no responsibility; without communication or means of communication with the Governor-General, he has raised and is raising large bodies of troops, passing all the best corps of the Punjab Irregular Force towards India.' Lawrence was taking a desperate gamble in sending the larger proportion of his most reliable troops south to relieve the beleaguered British force outside Delhi and banking on the ability of the remainder to stamp out rebellion among the many unreliable regiments of the Bengal Army remaining in the Punjab, scattered across the country at some fifteen stations, an average of two regiments at each.

While Chamberlain remained in Rawalpindi to allow the remainder of the Movable Column to join him, the Guides pushed on – not to Lahore, but to help bolster the field force being assembled in Amballa by General Anson. They rested on 19 May and resumed their march that same night:

20th Reached Mandra, 20 miles, at 5 a.m., having marched at 10 p.m. last night. Great difficulty in keeping awake; obliged to get off and walk; that succeeded in making me hot; mounted again, nearly fell off, eyes closed of themselves. Halt for ten minutes, Battye and Hawes on the ground asleep before stretched out . . . Men very cheerful and ready to go anywhere; none admit themselves too knocked up or too stiff to proceed.

21st Sohawah, 24 miles, crossed the Bakrialla; ravines and roads broken and intricate; spent a burning day: marched at 8 p.m., wind scalding.

So it goes on, night after night. On 3 June Daly notes: 'a few weeks ago how hard and strange we should have thought thus sleeping in the open without any other pillow than a stone; now our great object is to get down, sleep is never far from us'. They were now bypassing Amballa and proceeding directly south towards Delhi to link up with Anson's field force, with the objective of retaking the Mughal capital. This force, now under the command of Barnard, had moved out of Amballa to rendezvous with a siege train coming from Meerut at Alipur, ten miles north of Delhi.

Three days later, with the Sutlej crossed and Delhi less than a hundred miles away, the Guides began to suffer their first casualties: 'Cholera appeared amongst us this evening and attacked three Gurkhas; 1 cook died, 7 or 8 men under its pressure by sunset; obliged to leave 5 men behind.' A day further on and the Guides found themselves forced to fight a local action against a hostile village, losing one man killed and three wounded.

At midnight that same day, 7 June, General Barnard's Delhi Field Force, now consisting of six hundred cavalry, twenty-four hundred infantry, twenty-two field guns and a siege-train made up of eight 18-pounders and sixteen 8-inch and 5½-inch mortars, advanced down the Delhi road from Alipur. William Hodson and his scouts had gone on ahead and reported that the rebels were massed in strength on both sides of the road at the village of Badli-ki-Serai, about half-way between Alipur and Delhi. A three-pronged attack, culminating in a successful charge on the enemy's guns by the Scots of HM 75th Foot (later The Gordon Highlanders), forced the rebel sepoys into retreat, leaving thirteen guns on the ground. Continuing his advance, General Barnard soon came in sight of the thorn-covered spine of high ground outside Delhi known as the Ridge. Dividing into two columns, his men assaulted this two-mile rise from both ends, driving off its defenders and meeting at a midway point along the ridge beside a large building known as Hindu Rao's House.

This 'Ridge' was no more than a narrow outcrop of rock that ran north and south for a distance of about two and a half miles. At its highest point, where the ornamental signalling tower known as Flagstaff Tower had been built, it was no more than sixty feet above the plain. End-on rather than broadside-on to the city of Delhi though it was, its southern end surrounded on three sides by the suburbs of Delhi and walled vegetable gardens, it nevertheless provided the Field Force with a natural defensive position. 'I have frequently wandered over the Ridge since 1857,' wrote Fred Roberts many years later, 'and thought how wonderfully we were aided by finding a ready-made position − not only a coign of vantage of attack, but a rampart of defence.' His concise description of the British positions on Delhi Ridge cannot be bettered:

The main piquet was established at Hindu Rao's house, a large stone building, in former days the country residence of some Mahratta Chief, where the Sirmur Battalion [later the 2nd King Edward's Own Gurkha Rifles and today the 1st Battalion, Royal Gurkha Rifles, still serving with the British Army], two companies of the 60th Rifles [later the King's Royal Rifle Corps], and two of Scott's guns had been placed. About one hundred and eighty yards further to the left [north] was the observatory, near which our heavy gun battery was erected. Beyond the observatory was an old Pathan mosque, in which was placed an Infantry piquet with two field-guns. Still further to the left [north] came Flagstaff Tower, held by a party of Infantry with two more field-guns. At the extreme right [the southern end] of the Ridge, overlooking the trunk road, there was a strong piquet with a heavy battery. This was the weak point of our defence . . . a succession of houses and walled gardens, from which the rebels constantly threatened our flank. To protect this part of the position as much as possible, a battery of three 18-pounders and an Infantry piquet was placed on what was

12. Major-General Reynell Taylor: a photograph probably taken in 1877 at the end of his military career in India, when he was 55

13. John Nicholson, clean-shaven and ill-at-ease, photographed in London
for his mother during his home leave in 1851

14. Assistant Commissioner Muhammad Hayat Khan: the photograph is a *carte de visite* probably taken in Lahore after he formally joined the Punjab Commission in 1862

15. Colonel Harry Lumsden with British and Native Officers of the Queen's Own Corps of Guides: the photograph was probably taken shortly before Joe Lumsden finally relinquished command of the Guides in 1861 at the age of 40

16. 'A most grand fellow': a pen-and-ink sketch of Colonel Frederick Mackeson, pasted into an album by C.G. Pearse, who had served as his Assistant in Hazara

17. British and Native Officers of Hodson's Horse (together with a stray bugler), photographed by Felice Beato in March 1858 soon after the recapture of Lucknow from the mutineers. The officer standing in the centre is Assistant Surgeon Lieutenant Mecham; the seated officer may well be Major Henry Daly, then in temporary command of Hodson's Horse following Hodson's death on 9 March

18. 'Hodson's Horse at Rhotuck': Major William Hodson leads his irregulars into action at Rhotak on 16 August 1857. Lithograph by G.F. Atkinson, 1857

19. The British Camp outside Delhi, with the Ridge in the background: from Turnbull's *Sketches of Delhi*, 1857

20. The Kashmir Gate at Delhi, showing the breach made for the assault of the city by Nicholson's column: from Turnbull's *Sketches of Delhi*, 1857

21. 'Bobs Bahadur': Field Marshal Lord Roberts of Kandahar, Pretoria and Waterford, VC, Commander-in-Chief India 1885-93, Ireland 1895-9, South Africa 1899-1901: the photograph shows Fred Roberts with his staff officers in South Africa, flanked by a Sikh and a Pakhtun orderly

22. Veterans of the Mutiny: a photograph taken at a Bengal Army reunion held at the Star
and Garter in Richmond in 1859. In this group are: (*back row, left to right*) Lt Clement
Smith (27th Bengal Native Infantry); Brig. John Coke (1st Punjab Infantry, 'Coke's
Rifles'); Capt. Dighton Probyn, VC ('Probyn's Horse', later 11th KEO Lancers);
Major Henry Daly (1st Punjab Cavalry, 'Daly's Horse'); Capt. Charles Batchelor;
Major Clem Browne (DC, Cis-Sutlej); Depuis; (*front row, left to right*) unknown officer;
unknown officer; Col. Herbert Edwardes (Commissioner, Peshawar); Col. George
Lawrence (Resident, Mewar); Capt. Alfred Wilde (2nd Punjab Cavalry, 'Wilde's Cavalry'
Capt. Herbert Clogstown, VC (2nd Hyderabad Cavalry)

23. Native Officers of Queen Victoria's Own Guides' Cavalry: a photograph taken by
J. Burke in Afghanistan during the Second Afghan War. Fourth from the right is the son
of Gulbaz Khan, one of Harry Lumsden's first recruits. His grandson, Major-General
Jehan Zeb Khan, commanded the Guides' Cavalry in the 1960s

known as the General's Mound, with a Cavalry piquet and two Horse Artillery guns immediately below. In front of the Ridge, the ground was covered with old buildings, enclosures, and clumps of trees, which afforded only too perfect shelter to the enemy when making their sorties.

On 9 June – the day following the Delhi Field Force's capture of the Ridge – the Guides finally ended their march, coming into sight of the British camp 'as firm and light as if they had marched but a mile'. They had started out from Hoti Mardan six hours after receiving orders and, with three halts made by order, had nevertheless marched five hundred and eighty miles in twenty-two days – the equivalent of twenty-two of today's marathons completed in as many days, but in full marching order (arms carried and rations and ammunition in packs), during the fast of Ramadan and all in the hottest month of the Indian calendar.

One of the first British officers to ride out to greet the Guides' column as it entered General Barnard's camp outside Delhi was their former commandant, Major William Hodson. As soon as he was spotted, sepoys and sowars broke ranks and swarmed round him, puzzling the many spectators who had understood him to be held in deep dislike by the men of his former command. Hodson, profoundly moved by this spontaneous display of affection, hurried back to his tent to scribble a short letter in pencil to his wife in the hills – he wrote her at least one letter every day. 'It would have done your heart good to see the welcome they gave me,' he said, 'cheering and shouting and crowding round me like frantic creatures. They seized my bridle, dress, hands, and feet, and literally threw themselves down before the horse with the tears streaming down their faces. Many officers who were present hardly knew what to make of it, and thought the creatures were mobbing me; and so they were, but for joy, not for mischief.'

Hardly had Hodson finished writing these lines when bugles rang out to sound the alarm: the Delhi mutineers had launched a massive attack on the piquets at the southern end of the Ridge. These, less than half a mile from the walls of Delhi, were always the most vulnerable to attack, both on this day and for the sixteen weeks that followed. The Guides had only just reached their allotted camping ground, in the open plain behind and slightly to the west of the northern end of the Ridge, when a staff officer galloped up to Daly and asked how soon they could go into action. 'In half an hour,' Daly replied, and in half an hour his hundred and fifty sowars were indeed charging into action, with a second cheer for Hodson as they rode up to give him their support. He was already embroiled in hand-to-hand combat, fifty or so Sikh horsemen from Jindh at his side. A somewhat disturbing picture of Hodson in action has been left by an eye-witness, an engineer officer named Charles Thomason: 'I shall never forget Hodson's face. It was smiles all over. He went round and round the man, who in the centre of the circle was dancing *more Indico*, doing his best to cut Hodson's reins. This went on for a short time, when a neat point from Hodson put an end to the performance.'

Within half an hour the enemy had been driven back to the shelter of the walls of Delhi – but at a price. Henry Daly's diary for that first day at Delhi ends thus: 'The men hotly engaged, Battye mortally wounded – noble Battye ever in front; Khan Singh Rosa hard hit; Hawes clipt across the face with a sword and many good men down. Men behaved heroically, *impetuously*.' His second-in-command, Lieutenant Kennedy, had also been wounded, while Daly himself had had his horse killed under him and taken a wound in the calf from a spent round. In a letter to his wife in Murree Daly expanded on 'Poor gallant Battye . . . The last time I saw him in the fight I shouted to him, "Gallant Battye, well done, brave Battye." He was buried the day after our arrival, and at about the time we had marched past the burial ground the day before.'

This was the young man who had been so keen to write Horace's *Dulce et decorum est pro patria mori* on the wall of the officers' billiard-room in the mess at Hoti Mardan. Shot through the groin, he died murmuring those same seductive words.

When Herbert Edwardes returned from Rawalpindi to Peshawar on 21 May he found John Nicholson 'immersed in cares and anxieties . . . the regiments talking big, and the natives of the district wearing that consciousness of impending difficulty to their European rulers which is so sure a herald of crisis'. The Pakhtuns were not coming forward to enlist as Nicholson had hoped, and the intelligence being gleaned on all sides was exceedingly ominous: a detachment of the 55th BNI sent from Nowshera to Hoti Mardan to take the place of the Guides was said to be on the verge of mutiny, and four of the eight Bengal Army regiments quartered in Peshawar were showing signs of following suit. That night he and Nicholson went to bed fully dressed, swords and pistols by their bedsides. At midnight they were roused by a messenger from the commander of the military cantonment at Nowshera: the sepoys of the three Bengal Army regiments stationed there had turned against their officers. It was imperative to act before the Peshawar garrison heard of this and followed suit. They roused Brigadier Cotton in his bungalow and told him the only course was to disarm the four suspect native regiments at daybreak.

The commanding officers of every regiment in Peshawar, eight native and two British, were now woken and summoned to Cotton's bungalow. 'A most painful scene ensued,' recorded Edwardes. 'The commandants of those regiments which were to be disarmed unanimously and violently declared their implicit confidence in their men. One advised conciliation, and another threatened us that his men would resist and take the guns.' Angry words were exchanged as the colonels protested the innocence and unswerving loyalty of their men. But Nicholson, unmoved, enraged the officers still further by producing a packet of intercepted messages and intelligence reports. 'Perhaps these letters will interest you,' he suggested. The arguments continued until Edwardes forced a conclusion by stating that the matter rested entirely with Brigadier Cotton. All present now turned to him: he declared unequivocally that the four native regiments must be disarmed – 'No more discussion, gentlemen! These are my orders and I must have them obeyed!'

The meeting broke up at six in the morning and an hour later the troops began to form up on the open parade grounds in front of their respective lines. The two British infantry regiments – HM 70th Foot and HM 87th – were posted at either end of the cantonments, each with half the British-manned artillery, guns primed and muskets loaded. Cotton and Edwardes starting at one end and Nicholson at the other, they rode down the regimental lines, each party escorted by a troop of irregular cavalry and with empty artillery ammunition wagons following on behind. As each suspect regiment was approached the order was given to step forward and pile arms. Taken by surprise, the sepoys responded automatically. 'It was a painful and affecting thing to see them putting their own fire-locks into the artillery wagons,' wrote Edwardes to his wife, 'weapons which they had used honourably for years. The officers of a cavalry regiment, a very fine set of fellows, threw in their own swords with those of their men, and even tore off their spurs. It was impossible not to feel for and with them; but duty must be done, and I know that we shall never regret the counsel that we gave.'

The culmination of the morning's events was a public execu-tion. Letters from the Subadar-Major of the 51st BNI calling on the men of another regiment, the 64th, to join him in an uprising planned for 22 May had been intercepted by Nicholson's police. The Subadar-Major had then made a run for it into Afridi country but the Afridi very wisely decided that their laws of sanctuary did not apply in this case, and returned him bound and trussed to the DC's office. After a brief drumhead court martial, the Subadar-Major was marched before each regiment on parade before being hanged before the entire garrison.

The effect of what John Lawrence later described as a 'master stroke' was dramatic. 'As we rode down to the disarming,' Edwardes's letter continued, 'a very few chiefs and yeomen of the country attended us, and I remember judging from their faces that they came to see which way the tide would turn.' By the time the parade was over 'the air was cleared, as if by the thunderstorm. We breathed freely again . . . Hundreds of Khans and Urbabs [land-owners], who stood aloof the day before, appeared as thick as flies, and were profuse in offers of service. They had not calculated on our having so much pluck.' Levies soon began to arrive from the outlying districts, even from those areas which had lately been the scene of tribal disturbances. One morning a large crowd of armed Afridi caused alarm in the cantonment by pushing their way past the sentries posted at one of the main roads and asking which of the bungalows belonged to Edwardes Sahib. Worried chaprassis hurried to convey the news to Edwardes; coming out to meet the Afridi, he learned that they had come to enlist. Many were outlaws who had fled to the hills to escape justice and who now saw a chance to clear the slate by offering their services. 'I went among them', wrote Edwardes, 'and picked out their youths, and enrolled them as recruits; then brought the older ones, weather-beaten, scarred, and scored with frays, into our willow-walk in the garden, set them down in the shade, and, after talking to them, dismissed them to their hills again with a rupee each, quite satisfied that they had been honourably treated. I was not sorry, however, to get them out of the cantonment.'

Meanwhile, at Hoti Mardan a detachment of the 55th BNI sent up from Nowshera under its colonel to man the fort in the absence of the Corps of Guides was now joined by the bulk of their regiment; these men, mostly Hindu, had refused to obey their officers, and followed the detachment to Mardan to persuade their comrades to join them in open mutiny. Their colonel, like so many others in cantonments and stations all over northern India at this time, declined to believe that any of his men were less than loyal. He had previously been warned by the Sikhs in his regiment that the Hindu element was not to be trusted, but had declared that he would stake his life on their staunchness: with the greater part of his regiment now gone over to the rebels, he put a pistol to his head and blew out his brains.

But nemesis for the mutineers of the 55th was swift, and delivered in awful measure. At midnight on 24 May Nicholson set off with one of the two British infantry regiments in Peshawar and two squadrons of irregular cavalry. At daybreak his force was spotted from the walls of the fort at Hoti Mardan by sentries of the 55th and the alarm was sounded. Soon afterwards the mutineers were seen marching out of the fort in good order with their regimental colours flying, apparently aiming for the safety of the mountains of Swat to the north. The colonel of the British infantry regiment called a halt; his men had marched through the night and were in no condition to pursue the enemy, particularly now that the sun was up. Nicholson thought otherwise. He had a posse of his own Pakhtun mounted police with him as well as a squadron of Multani horse, which he considered quite adequate to the task of chasing the mutinous 55th. In the words of Edwardes, he spurred his men forward and 'hurled himself like a thunderbolt on the route of a thousand mutineers'. The 55th BNI was a well-disciplined regiment: when Nicholson on his grey charger was observed galloping up behind the column at the head of his small force, it halted on the command of its Native Officers and reformed in orderly fashion to receive cavalry. But before the sepoys had time to load and present, Nicholson was upon them. The line broke, and from that moment all thoughts of discipline ended as the sepoys scattered and ran. It then became a chase through the surrounding countryside which continued throughout the rest of day. The rebels were pursued and sabred or speared without mercy. As Edwardes put it in his official report, 'They were hunted out of villages, and grappled with in ravines, and hunted over the ridges all that day from Fort Mardan to the borders of Swat, and found respite only in the failing light.' Nicholson's party returned to Mardan exhausted and saddle-sore after some twenty hours of riding. They brought with them a hundred prisoners, two hundred captured muskets, and the colours of the 55th. In a brief note to Edwardes, Nicholson commented that some of the mutineers had fought with stubborn courage, 'as men always do who have no chance of escape but their own exertions'. He himself had cut down a large proportion of the hundred and fifty dead. Another twenty sepoys were caught and brought in by local villagers and levies over the next few days.

All one hundred and twenty prisoners of the 55th were condemned to death. As every soldier knew, the Articles of War laid down only one punishment for mutiny, the only variable being the mode of execution. Hanging was reserved for common criminals and for those soldiers like the Subadar-Major of the 51st BNI in Peshawar who were deemed to have behaved in a particularly unsoldierly way. Death by firing-squad was the military norm, but in India the British chose to follow Mughal custom where native troops were concerned, and 'blowing away' was the method: the condemned man was tied to the muzzle of a cannon and blown apart. This was considered to be highly effective, in that it combined maximum effect with minimum suffering – and it was regarded by sepoys as infinitely preferable to death by hanging. However, one hundred and twenty executions seemed excessive, even to John Nicholson, unswerving as he was in his belief that only one punishment fitted the crime, and he wrote to Edwardes to suggest that some of the condemned should be spared: 'I must say a few words for some of the 55th prisoners. The officers of that regiment all concur in stating that the Sikhs were on their side to the last. I would, therefore, temper stern justice with mercy, and spare the Sikhs and young recruits. Blow away all the rest by all means, but spare boys scarcely out of their childhood, and men who were really loyal and respectful up to the moment when they allowed themselves to be carried away in a panic by the mass.' In the end, John Lawrence's suggestion that a third of the number should be put to death was agreed upon, so forty of the most serious offenders were selected for execution.

On the morning of 10 June the troops in Peshawar turned out on the main parade ground opposite the European Infantry Lines (the triangle of land between the Old Jamrud Road and the Khyber Road, now occupied by the Khyber Colony) and formed into three sides of a square to witness punishment. Thousands of local inhabitants also gathered for the bloody spectacle of forty men being blown to bits. Even thus limited in numbers, the terrible fate of the men of the 55th BNI was an exercise in Old Testament vengeance that must have sent a chill into the heart of every mutineer or waverer in the ranks of the EICo's army in the Punjab – as, indeed, it was intended it should.

Revenge was very much on the minds of men like Nicholson at this time, when every post horse from down-country brought fresh news of killings of European men, women and children at one station or another. 'Let us propose a Bill for the flaying alive, impalement, or burning of the murderers of the women and children of Delhi,' wrote Nicholson to Edwardes at one point. 'I wish that I were in that part of the world, that if necessary I might take the law into my own hands.' Edwardes refused to be drawn, and Nicholson wrote to him again: 'You do not answer me about the Bill for a new kind of death for the murderers and dishonourers of our women. I will propose it alone if you do not help me. I will not, if I can help it, see fiends of that stamp let off with a simple hanging.' The subject continued to prey on Nicholson's mind and he refused to let the matter go, urging Edwardes to put aside any religious scruples he might have. 'As regards torturing the murderers of women and children . . . We are told in the Bible that stripes shall be meted out according to faults, and, if hanging is sufficient punishment for such wretches, it is too severe for ordinary mutineers. If I had them in my power today, and I knew that I were to die tomorrow, I would inflict the most excruciating tortures I could think of on them with a perfectly easy conscience . . . We have different scales of punishment for different kinds of theft, assault, forgery, and other crimes – why not for murder?'

Throughout this one-sided debate Nicholson was busily engaged with his police in rooting out potential troublemakers from among the ranks of the 64th BNI, which since the discovery of the Subedar-Major's letters had been broken up and its several companies dispersed to different posts along the border with Swat. Disloyal elements among them, so Nicholson believed, were trying to win the Swati over to their cause. 'I am strongly inclined to believe that we should not merely disarm but disband that corps and the 10th Irregular Cavalry,' he wrote to Edwardes on 30 May. 'There is no doubt that they have both been in communication with the Akhund of Swat . . . I believe we did not pitch into the 55th one day too soon. That corps and the 64th were all planning to go over to the Akhund together. I have a man who taunted my police on the line of march with siding with infidels in a religious war. May I hang him?' It says much for Edwardes that he was able to keep his bloodthirsty DC in line without losing his respect and friendship. The men of the 64th BNI were eventually disarmed and sent back to their villages without further bloodshed, and by 9 June Nicholson had returned to Peshawar looking for new work to do.

The strength of the bridges built by Edwardes and his colleagues along the frontier now became apparent. In Hazara, Edwardes's successor found the Hazarawals loyal to a man: 'Here I am tranquil,' wrote John Becher to Edwardes, 'only that, of course, there is excitement among the people. Chiefs and people flock in. They are in the most loyal spirit, desirous only to be employed more than I can employ them. If I ask for two horsemen I get ten supplied.' Richard Pollock, who had followed John Nicholson as DC in Bannu, had the same message: 'Nothing could really have been better than the feeling exhibited by the headmen of this district. They could hardly conceive that anyone would dare perpetrate the enormities they heard of, but begged to be employed if they could be of any use.' Major Henderson, standing in for John Coke in Kohat, was equally buoyant: 'If you want more men, tell me and you shall have them at once.'

In Peshawar itself crowds of Pakhtuns daily besieged the Commissioner's bungalow in the cantonment, some for news from Delhi but others bringing horses and weapons in the hope of being recruited as irregulars. As Edwardes reported to his wife, these occasions did much to lift his spirits:

The first horseman would be brought up. The beast perhaps would not move. The rider, the owner, and all the neighbours would assail him with whips, sticks, stones and Pashto reproaches that might have moved a rock; but nothing would do until the attempt was given up, and the brute's head turned the other way, when he went off at a gallop amid roars of laughter from the Pathans, who have the keenest perception of both fun and vice. No. 2 would make a shift to come up, but every man and boy in the crowd could see that he was lame on two or three legs. Then the argument began; and leg by leg, blemish by blemish, the animal was proved by a multitude of witnesses (who had known him for very many years) to be perfectly sound. And so the enlistment went on from day to day affording immense occupation, profit and amusement to the people, and answering a great many good ends. Now and then an orderly of the Hindustani Irregular Cavalry, admirably armed and mounted, would pass the spot and mark his opinion of the 'levies' by a contemptuous smile. But nevertheless he told his comrades in the lines that the country people were all with the English and that it was of no use to desert or to intrigue.

From across the border came perhaps the best signs of all. 'How valuable is now our friendly policy with Afghanistan,' wrote Edwardes to his wife early in June. Soon he was able to pen a gentle 'told-you-so' to Sir John Lawrence in Lahore, pointing out how that policy was proving to be 'a perfect Godsend to us. It keeps all above us quiet in a wonderful way . . . It is clear that, if we had been on bad terms just now with Kabul, we should have lost, first Peshawar, and then the Punjab, and all India would have reeled under the blow.' Even John Nicholson had to concede that Edwardes's policy of friendship had paid off handsomely, owning to Edwardes that he had never thought to see 'such solid advantage from our alliance with Dost Mohammad as we are doing at the crisis, in the perfect peace of our border; so that we are left at liberty to contend with our own Sepoys.'

With the disarming of two doubtful BNI regiments in Multan by Neville Chamberlain's younger brother Crawford and his 'Yellow Boys', the Punjab frontier was secured. On 10 June Nicholson found time for a short letter to reassure his mother: 'I just write a few lines to tell you that we are quiet here, and have made ourselves secure by disarming all the disaffected native regiments. Charles is with a wing of his regiment in the neighbourhood of Lahore. Do not be under any apprehension about either of us. I consider we are stronger in the Punjab at this moment than in any other part of the Bengal Presidency.' An equally reassuring if similarly brief letter went to Emma Edwardes in England: 'Dear Herbert and I are very well and have made ourselves very strong here . . . Do not therefore be uneasy about us. We have no fears for the result ourselves. With God's blessing we shall emerge from this crisis stronger than we have ever been in India before.' Whether he and Edwardes really felt as confident as their letters suggest is open to doubt.

While the threat of mutiny in northern Punjab had been all but removed, elsewhere the picture was very different. Outside Delhi the British on the Ridge clung to their defences, facing almost daily assaults on their positions and forced to watch helplessly as new regiments marched in through the gates of the city below them to swell the numbers of the mutineers: three regiments of infantry from Jullunder, others from Ferozepore, Philour and Rohtak – and at least another half dozen more reported to be on their way. They knew that unless their own numbers could be signficantly built up within a matter of days, they would be annihilated. Such help must come from the Punjab: elsewhere in Upper India all the EICo's key military stations – Agra, Gwalior, Fatehgar, Bareilly, Cawnpore and Lucknow – which might have been expected to send British troops to Delhi were themselves under siege by rebels. There was no hope of speedy relief from Bengal.

This was the background to a disturbing letter received by Edwardes in Peshawar on 11 June, in which Sir John Lawrence asked him to consider 'what should be done in the event of a disaster at Delhi'. Delhi was the corner-stone of British rule in India; if Delhi were lost, then all was lost. Everything that could be done to recapture and to hold Delhi must therefore be done: 'all our safety depends on this'. To release British troops and loyal levies from the Punjab for use in Delhi, he proposed the abandonment of Peshawar and the trans-Indus frontier region: 'The important points in the Punjab are Peshawar, Mooltan, and Lahore, including Umritsar. But I do not think we can hold Peshawar and the other places also in the event of disaster. We could easily retire from Peshawar early in the day.' He suggested they 'make a merit of necessity' and invite Amir Dost Mohammad Khan to hold the Vale of Peshawar and the trans-Indus as a friend, with the promise of its unchallenged possession once the crisis was over.

Lawrence's proposal staggered Edwardes, whose first comment was that 'unless this had been in his own handwriting, I would not have credited it'. It appeared to him an extraordinary lapse of judgement, even an act of weakness. Consulting immediately with Nicholson and Cotton, he despatched a strongly-worded protest on behalf of the three of them: 'We are unanimously of opinion that with God's help we can and will hold Peshawar, let the worst come to the worst, and it would be a fatal policy to abandon it and retire across the Indus. It is the anchor of the Punjab, and if you take it up the whole ship will drift to sea.' The spectre of Afghanistan, never far back in their minds, had once more loomed to the fore: 'As to a friendly transfer of Peshawar to the Afghans, Dost Mahomed would not be a mortal Afghan – he would be an angel – if he did not assume our day to be gone in India, and follow after us as an enemy. Europeans cannot retreat – Kabul would come again!' This first, heated riposte was swiftly followed by others equally passionate: to surrender Peshawar would be 'certain ruin'; they must 'stand or fall at Peshawar. It must be done somewhere; let us do it in the front, giving up nothing'; 'Let us hold the frontier province, at all events . . . It is absurd to engulf *everything* in the Delhi whirlpool.' At Edwardes's shoulder as he pens these letters the figure of John Nicholson is plain, standing with his arms folded, his face pallid and stern, and behind him his ancestors in their ranks, all grim-faced and muttering 'No surrender! No surrender!'

Despite this barrage of protests, Sir John Lawrence clung to his view. He wrote to Lord Canning in Calcutta, asking for full powers to take whatever decision he should deem fit. At first he omitted to pass on Edwardes's letters to the Governor-General, but when Edwardes discovered this he demanded that Lord Canning should know how strongly he and other officers felt on the issue. The answer, when it finally came, was short and to the point: 'Hold on to Peshawar to the last. Give up nothing.'

Even as this debate rumbled on, the British contingent on Delhi Ridge was being steadily reinforced, Lawrence pushing troops south as fast as the situation in the southern Punjab allowed. Hard on the heels of the Guides came other units detached from Neville Chamberlain's Movable Column and sent on ahead: first the 4th Sikhs and a squadron of Skinner's Horse under Lieutenant John Watson; then, a fortnight later, John Coke and his Rifles. After them came other units of the Punjab Irregular Force in dribs and drabs from wherever they could be spared: a squadron of the 2nd Punjab Cavalry under Lieutenant Charles Nicholson (John's brother), with Lieutenant Dighton Probyn as second-in-command; a squadron of the 5th Punjab Cavalry under Lieutenant John Younghusband; then two more full regiments of Punjab irregulars – the 2nd Punjab Infantry under Captain Green and the 4th under Captain Alfred Wilde.

The core of the Movable Column itself, diverted first to one hot-spot and then to another, came on more slowly. It now consisted of two British and two native units: HM 52nd Light Infantry (which became the Oxfordshire Light Infantry and survives today as the 1st Battalion, the Royal Green Jackets) and a troop of horse artillery; a wing of the 9th Bengal Light Cavalry and the 35th BNI. While the other native troops of the Movable Column had been overwhelmingly non-Hindu – mostly Sikhs, Punjabi Muslims, Pakhtuns and Afghans, as well as non-Brahmin Gurkhas and Dogra Hindus – these last two units contained a preponderance of Hindu Brahmins and Rajputs.

The command of the Movable Column was retained by Neville Chamberlain, promoted (at Sir John Lawrence's insistence, and over the heads of a dozen more senior officers) to the rank of field brigadier. At Wazirabad his authority was challenged by Colonel George Campbell, commanding officer of HM 52nd Light Infantry, who for a period took to his bed in a huff and refused to acknowledge Chamberlain as his senior officer. Underlying what Fred Roberts calls 'so puerile a sentiment' was the widespread feeling among Queen's Service officers that they were a cut above those of John Company – a prejudice that continued to be held by some British Army officers (Winston Churchill, for one) right up to the end of the Second World War. However, of far more serious concern to Chamberlain was the doubtful loyalty of the two units of native regulars in his column. Believing they were awaiting an opportunity to break away and make for Delhi, he asked Roberts to put out spies to watch the men's behaviour in camp – a wise precaution, for in the middle of the night of 8 June Roberts was roused by one of his men and told that the 35th intended to mutiny at daybreak. Roberts immediately woke Brigadier Chamberlain, who in turn summoned all the officers of the regiment from their camp beds. At dawn that morning all the sepoys of the 35th were called to parade, and two of their number were found to be carrying loaded weapons. A drumhead court martial was immediately assembled on the spot, with Native Officers from Coke's Rifles acting as members of the court. The two men were found guilty of mutiny and sentenced to be blown away.

As soon as the sentence had been carried out, Chamberlain addressed the shocked and silent ranks of the 35th BNI as they stood paraded on the punishment square. 'I call upon you to remember that each one of you has sworn to be obedient and faithful to your salt,' Roberts reports him saying. 'Like you, I have sworn to be faithful and do my duty, and I will fulfil my vow by blowing away every man guilty of sedition and mutiny, as I have done today. Listen to no evil counsel, but do your duty as good soldiers.' Young Fred Roberts had been watching the reaction of the sepoys to the execution and the speech that followed. 'They looked more crest-fallen than shocked or horrified,' he noted perceptively. 'We soon learnt that their determination to mutiny, and make the best of their way to Delhi, was in no wise changed by the scene they had witnessed.'

That evening the Movable Column set out for Amritsar, where Chamberlain learned that the Adjutant-General of Sir Henry Barnard's Delhi Field Force had been killed, and that he was to take his place. To avoid any further disputes about rank, he was now promoted brigadier-general, effectively making him the sixth most senior officer on the Delhi Ridge. Before setting off he wrote to his mother and sisters in England to assure them that, despite the evidence to the contrary, all was well: 'At Delhi they are only keeping their heads above water, but . . . though we are few, we do not in the least despair, and with the blessing of God the whole country will be at our feet by Christmas Day . . . Do not fear for me. I shall be as safe at Delhi as here – unless it pleases God that my bones shall rest here, and if it is His will why repine? We must all go sooner or later, and to die doing one's duty is the best of deaths.'

To his initial disgust, Fred Roberts was ordered to remain behind with the column, so as to provide some continuity for Chamberlain's successor. His disappointment evaporated when he heard that the new commander of the Movable Column was to be his hero, John Nicholson.

The news of his appointment and promotion to brigadier-general – a prodigious leapfrog for a man still down in the Indian Army List as a captain – reached Nicholson in Peshawar on 14 June, and he made immediate preparations to leave that night. At his request, the son of the man who had saved his life at the Margalla *burj* some years before had been given the post of police *darogah* or superintendent in Peshawar; Muhammad Hayat Khan, now grown into a tall, full-bearded and silent giant of the same mould as his patron, was summoned to join him with as many armed horsemen as he could raise.

That evening Nicholson and Edwardes dined together a last time, then exchanged gifts. Edwardes presented Nicholson with a little travelling clock he had owned for some years, and Nicholson gave his friend a silver drinking-cup, a treasured possession of his during his time in Bannu. The two shook hands outside the Commissioner's bungalow before Nicholson mounted his grey charger and, with Muhammad Hayat Khan at his side, rode out of the compound into the night. Edwardes then returned to his bungalow, sat down at his desk and picked up a pen. 'So there goes dear fine Nicholson,' he wrote. 'A great loss to me, but a still greater gain to the State at this crisis. A nobler spirit never went forth to fight his country's battles.'

At Rawalpindi Sir John Lawrence was waiting to give Nicholson a final briefing before he continued on his way to join the Movable Column south-east of Lahore. Nicholson had never forgiven Sir John for usurping his old chief, and had not learned to like him; indeed, he had taken to calling him an 'old woman', and only weeks before had been on the point of resigning from service in the Punjab and applying to join Sir Henry Lawrence in Oude. He now took the opportunity to quarrel with Sir John face-to-face over what he saw as the latter's continuing pusillanimity in the matter of abandoning Peshawar. However, as he continued his journey Nicholson evidently suffered a twinge of remorse over his hostility, because he sent back to Rawalpindi a message which came as close to saying 'sorry' as he ever managed: 'I forgot before starting to say one or two things I had omitted saying,' his letter reads in part. 'One was to thank you for my appointment. I know you recommended it on *public* grounds but I do not feel the less obliged to you. Another was to tell you I have dismissed old grievances, whether real or imaginary, from my mind, and, as far as I am concerned, bygones are bygones. In return I would ask you not to judge me over-hastily or harshly.'

Nicholson caught up with the Movable Column on 20 June. His actions in the Vale of Peshawar had gained him an unparalleled reputation for ruthlessness and won him widespread admiration among the rank and file of the British troops in India. One of the youngest officers of HM 52nd Light Infantry was Ensign Reginald Wilberforce, aged nineteen, son of the famous Bishop of Oxford, Samuel Wilberforce. He too fell under the Nicholson spell, being particularly struck by Nicholson's 'dark grey eyes with black pupils' which were said to 'dilate like a tiger's' when he was excited. In a rich (perhaps over-leavened here and there) memoir of his regiment's part in the Indian Mutiny campaign, Wilberforce records that within hours of Nicholson joining the column at Jullunder he overheard the following exchange between two of his men:

'Jack, the General's here.'

'How do you know?'

'Why, look there; there's his mark.'

The 'there' the fellow-soldier was told to look at was a pair of gallows, each of which was adorned with six hanging mutineers, while close by were several bullock-carts, all filled with sepoys who had revolted, and who were waiting their turn . . . Few courts martial were held by Nicholson; his dictum 'the punishment of mutiny is death' obviated any necessity for trial.

Accompanying Nicholson as his bodyguards and scouts was what Ensign Reginald Wilberforce describes as a 'motley crew' of frontier horsemen. 'They came out of a personal devotion to Nicholson,' he records. 'They took no pay from the Government, they recognised no head but Nicholson, and him they obeyed with a blind devotion and a faithfulness that won the admiration of all who saw them. These men, some 250 in number, mounted on their wiry ponies, surrounded the Column like a web; they rode in couples, each couple within signalling distance of the other, and so circled the Column round for many a mile.' Chief among this motley crew was 'a huge Pathan, black-whiskered and moustachioed; this man never left his [Nicholson's] side, he slept across the doorway of Nicholson's tent, so that none could come in save over his body. When Nicholson dined at mess this Pathan stood behind his chair with a cocked revolver in one hand, and allowed none to pass a dish to his master save himself.' This was, of course, Muhammad Hayat Khan, and though his devotion appears slavish to us, his grounds for concern were real enough. Soon after Nicholson joined them an attempt was made to poison not only him but all the British officers of the Movable Column – who, in true Nicholson style, were the last to know. One evening their dinner was inexplicably delayed; a messenger sent to the cooking tent returned with the information that it would be served a little late. Half an hour later Nicholson himself walked into the mess-tent with an apology: 'I am sorry, gentlemen, to have kept you waiting for your dinner, but I have been hanging your cooks.' It transpired that one of Nicholson's scouts – 'spies' might be a more accurate description – had learned that aconite was to be added to the soup on the menu at dinner that night. Once the dish had been made, Nicholson rounded up all the cooks and demanded they taste it. They refused, on the grounds that it was against their caste. He then got hold of an unfortunate monkey and force-fed it some soup. It died. Within minutes, as one of the officers present put it, 'our regimental cooks were ornamenting a neighbouring tree'.

The Movable Column had been diverted to Jullunder because of continuing disturbances since the mutiny, two weeks earlier, among three native regiments. At Jullunder it was joined by a second Bengal Army regiment, the 33rd BNI. Nicholson was not happy about this. The British element in the column, represented by HM 52nd Light Infantry and a troop of horse artillery, was now outnumbered two to one by native troops. He concluded, on his own initiative and without consulting any of his other officers, that both native infantry regiments should be disarmed. As the column was proceeding south towards Philour, Nicholson ordered HM 52nd and the artillery to push on ahead with him to a point on the road he and Lieutenant Roberts had earlier reconnoitred. 'When they reached the ground we had selected they took up a position on the right of the road,' narrates Fred Roberts, 'the two batteries in the centre and the 52nd in wings on either flank. The guns were unlimbered and prepared for action.' Only now were the commanding officers of the 52nd and the horse artillery troop told what was afoot: that the two BNI regiments following on behind were to be disarmed on the road, and that if they showed signs of resistance, they were to be fired upon.

When the first, the 35th BNI, reached the point in the road Nicholson had indicated, Roberts was sent forward to tell its commanding officer to direct his men to pile their arms and remove their belts. This officer, kept as much in the dark as the other commanders, was heard by Roberts to mutter, 'Thank God!' The order was obeyed and carried out without dissent, and as the disarming of the 35th was completed, the 33rd BNI marched into sight. They were treated in the same way, this time to the accompaniment of angry protests from their British officers. Their colonel, Robert Sandeman, had been with the regiment for more than thirty years and had commanded it throughout both Sikh Wars. Fred Roberts records that on hearing Nicholson's order, Colonel Sandeman exclaimed, 'What! Disarm my regiment? I will answer with my life for the loyalty of every man!' and when Lieutenant Roberts repeated the order 'the poor old fellow burst into tears'. Also present in the regiment that day was the colonel's son, Ensign Robert Sandeman, who later became one of the greatest of the second wave of frontier politicals, extending British authority deep into Baluchistan.

These proceedings had been watched from the side of the road by an old Sikh colonel who had fought against the British at Gujrat. When all was done and the disarmed sepoys had marched away with Nicholson's threats to hang anyone who dared to desert still ringing in their ears, this old soldier rose from his seat remarking that Nicholson had drawn the fangs of fifteen hundred serpents. To Roberts, Nicholson's instinct appeared almost uncanny: 'He seemed always to know exactly what to do, and the best way to do it.' What he found particularly surprising was that Nicholson, after spending so many years as a civilian administrator, should think and act like a soldier. But here 'Bobs Bahadur', even as a wise old warrior, was wide of the mark. Soldiers have rules and stick to them, whereas Nicholson had no time for rules. If he followed any code at all, it was that of the tribesmen he knew so well: kill, or be killed.

Before the purged but much weakened Movable Column could move on to Delhi Ridge there was still a deal of unpleasant work to be done in the Punjab. In Sialkot, the capital of Reynell Taylor's district, the local brigade commander had refused to disarm his native regulars. On the morning of 9 July half the brigade rose in revolt, killing him and a number of civilians, and before the day was out a well-armed rebel force of eleven hundred horse and foot had started out for Delhi. Included among this force were members of the second wing of the 9th Bengal Light Cavalry – the other half of the last Bengal Army unit still remaining in the Movable Column. When Nicholson got the news he kept it to himself. The Movable Column was then in Amritsar, after a fortnight spent rushing from one danger spot to another. This was still the hottest time of the year, the temperature still rising before the advent of the Rains, and to spare the men of HM 52nd Nicholson had created a 'flying column', buying up a number of ponies and *ekkas*, small pony-carts capable of carrying four persons and a driver. Nevertheless, it had still been an exhausting two weeks, and officers and men were looking forward to a restful night in barracks. Throughout dinner in the officers' mess that evening Nicholson was his usual silent self, but at half-past eight he checked his watch, lifted his head and spoke: 'Gentlemen, I do not want you to hurry your dinner, but the column marches in half an hour'. At nine p.m. the sowars of the 9th Bengal Light Cavalry's wing with the column were surrounded in their barrack quarters, disarmed, and placed under guard. Once this had been done the ponies of the flying column were harnessed to their carts and the march commenced.

Nicholson had concluded that the Sialkot mutineers would be moving east towards Gurdaspur in the hope of persuading the troops stationed there to join them. Although Gurdaspur was forty-four miles away he calculated that it might just be possible, if they hurried, to intercept the mutineers before they got there. At 8 a.m. the following morning the flying column halted for two hours at Patiala, where rations of bread, milk and rum were served out. After another three hours of marching under the full blaze of the sun the column came to a grove of trees. The officers of HM 52nd Light Infantry begged for an hour's rest in the shade, which Nicholson grudgingly allowed. Waking up after half an hour or so, one of the officers noticed that Nicholson was not with them: he was still seated on his horse in the middle of the road, in the full glare of the July sun. He made no outward sign, but the rebuke was patent.

The 'flying column' trundled into Gurdaspur shortly before 6 p.m., having covered the forty-four miles in eighteen hours. To Nicholson's satisfaction, they had beaten the Sialkot mutineers to it. Early next morning he led his force some twelve miles west to the banks of the Ravi River at a crossing-point named Trimmu Ghat, where they found the mutineers drawn up in line waiting for them – a thousand infantry in the centre and the remaining wing of the 9th Bengal Light Cavalry on their left. As a result of their march the day before large numbers of the 52nd had gone down with heat-stroke and exhaustion, so that they now could muster no more than two hundred and twenty men. However, they were armed with the new rifled Enfield and had the support of the nine guns of the horse artillery troop, disposed at intervals between sections of the infantry, to say nothing of Nicholson's mounted Punjabis and Pakhtuns hovering on their wings.

When Nicholson's force had advanced to within musket range, the enemy infantry fired a single volley down the line and charged, while the sowars of the 9th Bengal Light Cavalry spurred forward their horses and charged the column's right flank. The 52nd stood firm, forming squares to receive the enemy's horse and firing controlled volleys by ranks. 'For about ten minutes they stood up very well indeed,' wrote Nicholson of the mutineers in his official report, 'many of them advancing boldly up to the very guns. Meanwhile the cavalry had made several rushes in detached parties on our flanks and rear, but had always been repulsed by the file-firing of our infantry.' A more colorful account of the battle comes from Reginald Wilberforce, who writes (quite incorrectly) of the engagement being 'probably the only instance in the mutiny when Englishmen and sepoys actually crossed bayonets in the open'. During a momentary lull in the battle he observed two men of Nicholson's bodyguard challenge two troopers of the Bengal Light Cavalry to single combat:

> The challenge was accepted, and the four rode at each other, the Pathans on their ponies, their tulwars waving in circles round their heads, their loose garments flowing. The Bengalees sat erect on their big horses, their swords held ready to deliver the 'point', a stroke no regular cavalryman comprehends, and he does not in his sword exercise learn to parry the thrust. For a moment all eyes were on the four combatants: the thrust was delivered, but instead of piercing the bodies of the Pathans, it passed over them, for they threw themselves back on their ponies, their heads in the crupper, their feet by the ponies' ears, and in that position swept off the heads of the Bengal cavalrymen. Instantly the ponies wheeled round, the men straightened themselves in their saddles, and they passed away from our vision.

The sepoys were driven back and eventually broke ranks, running towards the river with Nicholson's horsemen at their heels. By a cruel stroke of ill-fortune, the rebels now found themselves unable to cross the river: quite by accident they had retreated onto a large island covered in thick brushwood, and the water on the far side was too deep to ford. Realising that his prey was trapped, Nicholson posted a guard at the ford and led his men back to Gurdaspur to rest and recover. Three days later they returned and set about a mopping-up operation that resulted in the death of virtually every one of the 1,100 mutineers. At the first engagement, at Trimmu Ghat, Wilberforce had seen Nicholson cleave a man's head in two with his sabre; here he saw him rise in his stirrups and deliver such a mighty blow that he actually severed his unfortunate victim in two, finishing with the remark, 'Not a bad sliver, that.' According to Nicholson himself, 'The real business was over in a few minutes without any check, and with a loss to us of only six wounded. A few resolute men among the mutineers died manfully at the gun; the rest fled, and were either slain on the bank or driven into the river.' Of the Movable Column's forty-six casualties, more than half were deaths caused by sunstroke and dehydration.

News of this deadly operation spread to every corner of the Punjab and beyond, providing much-needed comfort to the British and their allies. In Rawalpindi, Sir John Lawrence was moved to comment that had other commanders acted with the same energy shown by Nicholson, Delhi would long since have fallen into their hands; Lord Canning, at the other end of the country, noted that Nicholson, 'sweeping the country like the incarnation of vengeance, had struck terror into wavering hearts'. The 'incarnation of vengeance' had by now acquired quite a following. As he progressed through the countryside Sikhs gathered by the roadside to do him homage as he passed on his grey mare. At his camps they called in groups to pay their respects, and were shepherded into his tent by his Pakhtun bodyguard a dozen at a time. Wilberforce noticed that Nicholson raised no objection provided they sat quietly – but if they prostrated themselves, or began chanting, they were taken away and whipped: 'This was an offence, against the committal of which warning had been given, and the penalty never varied: three dozen lashes with the cat-o'-nine-tails on the bare back. This they did not mind, but on the contrary rejoiced in the punishment.'

The ruthlessness Wilberforce and others so admired was accompanied by arrogance and insubordination. Command of the Movable Column gave Nicholson the excuse to do more or less as he pleased, challenging or ignoring Sir John Lawrence's orders, demanding that more troops be sent to join him, or ordering them to be repositioned wherever he felt they ought to go. A point came when the Chief Commissioner had lost track of Nicholson's movements entirely. A peremptory note demanded a reply to his letters by return: 'You are to inform me, without delay, where you are and what you are doing, and to send me a return of courts-martial held on insurgent natives, with a list of the various punishments inflicted.' Whether this reprimand was given before or after the episode of the regimental cooks is uncertain, but Nicholson's reply was little calculated to put Sir John's mind at rest: he simply turned the letter over, and on the back noted where he was, and the date. Underneath he scrawled 'The punishment of mutiny is death'. He then added his signature, re-sealed the letter, and had it returned to its sender.

Lawrence could only make the best of this insubordination. 'I fear you are incorrigible,' he wrote on 4 August, after learning that Nicholson had gone against orders and commandeered a body of British gunners from Philour to strengthen his column. 'So I must leave you to your fate. But depend on it, you would get on equally well, and much more smoothly, if you worked *with* men rather than against them.'

Nicholson was by now at Amballa, in response to an urgent appeal from General Barnard with the Delhi Field Force to bring his Movable Column down to Delhi Ridge as soon as possible. On 7 August he set out for Delhi by mail-cart, leaving the column to follow on behind.

12

'Like a King coming into his own'

DELHI RIDGE, AUGUST–SEPTEMBER 1857

> When Nikal Seyn to Delhi came, right solemnly he swore:
> 'If God will only spare my life, her name shall be no more.
> Proud Jumna's flood shall wash her streets, her battlements
>   I'll raze,
> And nought but blackened mounds shall meet the
>   wandering traveller's gaze'.
>   English translation of a Punjabi ballad heard
>   sung on the streets of Delhi in the 1890s

SINCE TAKING Delhi Ridge two months earlier, the Delhi Field Force had been unable to do more than hold its position. Repeated attacks from the city had been beaten off, with heavy losses among the enemy but also at high cost to the defenders. The overwhelming numerical supremacy of the mutineers, combined with the strong defences of the city – seven miles of walls twenty-four feet high protected by deep ditches, with heavily fortified bastions at each gate topped by a total of 154 heavy guns – had made it impossible for the Delhi Field Force to carry out General Barnard's plan to bring their siege guns to bear on the city's Kashmir Gate and force a breach. 'The whole thing is too gigantic for the force brought against it,' the general had written in answer to Sir John Lawrence's complaints about lack of action. 'You may ask why we engage in these constant attacks. The reason simply is that when we are attacked we must defend ourselves.'

A critical point was reached on 19 June when, as recounted by Fred Roberts, 'the rebels issued from the city in great force, and threatened nearly every part of our position. The fighting was severe throughout the afternoon, the piquets having again and again to be reinforced.' As the afternoon wore on, more and more sections of infantry held in reserve had to be committed to the front, leaving the Delhi Field Force's positions dangerously exposed at the rear. Then, an hour before dusk, a large body of insurgents appeared quite unexpectedly behind them, having made its way round the southern perimeter of the Ridge unobserved. 'The move was a surprise which almost overwhelmed us,' Henry Daly wrote some weeks later. 'We had nothing at first but a portion of the 9th Lancers, the Guides' Cavalry, and 4 guns, wherewith to meet and repel the attack.' Daly's horsemen and a troop of Bengal Horse Artillery commanded by Major Harry Tombs found themselves facing a mass of infantry and cavalry, as well as six or eight guns, already positioned and firing. In an effort to hold up the enemy's advance he ordered his Guides' Cavalry to attack its left flank while he remained with half a dozen sowars to give some slight protection to their own four guns. His own position very soon came under attack. 'The enemy,' continues his account, 'observing our weakness and the absence of infantry, were now closing on us in such numbers that Major Tombs said to me, "I fear I must ask you to charge to save our guns." I was the only British officer with the cavalry, a few Guides only; with these I broke through the infantry and reached the enemy's guns. This diversion cleared our front.'

What this reticent account omits to mention is that Daly's charge with his few sowars into the teeth of the enemy's battery, little less than suicidal, not only saved Major Tombs's four precious guns but checked the enemy's attack. Two of the Guides cavalrymen who charged with Daly were killed outright and the rest were wounded; Daly himself was brought down by a bullet in the shoulder that threw him from his horse and rendered his left arm useless for the rest of his life. At dusk his men came looking for him and at first could not find him – until one of the enemy called across and pointed out where he lay. This rebel was a young man whom

Henry Daly had found in great poverty some ten months earlier and made a jemadar in the 1st Oude Irregular Cavalry. He was a grandson of Shah Shuja-ul-Mulk, the old Emperor of Delhi and, according to a note written by Mrs Daly, had joined the rebels 'almost by compulsion'. The note adds that, to her great regret, he was captured after the taking of Delhi and hanged.

That night General Barnard visited Daly in the sick tent, thanked him for his action and expressed his regret that the newly instituted gallantry medal, the Victoria Cross, could not be awarded to officers in the service of the EICo. (It remained exclusive to the Queen's Army until the following year, one further source of discontent among EICo officers.)

William Hodson, meanwhile, had been having a fine time setting up and running the Delhi Field Force's intelligence department, operating a highly effective network of spies, scouts and 'writers' who daily sent out details of what was happening inside the city and at court in the Red Fort. His operatives were in the main irregular cavalrymen recruited during the previous few weeks into Hodson's Horse, mostly Sikhs from the Amritsar, Jindh and Lahore Districts of the Punjab raised in small rissalahs by prominent local Sikh sirdars. One such, Sirdar Man Singh, formerly of Chamberlain's Punjab Police, became the corner-stone of the corps, raising the first troop and going on to become for more than two decades the regiment's most senior Native Officer. Punjabi Muslims were also well represented and one of these, Rajab Ali, became Hodson's chief intelligence officer or spymaster, sending members of his team into Delhi in the guise of mutineers and debriefing them on their return. Hodson revelled in his own night-time reconnaissances. At an early stage of the siege he took a party of horrified engineer officers right through the enemy-occupied area surrounding the southern end of the Ridge and then up to the walls of the city itself. 'Hodson led the way,' recorded one of that party (his friend Charles Thomason), 'and, chatting merrily, took us straight into the Sabzi Mandi. As we went along the narrow street many of the enemy, with muskets and cross-belts, put their heads over parapets on the houses right and left and bobbed down again. Both Champain . . . and Salkeld looked glum as we advanced further and further, for neither had brought arms.' As the party came up to the Mori Bastion, jutting out from the north-west corner of the city wall immediately facing Delhi Ridge, Hodson spotted an old lady crossing the road ahead of them, greeted her with a warm smile and began chatting to her in Urdu. This went on for a minute or two, until one of the party suggested that 'the place was hardly well chosen for a flirtation'. They then returned to camp by the same route, everyone but Hodson thoroughly shaken. The direct outcome of this reconnaissance was a proposal by some of the younger officers, led by Hodson, that the city should be assaulted at once and without any further delay. This was put to General Sir Henry Barnard, who in his exasperation told them to bring him a plan of attack, and he would consider it. 'Times must be changed,' Hodson wrote to his wife, 'when four subalterns are called upon to suggest a means of carrying out so vital an enterprise as this.'

Their plan was hastily and badly conceived, but Barnard gave it his approval and an assault on the city was ordered for dawn on 13 June. Calling for every able man with the Delhi Field Force to join in a massed attack on the city, it relied for success on surprise and numbers rather than on the usual technique of first creating breaches in the walls. Had it proceeded, it would almost certainly have failed, with disastrous consequences. In the event, the assault had to be called off at the last minute because, in their concern to keep it a surprise, those responsible for executing the plan had omitted to inform a number of regimental commanders. Woken in the middle of the night and ordered by excited junior officers to withdraw their men from their piquets in order to make an immediate assault on Delhi, some quite understandably balked and refused to budge, so that after a chaotic few hours of orders and countermands the whole business was dropped.

Following this fiasco morale, already low, plunged lower still. The Rains were late, and the ground on which the British were camped had now become as hard as rock. It was impossible to dig proper graves for their own dead; of necessity, the remains of the enemy, as well as numerous corpses of horses, camels, even elephants, lay where they had fallen, becoming daily more bloated, blackened and foul-smelling, and generating such swarms of flies that they 'literally darkened the air, descending in myriads and covering everything'. It was impossible to eat without having constantly to wave flies off one's food, and the drinking water, drawn from tanks sited near the camp's latrines, soon became foul. Cases of cholera became increasingly common and, together with heat apoplexy, began to claim more casualties than the fighting. On 5 July cholera gained its most senior victim, General Sir Henry Barnard, whose death started a new leadership struggle among the senior officers of the Delhi Field Force. His immediate successor was old General Reed, who had earlier stepped aside in favour of Barnard but now felt strong enough to resume command. In this he was seriously mistaken. 'Too ill and feeble', wrote Neville Chamberlain, 'to discharge the duties of his position', he remained nominally in charge but left all decisions to his Chief of Staff, Brigadier-General Neville Chamberlain. 'So certainly was my position recognised by poor General Reed,' wrote Chamberlain, 'that all the Staff were in attendance upon me. All reports were addressed to and received by me, and I issued orders without reference to anyone, merely telling the General what was going on.'

Meanwhile, the leadership of the Corps of Guides had also changed hands. Henry Daly's shoulder wound meant it would be months before he could mount a horse again, and the other surviving British officers in the Corps were too inexperienced to take command. Who else was there but its former commander, William Hodson? So for five glorious weeks Hodson was in his element – leading the Guides into battle *and* running his intelligence network, with his own Hodson's Horse in the care of Sirdar Man Singh. During those five weeks he was, by all accounts, consumed with a manic energy, as though making up for lost time. Three eye-witness accounts of this period paint an indelible image of the man, and the respect he commanded. 'He is scarcely out of the saddle day or night,' wrote one officer in a letter. 'He is always on the move . . . Even when he might take rest he will not, but will go and help work the batteries, and expose himself constantly, in order to help relieve some fainting gunner or wounded man.' A second officer noted that Hodson was one of the few officers who was always saluted by the British soldiery: 'Hodson never passed down the lines without every man rendering to him that mark of respect. The soldiers loved him as their own. "There goes that 'ere

Hodson," said a drunken soldier, as he cantered down the lines. "He's sure to be in everything: he'll get shot, I know he will."' A third describes him as being 'as happy as a king' whenever he was in action: 'I fancy I see him now, smiling, laughing, parrying most fearful blows as if he were brushing off flies, calling out all the time, "Why, try again now"; "What's that?"; "Do you call yourself a swordsman?" etc. . . . It always seemed to me that he bore a charmed life.'

The arrival at the end of June of Major John Coke with his seven hundred riflemen in their dark green uniforms provided a much needed boost to morale. His numbers had lately been swelled by the addition of a troop of eighty Afridi horse under the command of a chief from Kohat, Mir Mubarak Shah, 'a grand speciment of a frontier Khan' who had felt it incumbent on him to ride more than six hundred and fifty miles to be at his friend's side at Delhi. Like the Guides before them, Coke's Rifles were almost at once thrown into battle, sent out to clear a rebel force coming up to threaten their right flank. Among those killed in this first engagement was Mir Mubarak Shah.

Coke's Rifles, together with the other reinforcements from Nicholson's Movable Column, raised the Delhi Field Force numbers to almost six thousand six hundred, but they were still outnumbered and outgunned many times over by the reinforcements the rebels continued to receive. 'Mutineers from Jullundur, Nasirabad, Nimach, Kotah, Gwalior, Jhansi and Rohilkand arrived at about this time,' wrote Fred Roberts. 'We could distinctly see them from the Ridge, marching in perfect formation, with their bands playing and colours flying. Indeed, throughout the siege the enemy's numbers were constantly being increased, while they had a practically unlimited number of guns, and the well-stocked magazine furnished them with an inexhasustible supply of ammunition.' A curious contrast between the two armies became increasingly marked: while the uniforms of the British forces grew shabbier and dustier by the day, so much so that one of the two Bengal Fusilier regiments present became known as the 'Dirty Shirts', the rebels made a deliberate point of turning out to the attack smartly dressed in their new uniforms – for the heavy red coats and black shakos of John Company's army had been abandoned for starched white tunics and black pill-box caps – 'a garish contrast to the dingy dress of their foes'.

On 14 July the mutineers made a series of concerted rushes from several sides which advanced their positions at the southern end of the Ridge, in the area of suburbs and market gardens known as Sabzi Mandi. Chamberlain decided that they must be driven back to the walls of the city before they could consolidate these new positions, and for some reason chose to lead a counter-attack in person. Fred Roberts also took part. 'We had great difficulty in driving the enemy back,' he wrote. 'They contested every inch of the ground, the many serais and walled gardens affording them admirable cover; but our troops were not to be withstood; position after position was carried until we found our-selves in sight of the Lahore gate and close up to the walls of the city.' At this point Chamberlain's enthusiasm got the better of his judgement. Roberts saw him setting his troops 'a splendid exam-ple', jumping his horse over a wall lined by the enemy and calling on those behind to follow him. However, 'in our eagerness to drive the enemy back we had . . . come too far. Musketry from the walls and grape from the heavy guns mounted on the Mori and other bastions committed terrible havoc. Men were falling on all sides.'

Also involved in this unwise assault was William Hodson, who described it as 'one of the sharpest encounters we have yet had . . . Shebbeare [commanding the Guides' Infantry] got wounded early in the fight, so I led the Guide infantry myself . . . We got within thirty yards, but the enemy's grape was too much for our small party. Three of my officers, Shebbeare, Hawes and De Brett, slightly wounded, and several men. Of the Fusiliers who were with us some 60 men were wounded; Daniell's arm broken by a shot, Jacob's horse shot dead under him, Chamberlain shot through the arm, little Roberts wounded, and several more. Everybody wonders I was not hit – none more than myself. God has been very merciful to me.'

Chamberlain, as he turned in his saddle to give the order to retire, had received what he described as a 'tap on my shoulder', which shattered the bone. He was carried back to camp in a *doolie* or covered stretcher. 'It was one of those charming evenings we sometimes have during the rainy season,' he wrote two months later to one of his sisters. 'As I was being borne back to camp, I could not avoid contrasting the exquisite beauty and calm of Nature with the scene I had left . . . After the surgeons had examined the wound and removed as much of the fractured bone as they could, I was left to myself, and the next two or three days in a half state of stupefaction from morphia. From this time until the bone had sufficiently united to allow me to sit up, I was fixed to the broad of my back.' For eight weeks Chamberlain was so fixed, 'my interest in the struggle being confined to listening to the fire, and afterwards being told what had gone on'. This gave him plenty of time to reflect on what might have been, had he acted more wisely.

The loss of Chamberlain to injury was the final straw for General Reed, who now suffered a total collapse and announced his departure for Simla. Before quitting camp on 16 July he made over command of the Delhi Field Force to Colonel Archdale Wilson, his commander of artillery and the man who as brigade commander at Meerut had failed to act against the original mutineers. This appointment so enraged two more senior officers in camp who felt they were better fitted for the job that they too upped and left. 'We are in a nice fix here,' wrote Hodson to his wife on 16 July. 'Our rulers will now less than ever decide on a bold course; and, truth to tell, the numbers of the enemy have [been] so rapidly increased, and ours so little replenished in proportion, and our losses, for a small army, have been so severe, that it becomes a question whether we can risk an assault. Would to Heaven it had been tried when I first pressed it!'

For all Hodson's doubts, Wilson proved a better commander than his predecessors: he reorganised and strengthened the defences, and imposed more discipline in camp, sending out working parties to bury or burn the cadavers and improving the camp's sanitation – not before time, as the Rains had by now arrived, bringing an end to the debilitating temperatures but adding greatly to the sickness in camp. More than a third of the Delhi Field Force were soon on the sick list, including over one thousand of the British troops. One of the worst affected regiments was HM 52nd Foot; Ensign Wilberforce writes that

within twenty days of their arrival they had almost half the regiment – three hundred and forty men – on the sick list, mostly
suffering from fevers, and had buried many victims of cholera.
News of the terrible massacres at Cawnpore, received in early
August, plunged the camp to a nadir of depression. The rebels
now began a fresh series of concerted attacks with the aim of
gaining control of the area between the Ridge and the city's
Kashmir Gate, much of it taken up by the burnt-out remains of
Delhi's civil station. A night counter-attack cleared much of the
ground and captured four guns, but among the casualties was the
commander of the attacking force, the newly promoted Colonel
John Coke, who now joined Daly and Chamberlain among the
ranks of the sick and wounded. The scene was set for the arrival
of John Nicholson, followed some days later by his Movable
Column, welcomed into camp on 13 August by a band playing
martial airs and by every man who was on his feet and not on
guard. On the final leg of its journey the column had been
greatly strengthened by further troops from the Punjab: two regiments of irregular infantry, the 2nd (Green's Rifles) and 4th
(Wilde's Punjabis); a wing of the 1st Baluch Regiment; two
hundred newly-raised Multani cavalry; four hundred Punjab
Police; and a field battery – in all, nearly four thousand men,
bringing up the numbers on the Ridge to over ten thousand.
Spirits soared, as much at the prospect of decisive leadership as
from the addition to their numbers.

Nicholson's arrival plainly induced a strong feeling of *deus ex
machina*. In almost every one of the numerous personal accounts of
these stirring events, he figures as almost superhuman, a giant in
every respect, imbued with every martial virtue. To Daly he
seemed 'by grace of God . . . like a King coming into his own'. He
was what everyone had been praying for: a war leader who seemed
invincible, almost godlike in his moral strength. 'Nicholson is a
host in himself,' noted Hodson, 'if he does not go and get knocked
over as Chamberlain did. The camp is all alive at the notion of
something decisive taking place.' Almost immediately he was
spotted going over every foot of ground held by the Delhi Field
Force. The anonymous author of a privately-published account of
the siege describes how

a stranger of very striking appearance was remarked visiting all our pickets, examining everything, and making most searching enquiries about their strength and history. His attire gave no clue to his rank; it evidently never cost the owner a thought . . . It was soon made out that this was General Nicholson, whose person was not yet known in camp; and it was whispered at the same time that he was possessed of the most brilliant military genius. He was a man cast in a giant mould, with massive chest and powerful limbs, and an expression ardent and commanding, with a dash of roughness; features of stern beauty, a long black beard, and deep sonorous voice. There was something of immense strength, talent, and resolution in his whole frame and manner, and a power of ruling men on high occasions which no one could escape noticing.

The same writer goes on to speak of Nicholson's 'imperial air, which never left him, and which would have been thought arrogance in one of less imposing mien'. To many senior officers, arrogant was exactly what Nicholson was. On their initial encounter Major Charles Reid, whose Sirmur Rifles held Hindu Rao's house on the right of the British line, concluded that he had never in his life met a man he so disliked at first sight: 'His haughty manner and peculiar sneer I could not stand.' Colonel Campbell and the company commanders of HM 52nd Light Infantry, having spent several trying weeks with Nicholson, loathed him so much that they refused to serve under him after their arrival on Delhi Ridge. Junior officers and other ranks took him to their hearts, however. One eye-witness writes of Nicholson passing a guard-post of HM 52nd and being saluted by a sentry who called out to a colleague, 'Jack, here's the General. Present arms.' To which Nicholson replied, 'Thank you, but I am not General, only Captain Nicholson.'

Nicholson posed a problem for General Archdale Wilson. Although Wilson had been appointed commander of the Delhi Field Force and was the senior of the two, Nicholson carried with him his own authority – and was transparently the more experienced and abler man. Aside from the fiasco at Meerut, Wilson's only experience of war had been the siege of Bharatpur more than thirty years previously, in 1826, as a lieutenant of artillery. Jealous of Nicholson's reputation and, more reasonably, determined that there should be only one commander in camp, he kept his rival at arm's length, refusing to discuss his plans with him. Nicholson was placed in command of a number of irregular corps and left to his own devices. To begin with this suited Nicholson, who was content at first to get to know the troops and their commanders. But as it became increasingly apparent that Wilson was failing to take control of events, so Nicholson's authority, however unacknowledged formally, began to extend itself until, as Henry Daly wrote, he had 'virtually assumed command of the Force; for it was an open secret that it was *his* will that the ostensible General – the unfortunate Archdale Wilson – was constrained to obey, and that it was *his* leading that the army was prepared to obey.'

Nicholson remained full of optimism. 'Our position is a perfectly providential one,' he wrote to Herbert Edwardes in Peshawar on 28 August. 'We could not have found one better suited to our requirements. Had the ground been of an ordinary character, we must have abandoned it long ago; but the ridge, with the strong buildings on it in front, and the river and canal protecting our flanks and rear, has saved us. I think Wilson has hitherto had considerable cause for anxiety. Had the enemy had the enterprise to detach a strong force to his rear, we could not have sent more than five or six hundred men against it. It is too late for them to try that game now, and they know it, and are at their wits' end to devise some new plan of action. When the second siege train from Firozpur arrives, I believe we shall go in.'

To John Lawrence, now back once more in Lahore, Nicholson wrote to urge him to maintain the pressure on Wilson: 'Wilson says that he will assume the offensive on the arrival of the heavy guns [from Firozepore] but he says it in an undecided way, which makes me doubt if he will do so if he is not kept up to the mark. Do you therefore keep him up to it. He is not at all equal to the crisis, and I believe he feels it himself . . . Wilson will take no responsibility on himself, and it seems to me that he is becoming jealous of me, lest I should earn more than my share of kudos. He will not even show me the plan of the assault now, though I feel sure his nervousness will make him do so before the time comes.'

It cannot have been easy for Wilson, still having to fend off almost daily attacks on their position, to have this restive 'genius for war' (as Daly describes Nicholson) prowling round his tent; he had a further source of irritation in William Hodson. For several weeks groups of wild-looking freebooters from the Punjab had been riding into camp to enlist in Hodson's Horse, drawn by promises of booty. Their presence became too much for General Wilson, who claimed that Hodson was causing 'great anxiety by exceeding his orders'. He was ordered to relinquish command of the Guides and to concentrate his efforts on bringing discipline to his own regiment. The Corps of Guides was thereupon split into two separate units, the Cavalry to become part of the Field Force's cavalry brigade and the Infantry to be attached to the Sirmoor Rifles.

Hodson took the loss of the Guides' command with remarkably good grace and turned all his energies to shaping his still untried corps of irregular horse into the toughest cavalry unit in the country. He poached dynamic young British officers from other units and brightened up the drab khaki tunics of his men by kitting them out in the brightest scarlet turbans and sashes he could find, a distinctive touch that quickly gained them the nickname of 'the Flamingos'. However, if Henry Daly's account is to be believed, some of Hodson's newest recruits were distinctly lacking not only the martial skills but even the accoutrements of their predecessors, so that mounts and weapons had to be found for them. 'Many of the men,' Daly wrote in a private note on Hodson's Horse for his successor, 'hastily collected, caught at the plough's tail, cut a ludicrous figure mounted on the big, obstinate stud horses with English saddles, bumbling through the Delhi camp; the regiment then acquired a nickname which it long retained, "the Plungers".'

The blooding of the new corps was on 16 August, when Hodson rode out of camp at the head of three hundred horse with orders to strike at a party of mutineers from Delhi who were said to be collecting reinforcements at Rohtak, forty-five miles away to the north. To bolster the new recruits, a third of Hodson's force was made up of Guides' Cavalry and horsemen from Nicholson's Pakhtun irregulars. The monsoon was now at its height, turning the roads into mud and streams into torrents, but Hodson and his men pushed on, reaching Rohtak after several lively skirmishes on the way. The mutineers turned out to be in possession of the town, in far larger numbers than had been reported and well dug-in behind strong defences. Without guns or infantry, a direct assault was out of the question, so Hodson devised a ruse to draw the enemy out into the open – a half-hearted attack, followed by a confused retreat. This was a risky strategem when the bulk of his troops were still unfamiliar with field movements, but it worked perfectly: 'The enemy moved out the instant we withdrew, following us in great numbers, yelling and shouting and keeping up a heavy fire of matchlocks . . . I continued to retire until we got into open and comparatively dry ground, and then turned and charged the mass, who had come to within 150 to 200 yards of us. The Guides, who were nearest to them, were upon them in an instant, closely followed by, and soon intermixed with, my own men. The enemy stood for a few seconds, turned, and then were driven back in utter confusion to the very walls of the town.' In his report Hodson had warm words for the Guides' Cavalry, who 'behaved with their usual dashing gallantry', but was unstinting in his praise for the sowars of his own Horse, who 'not only remained under fire unflinchingly, but retired before the enemy steadily and deliberately, and when ordered, turned and charged home boldly'. It was a good beginning.

Although Hodson's ride to Rohtak won him universal praise, it also marked the start of a second and more fatal decline in his already clouded reputation. On their way north his cavalry had captured a mutineer named Bisharat Ali, a rissaldar in the 1st Punjab Cavalry and an old friend of Neville Chamberlain. Having been caught red-handed, as it were – leading a party of deserters from his own regiment – he was summarily tried by Hodson, and shot. This was standard practice in a war where every deserter or mutineer was considered fair game for instant execution – John Nicholson was doing no less, and in Peshawar Herbert Edwardes had issued a proclamation that any deserter found could be killed and his property seized by his captors. Neville Chamberlain did not accept Bisharat Ali's guilt, however, and camp gossip had it that Hodson had shot Bisharat Ali out of personal enmity – something to do with a loan on which the one had stood surety for the other in earlier days. Nothing more came of it, but the rumour festered, preparing the ground for subsequent allegations – tales of looting and double-dealing of one sort or another – to be taken seriously by men who should have known better.

A week after Hodson's sortie it was Nicholson's turn to take the field, on a larger scale. The all-important siege-train from Ferozepore was now trundling slowly down the Grand Trunk Road towards Delhi, long lines of bullocks dragging the heavy guns that would enable them to invest the city in earnest. The mutineers got wind of its approach, and on 24 August a force of seven thousand men with thirteen guns was sent out to intercept it. Wilson's first real instruction to Nicholson ordered him to pursue the rebels and stop them before they could reach the siege-train. On the morning of 25 August Nicholson marched north with a mixed force of about two thousand five hundred men – nearly all Punjab irregulars, with the exception of three troops of horse artillery and two companies of British infantry drawn from HM 61st Foot (now the Gloucestershire Regiment). He had with him his younger brother, Lieutenant Charles Nicholson, at the head of a troop of the 2nd Punjab Cavalry, and also the younger brother of Harry and Peter Lumsden, Lieutenant William Lumsden, now promoted to lead Coke's Rifles in place of their wounded commander.

It was John Coke's view that 'there was not another man in camp, except perhaps Chamberlain, who could have taken that column to Najafgarh'. Ignoring Wilson's orders to stick to the roads, Nicholson led the column on a short-cut that took them through flooded countryside where the guns drawn by the horse artillery had frequently to be manhandled out of the mud. A gunner officer later told Coke that 'at one time the water was over his horses' backs, and he thought they could not possibly get out of their difficulties. But he looked ahead and saw Nicholson's great form riding steadily on as if nothing was the matter, and he felt sure that all was right'. After nine miles of this the column stopped for a rest while Nicholson rode forward with some of his own men to scout out the ground ahead. They learned that the mutineers had halted at the town of Najafgarh, twelve miles distant, and were taking up defensive positions on the far side of a drainage canal.

Returning to the column, Nicholson gave the order to resume the march, ignoring the protestations of the colonel of the 61st that his men were too exhausted to go on.

Another nine miles of desperately hard going, with the rain falling in torrents and the ground little better than a morass, brought them to the canal. The rebels' position extended along the far bank for a mile and a half, from a bridge over the canal on the left to the town of Najafgarh on the right. In the expectation that Nicholson's column would attack across the bridge, their guns had been concentrated between the bridge and an old serai at the centre of their position, all protected by entrenchments with parapets and embrasures. Nicholson chose instead to march round to the east and, having successfully dragged his sixteen horse-drawn guns across a flooded nullah, attack from the side, between the serai and the town. Before ordering the advance to be sounded, Nicholson rode along the lines on his grey charger and spoke to each company and troop in turn. To the men of the 61st he spoke of Chilianwala, reminding them of the words that Sir Colin Campbell had spoken to them before their charge there: 'Hold your fire until twenty or thirty yards, then fire and charge.' At this point an incident not mentioned in any official report took place: one of the enemy's 'picked men' came swaggering forward and challenged Nicholson to mortal combat. The doughty Muhammad Hayat Khan immediately fell upon the man with a blow from his tulwar that killed him instantly.

The bugles were now sounded, the guns on both sides thundered, and the infantry swept forward, Nicholson leading the way. The serai was taken within minutes, and the gun batteries beyond it. The line then turned and swept along the rear of the enemy's defences, giving only the luckier rebels time to retreat across the bridge. Thirteen guns were seized, with all the enemy's ammunition and supplies, and about nine hundred rebels killed – at a cost of thirty dead on Nicholson's side. One was Lieutenant William Lumsden. Nicholson's first act on returning to Delhi was to write to Joe Lumsden in Kandahar with the news of his youngest brother's death and the manner of his dying – at the head of his regiment and uttering words of encouragement to his men. Short and to the point, the letter closed, 'Give my love to Peter; you have my sympathy with you more than I can express. Ever, dear Joe, Yours very sincerely, J. Nicholson.'

The victory caused great jubilation in the camp outside Delhi. General Wilson was generous in his tributes to Nicholson who, for his part, was quick to express his 'extreme satisfaction' at the conduct of his troops. From Lahore Sir John Lawrence sent his congratulations, adding, 'I wish I had the power of knighting you on the spot; it should be done.' From Peshawar came a letter from Herbert Edwardes, less fulsome because chiefly and somewhat emotionally devoted to the news from Lucknow of the death of their first and greatest chief, Sir Henry Lawrence. Nicholson took it over to read to Chamberlain and Daly in the hospital lines at what must have been a very sombre gathering. He promised to have copies made for them but never found time to do so, and the letter was lost. Edwardes's letter to Joe Lumsden on the subject survives, and was presumably in a similar vein: 'We have all lost a friend, a master, an example – a second father. The Punjab, India, England has lost the noblest of public servants. Anything so distressing as this I have not yet heard, though Heaven knows there has been no lack of bloodshed. Thousands, black and white, will mourn him. For him we cannot grieve, for he was a humble and sincere Christian, prepared to die at any time, and he has died at last for his country. But, for ourselves, we must lament all our lives, for we shall never see his like again.'

Of all the Young Men, only William Hodson appears to have been unmoved by the death of 'dear Sir Henry'. To judge from his reply to Edwardes of 1 September, Nicholson was all but unmanned by his loss. With Sir Henry gone, he now had only Edwardes as his model: 'If it please Providence that I live through this business, you must get me alongside you again, and be my guide and help in endeavouring to follow his example; for I am so weak and unstable that I shall never do any good myself. I should like to write you a long letter, but I cannot manage it. God bless you, dear Edwardes. Ever yours affectionately, J. Nicholson.'

The rains had turned the Delhi Field Force's camp, sited in the lee of the ridge and out of range of the enemy's guns, into a sea of sludge surrounded by overflowing drains. Disease continued to claim as many victims as the rebel artillery and musket fire. 'Nothing is going on here of public importance,' wrote Hodson to his sister on 3 September. 'Everything is stagnant save the hand of the destroying angel of sickness: we have at this moment 2500 in hospital, of whom 1100 are Europeans, out of a total of 5000 men [i.e., Europeans], and yet our general waits for this and that arrival, forgetful that each succeeding day diminishes his force by more than the strength of the expected driblets. He talks now of awaiting the arrival of three weak regiments of Gulab Singh's force under Richard Lawrence [a fourth Lawrence brother, seven years younger than John], who are marching from Umbala . . . The train will be here tomorrow or next day, and I hope our general will not lose a day after that.'

The mile-long siege-train rolled into camp on 4 September: no fewer than sixty howitzers and mortars, together with hundreds of bullock-carts loaded with round shot, grape canisters and shells. The scene was now set for the last act of the drama of Delhi. Nicholson's first two military actions – the breaking of the mutineers at Hoti Mardan, and the destruction of the enemy force at the crossing of Trimmu Ghat – had been largely instrumental in halting the drift into rebellion in the Punjab. His third and much larger engagement at Najafgarh had isolated and paralysed the mutineers at Delhi. Now there remained only the taking of Delhi itself, and here Nicholson's role was again to prove pivotal.

Nicholson himself believed that the men chiefly responsible for the taking of Delhi were the engineers – in particular, the Field Force's chief engineer, Lieutenant-Colonel Richard Baird-Smith. For the previous seventeen years Baird-Smith had been mainly occupied building canals in the Punjab: an unlikely hero on the face of it, but he was a forceful character, and had no time for the 'croakers' among the senior ranks who were all for retiring, or holding on for more reinforcements. From the moment of his arrival in camp he had made a nuisance of himself, bombarding the Field Force's headquarters with plans for assault and keeping General Wilson under constant pressure. At Baird-Smith's side as his executive assistant was another Punjabwallah, and an equally forceful character: Lieutenant Alex Taylor, the young Public Works Department engineer who had built the new road from Rawalpindi to Peshawar and was now the Field Force's 'Director of Tunnels'. Between them, these two men oversaw a series of miracles performed by the hundreds of native sappers, miners and pioneers in the force, whether it was blowing up bridges in the surrounding area, strengthening the camp's defences, laying new trenches, or building up emplacements for the siege batteries.

With the arrival of Nicholson the two engineers gained their most powerful ally: unlike General Wilson, he was prepared to work closely with them as they drew up their plans for breaching the city walls prior to an assault on Delhi. 'The Engineers have consulted me about the plan of the attack, though Wilson has not,' Nicholson wrote to Sir John Lawrence three days after the arrival of the siege-train. 'They tell me they proposed to him that I should be consulted, and that he maintained a chilling silence. I imagine it is as I supposed – that he is afraid of being thought to be influenced by me. I care little, however, whether he receives my suggestions direct or through the Engineers. Like Barnard, he talks about the "gambler's throw"!'

The engineers maintained their pressure on General Wilson, and on 8 September Nicholson wrote again to John Lawrence with news that Baird-Smith's plans had been grudgingly accepted by Wilson. Hodson's spies having reported that the mutineers were expecting the assault to come from the west, at the Kabul Gate, where the British positions were closest to the city wall, Baird-Smith had therefore proposed to Wilson that the main assault should be directed against the city's northern defences, concentrating on the Kashmir Gate and the section of the wall between that and the river. This would mean taking the open no-man's-land below the Delhi Ridge and setting up four batteries of siege guns as close to the walls as they could bring them. 'We break ground with No.1 heavy battery at 650 yards tonight,' wrote Nicholson to Lawrence. 'Nos 2 and 3 tomorrow night at 550 and 350. Batter on the 9th and go in on the 10th. I can't give you the plan of attack, lest the letter should fall into other hands.' He added that General Wilson was losing his mind: 'Wilson's head is going: he says so himself, and it is quite evident he speaks the truth.'

A quite extraordinary confrontation was indeed now taking place between Wilson on the one hand and his Chief Engineer and John Nicholson on the other, much of it through intermediaries, since Wilson was doing his best to avoid both. A near-fatal attack of cholera had left him dispirited, and unwilling to commit himself to any one course of action. 'Don't drive me so,' the wretched commander wrote to Baird-Smith. 'I have already more than I can manage, and my head gets into such a state that I feel nearly mad sometimes.' As far as Baird-Smith was concerned, Wilson *was* mad – or, as he put it, 'off his head'. He had nothing but contempt for him, writing later that Wilson had been 'so uniformly obstructive by his dread of responsibility and his moral timidity that I say as little about him as I can . . . I believe his mind to have been a little off its usual balance all the time we were at work, and he was literally more difficult to deal with than the enemy. It was only by constantly reminding him that if he interfered with my plans, I would throw the whole responsibility for the consequences on him, that I could get on at all.'

Their differences came to a head on 7 September, when a general council of war attended by all the senior officers in camp took place in General Wilson's tent. Fred Roberts had sufficiently recovered from the bullet wound in his back to serve as Nicholson's staff officer, and it is he who relates how close Nicholson came to leading a mutiny. 'As his staff officer I had been fortunate to gain his friendship,' he writes:

On this occasion I was sitting in [Nicholson's] tent before he set out to attend his council. He had been talking to me in confidential terms of personal matters, and ended by telling me of his intention to take a very unusual step should the council fail to arrive at any fixed determination regarding the assault. 'Delhi must be taken,' he said, 'and it is absolutely essential that this should be done at once; and if Wilson hesitates longer, I intend to propose at today's meeting that he should be superseded.' I was greatly startled, and ventured to remark that, as Chamberlain was hors de combat from his wound, Wilson's removal would leave him, Nicholson, senior officer with the force. He smiled as he answered: 'I have not overlooked that fact. I shall make it perfectly clear that, under the circumstances, I could not possibly accept the command myself, and I shall propose that it be given to Campbell, of the 52nd.

313

Roberts walked over with Nicholson to Wilson's staff tent and then waited outside in a state of great excitement while the council of war deliberated. When Nicholson emerged he learned, to his relief, that Wilson had capitulated. He had been forced to accept Baird-Smith's plan of assault in every respect while insisting that, should it fail, Baird-Smith and not he, the commander of the Delhi Field Force, should take the blame. Nicholson's triumphant letter to John Lawrence says it all:

The game is completely in our hands . . . After making all kinds of objections and obstructions, and even threatening more than once to withdraw the guns and abandon the attempt, Wilson has made everything over to the Engineers, and they, and they alone, will deserve the credit for taking Delhi. Had Wilson carried out this threat of withdrawing the guns, I was quite prepared to appeal to the army to set him aside and and elect a successor. I have seen lots of useless generals in my day; but such an ignorant, croaking obstructive as he is, I have hitherto never met with . . . The purport of his last message in reply to the Engineers ran thus: 'I disagree with the Engineers entirely. I foresee great, if not insuperable, difficulties in the plan they propose. But as I have no other plan myself, I yield to the urgent remonstrances of the chief engineer.' The above are almost the very words used by him, and yet he never even examined the ground on which the Engineers proposed to erect the breaching batteries.

Though Wilson may not have examined the ground before the Kashmir Gate, Nicholson and Taylor certainly had. Before drawing up his plans for the assault here, Alex Taylor had made a daring night reconnaissance of an area of the civil lines below the Delhi Ridge known as Ludlow Castle, which at that time was still in enemy hands. His plans were rejected by Wilson, who refused to believe his claim to have made a personal inspection of the ground. When Nicholson heard of this, he at once offered to go out with Taylor on a further reconnaissance – an offer that Wilson accepted with alacrity, despite the risk of losing such a senior officer on so dangerous a mission. The two men slipped over the outer perimeter at midnight and not only surveyed the enemy positions at Ludlow Castle but got as far as an old Mughal summer palace close to the Kashmir Gate. One – possibly suspect – account of this foray has it that Nicholson, forewarned by Hodson's spies that the sentries manning the bastions above the Kashmir Gate were Sikhs, took advantage of this to climb up onto a section of the city walls beside the gate, making no attempt to hide himself. He was seen and recognised by the sentries as Nikal Seyn, but such was his reputation that none dared fire on him. Whatever the truth of this story, Taylor's report proved of enormous value in the subsequent capture of Ludlow Castle and the siting of the four siege batteries.

The first of these batteries was to be placed just below and east of the Ridge, positioned to reduce the powerful Mori Bastion directly to its front at a distance of half a mile and to provide covering fire for the second and subsequent batteries. Made up of four 24-pounders, five 18-pounders and one 8-inch howitzer, it was raised by Taylor and his pioneers in a single night. In a vivid personal memoir written twelve years after these extraordinary events, General Richard Barter, at the time of the siege adjutant of HM 75th Foot, describes the dramatic impact made by the battery when it first opened up on the morning of 8 September:

> We were all up early to see the ball open. The Moree proceeded to administer its usual morning dose to the piquets, but the smoke had scarcely spurted from its embrasures when the leafy screen was torn from our battery and we could see the iron hail strike the wall, sending up clouds of dust and bringing the masonry down into the ditch. It must have been an astonisher to the fellows in the bastion, but they quickly recovered from their surprise and turning the guns on the battery commenced a regular duel with it; our fellows continued to fire salvos, that is, all the guns fired together like an Infantry volley, and the effect of such a weight of metal striking the walls at once soon became apparent, for the Moree began to look like a large heap of earth, and gun after gun was disabled in the front of it till at length not one was fit for service.

The element of surprise was now lost, of course, so that the erection of the other three batteries, each closer to the walls and more exposed than the last, could only be achieved at high cost. Fred Roberts, an artilleryman by training, was put in charge of some of the guns of Number 2 battery and describes how scores of unarmed native pioneers were hit in the process of setting it up: 'With that passive bravery so characteristic of Natives, as man after man was knocked over, they would stop for a moment, weep a little over a fallen friend, place his body in a row along with the rest, and then work on as before.' As the British attack now seemed almost certain to come from this quarter, the rebel sepoys lined the city's northern walls, towers and trenches with every gun, rocket-launcher and musket they could collect, and maintained such 'a perfect storm of musketry' that the establishment of the last two batteries took far longer than planned. Throughout this period Nicholson consulted with Baird-Smith to refine the details of the coming assault, which would depend on two breaches being made on the four-hundred-yard section of wall between the Kashmir Gate and the Water Bastion and the doors of the Gate itself being blown open. Neville Chamberlain wrote that 'from the day of the trenches being opened to the day of the assault he was constantly on the move from one battery to another; and when he returned to camp he was constantly riding backwards and forwards to the chief engineer, endeavouring to remove any difficulties'.

On the morning of 13 September all the senior commanders bar Nicholson were summoned to headquarters to hear General Wilson read out the general orders for the assault, provisionally set for dawn the following day, 14 September. To the great satisfaction of most of those present, it was to be under the command of Brigadier-General John Nicholson, and would consist of four columns, with a fifth held in reserve. The first two would attack the Kashmir Bastion and Water Bastion breaches, the third the Kashmir Gate, and the fourth, acting in some respects as a diversion, would attempt an assault on the unbreached Kabul Gate west of the Mori bastion, this attempt being dependent for its success on the Kabul Gate being taken from the inside by one of the other columns. Each column was to comprise three regiments of infantry – now reduced, by sickness and casualties, to between three hundred and four hundred men each, so that no single column would be more than one thousand strong. Success would depend entirely on the assault being delivered with such speed and ferocity that the defenders would have no time to exploit their numerical advantage before at least a corner of the city had been taken.

As well as commanding the general assault, Nicholson was to personally lead the first column. Made up of one Scots regiment, HM 75th Foot, the 1st Bengal Fusiliers and the 2nd Punjab Infantry, No. 1 Column was to storm the breach made near the Kashmir Bastion. Now commanded by John Nicholson's brother, Lieutenant Charles Nicholson, Coke's Rifles were to form part of No. 3 Column, storming the Kashmir Gate itself once the gates had been blown open by charges laid by a party of sappers. The Guides' Infantry were to make up part of No. 4 Column, spear-headed by the Gurkhas of the Sirmur Rifles, while the Guides' Cavalry, together with Hodson's Horse and the 1st, 2nd and 5th Punjab Cavalry, were to form part of Brigadier Hope Grant's cavalry brigade, in support of the fourth column.

While the order of battle was being given out, Nicholson went out to watch as the last breaching battery, advanced to within a hundred and sixty yards of the Water Bastion, fired its opening salvos, before hurrying to Neville Chamberlain's bedside to urge him to exert all his influence to prevent Wilson from any further backsliding. As soon as he knew that Wilson had confirmed his position as overall commander of the assault, he called together the senior officers of all the regiments involved for final briefings from their respective column commanders. Young Captain Richard Barter of HM 75th Foot attended the briefing in Nicholson's tent: 'On a table before him was a map of the city and he stood up, his right foot on his chair, and explained what we were expected to do in a clear and lucid manner. Each man to carry two hundred rounds of ammunition in his pouch and haversack, we were to take the breach to the right of the Kashmir bastion known as the main breach, by assault and escalade.' General Nicholson himself was to be distinguishable by his standard, a green flag which one of his 'Afghan followers' would carry to point out his position: doubtless this 'Afghan' was Muhammad Hayat Khan. According to Barter, 'the General had a wonderful idea of the Frontier men and considered them, I am told, superior to British soldiers. They most certainly did splendid service in Delhi and on every other occasion when I saw them in action, but to compare them with the British soldier is going rather too far.'

In that last magical hour of the day known as the *hawa khana*, the time of 'breathing the air' that comes just before sunset in India, Nicholson rode beside Chamberlain as he was carried in a doolie along the Ridge to the roof of Hindu Rao's house, where they were joined by Henry Daly and another invalid, Risaidar Khan Singh Rosa of the Guides. From here they were to keep an eye on events on the right of the Ridge. After bidding farewell to his friends, Nicholson joined the engineer Alex Taylor on a final tour of the four batteries, to determine whether sufficient damage had been done to allow the attack to proceed the next morning. 'He was evidently satisfied,' wrote Fred Roberts, 'for when he entered our battery he said: "I must shake hands with you fellows; you have done your best to make my work easy tomorrow."'

Soon after dark, four of Taylor's engineer officers crept up to the ditch below the city walls and returned to confirm that the two breaches in the city wall – one beside the Kashmir Bastion and one a little further along the wall, near the Water Bastion – were indeed large enough to be stormed. At midnight Baird-Smith reported this to General Wilson, adding that the breaches should be assaulted without delay. Still protesting that it was against his wishes, Wilson gave the order to proceed.

In the final hours before forming up for the attack, every man taking part in the assault made his own personal preparations, writing last letters and wills. Those who still had any put on fresh clothing, partly to keep any wounds they might suffer as clean as possible but also out of self-respect. Captain Barter wound two turbans round his forage cap to give his head some protection from sword cuts, and tucked his wife's last letter from the Hills into the folds. 'There was not much sleep that night in our Camp,' he later recalled in his memoir:

> I dropped off now and then but never for long and when I woke I could see that there was a light in more than one of the

officers' tents and talking was going on in a low tone amongst the men, the snapping of a lock or springing of a ramrod sounding far in the still air telling of preparation for the approaching strife. A little after midnight we fell in as quietly as possible on the left of our tents; by the light of a lantern the orders for the assault were then read to the men. They were to the following purport: 'Any officer or man who might be wounded was to be left where he fell: no one was to step from the ranks to help him as we had no men to spare . . . There was to be no plundering, but all prize taken was to be put into a common stock for fair division after all was over. No prisoners were to be made, for we had no one to guard them, and care was to be taken that no women or children were injured.' To this the men at once answered, 'No fear, sir.' The officers now pledged their honours on their swords to abide by these orders, and the men then promised to follow their example.

After prayers had been said by a chaplain, the Highlanders of the 75th marched out of camp and across the Ridge, to take their allotted place in the trenches at the head of No. 1 Column. The assault was planned to begin at dawn but it took longer than expected for some of the regiments to reach their positions, so that the sun was already high in the sky when John Nicholson gave the signal to begin. On his command, the guns and mortars of the breaching batteries fell suddenly and dramatically silent. After a few seconds the sound of cheering was heard as the front ranks of the two columns poised below the two breaches in the walls climbed over the parapets and began to run across open ground.

Fred Roberts from his gun battery at Ludlow Castle, and Neville Chamberlain and Henry Daly further away on Delhi Ridge, watched the assault begin. Roberts has provided the most compelling account:

No sooner were the front ranks seen by the rebels than a storm of bullets met them from every side, and officers and men fell thick on the crest of the glacis. Then, for a few seconds, amidst a blaze of musketry, the soldiers stood on the edge of the ditch, for only one or two of the ladders had come up, the rest having been dropped by their killed or wounded carriers. Dark figures crowded on the breach, hurling stones upon our men and daring them to come on. More ladders were brought up, they were thrown into the ditch, and our men, leaping into it, raised them against the escarpe on the other side. Nicholson, at the head of a part of his column, was the first to ascend the breach in the curtain.

After a few desperate minutes of hand-to-hand fighting, both breaches were taken and the ramparts on either side cleared. While this was going on a party of ten sappers, together with a bugler of HM 52nd Foot, ran for the Kashmir Gate carrying powder bags and slow-matches to blow open the doors. One beam of the bridge over the ditch still remained in place, which allowed the survivors to reach the gate and place the explosives. The noise of battle was so great that the bugler had to sound the advance three times before his call was heard by the 52nd, who then advanced, with the sepoys of Coke's Rifles under Charles Nicholson hard on their heels. Among the latter was one Subedar Rattan Singh, a Sikh from Patiala who had been invalided out of the regiment several years before. As Coke's Rifles marched through Patiala *en route* to Delhi three months earlier, this old gentleman had been seen standing by the roadside with two swords in his belt. When Major Coke asked him what he was doing, he answered that he had come to rejoin his regiment: 'What! My old corps going to fight at Delhi without me! I hope you will let me lead my old Sikh company into action again. I will break these two swords in your cause.' Coke had allowed him to rejoin, and he had fought very gallantly throughout the siege. On the morning of the assault he had fixed it so that his own company should be at the head of the column. He was among the first of his regiment to be shot down as they fought their way through the Kashmir Gate.

The three columns met in the open ground between the Kashmir Gate and St James's Church, then separated again to clear different sectors of the city. Nicholson had given his own column the task of clearing the ramparts of the Shah Bastion and then the Mori Bastion and Kabul Gate beyond, with the aim of uniting with the fourth column as it fought through the outer surburbs of

Kishenganj and Paharipur. Once the Kabul Gate had been taken they would push on to secure the Lahore Gate, about six hundred yards south of the Kabul Gate.

Within an hour the ramparts as far as the Kabul Gate had been taken, and the British colours were hoisted on top of its tower. But at this point the advance towards the Lahore Gate fizzled out, halted by a determined rebel stand at the strong-point of the Burn Bastion, midway between the Kabul and Lahore Gates. Soon afterwards the tall figure of John Nicholson was spotted on the walls of the Mori Bastion by Brigadier Hope Grant, commander of the cavalry brigade supporting the fourth column outside the walls. In the confusion of the assault, Nicholson had become separated from his standard-bearer and bodyguard, the presumed Muhammad Hayat Khan; he now called down to Grant that all was going well, and that he was on his way to attack the Lahore Gate.

Within the city's walls the assault was progressing more or less according to plan, but this was not the case outside. The fourth column's attack had failed: the Sirmur Rifles at its centre had met unexpectedly heavy opposition as they attempted to clear the two suburbs outside the Kabul Gate, and on their right flank the Kashmir contingent under Richard Lawrence had buckled and was now in retreat, having abandoned its guns. A well-organised rebel counter-attack was now pushing the entire column back to its starting point in the gardens of Sabzi Mandi. Major Reid of the Sirmur Rifles, leading the fourth column, had been severely wounded, as had a number of other senior officers. Richard Lawrence attempted to assume command, but a Captain Muter of HM 6th Foot refused to take orders from him and issued his own, countermanding Lawrence's. From their position on the roof of Hindu Rao's house, Chamberlain and Daly watched with growing concern. 'We saw the repulse of Reid's column,' wrote Chamberlain, 'and could not fail to admire the conduct of the mutineer native officers as they rode along in front of their regiments endeavouring to incite their men to press home their advantage against the Cashmere Contingent . . . The Jummoo troops bolted, lost the whole or a portion of their guns, came back on our men, created a panic, and we were driven back in confusion, leaving our killed and some wounded (I believe) behind . . . So critical did affairs then look that it seemed possible the enemy might succeed in passing through, or might turn our right defences and attack them from the rear.' Seeing what was happening – or, more accurately, listening to a running commentary from the slightly less incapacitated Henry Daly – Neville Chamberlain decided to intervene: 'At such a crisis it was not a time to think of arms or weak legs or anything else, so down I hurried in a litter and took command, and got the corps separated and told off the different defences.' Few field commanders before or since can have ordered their troops about a battlefield while lying supine on a stretcher.

All this time, Grant's six-hundred-strong cavalry brigade had been standing idle, unable to charge to the rescue of Reid's column because of the built-up nature of the ground before them. They had come round on the far right to a position immediately to the front of and less than five hundred yards from the Lahore Gate. Here, for no good reason that William Hodson could determine, they were forced to sit in their saddles for almost two hours under what he describes, somewhat incoherently, as 'the heaviest fire troops are often exposed to, and that, too, without the chance of doing anything about preventing the enemy coming on . . . My young regiment behaved admirably, as did all hands. The loss of the party was, of course, very severe.' The failure of Reid's column to hold the ground in front of the Kabul Gate, combined with Nicholson's failure to progress along the ramparts beyond that same point, meant that the heavy guns of the Burn Bastion and the Lahore Gate – both untouched by the Delhi Field Force's siege batteries – were able to pour grape down onto Grant's cavalry paraded beneath their walls, inflicting appalling casualties among men and horses.

The cavalry included many of Nicholson's oldest and most loyal allies from the Frontier, and possibly their plight was the spur that drove him to what he now did; or it may be that, having told General Wilson his column would take the Lahore Gate, he was determined they should do so, come what may; or again, perhaps it was a simple matter of temperament, and Nicholson never considered that his luck must one day run out.

To reach the Burn Bastion from the Kabul Gate meant proceeding down a single narrow lane some two hundred yards long, with the city wall on the right and a terrace of single-storey flat-roofed houses on the left, each topped with low walls – ideal vantage points for sharp-shooters; at the far end, a 24-pounder had been turned to fire grape down the lane. It was nothing less than a death-trap. A party of the 1st Bengal Fusiliers had already attempted one direct attack up the lane and had been driven back to the Kabul Gate. A larger group from the same regiment then gathered under their commander to make a second assay. He and several of his officers dashed into the lane and within seconds were shot down, one after the other. The men following them wavered, and retreated to safety.

John Nicholson now strode onto the scene. Calling upon the demoralised fusiliers to follow him, he stepped out into the lane, and a fresh hail of grape and musket balls. He was half-way down when he realised he was not being followed. He stopped and turned to call the men behind to come on, waving his tulwar above his head as he did so. At that moment a sepoy lying on the roof of one of the houses lining the lane fired down on him, the ball striking his body with an audible thud and entering his exposed right side, below his armpit. Someone nearby exclaimed that he was hit, to which Nicholson replied irritably, 'Yes, yes.' Then his knees buckled and he began to sink to the ground. A sergeant of the 1st Bengal Fusiliers caught him and dragged him into a small recess immediately under the wall. Here he lay for some time, refusing to be moved, saying only that he would stay there till Delhi had been taken. Eventually he was carried back to the Kabul Gate and placed in a doolie. Two doolie-bearers were found and ordered to take him to the field hospital beyond Delhi Ridge, but at some point short of the Kashmir Gate they abandoned their charge by the side of the street – which was where Fred Roberts, sent out by General Wilson to establish the truth behind rumours of Nicholson's wounding, found him.

13

'Our best and bravest'

THE AFTERMATH, SEPTEMBER 1857 ONWARDS

That friend who is not faithful is no friend at all.
That act which is but short-lived is no work at all.
Khushal Khan Khattak

IT TOOK a week of fierce street-fighting to recapture Delhi. As soon as the Kashmir Gate had been secured, General Wilson came down from the Ridge to make his headquarters in St James's Church, just inside the walls of the city. But the setback to No. 4 Column and the slow progress made by the other columns in their drive into the heart of the city 'appeared to crush all energy and spirit out of him'. Fred Roberts saw how dejected he was: 'Despite the objections of all his staff officers Wilson became more than ever convinced that his wisest course was to withdraw from the city.' Only the combined efforts of Neville Chamberlain and Richard Baird-Smith prevented him from giving the order to retire. Chamberlain sent Wilson a strongly-worded despatch urging him to stay put, for the mutineers were now 'like a rope of sand' and would become more disorganised and demoralised with every passing hour. Baird-Smith, despite a severe leg wound, told the General to his face that they *must* hold on. And when news of Wilson's wavering reached Nicholson's ears as he lay dying, he struggled to sit up in his cot and roared out the last in his tally of insubordinations: 'Thank God I have strength yet to shoot him, if necessary.'

The retaking of Delhi did not end the Sepoy Mutiny, but did signal its ultimate failure. The blow to the rebels and the boost given to the British in India and their allies was enormous. A strong fortress defended by more than thirty thousand desperate and well-armed men had been taken by a force never more than a third of their number. While it is true that the shock troops of the three columns which first broke into the city were mostly British – the three Queen's regiments of HM 75th Foot, 8th Foot and 52nd Light Infantry, together with the EICo's 1st and 2nd Bengal Fusiliers – more than four-fifths of the Delhi Field Force were native troops, mostly irregulars drawn from the Punjab and beyond. According to Fred Roberts, the four units most constantly engaged in fighting were the British riflemen of HM 60th, the Gurkhas of the Sirmur Rifles, and the Pakhtuns, Sikhs and Punjabi Muslims of the Corps of Guides and Coke's Rifles. The Guides came to Delhi with five hundred and fifty men and suffered three hundred and nineteen casualties; Coke's Rifles arrived with six hundred and sixty-four sepoys and had two hundred and eight killed or wounded; two of its three British officers were killed and the third, John Coke, was wounded. Of the five British officers who then replaced these three before the assault, one was killed and the other four wounded. One of the latter was Charles Nicholson, who had to have an arm amputated. Unusually for an attacking force, the artillery, engineers, sappers and pioneers also sustained very heavy casualties, with losses amounting to nearly seven hundred killed or disabled. It is not known how many native camp-followers – the water-carriers, stretcher-bearers, porters, grooms, animal-transport drivers and others – died or were maimed for life.

John Nicholson took nine days to die. After examination by the surgeons he was taken to Daly's tent, and that same evening his brother Charles, now minus his right arm, was placed by his side. 'How the two brothers loved each other!' wrote Daly later, recalling that in the days before the assault 'the great one used to come down and see me when I was wounded, and the little one found out the hour, and used to drop in as if by accident and say, "Hilloa, John, are *you* there?" And John would say, "Ah, Charles, come in!" And then they'd look at each other. They were shy of giving way to any expression of it, but you saw it in their behaviour to one another.'

On his first visit Neville Chamberlain found John 'helpless as an infant, breathing with difficulty, and only able to jerk out his words in syllables at long intervals, and with pain'. From the outset the case had been diagnosed as hopeless, with little to be done other than giving heavy doses of morphine to limit the pain. Though reduced to a state of stupor for most of the time, Nicholson was yet able to fire a shot from his pistol through the side of the tent to shut up his horsemen, gathered in apparently noisy vigil outside. He was also able to dictate to Chamberlain a number of messages. One of the first was to his old enemy Sir John Lawrence, begging him to depose Wilson and appoint Chamberlain in his place. Others were more personal, chiefly for his mother and for Herbert Edwardes. In the last of these he asked Chamberlain to tell his dearest friend that 'if at this moment a good fairy were to grant me a wish, my wish would be to have him here, next to my mother'. When these words had been written down he added, 'Tell my mother that I do not think we shall be unhappy in the next world. God has visited her with a great affliction; but tell her that she must not give way to grief.'

Edwardes's last response, telegraphed to Chamberlain, was 'Give John Nicholson our love in time and eternity, and read him Acts xvi. 31 and Rom. x. 9. God ever bless him. I do not cease to hope and pray for him as a dear brother.' Both New Testament texts refer to salvation through Jesus Christ: 'Believe in the Lord Jesus Christ and thou shalt be saved.' A second telegraph, from John Lawrence, had also an evangelical ring: 'Give my love to Nicholson and say how deeply we shall deplore his fall. He is a noble fellow. Tell him to think of his Saviour and pray for His aid which alone can save him.'

If prayers and thoughts of salvation crossed Nicholson's mind as he lay in a fog of morphia, nothing is known of them. He was tended throughout by Muhammad Hayat Khan, who washed him, gave him water, and saw to it that he was not troubled by unwanted visitors. Told on 20 September that the city was now entirely in British hands, he replied, 'My desire was that Delhi should be taken before I die and it has been granted.' When Chamberlain saw Nicholson on the evening of 22 September he was unable to say more than a few words: 'Death had now come to claim him. Every hour he became weaker and weaker, and the following morning his soul passed away to another and better world.'

Nicholson's death brought expressions of grief pouring in from quarters both expected and unexpected. The most heartfelt came from Peshawar. 'I feel as if all happiness had gone out of my public career,' telegraphed Herbert Edwardes to Chamberlain:

> Henry Lawrence was as the father, John Nicholson the brother, of my public life . . . Never, never again can I hope for such a friend. How grand, how glorious a piece of handiwork he was! It was a pleasure even to behold him. And then his nature was so fully equal to his frame! So undaunted, so noble, so tender, so good, so stern to evil, so single-minded, so generous, so heroic, yet so modest. I never saw another like him, and never expect to do so. And to have had him for a brother, and now to lose him in the prime of life. It is an inexpressible and irreparable grief.

Even the hard-bitten William Hodson was much affected, writing to his brother before the gravity of Nicholson's injuries was made known that he would gladly give a year's pay to have him restored to health. He mourned his death with equal feeling, declaring that, 'with the single exception of my ever-revered Sir Henry Lawrence and Colonel Mackeson, I have never seen his equal in field or council. He was pre-eminently our "best and bravest", and his loss is not to be atoned for in these days.' Others among the Young Men added their words of praise and their expressions of loss. Only Sir John Lawrence was less than fulsome, although he too acknowledged that Nicholson had been the major architect of their success at Delhi and the 'life and soul of the army'.

The burial of the 'hero of Delhi' took place at daybreak on the following day, 24 September. A new graveyard had been prepared on the open land between the ruins of the Kashmir Gate and Ludlow Castle – ground across which Nicholson and men of No. 1 and No. 5 Columns had charged ten days before. 'No band played the Dead March,' recorded Ensign Wilberforce. 'No volleys of musketry were fired over the Great General. Chief amongst his mourners stood Neville Chamberlain, his devoted friend; and surrounding the open grave were officers and men, some with sunburnt faces, some bleached white with fever and sickness, their plain khaki uniforms contrasting with the picturesque dresses of Pathans and Afghans, and others of his Multani Horse [more correctly, the mixed Punjabi and Pakhtun horse].' Only after the coffin had been lowered into the ground and the grave filled in did these last give way to their grief:

> Throwing themselves on the ground, they sobbed and wept as if their very hearts were breaking; and be it remembered that these men held the creed, that a man who shed tears was only fit to be whipped out of his village by the women. Probably not one of these men had ever shed a tear; but for them Nicholson was everything. For him they left their frontier homes, for him they had forsaken their beloved hills to come down to the detested plains; they acknowledged none but him, they served none but him. They believed, as others, that the bullet was not cast, the sword not ground, that could hurt him; over and over again in the frontier skirmishes they had seen Nicholson pass unharmed where others must have been killed; and now that the earth was placed on his coffin, they threw their tradition of manhood to the wind.

Neville Chamberlain had appropriated from the Red Fort a large white marble slab which had served generations of kings as a garden seat. This he ordered to be placed over Nicholson's grave, bearing the following brief inscription:

THE GRAVE

OF

BRIGADIER-GENERAL JOHN NICHOLSON

WHO

LED THE ASSAULT AT DELHI

BUT FELL IN THE HOUR OF VICTORY

MORTALLY WOUNDED

AND DIED SEPTEMBER 23, 1857

AGED 35.

The last line was incorrect: Nicholson was thirty-four at his death.

Fred Roberts was among those absent from the interment. As it took place he was marching out of the city as part of a relieving force of 2,650 headed for Lucknow and Cawnpore. 'Our way from the Lahore Gate by the Chandi Chauk led through a veritable city of the dead,' he wrote. 'Not a sound was to be heard but the falling of our own footsteps; not a living creature was to be seen. Dead bodies were strewn about in all directions, in every attitude that the death–struggle had caused them to assume, and in every stage of decomposition. We marched in silence, or involuntarily spoke in whispers, as though fearing to disturb those ghastly remains of humanity . . . Our horses seemed to feel the horror of it as much as we did, for they shook and snorted in evident terror.'

From Delhi Lieutenant Fred Roberts marched away to fame, honour and great personal popularity, both in India and in Britain. He took part in numerous military actions at Lucknow, Cawnpore and elsewhere in Oude and central India, winning the Victoria Cross for valour in recovering a standard. He went on to campaign as far afield as Abyssinia and Assam before returning to the Frontier in 1878 to command the former Punjab Irregular Force – by then renamed the Punjab Frontier Force, the Piffers. This fortunate timing gave him the opportunity to lead the Kurram Field Force and then the Kabul Field Force during the Second Afghan War, where he made his name as a fighting general with his 'march on Kandahar' from Kabul in 1880. He became Commander-in-Chief in India in 1885 – the 'Bobs Bahadur' of Rudyard Kipling's barrack-room ballads, genuinely beloved of his troops, despite his hard line on drink and prostitutes – and finally left India in the spring of 1893 after forty-one years of military service. He was made a Field Marshal in 1895 and four years later went out to South Africa as C-in-C to direct the conduct of the Boer War. In 1901 he was created Earl Roberts of Kandahar, Pretoria and Waterford. Two years later he paid his brief visit to the home town of the hero of his youth, the man whom he had first met almost half a century before, while camped in the hills outside Peshawar. He died in comfortable old age at Waterford in 1914, aged 82.

Many of the young officers of Roberts's generation who fought at Delhi and survived rose to become distinguished generals: Lieutenant Alex Taylor of the Engineers, for example, retired to England in 1880 as General Sir Alexander Taylor and was president of the Royal Engineering College at Cooper's Hill for almost two decades; Lieutenant Alfred Wilde returned to the Frontier to command the 4th Punjab Infantry (Wilde's Rifles), the Guides and then the Piffers, leading the Hazara Field Force in the Black Mountain campaign of 1868 before retiring as Lieutenant-General Sir Alfred Wilde; Captain George Green of the 2nd Punjab Infantry (Green's Punjabis) recovered from wounds sustained at Delhi in time to take part in the relief of Lucknow, retiring as General Sir George Green in 1877; Major John Vaughan of the 5th Punjab Infantry (Vaughan's Rifles) also led his regiment to Lucknow, and later commanded a brigade in the Black Mountain War of 1868 before retiring as Major-General Sir John Vaughan; Lieutenant Dighton Probyn of the 2nd Punjab Cavalry (Probyn's Horse) went on to win a VC at Agra and retired after many years of frontier service to become Keeper of the Privy Purse to King Edward VII as General Sir Dighton Probyn. The list could be continued.

Lieutenant Charles Nicholson was not so fortunate. He survived the amputation of his arm but never fully recovered his health. He sailed back to Ulster on sick-leave, then went briefly to America where he met and married a distant cousin. In 1862 he was offered the command of a Gurkha regiment and so returned to India with his wife. On the fifth day of their journey up-country he collapsed and died in a roadside dak-bungalow, aged thirty-three. He was the fourth and last of the Nicholson brothers to die in India. Four out of four.

As to the more senior officers at Delhi, the ineffectual Archdale Wilson went on to command the artillery at the taking of Lucknow but then left India as soon as decency permitted. He returned to England with a baronetcy for his pains to write two self-justifying volumes about his leadership. He also retired a full general, on the 'Buggins' turn' principle. The man who had actually earned the plaudits given to Wilson, Richard Baird-Smith, never received public recognition. He returned to his post with the Public Works Department in Lahore but never recovered his health after Delhi and died in 1861 on his way home to England. A plaque was later erected to his memory in St Paul's Cathedral, Calcutta. The gallant and peppery John Coke survived the wound he received at the assault on Ludlow Castle and returned to command the 1st Punjab Infantry in Kohat for another year, but was another whose health was undermined. He went home to England and semi-retirement as a Major-General and a KCB, later becoming High Sheriff of Herefordshire.

Among John Nicholson's friends, the now fragmenting inner circle of Henry Lawrence's Young Men, fortunes were mixed. Neville Chamberlain went on to achieve unwanted fame as the most wounded officer in the Indian Army. After Delhi he wrote to his brother Crawford that he had no wish for further active service, hoping rather 'to turn my sword into a shepherd's crook', although 'if duty requires the sacrifice I cannot repine' – and duty did indeed require more from him. Returning to the Frontier, he commanded brigades in the Waziri campaign of 1860 and the much more serious Umbeyla campaign in 1863. This last, fought against the combined Swati and Yusufzai in the Malakand hills overlooking the Vale of Peshawar, involved Reynell Taylor as the senior political officer and Alexander Taylor as the senior engineer, as well as many other familiar 'names' from the Piffers, including Colonels Wilde, Vaughan, Probyn, Brownlow and the one-armed Sam Browne. It was in this campaign that Sir Neville Chamberlain received the last wound of his military career, while personally leading an assault against the notorious Crag Piquet, a well-aimed jezail bullet in the right arm once again forcing him to relinquish command at a critical stage. After a six-year spell in the south as Commander of the Madras Army, Chamberlain was back on the Frontier in 1878 leading a political mission to the Amir of Afghanistan. The blocking of that mission by the Afghans halfway up the Khyber at Ali Masjid – the very spot where thirty-six years earlier Chamberlain had seen his friend John Nicholson bury his brother Alexander – gave grounds for the Viceroy, Lord Lytton, to launch the Second Afghan War. Though far from the 'signal catastrophe' of the First, it was almost a carbon copy, comprising the ritual killing of the British envoy (Colonel Cavagnari) and his escort (four British officers and sixty-eight men of the Corps of Guides) in Kabul, an invading army besieged (General

Roberts at Sherpur), a military disaster (an army of two thousand five hundred men destroyed at Maiwand) and a concluding British victory (Roberts' march to Kandahar). Chamberlain served as a member of the Viceroy's Supreme Council during the war, then retired to England in 1881. After being made a Field Marshal in 1900 he spoke out against the conduct of the South African War. He and his younger brother, General Sir Crawford Chamberlain, both died in 1902, aged 82 and 81 respectively. Whatever would the elder brother make of the fact that he is best-known today as the inventor of snooker (in fact, devised by a nephew, Colonel Sir Neville Chamberlain, in Bangalore in 1875)?

Now to the ill-starred William Hodson. After coming unscathed through that futile parade of Hope Grant's cavalry brigade outside the Lahore Gate and, before that, at least a score of cavalry actions in and around Delhi, it must have seemed to him, as to his Flamingos – his Plungers – that he bore a charmed life. But while no one questioned his bravery or his fighting ability, what was increasingly a subject of gossip and innuendo was his doubtful morality. At Delhi he had lived life on the edge, flitting from one role to another, revelling in the murky business of information-gathering, doing the Field Force's dirty work, spending much of his time huddled with mysterious native couriers and irregulars whose loyalties were uncertain. Like Nicholson, he had no time for *politesse*, or political niceties; but he lacked Nicholson's over-whelming presence and authority. Loved by his men, he was always distrusted by the British officers.

Nicholson's death in no way deterred him from carrying on his war against the rebels with the same blood-thirsty bravado he had hitherto displayed. On the day following the storming of the city Hodson learned that the old Mughal Emperor, Shah Bahadur, together with his sons and entourage, had fled from the Red Fort to the Tomb of Humayun, five miles beyond the southern gate of Delhi. Immediately he applied to General Wilson for permission to go out with a small force of his horse to capture the king and bring him back a prisoner. Wilson would have none of it, describing it as too dangerous, so Hodson appealed to Neville Chamberlain. He agreed it was a risk worth taking, and argued

Hodson's case. 'I went to General Wilson,' wrote Chamberlain, 'and urged on him the necessity of the endeavour being made. He said angrily that I was urging him to assent to a thing that I would not myself undertake. I kept my temper with great difficulty. After my continuing to urge the point he at length agreed.'

Hodson and a hundred of his men rode out to the white marbled tomb of Emperor Humayun, negotiated the surrender of the old man and part of his court, and escorted them back to Delhi, followed by a large crowd of angry retainers and supporters. Hodson then went again to Wilson, for permission to return to Humayun's Tomb and bring back into custody the Emperor's two sons, widely believed by the British to have had a hand in the massacre of British prisoners in the Red Fort during the early days of the uprising. Once again Wilson bowed to applied pressure, with the caveat 'but don't let me be bothered with them'. Like the knights who murdered Thomas à Becket, Hodson took the general at his word. Returning to the tomb, he found a large and hostile crowd gathered. Again he negotiated, with the warning that he had come to 'seize the Shahzadas [sons of the king] for punishment, and intended to do so dead or alive'. After two hours of 'wordy strife and very anxious suspense', the two princes and a grandson of Shah Bahadur gave themselves up, asking whether their lives had been promised by the Government. 'Most certainly not' was Hodson's answer, and he placed them under armed guard in a cart. While his prisoners were being escorted back to Delhi, Hodson stayed behind to collect up arms from the crowd gathered at Humayun's Tomb; by the time he and the rest of his sowars caught up with the prisoners and their escort, it was to find them surrounded by an angry mob. Later he claimed that he had no time to think twice: 'I came up *just in time*, as a large crowd had collected and were turning on the guard. I rode in among them at a gallop, and in a few words I appealed to the crowd, saying that these were the butchers who had murdered and brutally used helpless women and children, and that the Government had now sent their punishment: seizing a carbine from one of my men, I deliberately shot them one after another.' Hodson's argument that he 'had no time for deliberation' was backed up by his men – but there were other eye-witnesses, British officers who claimed to have seen him strip the princes of their jewelled arm-bands and silk clothes before he shot them.

There can be no doubt that in the first instance Hodson's killing of the three princes in cold blood was widely applauded by his brother officers. Once the city had been taken, however, and passions had had time to cool, attitudes changed. As Fred Roberts put it, by this act Hodson 'did . . . give colour to the accusations of blood-thirstiness which his detractors were not slow to make'. In justifying his actions to his wife soon after the event, Hodson made it plain that he had had no qualms about 'destroying the enemies of our race', adding that he was prepared to have 'all kinds of bad motives attributed to me, for no man ever yet went out of the beaten track without being wondered at and abused; and so marked a success will make me more enemies than friends.'

He was right. From that time onwards Hodson was marked out as a pariah, his every action cast in a bad light. Just as every narrative of the siege of Delhi carries glowing accounts of Nicholson's feats, so many of these same accounts include stories, almost invariably told at second or third hand, of Hodson's dastardly deeds. He was said to be as much interested in plunder as in killing – a curious twist of hypocrisy in view of the looting indulged in by all ranks, British and native alike. In this respect, the worst that can be said of Hodson is that he turned a blind eye to looting among his irregulars; this was, after all, what many had left the Punjab for, and a small perk for all the risks they took. The official rule at Delhi was that all plunder was to be shown to the prize agents, where 'it was divided into two shares, one share being given to the finder, the other to the prize fund'. However, as far as many soldiers were concerned it was very much a case of finders keepers, and the irregulars were well to the fore. The numerous surviving personal testimonies of the capture of Delhi make it clear that looting was more than widespread – it was all-pervading. The Gurkhas of the Sirmur Rifles were conspicuous plunderers, and even those golden boys of the Frontier Irregulars, the Corps of Guides, did more than their share – as a jocular letter from Herbert Edwardes to Joe Lumsden testifies. This was written on 23 January 1858, as the Guides were preparing to make a triumphant return to Peshawar: 'The whole border is in commotion about the wealth of the Guides, who have brought countless fair ladies and splendid byles [bullock carriages] with red curtains and fat bullocks from the precincts of the palace [the emperor's palace in Delhi]. Every man is said to be a Croesus. The tales are endless. It is like the return of the crusaders.'

At least part of the ill-will directed towards Hodson after Delhi can be linked to the expansion of Hodson's Horse, for the regiment attracted so many volunteers that it had to be divided first into two and then into three battalions. In the aftermath of the city's capture these ill-disciplined irregulars were badly needed, doing valuable service in the months that followed, working their way across the countryside like a plague of locusts on the flanks of the British forces closing in first on Cawnpore and then on Lucknow. Here the most terrible retribution took place, and hundreds, if not thousands, of innocent men were shot, bayoneted or strung up for no better reason than that they were there. 'I never let my men take prisoners,' wrote Hodson at this time, 'but shoot them at once.' Again Hodson was doing nothing that other officers of the British regiments and their men were not doing. Revenge was the order of the day, and those who marched on Cawnpore were merciless.

Hodson's end came on 9 March 1858 as he and his men were clearing a building of mutineers in the grounds of Begum Kothi, part of the palace of the Nawab of Oude in Lucknow. While breaking down a door he received a musket ball in the chest at nearly point-blank range, and died the following day. Almost immediately it was rumoured in camp that Hodson had been engaged in looting. This was plain nonsense, as a number of British officers and men later testified, but Hodson now had few champions to speak up for him. When his immediate property and effects were auctioned, according to military custom, the total sum raised to be sent to his widow was £170 – hardly representative of a king's ransom in loot. Susan Hodson was forced to apply to the EICo's Corporate Fund for financial assistance to pay for her passage home to England, and was only rescued from poverty when a special pension was awarded by the Secretary of State for India 'in testimony of the high sense entertained' of her late husband's services. Hodson is still widely perceived as the black sheep in the British fold, but in truth he is closer to being the obverse of the one coin, that side of themselves which the British in India preferred not to see.

The man who took over Hodson's Horse was – who else could it have been? – Henry Daly. Despite having lost the movement in his left arm he had been able to rejoin the fighting in time to take part in the recapture of Lucknow and the subsequent mopping-up operations in Oude. He was given the command the day following Hodson's death, and did his best to bring the regiment to a greater state of order and discipline. Although six British officers were attached to Hodson's Horse, they had been allowed little say in the running of its affairs. 'No European officer knew anything of the affairs of the regiment,' Daly wrote in a memorandum. 'Everything was done by himself.' Mixed up among the officially enlisted men were large numbers of freebooters: 'Plunder and the tales of golden floods had enticed many of the relatives and friends of the sowars from the Punjab; the lines of the regiment were full of these amateurs; they wore the uniform and have sometimes, in the absence of the sowars, actually attended parades and taken duty. In a skirmish I was at first surprised to see the great array at the commencement; their occupation, however, quickly thinned the gathering. I had much difficulty in breaking through this combination.' Daly applied a firm hand and sent numbers of supernumeraries on their way, then reorganised the regiment into three battalions, each with a Sikh sirdar as its subadar. It is worth noting that while Daly found the corps' accounts apparently a shambles, the same experience as Hodson's when he first took command of Lumsden's Guides, a detailed examination proved everything to be in order. The examination was carried out by Lieutenant R.B Anderson, younger brother of Daly's best friend William Anderson, murdered at Multan in 1848. Daly was subsequently given command of the Central India Horse in 1861. He later returned to civil administration, but never on the Frontier, in 1871 becoming Agent for the Governor-General for the princely states of Central India. He too got his 'K', and retired to England in 1882 as General Sir Henry Daly. Just before he retired he lost his wife, who died in Bombay before she could board the ship for home. There are few details of the marriage, but the relationship is known to have been close. After Susan Daly's death Henry wrote to a friend that 'my life in India seems a thing of yesterday, and when I call up the incidents and time, it is passing strange, for, until this dark blow came, I felt no older or colder than when I landed a boy of seventeen'. A son born to the Dalys followed their footsteps in India and became a highly regarded political agent.

Among those who fought beside Nicholson at Delhi, one last name remains to be considered. After the burial of his liege lord and protector, Muhammad Hayat Khan went home to Hasan Abdal with his half-brother, also one of Nicholson's band. According to Ensign Reginald Wilberforce, most of Nicholson's horsemen decamped soon after his burial: 'These men never took any pay whatsoever for their services, and when, a few days after Nicholson's funeral, an order was received by them from headquarters to march somewhere – I do not know where – they returned for answer that they owned no allegiance to the English Government; that they had come down to protect and serve Nicholson, and to loot Delhi, both of which they did to the best of their ability. And when they had collected up as much plunder as they could, they marched back again, up country, to their own homes, carrying their plunder with them.'

Once peace had been restored to the Punjab, Muhammad Hayat Khan was given a grant of land and a position as a *tahsildar* or revenue officer. In 1861 he was appointed Extra Assistant Commissioner, first at Shapur, then at Bannu; in 1872 he became an Assistant Commissioner, and in 1877 was made a Companion of the Star of India. He was by then the right-hand man of Louis Cavagnari, Commissioner of Kohat between 1866 and 1877, and played an important role as interpreter in negotiations with the Afghans in the late 1870s. He then acted as a Political Assistant to General Roberts, with first the Kurram Field Force and then the Kabul Field Force between 1878 and 1880, taking part in Roberts's march on Kandahar. Subsequently he became a Divisional Judge, and in 1899 was awarded the title of Nawab. He died at home in Hasan Abdal in 1901, the greatly respected patriarch of his family.

Of the younger politicals who followed Nicholson and his peers into the Punjab as their assistants and, fleetingly, into this book – Pearse, Cocks, Bowring, Pollock, Herbert, Coxe and others –

none achieved a like fame. Perhaps this was inevitable. The times had changed. Compared with the major upheavals their predecessors went through – the First Afghan War, the First and Second Sikh Wars and the Sepoy Mutiny – theirs was an era of tranquillity. But there were frontier campaigns still to be waged against the more troublesome Pakhtun tribes, and the Corps of Guides and the other Piffer regiments were still called out to spearhead punitive expeditions into the mountains. In these campaigns Harry 'Joe' Lumsden played his part. He and his brother Peter returned to Peshawar from Kandahar in mid 1858 and both had a hand in rebuilding the much-fragmented Corps of Guides – now renamed The Queen's Own Corps of Guides – before going their separate ways. Joe resumed command of the Corps and served under his old friend Brigadier Sir Neville Chamberlain in operations against the Waziri in 1860. Later that year an attempt was made on his life by a religious fanatic and he was lucky to escape with only a severe wound to his left arm. In March 1862 he ended his connection with his beloved Guides when offered the command of the Nizam of Hyderabad's army in southern India. He retired as a full general and Knight Companion of the Star of India and died at home in Scotland at the age of 75. In his retirement he spoke often of the Guides, but if he harboured regrets over his absence from what was always remembered as the Corps' finest hour, they went with him unspoken to his grave.

Another of the Young Men not at Delhi in the summer of 1857 was Reynell Taylor, busy with problems of his own in Kangra. In later days Taylor came to be known as the 'Bayard of the Punjab', more for his essential decency than for any qualities of the *chevalier*. He returned to Bannu and the lands of the Derajat west of the Indus as Commissioner in 1859, and for the next seventeen years had a succession of senior postings in the Punjab as Commissioner: Peshawar in 1862, Amballa in 1865, Amritsar in 1870. He retired to England as, yes, a general (a Major-General, in fact), but without a knighthood. He deserved better. Of the wife he took to India when she was so young, regrettably little is known.

The second master of the Young Men, Sir John Lawrence, went on to far greater things. He became the first Lieutenant-Governor of the Punjab in January 1859, when British India ceased to be a property of the East India Company and became part of Queen Victoria's dominions. At the end of 1863 he was appointed Viceroy of India in succession to Lord Elgin. His viceroyalty was characterised by a policy of non-interference in the affairs of his Afghan neighbour summed up in the happy phrase 'masterly inactivity'. He preferred to concentrate his efforts on consolidation and on basic necessities or desiderata such as sanitation, irrigation, and the extension of the railway system. As he grew older he became increasingly convinced, like his brother Henry and their common lieutenant, Herbert Edwardes, that British rule in India was part of God's purpose: 'We have not been elected or placed in power by the people, but we are here through our moral superiority, by the force of circumstances and by the will of Providence.' He retired from India in 1869 and on his return to England was created Baron Lawrence of the Punjab and Grateley (according to the *Dictionary of National Biography*, 'a small estate on Salisbury Plain left him by his sister, Mrs Hayes'). He died in 1879, and lies buried in Westminster Abbey. His eldest brother George, who had been Peshawar's first Resident, served as Agent to the Governor-General in Rajputana for several years after the Mutiny before resigning on the grounds of ill-health in 1864. He was created a Knight Commander of the Star of India in 1866 and, having retired from the army, was appointed an honorary Lieutenant-General in 1867. He outlived John by five years, dying in 1884. Brother Henry lies buried in the grounds of the Residency at Lucknow, an epitaph he composed himself inscribed on his tombstone: 'Here lies Henry Lawrence who tried to do his duty'. His wife, the doughty Honoria, had died of cancer in 1854.

Lastly there is Herbert Edwardes, who after the great promise of his early years never really came into his own. Lonely and worn down by the strains of holding Peshawar and northern Punjab together through the Mutiny, desperate to return to his wife and family in England and recover his health, he was forced to stay on in India until the middle of 1859, by which time he was close to collapse, both physically and mentally. He spent two years in England regaining his health, during which time he was created a Knight of the Bath. When he and his wife returned to India in 1862 he might have expected something a little more prestigious than the Commissionership of Amballa. He was, after all, a 'born ruler of men', as Sir John Lawrence had put it – and as his record showed. Yet he was denied the higher office that his talents demanded. His three years at Amballa were, by his own admission, 'the most burdensome and unhappy of my public life'. What made them so was 'the state of *machinery* to which we had all been reduced, and the daily sense that I had less power than I had eighteen years before, when dear Sir Henry Lawrence sent us forth to do our best for chiefs and people, and supported us doing it'. Later there was talk of the governor-generalship of the Punjab, but when the office was finally offered him by Sir John Lawrence, his wife's and his own increasing ill-health forced him to turn it down and seek early retirement instead. It may be that this lack of promotion was linked to the zeal – if not zealotry – with which Edwardes urged the propagation of the Gospel and the setting up of various Christian projects in India. The triumphant outcome of the Sepoy Mutiny had left him in no doubt that 'the Giver of Empires is indeed God', and that He had awarded the government of India to Britain because 'England has made the greatest effort to preserve the Christian religion in its purest form'. However, excessive evangelising was now widely recognised as one of the factors that had destabilised the Bengal Army and precipitated the Sepoy Mutiny, and the new administration was in no mood to take any more risks with the religious sensibilities of the native peoples of the subcontinent. This did not, of course, prevent the Edwardeses making the propagation of evangelical Christianity, both at home and in India, the central feature of the rest of their lives. Herbert Edwardes never fully regained his health and finally succumbed to an attack of pleurisy in London in December 1868. A life of his great mentor Sir Henry Lawrence, on which he had been working for some years, was left unfinished. He was forty-nine. His devoted widow Emma then made it her life's work to perpetuate her late husband's memory in print, in the form of the two-volume work *Memorials of the Life and Letters of Major-General Sir Herbert Edwardes*, published in 1886.

After Independence the grand obelisk erected over the grave of the assassinated Frederick Mackeson in Peshawar's Kampani Bagh was pulled down. A car park now covers his mortal remains. At the Margalla Pass a memorial tower of stone is still referred to as the Nicholson burj but few can tell you who this Nicholson was or what he did. The true memorial of these men is the Frontier. They did not demarcate its borders, nor did they create the North-West Frontier Province of Pakistan as it is today. But, in establishing the ground rules of local government and giving the borderland between Afghanistan and the Indian subcontinent its own distinct identity, they *made* the Frontier. In doing so they helped to preserve the tribal culture of the Pakhtuns, who today talk of Pakhtunkwa – the country of the Pakhtuns – and see themselves as a people, despite being divided between two nation states. Whether this is a plus or a minus in the greater scheme of things, only time and history will tell.

Acknowledgements

THIS BOOK could not have been written without the help of a great many kind people in Pakistan who opened their doors to me in the best traditions of Pakhtun *melmastia* and also shared their knowledge with me. I listened and tried to learn, but ultimately the views expressed and the conclusions reached are mine alone.

My informants and hosts fell into two groups, official, and non-official or retired. Among the former I wish to thank: His Excellency Lieutenant-General (Rtd) Mohammad Arif Bangash, Governor of the North West Frontier Province; Javed Iqbal, Secretary to the Governor; Shafiquzzaman, Director of Press Information; Mir Laig Shah, Commissioner of Peshawar Division; Sahibzada Mohammad Khalid, then Commissioner of Kohat Division; Raffat Pasha, D.I.G. Police, Kohat; Major Attaullah Khan, Commissioner of Bannu Division; Mohammed Jehanzeb Khan, Deputy Commissioner of Bannu; and Gulzar Khan, Commissioner of Afghan Refugees.

Among the latter, I wish to express my thanks to Dr Humayan and Mrs Munawar Khan; Begum Mahmooda Salim of the Khattars of Wah; Major-General (Rtd) Jehanzeb Khan, former Colonel of the Corps of Guides Cavalry; Brigadier (Rtd)

Mohammad Ishaq, former Commandant of the Punjab Frontier Force Regiment; Omar Khan Afridi and his cousins Amjad Khan Afridi and Malik Nadir Khan; Azam and Parveen Khan; Aurangezeb Khan, Khan of the Mashwanis; Mamood Raza of Sirikot; and, in particular, Bashir Ahmad of Mansehra and his nephew Major Tariq Mahmood, without whose encouragement, enthusiasm and support my chapters on James Abbot and the people of Hazara could not possibly have been written. Thanks in large measure are due, too, to Rahimullah Yusufzai, doyen of the Peshawar press corps, who not only took me into Afghanistan but, more importantly, got me safely out again.

In Delhi I enjoyed the hospitality of Jonathan Mermagan and my old drinking partner, photographer Aditya Patankar, and drew on the local knowledge of Nigel 'Hanklin-Janklin' Hanklin, for which many thanks.

In England I received valuable advice and support from Louise Nicholson, Sue Farrington ('the cemetery lady') and Theon Wilkinson, MBE (founder and for a quarter of a century now honorary secretary of that remarkable body of ancestor-worshippers, the British Association for Cemeteries in South Asia). My thanks go also to the directors and staff at what was the India Office Library and Records – now the Oriental and India Office Collection at the new British Library – and at the National Army Museum.

In Northern Ireland I drew on the local knowlege of Deirdre Armstrong and others at the South Eastern Education and Library Board, Ballynahinch and of Brenda Collins at the Lisburn Linen Centre and Trevor Neill of the Lisburn History Society. In the Republic I enjoyed a correspondence with my distant Hogg relative, William Nicholson.

My special thanks to two fellow-travellers: photographer Richard Davies, and my wife Liz. Lastly, my thanks to Roger Hudson for reading my manuscript, and especially to Liz Robinson, most meticulous of editors.

Glossary

akhund (P.):   religious teacher or saint

ayah (H.):   child's nurse, originally Portuguese

badal (P.):   revenge

badragga (P.):   tribal escort

bagh (P.):   garden

banya (H.):   banker, money-lender, usually Hindu

cantonment: in the Anglo-Indian context, standing camp or military quarter of *station*

civilian: in the Anglo-Indian context, an administrative officer of the EICo

civil lines: area of *station* where *civilians* lived

Cold Weather: the winter months between October and March

duffardar (A.):   commander of a small body of cavalry, equivalent of an infantry *havildar*

darrah (P.):   mountain pass, thus Darra

dekshi (H.):   cooking pot

Eid (A.):   Muslim festival marking end of *Ramadan*

ghar (Pu.):   mountain, thus Spin Ghar, White Mountain, also known as Safed Koh

ghazi (A.):   Islamic fighter for the faith

hookah (H.):   water-cooled pipe for smoking, also known as hubble-bubble

Hot Weather: the summer months between April and September

hujra (Pu.):   village guest-house, community centre

insaf (A.):   justice

jagir (P.):   assignment of land/land revenue, thus *jagirdar* (P.), landholder

344

Glossary

jehad (A.):	holy war
jemadar (H.):	native officer in army or police
jirga (Pu.):	*Pakhtun* tribal assembly
kafila (A.):	caravan
Kaka (Pu.):	uncle
Khalsa (A.):	pure, in the Punjab associated with the Sikh confederation, thus *Khalsa dal* – the Sikh army
khan (Pu.):	king, thus head of clan or tribe
khassedar (P.):	tribal policeman
kotal (P.):	summit of pass, thus Landi Kotal
kutcherry (H.):	administrator's office or court house, also spelt *cutcherry*
lashkar (P.):	tribal army
lungi (H. & P.):	waistcloth; also allowance paid to *malik* by government
malik (A.):	king, thus headman of village
maqbara (A):	tomb
masjid (A.):	mosque
maulvi (A.):	Muslim priest or learned scholar
melmastia (Pu.):	protection, thus hospitality
misl (A.):	Sikh cohort within *Khalsa dal*
Mohuram (A.):	Muslim month of mourning and fasting to commemorate assassination of Hussain, grandson of the Prophet Mohammed
mujaddid (A.):	reformer, thus *mujahidin* (A.): holy warriors
mullah (A.):	'one who shows', thus a religious teacher who leads prayers in the mosque
munshi (H.):	language teacher, translator or scribe
musasahib (A.):	aide
Muslim (A.):	one who submits, thus follower of Islam; on Indian subcontinent *Mussulman*
nang (Pu.):	personal honour, the key element in *Pakhtun* society
nizam (P.):	governor
Pashtu (Pu.):	language of the *Pakhtuns* as spoken by south-western tribes, also *Pakhtu*
Pakhtun (Pu.):	Pathan, thus *Paktunkhwa* (Pu.), the way of the Pathans, and *Pakhtunwali* (Pu.), Pathan code. The *Pakhtun* tribes claim a common ancestor named Qais, who lived at the time of the Prophet
pagri (H.):	head-cloth worn as turban
pir (P.):	saint, thus *pirzada* (P.), descendant of saint
Punjab (H.):	five rivers, thus land of the five rivers between the Indus and Sutlej, thus *Punjabi*, the people and language of the Punjab
Qur'ān, Koran (A.):	the words of Allah, as dictated by the angel Gabril to the last Prophet Mohammad
Rains:	the summer monsoon, usually affecting the Punjab from mid July to the end of September
rawaj (P.):	customary law, takes precedence among *Pakhtuns* over *Shariat*
risala (A.):	troop of irregular horse recruited by or under the authority of a *risaldar*, native subaltern of horse

Glossary

saheb (A.):	master, title applied to man of rank; later applied, as Sahib, to denote Europeans
salaam alaikum (A.):	peace be on you: Islamic greeting
sanad (A.):	grant
sangar (Pu.):	stone breastwork
sarai, serai (A):	inn, thus caravanserai
Saiyyid (A.):	descendent of the Prophet Mohammad, also *Said*
sepoy (P.):	native foot soldier, from Persian *sipahi*, army
Shariat (A.):	Islamic law based on the Koran
shah (P.):	king
sher (P.):	lion or tiger, often used as title
shikar (P.):	hunting, thus *shikari* – hunter
Sikh (H.):	disciple, thus applied to followers of the Sikh religion originating from the teachings of Guru Nanak
silladar (P.):	bearer of arms, but applied to *sowar* or trooper of irregular horse who brings his own mount and arms
sirdar, sardar (P.):	commander, but in the Punjab applied to leaders of the Sikh *misls*
sowar (P.):	horseman, thus native cavalry trooper
subedar (P.):	chief native officer of a company of *sepoys*
station:	in the Anglo–Indian context, a place where British officials live and work
Talib-ul-ilm (A.):	searcher after knowledge, thus *Taliban* (A.) – ordained, searchers after knowledge
tulwar (A.):	curved sabre
ulema (A.):	learned man
wazir (A.):	minister; also *vizier*
zai (Pu.):	son, thus *Yusufzai*, Sons of Joseph
zamin (P.):	land, thus *zamindar* (P.), landowner
zan (P.):	women, thus *zanana* (P.), women's quarter or harem
zar (P.):	gold

Select bibliography

Manuscripts and albums in the Oriental and India Office Collection at the British Library

Abbott, Sir James, Huzara and its Place in the Second Sikh War, MSS Eur. C.225
 The Chiefs of Hazara AD 1850, memorandum, MSS Eur. C.120
Bowring, L.B., Memoir of Service in India, MSS Eur. G. 91
Curzon, Lord, Collection, MSS Eur. F. 111–112
Edwardes, Sir Herbert, Collection, C. 183
 Diary of an Expedition to Bunnoo, MSS Eur. E. 211
Keyes, Sir Charles Patton, Papers, MSS Eur. D. 1048
Lawrence, Sir George, Papers, MSS Eur. D. 830
Lawrence, Sir Henry, Collection, MSS Eur. F. 85
Lawrence, Honoria, Journals, Lawrence Collection, MSS Eur. F. 85
Lumsden, family, Papers, MSS Eur 368
MacNabb, Sir Donald, Albums, Photo 752
Pearse, General G.G.., Papers, MSS Eur. B. 115 & Eur. E. 205
Saunders, E.S., Collection, MSS Eur. J.713
Thomas, Werge, Collection, MSS F.171

Published sources (London, unless otherwise noted)

Abbott, James, Journey to Khiva, 1843
Ahmed, Akbar, Social and Economic Change in the Tribal Areas, Karachi, OUP, 1977
Aijuzuddin, F.S., Historical Images of Pakistan, Lahore, Ferozsons Press, 1992
——Lahore: Illustrated Views of the 19th Century, Ferozsons Press, 1990
Allen, Charles, Plain Tales from the Raj, Deutsch, 1975

Select bibliography

Baird, J.G.A., *Private Letters of the Marquis of Dalhousie*, 1910

Barter, Richard, *The Siege of Delhi: Mutiny Memoirs of an Old Officer*, Folio Society, 1984

Bellew, H.W., *A General Report on the Yusufzais*, Lahore, Government Press, 1864

——*The Races of Afghanistan*, Thacker, 1880

Bruce, Richard, *The Forward Policy and its Results*, Longman, 1900

Burnes, Alexander, *Cabool: A Personal Narrative of a Journey to and Residence in that City in the Years 1836, 1837, and 1838*, John Murray, 1843

Caröe, Olaf, *The Pathans 550BC – AD1957, with an Epilogue on Russia*, Karachi, OUP, 1983

Chamberlain, Sir Crawford, *Remarks on Captain Trotter's Biography of Major W.S.A. Hodson*, Edinburgh, 1901

Cunningham, J.D., *A History of the Sikhs*, 1918

Curzon, George, *Frontiers* (Romanes Lecture, 1907), Oxford, Clarendon Press, 1907

Daly, H., *Memoirs of General Sir Henry Daly*, 1905

Dani, Ahmed Hasan, *Peshawar, Historic City of the Frontier*, Peshawar, Khyber Mail Press, 1969

Diver, Maud, *Honoria Lawrence*, 1909

Durand, Henry, *The First Afghan War*, 1879

Dupree, Louis, *Afghanistan*, Princeton, PUP, 1973

Edwardes, Herbert, *A Year on the Punjab Frontier*, Bentley, 1851

——and Merivale, Herman, *Life of Sir Henry Lawrence*, 1872

Edwardes, Lady, *Memorials of the Life and Letters of Major-General Sir Herbert B. Edwardes by his Wife*, 1886

Elphinstone, Mountstuart, *An Account of the Kingdom of Caubul and its Dependence on Persia, Tartary, and India*, John Murray, 1815

Eyre, Vincent, *The Military Operations at Cabul, with a Journal of Imprisonment in Afghanistan*, Bentley, 1843

Forrest, G.W., *Selections from the Letters, Despatches and Other State Papers Preserved in the Military Department of the Government of India, 1857–58*, 1893

——*The Life of Field-Marshal Sir Neville Chamberlain*, 1909

Gambier-Parry, E., *Reynell Taylor: a Biography*, 1888

Gray, Ernest, *Nikkal Seyn: A Tale of John Nicholson, Hero of Delhi, Saviour of India*, Collins, 1947

Hibbert, Christopher, *The Great Mutiny, 1857*, 1978

Hodson, V.C.., *List of the Officers of the Bengal Army 1758–1834.*

Hodson, Revd G.H., *Twelve Years of a Soldier's Life in India: Hodson of Hodson's Horse*, 1859

Hudson, Roger (ed.), *The Raj: an Eye-Witness History of the British in India*, Folio Society, 1999

Jackson, D., *India's Army*, Samson Lowe, 1940

Kaye, Sir John, *A History of the War in Afghanistan*, Bentley, 1857

——*A History of the Sepoy War in India*, Bentley, 1864–76

——*Lives of Indian Officers, London*, Allen, 1867

——and Malleson, G.B., *History of the Indian Mutiny*, Bentley, 1891

Khan, Mohammed Said, *The Voice of the Pukhtoons*, Peshawar, Ferozsons Press, 1972

James Lawrence, *Raj: the Making and Unmaking of British India*, Little, Brown, 1999

Kipling, Rudyard, *Barrack-room Ballads*, Methuen, 1892

——*Kim*, Methuen, 1902

Select bibliography

Lawrence, Lt–Gen. George, *Forty-Three Years in India*, 1874

Lawrence, John, *Lawrence of Lucknow: A Story of Love*, Hodder, 1980

Lumsden, Gen. Sir Peter, *Lumsden of the Guides*, John Murray, 1899

Mason, Philip (as Woodruff, Philip), *The Men Who Ruled India*, 1953

——*A Matter of Honour*, Jonathan Cape, 1974

Moore, Surgeon-General Sir William, *A Manual of Family Medicine and Hygiene for India*, Churchill, 1872

——*Health Resorts for Tropical Invalids*, Calcutta, 1884

Miller, Charles, *Khyber: British India's North-West Frontier*, Macdonald, 1977

Pearson, Hesketh, *The Hero of Delhi: A Life of John Nicholson*, Collins, 1939

Punjab Government, *Gazetteer of the Bannu District*

——*Gazetteer of the Hazara District*

——*Gazetteer of the Kohat District*

——*Gazetteer of the Lahore District*

——*Gazetteer of the North-West Frontier Province*

——*Gazetteer of the Peshawar District*

——*Records*, Vol. IV: *Journals and Diaries of the Assistants to the Resident at Lahore 1846–1849*

Raikes, Charles, *Notes on the Northwest Provinces*, 1852

——*Notes on the Revolt in the North-western Provinces of India*, 1858

Roberts, Field Marshal Earl, *Forty-One Years in India: from Subaltern to Commander-in-Chief*, Longman, 1908

——*Letters Written During the India Mutiny*, Longman, 1902

Smith, Bosworth, *Life of Lord Lawrence*, 1883

Spain, James, *The Pathan Borderland*, Hague, Monton, 1963

——*The Way of the Pathans*, Oxford, OUP, 1962

Thorburn, S.S., *Bannu: Or Our Afghan Frontier*, 1876

Trotter, Lionel, *The Life of John Nicholson*, John Murray, 1897

——*A Leader of Light Horse: The Life of Hodson of Hodson's Horse*, 1900

Warburton, Robert, *Eighteen Years in the Khyber, 1879–1893*, John Murray, 1900

Walker, Col. Thomas, *Through the Mutiny*, 1907

Watson, H.P., *Gazetteer of the Hazara District*, Punjab, 1908

Wilberforce, R.G., *An Unrecorded Chapter of the Indian Mutiny*, 1895

Younghusband, George, *The Story of the Guides*, Macmillan, 1908

Yule, Henry & Burnell, A.C., *Hobson-Jobson: a Glossary of Colloquial Anglo-Indian Words and Phrases*, 1886

INDEX

Index

NOTE: Ranks and titles are generally the highest mentioned in the text

Index

Index

Hodson, William (cont.)
Man Singh serves with, 175; in Second Sikh War, 187, 195–6; on senior officers at Chilianwala, 192; at annexation of Punjab, 207; testifies for Sundil Khan, 211; periodic ill-health, 222; administrative appointments, 229–30, 235; in action against Bori tribesmen, 234; and loss of daughter, 235; unpopularity among officers as commander of Guides, 235–6, 238, 332; warned by Lawrence and relieved of duties, 236–7, 253; charged with corruption, remanded to regiment and disgraced, 237–9; exonerated by Taylor's report on Guides, 258–60; pleads case with Anson, 260; appointed assistant quartermaster-general to Delhi relief force, 261; rides to and from Meerut, 261; raises Hodson's Horse, 262; role in Sepoy Mutiny, 265; in advance on Delhi, 271; meets Guides on arrival in Delhi (1857), 273; men's affection for, 273, 299–300, 332; fighting at Delhi, 274, 301, 307–8; penetrates into Delhi, 297–8; sets up intelligence department of Delhi Field Force, 297, 312; takes command of Guides at Delhi, 299; on leadership at Delhi, 302; on Nicholson's arrival at Delhi, 303; Wilson orders to relinquish command of Guides, 306; orders shooting of Bisharat Ali, 307–8; unmoved by death of Henry Lawrence, 310; on conditions at Delhi, 311; on assault on Delhi, 322; mourns death of Nicholson, 327; captures Mughal Emperor and kills sons, 332–4; arouses ill-will, 334–6; shot and killed, 335

Hodson's Horse (later 10th Bengal Lancers): raised (1857), 262; at Delhi, 297, 299, 306–7, 317; expansion, 335; Daly commands and reorganises, 336

Hogg family, 22

Hogg, James Weir (John Nicholson's uncle), 23–5, 34, 62

Hoti Mardan (village), Punjab, 100, 105, 267–9, 275, 277–8, 311

Imam-ud-Din, Sheik, 82–3

India: British forward policy in, 27

Indian Mutiny see Sepoy Mutiny (1857–8)

Indian Political Service: in NWFP, 17

Irregular Cavalry, 1st see Skinner's Horse

Islam: qualities, 13

Jacob, Lieut., 301

Jafir of the Dagger Hand (Hazara outlaw), 137–8, 169

Jalalabad, 39, 41–2, 44, 46, 69

Jammu: Nicholson serves in, 77; claims Kashmir, 82

Jehandad Khan, 139–40

Jehangir, Mughal Emperor, 60

Jeman Khan, Mir, 132–3

Jindan, Maharani, 80, 144, 153

Jinnah, Mohammad Ali (Qaid-i-Azam), 59

Jullal Khan, 170

Jundial Singh, 133, 140, 142, 159–60, 169

Kabul: occupied by British (1839), 32; British expelled from and massacred, 41; Nicholson taken to, 46–7; British reconquer, 49–50

Kader Khan, 236

Kandahar: garrison besieged and relieved (1842), 44, 46; military mission in, 257; Roberts's march to and victory at (1880), 332, 338

Kangra, 79

Karam Khan, Hassan, 166, 172–4

Kashmir: Henry Lawrence commands expedition to, 82–3; sale to Gulab Singh, 82; Nicholson in, 83, 86–7; incorporates Hazara, 131, 133

Kaye, John: letter from Henry Lawrence, 7; fire destroys Nicholson letters, 25–6; on disorder in Punjab, 62; on Abbott, 75; History of the War in Afghanistan, 41

Kennedy, Lieut. T.G., 257, 274

Kennedy (US soldier of fortune) see 'Canara, Colonel'

'khaki', 104, 212

Khalsa Dal, 28–30, 60–2, 80; see also Sikhs

Khan Khosh, Kowrah, 149

Khan Rosa Singh, Risaidar, 274, 318

Khan Singh, Sirdar, 146–50

Khan-i-Zamun, khan of Tarkhelis, 194

Index